HIPPOCRENE STANDARD DICT

ARABIC-ENGLISH

HIPPOCRENE STANDARD DICTIONARY

ARABIC-ENGLISH

John Wortabet and Harvey Porter

HIPPOCRENE BOOKS
New York

Second printing, 1995

Hippocrene paperback edition, 1993.

For information, address:
Hippocrene Books, Inc.
171 Madison Avenue
New York, NY 10016

ISBN 0-7818-0153-2

HIPPOCRENE STANDARD DICTIONARY

ARABIC-ENGLISH

قاموس عربي وانكليزي

ARABIC-ENGLISH DICTIONARY.

ا

أ	As a numerical sign = 1.
أ	Particle of interrogation.
أَبٌ مث أَبَوَانِ ج آبَاء	Father.
آبٌ	Month of August.
أَبَوِيٌّ	Fatherly, paternal.
أُبُوَّةٌ	Fatherhood.
أَبَدٌ	Time, eternity (future).
أَبَدَ ٱلآبِدِينَ	For ever.
أَبَداً	Ever ; always.
أَبَدِيٌّ وَمُؤَبَّدٌ	Eternal.
أَبَدِيَّةٌ	Eternity, perpetuity.
إِبْرَةٌ ج إِبَرٌ	Needle.
مِئْبَرٌ ج مآبِرُ	Needle-case.
إِبْرِيزٌ	Pure gold.
أَبْرَشِيَّةٌ	Diocese.
إِبْرِيقٌ ج أَبَارِيقُ	Water-jug.
إِبْزِيمٌ ج أَبَازِيمُ	Buckle, clasp.
إِبْطٌ ج آبَاطٌ	Arm-pit.
أَبِقَ يَأْبِقُ	To run away.
آبِقٌ	Runaway (slave).
إِبْلٌ	Camels (coll noun).
إِبْلِيسٌ ج أَبَالِسَةٌ	Satan.
أَبَّنَ	To praise the dead.
إِبَانَ	Time or season of a thing.
إِبْنٌ ج أَبْنَاء وَبَنُونَ	Son.
إِبْنَةٌ أَوْ بِنْتٌ ج بَنَاتٌ	Daughter.
أَبَنُوسٌ	Ebony.
أُبَّهَةٌ	Beauty. Greatness,
أَبَى يَأْبَى	To refuse, refrain.
أَبِيٌّ	Refusing, disdaining.

إباء	Refusal, rejection.
أتانٌ ج أُتُنٌ وآتُنٌ	She-ass.
أتونٌ ج أُتُنٌ	Oven, furnace.
أتَى يأتي	To come, arrive.
آتَى إيتاء	To give ; requite.
تأتَّى	To happen.
إتيانٌ	Arrival, coming.
آتٍ	Comer, one who arrives.
ألآتي	The future ; coming next.
أثَّ يئِث	To abound.
أثاثٌ	Household furniture.
أثِرَ يأثُرُ	To choose.
أثَّرَ في	To impress.
آثَرَ	To choose, prefer.
تأثَّرَ	To follow one's tracks
أثرٌ ج آثارٌ	Trace, impression.
تأثيرٌ	Influence ; impression.
مأثُرةٌ ج مآثِرُ	Memorable deed.
مؤثِّرٌ	Impressive.

أثْلٌ	A kind of tamarisk.
أثِمَ يأثَمُ	To sin.
أثَّمَ	To accuse of sin.
إثمٌ ج آثامٌ	Sin, crime.
أثيمٌ ج أثماء	Guilty.
مأثَمةٌ ومأثَمٌ ج مآثِمُ	Sin, crime.
أجَّ يؤُجُّ أجيجاً	To burn, blaze.
أجَرَ يأجِر	To pay ; let on hire.
آجَرَ	To pay, let for money.
إستأجَرَ	To hire, take on hire.
أجْرٌ ج أجورٌ	Recompense.
أجْرٌ وأُجرةٌ	Wages, salary.
آجُرٌّ	Baked bricks.
إيجارٌ	Lease, hire, rent.
أجيرٌ ج أجَراء	Hired labourer.
مؤْجِرٌ ومؤاجِرٌ	Landlord.
مُستأجِرٌ	Tenant.
إجّاصٌ وإنجاصٌ	Pear (fruit).
أجِلَ يأجَل	To delay, tarry.

To grant a delay.	أَجَّلَ
Appointed time.	الأَجَلُ
Cause, reason, sake.	أَجْلٌ
Postponed, future.	آجِلٌ
Thicket, jungle.	أَجَمٌ ج آجَامٌ
To unify.	أَحَّدَ وَوَحَّدَ
To unite with ; join.	إِتَّحَدَ بِ
One.	احَدٌ م إِحْدَى ج آحَادٌ
Sunday.	الأَحَدُ
Units.	آحَادٌ
Union ; agreement.	إِتِّحَادٌ
To take.	اخَذَ يأْخُذُ
To begin, to say.	أَخَذَ يَقُولُ
To seize, take hold of.	أَخَذَ بِ
To aid, assist.	أَخَذَ بِيَدِهِ
To blame.	آخَذَ مُؤَاخَذَةً بِ أَوْ عَلَى
To take to himself.	إِتَّخَذَ
Source. Way.	مَأْخَذٌ ج . مآخذ
To postpone.	أَخَّرَ تَأْخِيراً
To tarry, delay.	تَأَخَّرَ
Other, another.	آخَرُ م اخْرَى
End, last.	آخِرٌ ج أَوَاخِرُ
The future life.	اْلآخِرَةُ
Last, extreme.	أَخِيرٌ ج أَخِيرُونَ
At the end, finally, lastly.	أَخِيراً
Posterior part.	مُؤَخَّرٌ
Brotherhood.	إِخَاءٌ وَاخُوَّة
Brother.	أَخٌ ج إِخْوَةٌ وَإِخْوَانٌ
Sister.	أُخْتٌ ج أَخَوَاتٌ
Fraternal, brotherly.	أَخَوِيٌّ
Stable.	أَخُورٌ
To be educated.	أَدُبَ يأْدُبُ
To invite to a meal.	أَدَبَ يَأْدِبُ
To discipline, chastise.	أَدَّبَ
Become well-educated.	تَأَدَّبَ
Liberal education.	أَدَبٌ ج آدَابٌ
Polite literature.	عِلْمُ الأَدَبِ
Chastisement.	تَأْدِيبٌ

أَدَبِيٌّ Moral. Polite.

أَدِيبٌ ج أُدَبَاءُ Literary, learned.

إِدَامٌ Condiment, seasoning.

أَدَمَةٌ Human skin.

أُدْمَةٌ Dark or tawny colour.

آدَمِيٌّ Human being.

أَدَّى To give up, deliver.

أَدَّى إِلَى To bring to

أَدَاءٌ Payment, discharge.

أَدَاةٌ ج أَدَوَاتٌ Tool, utensil.

إِذْ When. Lo.

إِذَا Behold! When.

إِذاً وإِذنْ Therefore.

آذَارُ March (month).

أَذِنَ لِ يأذَن To give leave to.

أَذَّنَ To call to prayer.

إِسْتَأْذَنَ To ask permission.

إِذْنٌ Permission, leave.

أُذْنٌ وأُذُنٌ ج آذَانٌ Ear. Handle.

أَذَانٌ The Moslem call to prayer.

مِئْذَنَةٌ ومَأْذَنَةٌ ج مَآذِنُ Minaret.

مُؤَذِّنٌ One who calls to prayer.

آذَى إِيذَاءً To injure, annoy.

أَذًى وأَذِيَّةٌ Injury, damage.

مُؤْذٍ Hurtful, harmful.

أَرَبٌ ج آرَابٌ Need, want.

إِرْبًا إِرْبًا In pieces, limb by limb.

أُرْبِيَّةٌ Groin.

مَأْرَبَةٌ ومَأْرَبٌ ج مَآرِبُ Purpose.

أُورُبَّا Europe.

أُورُبِّيٌّ European.

إِرْثٌ (*See* وَرِث) Inheritance.

أُرْجُوَانٌ Purple (*n*).

أُرْجُوَانِيٌّ Purple (*adj*).

أَرَّخَ To date ; write a history.

تَأْرِيخٌ ج تَوَارِيخُ Epoch, history.

مُؤَرِّخٌ Historian.

مُؤَرَّخٌ Dated

إِرْدَبٌّ — Ardeb, (corn measure).

أَرْزٌ — Cedar or pine (tree).

أَرْزٌ وَأُرُزٌّ وَرُزٌ — Rice.

أَرْضٌ — Earth, soil, land.

أَرْضِيٌّ — Terrestrial.

أَرِقَ يَأْرَقُ — To be sleepless.

أَرَقٌ — Wakefulness; insomnia.

ارنبٌ ج أَرَانِبُ — Hare, rabbit

ازَبَ يَازِبُ ازْبًا — To flow.

ميزَابٌ ج مَيَازِيبُ — Drain.

ازَرَ — To assist, strengthen.

إِزَارٌ — A long wrapper, veil.

مُؤَازَرَةٌ — Succour, assistance.

مِئْزَرٌ ج مَآزِرُ — An apron.

أَزَلٌ وَأَزَلِيَةٌ — Eternity.

ازَلِيٌّ — Eternal (of past time).

أَزْمَةٌ — Distress; draught.

إِزَاءَ — In front, opposite to.

أَسَّسَ — To found.

تَأَسَّسَ — To be founded, built.

اسَاسٌ ج أُسُسٌ — Foundation.

اسَاسِيٌّ — Fundamental.

مُؤَسِّسٌ — Founder.

مُؤَسَّسٌ — Founded, established.

أَسْبَانَخ — Spinach, spinage.

اسْتَاذٌ ج أَسَاتِذَةٌ وَأَسَاتِيذُ — Master, professor.

اَسَدٌ ج اُسُودٌ — Lion.

اَسَرَ يَاسِرُ — To take captive.

إِسْتَأْسَرَ — To submit as a captive.

بِأَسْرِهِ — All, the whole of.

أَسْرٌ — Captivity, retention.

اسرَةٌ — Near relations.

أَسِيرٌ ج اسَرَاءُ وَأَسْرَى — Captive.

إِسْطَبْلٌ ج إِسْطَبْلاتٌ — Stable.

أُسْطُولٌ ج اسَاطِيلُ — Fleet.

أَسِفَ وَتَأَسَّفَ — To regret.

أَسَفٌ — Sorrow, grief, regret.

اَسَفِيّ وَيَا أَسَفَا — Oh ! Alas !

إِسْفَنْجٌ	Sponge.
إِسْكِلَةٌ ج أَسَاكِلُ	Harbour.
إِسْمٌ ج أَسْمَاءٌ	Name ; noun.
أَسِيَ يَأْسَى	To be grieved.
اسًى وَأَسًا	Grief, sorrow.
أَصُلَ يَاصُلُ	To be firmly rooted.
تَأَصَّلَ	To be firmly rooted.
إِسْتَاصَلَ	To extirpate.
أَصْلٌ ج أُصُولٌ	Root ; principle.
أَصْلِيٌّ	Radical, original.
أَصِيلٌ	Noble ; judicious.
الأَصِيل	Evening.
إِفْرَنْجٌ وَإِفْرَنْجَةٌ	Franks.
إِفْرَنْجِيٌّ	A European.
افُقٌ ج آفَاقٌ	Horizon ; region.
أَفَكَ يَأْفِكُ	To tell a lie.
إِفْكٌ وَإِفْكَةٌ	A lie.
أَفَلَ يَافُلُ	To disappear, set.
أَفْيُونٌ	Opium.
أُقْحُوَانٌ	Camomile.
اقّةٌ ج اقَقٌ وَاقَاتٌ	Oke.
أَكَّدَ	To assure.
تَأَكَّدَ	To be assured.
اكِيدٌ	Firm ; certain.
تَأْكِيدٌ	Assurance, certitude,
أَكَلَ يَأْكُلُ	To eat.
اكْلَةٌ	A morsel, mouthful.
آكِلَةٌ وَأَكَلَة	Corroding ulcer.
أَكِيلٌ وَأَكُولٌ	Glutton.
مَأْكَلٌ ج مَآكِل	Food.
أَكَمَةٌ ج آكَامٌ	Hill. Mound.
أَلْ	The (definite article).
الاَ	Is it not so ? Surely.
أَلاَّ أَنْ لا	That-not.
إِلاَّ	Unless, except.
أَلَّذِي مث أَللَّذَان ج أَلَّذِين	Who, which (*Masc*).
التي ج اللَّوَاتي	Who, Which (*Fem*).

أَلِفَ يَأْلَفُ	To be accustomed
آلَفَ	To be friendly.
أَلَّفَ	To compile a book.
تَأَلَّفَ	To be united.
إِلْفٌ وَأَلِيفٌ	Friend, companion.
أَلْفٌ ج أُلُوفٌ وَآلَافٌ	Thousand.
أُلْفَةٌ	Friendship, alliance.
إِئْتِلَافٌ	Accord, harmony.
تَأْلِيفٌ ج تَآلِيفُ	Compilation.
مَأْلُوفٌ	Customary, usual.
مُؤَالَفَةٌ	Friendship, familiarity.
مُؤَلِّفٌ	Author (of a book).
مُؤَلَّفٌ	Book. Composed.
أَلِمَ يَأْلَمُ	To suffer, feel pain.
أَلَّمَ وَآلَمَ	To pain, cause pain.
تَأَلَّمَ	To feel pain, ache.
أَلَمٌ ج آلَامٌ	Pain, grief, ache.
أَلِيمٌ وَمُؤْلِمٌ	Painful.
أَلْمَاسٌ	Diamond.
إِلٰهٌ ج آلِهَةٌ	A god, divinity.
اللّٰه	God ; the One True God.
أَلَّهَ	To deify.
اللّٰهُمَّ	O God !
أُلُوهَةٌ وَأُلُوهِيَّة	Divinity.
أَلْيَةٌ ج أَلَايَا وَأَلَيَاتٌ	Rump.
الأَيُّ ج الآيَاتٌ	Regiment.
إِلَى	To, unto, until.
إِلَى أَنْ	Until, till.
إِلَى مَتَى	Until when ? How long ?
أَمَّ يَؤُمُّ	To seek ; lead.
أُمٌّ ج أُمَّاتٌ وَأُمَّهَاتٌ	Mother.
أَمَامَ	Before, in-front.
إِمَامٌ ج أَئِمَّةٌ	Imam, leader.
أُمَّةٌ ج أُمَمٌ	Nation, people.
أُمِّيٌّ	Maternal, Illiterate.
أَمَّا	But, but as to.
إِمَّا ــ وَإِمَّا	Either, or.
أَمَدٌ ج آمَادٌ	Limit, end, term

أَمَرَ يَأْمُرُ	To order, command.
آمَرَ مُؤَامَرَةً فِي	To consult.
أَمْرٌ ج أَوَامِرُ	Command, order.
أَمْرٌ ج أُمُورٌ	Matter, affair.
إِمَارَةٌ	Prefecture, power.
أَمِيرٌ ج أُمَرَاءُ	Chief, prince.
أَمِيرُ أَلَايْ	Colonel.
أَمِيرُ ٱلْبَحْرِ	Admiral.
أَمِيرُ ٱلْمُؤْمِنِينَ	Caliph.
أَمِيرِيٌّ	Princely.
أَلْمَالُ ٱلأَمِيرِيُّ	Taxes.
مَأْمُورٌ	Sub-governor.
أَمْسِ	Yesterday.
أَمَلَ يَأْمُلُ	To hope, hope for.
تَأَمَّلَ	To meditate, reflect upon.
أَمَلٌ ج آمَالٌ	Hope, desire.
مَأْمُولٌ	Hoped, expected.
أَمُنَ يَأْمُنُ	To be faithful.
أَمِنَ يَأْمَنُ	To be or feel safe.
أَمَّنَ وَآمَنَهُ عَلَى	To entrust.
آمَنَ إِيمَانًا بِ	To believe in.
أَمَّنَهُ	To protect
إِئْتَمَنَ	To trust, rely upon.
أَمْنٌ وَأَمَانٌ	Safety, protection.
آمِنٌ	Safe, secure.
أَمَانَةٌ	Faithfulness, fidelity.
أَمِينٌ ج أُمَنَاءُ	Faithful.
أَمِينُ ٱلصُّنْدُوقِ	Treasurer.
آمِينَ وَأَمِينَ	Amen ; so be it.
إِيمَانٌ	Creed, belief.
مَأْمُونٌ	Trustworthy.
مُؤْمِنٌ	Believer, faithful.
أَمَةٌ ج إِمَاءٌ	Female slave.
أَنْ وَأَنْ	That (*particle*).
إِنْ	If. Not.
أَنَّ وَإِنَّ	Certainly, truly.
إِنَّمَا	Only , but. Verily.
أَنَّ يَئِنُّ أَنِينًا	To groan ; moan.

أَنَا ج نَحْنُ — I, we.

أَنْتَ ج أَنْتُم م أَنْتِ ج أَنْتُنَّ — Thou.

أَنْتُمَا — You two, both of you.

أُنْثَى ج إِنَاثٌ وأَنَاثَى — Female.

مُؤَنَّث — Feminine, effeminate.

أَلإِنْجِيلُ — The Gospel.

أَنِسَ يَأْنَسُ — To be polite, affable.

آنَسَ مُؤَانَسَةً — To be sociable.

آنَسَ إِينَاساً — To cheer.

أُنْسٌ — Social life. Cheerfulness.

إِنْسٌ — Mankind.

إِنْسَانٌ ج أُنَاسٌ — Man.

إِنْسَانِيٌّ — Human ; polite.

إِنْسَانِيَّةٌ — Humanity ; politeness.

أَنِيسٌ وَمُؤَانِسٌ — Friendly, gentle.

أَنِفَ يَأْنَفُ — To hate, disdain.

إِسْتَأْنَفَ — To recommence; appeal.

أَنْفٌ ج آنَافٌ وَأُنُوفٌ — Nose.

آنِفاً — Little while age.

أَنَفَةٌ — Dislike. Scorn.

أَنُوفٌ — Disdainful.

مَجْلِسُ ٱلْاسْتِئْنَافِ — Court of appeal

أَنِقَ بِ يَأْنَقُ — To be pleased.

تَأَنَّقَ — To be dainty.

أَنَامٌ وآنَامٌ — Men, mankind.

تَأَنَّى — To act deliberately.

أَنَاةٌ — Patience, deliberateness.

إِنَاءٌ ج آنِيَةٌ وَأَوَانٍ — Vessel.

تَأَنٍّ — Deliberateness.

مُتَأَنٍّ — Deliberate, careful.

أَنِيسُونٌ — Anise.

أَنَّى = مِنْ أَيْنَ — Whence ?

آهِ وَآهَا — Ah ! Alas !

أَهَّبَ — To equip, get one ready.

تَأَهَّبَ لِ — To get ready.

أُهْبَةٌ ج أُهَبٌ — Apparatus, tools.

أَهَّلَ لِ — To render fit for.

أَهَّلَ بِهِ — To bid welcome.

تَأَهَّلَ	To marry.
إِسْتَأْهَلَ	To deserve, merit.
أَهْلاً وَسَهْلاً	Welcome !
أَهْلٌ ج أَهَالٍ	Family ; relations.
أَهْلٌ لِ	Worthy of, fit for.
أَهْلِيٌّ	Domestic.
اهْلِيَّةٌ	Aptitude, fitness.
مُسْتَأْهِلٌ	Deserving, meriting.
أَو	Or, unless.
آبَ يَؤُوبُ إِيَاباً	To return.
إِوَز	Geese.
آسٌ	Myrtle.
آفَةٌ ج آفَاتٌ	Injury, damage.
آلَ يَؤُول	To result in.
أَوَّلَ	To explain, make clear.
آلٌ	Family ; kinsfolk.
آلَةٌ ج آلَاتٌ	Instrument.
آلِيٌّ	Organic.
أَوَّلُ ج أَوَائِل	First, beginning.
أَوَّلاً	Firstly, in the first place.
أَوَّلاً فَاوَّلاً	Successively.
اولَئِكَ	Those, these.
إِيَالَة ج إِيَالَاتٌ	Province.
تَاوِيلٌ	Interpretation.
مَآلٌ	End, result, issue.
آنٌ وَاوَانٌ	Time.
أَلآنَ	Now at present.
إِيوَانٌ إِيوَانَاتٌ	Porch, hall.
أَوَى يَأْوِي	To resort for shelter.
مَأْوًى ج مَآوٍ	Abode shelter.
إِبْنُ آوى	Jackal.
أَيْ	That is to say; namely.
أَيٌّ	Whoever, whichever.
آيَةٌ ج آيَاتٌ	Sign ; miracle.
إِيَّاهُ	Him.
إِيَّايَ	Me.
ايَّدَ	To strengthen, aid.
ايَّار	May (month).

أَيِسَ يَأْيَسُ	To despair.
إِيَاسٌ	Despair.
أَيِسٌ وَآئِسٌ	Despairing.
أَيَّلٌ وَإِيَّلٌ	Deer, stag.
أَيْلُولُ	September.
آنَ يَئِينُ	Its time comes.
أَيْنَ	Where ? whither ?
أَيْنَمَا	Whither ; everywhere.
إِلَى أَيْنَ	Whither ? where ?
مِنْ أَيْنَ	From whence ?

ب

ب	As a numerical sign 2.
بِ	With, during, by, at, in.
بِاللّٰهِ	By God !
بِمَا أَنْ	By reason of, inasmuch.
بَابَا ج بَابَاوَات	Pope ; father.
بَابَوِيٌّ وَبَابَاوِيٌّ	Papal.
بُؤْبُؤُ ٱلْعَيْنِ	Pupil of the eye.
بَابُوجٌ ج بَوَابِيجُ	Slipper.
بَابُونَجٌ	Camomile.
بَاذِنْجَانٌ	Egg-plant.
بِئْرٌ ج آبَارٌ	Well, cistern.
بَارَةٌ ج بَارَاتٌ	Para (coin).
بَارُودٌ	Gunpowder.
بَارُودَةٌ ج بَوَارِيدُ	Gun.
بَازٌ	Falcon, hawk.
بَازَارٌ	Market.
بَازِرْكَانٌ	Cloth-merchant.
بِئْسَ	Evil ! Bad, very bad. !
بَأْسٌ	Courage , boldness.
بَأْسٌ وَبُؤْسٌ	Misfortune.

Misfortune, distress.	اَلْبَأْسَاءُ
Unfortunate, poor.	بَائِسٌ
Pasha.	بَاشَا ج بَاشَاوَاتٌ
Sparrow-hawk.	بَاشَقٌ ج بَوَاشِقُ
Bunch of flowers, bouquet.	بَاقَةٌ
Bale (of merchandise).	بَالَةٌ
Okra.	بَامِيَا وَبَامِيَةٌ
Parrot.	بَبْغَاءُ ج بَبْغَاوَاتٌ
To cut off ; decide.	بَتَّ يَبُتُّ
Irrevocably; not at all.	اَلْبَتَّةَ وَبَتَّةً
To cut off; amputate.	بَتَرَ يَبْتُرُ
Virgin.	بَتُولٌ
Virginity.	بُتُولِيَّةٌ
To disperse, publish.	بَثَّ يَبُثُّ
To be divulged, spread.	إِنْبَثَّ
Pustule.	بَثْرٌ ج بُثُورٌ
To break out.	بَثَقَ يَبْثُقُ
To proceed from.	إِنْبَثَقَ مِنْ
To dawn.	إِنْبَثَقَ ٱلْفَجْرُ

Stork.	بُجَعٌ
To be great.	بَجُلَ يَبْجُلُ بَجَالَةً
To honour, praise.	بَجَّلَ
To be hoarse.	بَحَّ يَبَحُّ بَحًّا
Hoarseness ; rough voice.	بُحَّةٌ
Hoarse.	أَبَحُّ وَمَبْحُوحٌ
To investigate.	بَحَثَ عَنْ
To discuss.	بَاحَثَ وَتَبَاحَثَ
Examination, enquiry.	بَحْثٌ
Research.	مَبْحَثٌ ج مَبَاحِثُ
Discussion, controversy.	مُبَاحَثَةٌ
To scatter.	بَحْثَرَ
Sea.	بَحْرٌ ج أَبْحُرٌ وَبُحُورٌ
The Atlantic Ocean.	بَحْرُ ٱلظُّلُمَاتِ
The Red Sea.	اَلْبَحْرُ ٱلأَحْمَرُ
The Black Sea.	اَلْبَحْرُ ٱلأَسْوَدُ
The Caspian Sea.	بَحْرُ ٱلْخَزَرِ
The Pacific Ocean.	اَلْبَحْرُ ٱلْمُحِيطُ
The Mediterranean.	اَلْبَحْرُ ٱلْمُتَوَسِّطُ اوْ بَحْرُ ٱلرُّومِ

Basin, pool.	بَحْرَةٌ ج بِحَارٌ
Lake.	بُحَيْرَةٌ ج بُحَيْرَاتٌ
Nautical.	بَحْرِيٌّ
Sailor.	بَحْرِيٌّ ج بَحْرِيَّةٌ
Fortune, good luck.	بَخْتٌ
To swagger.	بَخْتَرَ وَتَبَخْتَرَ
To steam.	بَخَرَ يَبْخُرُ بَخْراً
To fumigate, steam.	بَخَّرَ
Steamship.	بَاخِرَةٌ ج بَوَاخِر
Vapour steam.	بُخَارٌ ج أَبْخِرَةٌ
Incense.	بَخُورٌ
Cyclamen (plant).	بَخُورُ مَرْيَم
Having a foul breath.	أَبْخَرُ
Censer.	مِبْخَرَةٌ ج مَبَاخِر
To diminish.	بَخَسَ يَبْخَسُ
Defective, low price.	بَخْسٌ
To be miserly.	بَخِلَ يَبْخَلُ
Avarice, stinginess.	بُخْلٌ
Miser ; miserly.	بَخِيلٌ ج بُخَلاءُ

To disperse ; squander.	بَدَّدَ
To be dispersed.	تَبَدَّدَ
To be arbitrary.	إِسْتَبَدَّ
By all means, necessarily.	لَا بُدَّ
To begin ; create.	بَدَأَ يَبْدَأُ
To give precedence.	بَدَّأَ
To create ; produce.	أَبْدَأَ
To begin, commence.	إِبْتَدَأَ ب
Beginning.	بَدْءٌ وَبَدَاءَةٌ
Initial, primary.	إِبْتِدَائِيٌّ
Principle.	مَبْدَأٌ ج مَبَادِئُ
Dissipation ; pride.	بَدْخٌ
To hasten towards.	بَدَرَ إِلَى
To hasten.	بَادَرَ وَابْتَدَرَ
Full moon.	بَدْرٌ ج بُدُورٌ
Thrashing-floor.	بَيْدَرٌ ج بَيَادِر
To originate.	بَدَعَ يَبْدَعُ
To originate.	أَبْدَعَ وَابْتَدَعَ
Innovation.	بِدْعَةٌ ج بِدَعٌ

Astonishing.	بَدِيعٌ
Rhetoric.	عِلْمُ ٱلْبَدِيعِ
Invention.	إِبْدَاعٌ وَٱبْتِدَاعٌ
Inventor. Creator.	مُبْدِعٌ
To change, exchange.	بَدَلَ يَبْدُلُ
To be changed or altered.	تَبَدَّلَ
To take in exchange.	إِسْتَبْدَلَ
Substitute.	بَدَلٌ وَبَدِيلٌ
Instead of.	بَدَلَ أَنْ
In exchange for.	بَدَلاً مِنْ
Reciprocity.	تَبَادُلٌ
Reciprocal	مُتَبَادِلٌ
Body, trunk.	بَدَنٌ ج أَبْدَانٌ
To come suddenly.	بَدَهَ ج يَبْدَهُ
Intuitive knowledge.	بَدَاهَةٌ
Intuitively.	بَدِيهاً . عَلَى ٱلْبَدِيهَةِ
Axiom.	بَدِيهِيَّةٌ
To appear.	بَدَا يَبْدُو
To make plain, reveal.	أَبْدَى
Nomads, bedouins.	أَلْبَدْوُ
Desert.	بَادِيَةٌ ج بَوَادٍ
Desert life ; desert.	بَدَاوَةٌ
Beduin ; nomad.	بَدَوِيٌّ
To be proud.	بَذِخَ يَبْذَخُ
Pride, haughtiness.	بَذْخٌ
To sow ; disperse.	بَذَرَ يَبْذُرُ
Seed, grain.	بَذْرٌ ج بِذَارٌ
Dissipation, prodigality.	تَبْذِيرٌ
Prodigal.	مُبَذِّرٌ
To give.	بَذَلَ يَبْذُلُ
Generous gift, present.	بَذْلٌ
To justify.	بَرَّرَ
To be justified.	تَبَرَّرَ
Goodness, piety.	بِرٌّ
Wheat.	بُرٌّ
Land as opposed to sea.	بَرٌّ
By land and by sea.	بَرًّا وَبَحْرًا
Just, pious.	بَارٌّ ج أَبْرَارٌ

External.	بَرَّانِيٌّ ج بَرَّانِيُّون
Wild (tree or animal).	بَرِّيٌّ
Desert, waste.	بَرِّيَّةٌ ج بَرَارِيٌّ
Justification.	تَبْرِيرٌ
To create.	بَرَأَ يَبْرَأ
To be innocent of. Recover from an illness.	بَرَأَ وبَرِئَ يَبْرَأ
To acquit.	بَرَّأَ من
Recovery, cure.	بُرْءٌ وبَرْءٌ
Innocent.	بَرِيءٌ ج أَبْرِيَاء
Immunity. Document.	بَرَاءَةٌ
Creator (God).	أَلْبَارِئ
Creature, creation.	بَرِيَّةٌ ج بَرَايَا
Native of Barbary.	بَرْبَرِيٌّ
Oranges.	بُرْتُقَانٌ وبُرْدُقَانٌ
Tower, castle.	بُرْجٌ ج بُرُوجٌ
Signs of zodiac.	بُرُوجُ الأَفْلاكِ
Man-of-war.	بَارِجَةٌ ج بَوَارِجُ
To part from.	بَرِحَ يَبْرَحُ

To continue, persevere.	ما بَرِحَ
To cause pain.	بَرَّحَ
Yesterday.	أَلْبَارِحُ وأَلْبَارِحَةُ
Day before yesterday.	أَلْبَارِحَةَ الأُولَى أَوَّلَ أَلْبَارِحَةِ
To become cold.	بَرَدَ يَبْرُدُ
To file (iron).	بَرَدَ
To make cool or cold.	بَرَّدَ
Cold.	بَرْدٌ
Hail ; hail stones.	بَرَدٌ
Fever and ague.	بُرَدَاءُ وبُرَدِيَّةٌ
Reed, papyrus reed.	بَرْدِيٌّ
Cold.	بَارِدٌ
Freshness, coolness.	بُرُودَةٌ
Courier, post.	بَرِيدٌ ج بُرُدٌ
File.	مِبْرَدٌ ج مَبَارِدُ
Donkey-saddle.	بَرْدَعَةٌ
To appear, issue.	بَرَزَ يَبْرُزُ
To go to battle.	بَارَزَ

أَبْرَزَ — To publish, bring out.
بِرَاز وَمُبَارَزَة — Combat, duel.
بُرُوز — Appearance.
مُبَارِز — Champion ; fighter.
بَرْزَخ ج بَرَازِخ — Isthmus.
بِرْسِيم — Alexandrian clover.
بِرْش — Stramonium.
أَبْرَش م بَرْشَاء — Piebald, spotted.
بِرِشْت — Soft-boiled egg.
بِرْشَان — Wafer.
بَرَص — Leprosy.
أَبْرَص م بَرْصَاء ج بُرْص — Leper.
بَرْطَل بَرْطَلَة — To bribe.
بِرْطِيل ج بَرَاطِيل — Bribe.
بَرَعَ يَبْرَع — To excel.
تَبَرَّعَ بِ — To bestow of free will.
بَارِع — Distinguished ; perfect.
بَرَاعَة — Distinction ; elegance.
بُرْعُم ج بَرَاعِم — Bud.

بُرْغُوث ج بَرَاغِيث — Flea.
بَرْغَش — Small flies ; gnats.
بَرْغَشَة — A small fly ; gnat.
بُرْغُل — Wheat coarsely ground.
بُرْغِيّ ج بَرَاغِيّ — Screw.
بَرَقَ يَبْرُقُ — To flash, lighten.
أَبْرَقَ — To flash, gleam.
بَرْق ج بُرُوق — Lightning.
بُورَق — Borax.
بَرْقَعَ — To veil the face.
بُرْقُع ج بَرَاقِع — A lady's veil.
بَرْقُوق — Yellow plum ; apricot.
إِبْرِيق ج أَبَارِيق — Ewer.
بَرَكَ يَبْرُكُ — To kneel.
بَارَكَ فِي أَوْ عَلَى — To bless.
تَبَرَّكَ بِ — To seek blessing.
تَبَارَكَ — To be blessed.
بَرَكَة ج بَرَكَات — Blessing.
بِرْكَة ج بِرَك — Pool, pond ; tank.

Blessed. مُبَارَك

Compasses. بِرْكَارٌ وَبِيكَارٌ

Volcano. بُرْكَانٌ ج براكين

To twist. بَرَمَ يَبْرُمُ

To make firm. أَبْرَمَ

Gimlet; augur. بِيرَمٌ وَبَرِّيمَة

Affirmed, assured. مُبْرَمٌ

Twisted cord. مَبْرُومٌ

Barrel ; cask. برميلٌ ج بَرَاميلُ

A kind of cloak. بُرْنُسٌ

Hat. بُرْنَيْطَةٌ

Space of time. بُرْهَةٌ

To prove بَرْهَنَ عَلَى أو عَنْ

To be demonstrated. تَبَرْهَنَ

Proof, evidence. بُرْهَانٌ ج بَرَاهِينُ

Demonstrated, proved. مُبَرْهَنٌ

Frame. بِرْوَازٌ ج بَرَاوِيز

To pare ; emaciate. بَرَى يَبْرِي

To vie with. بَارَى وَانْبَرَى

Creation, universe. بَرِيَّةٌ ج بَرَايَا

Mended or cut (pen). مَبْرِيٌّ

Linen or cotton clothes. بَزٌّ

Udder, nipple. بِزٌّ ج أَبْزَازٌ

Seed, grain. بِزْرٌ ج بُزُورٌ

A grain or seed. بِزْرَةٌ

To peep forth (sun). بَزَغَ يَبْزُغُ

Rising of sun or moon. بُزُوغٌ

To spit. بَزَقَ يَبْزُقُ بَزْقاً

Spittle, saliva. بُزَاقٌ

Snail. بَزَّاقَةٌ (*coll.* بَزَّاقٌ)

Spittoon. مَبْزَقَةٌ

To split. Tap a cask. بَزَلَ يَبْزُلُ

Perforator. بِزَالٌ وَمِبْزَلٌ

Buckle. إِبْزِيمٌ

Bath-tub. الإِبْزَنُ ج أَبَازِنُ

Cat. بَسٌّ م بَسَّةٌ (بُسَيْنٌ م بُسَيْنَةٌ)

Garden ; orchard. بُسْتَانٌ ج بَسَاتِينُ

Gardener. بُسْتَانِيٌّ

بَاسور	Piles.
بَسَطَ يبسُطُ	To spread out ; cheer.
إنبَسَط	To be cheerful, merry.
بِسَاط ج بُسُط	Carpet.
بَسِيط ج بُسطاء	Simple.
ألبَسِيطة	The Earth.
إنبِسَاط وبسْط	Cheerfulness.
مبْسوط	Extended ; happy.
بَسَقَ يبْسق بَسقاً	To spit.
بَسُل يبْسل	To be brave.
بَاسِل ج بسلاء	Bold, brave.
بسَالة	Bravery ; heroism.
بَسَم يَبْسِم وتَبَسَّم وا بتَسَم	To smile.
تبَسُّم وابتِسام	Smile.
بَش	To be cheerful.
بَشَاشَة	Cheerfulness of face, gentleness.
بَشَر يبْشِر	To rejoice at.
بَشَّر	To announce good news.
باشَر	To manage an affair.
بَشَرَة	Epidermis ; cuticle.
بَشَر	Man ; mankind ; humanity.
ألبَشَر	Mankind, men.
بُشْرى	Good news.
بَشَريّ	Human.
بِشَارة ج بشائر	Good news ; gospel.
بَشِير	Bearer of good news.
مُبَشِّر	Announcer of news ; preacher.
بَشِعَ يبْشع	To be ugly, deformed.
بَشَاعة	Bad taste (food); ugliness.
بَشِع وبَشِيع	Ugly ; repulsive.
بَشَم	Indigestion.
بَشْنِين	Lotus (plant).
بَصَّ يبِصُّ	To shine, glitter.
بَصَّة	A live coal.
بَصَّاص ج بَصَّاصون	Spy.
بصر يبْصر بصر يبْصر	To see.
تَبَصَّر	To consider, observe.
بَصَر ج أبصَار	Sight.

بَصِيرٌ ج بصراء	Intelligent.
تَبَصُّرٌ	Consideration ; reflection.
بصق يَبْصُق بصقًا	To spit.
بُصَاق	Spittle, saliva.
بَصَلٌ	Onion ; bulb.
بضَعَ يبضَع	To cut, incise.
بِضْعٌ وبِضْعَةٌ	A small number.
بِضْعَةَ أيامٍ	A few days.
بِضَاعة ج بَضَائِع	Merchandise.
مِبْضَعٌ ج مبَاضِع	Knife ; lancet.
بط يَبُطُّ	To lance a tumour.
بطةٌ ج بَطٌّ	Duck.
بَطةٌ ج بُطَطٌ	Bottle.
بَطؤَ يَبْطُؤُ	To linger.
تَبَاطَأَ في	To be slow, dally.
بطَاء وبطْء وبُطوء	Slowness.
بَطِيء	Slow, tardy, dilatory.
بطحاء وبَطِيحَة	Water-course.
بِطِّيخٌ أحْمَر	Water-melon.
بِطِّيخٌ أَصْفَر	Musk-melon.
بطِرَ يبطَر بَطَرًا	To exult.
بَطَرٌ	Exultation. Wantonness.
بَيْطَرَ	Toshoe animals
بِيْطارٌ ج بياطِرة	Farrier.
بَيطَرَةٌ	Veterinary art .
بطّاريّةٌ	Battery (of cannons).
بطرِكٌ ج بطارِكَةٌ	Patriarch.
بَطْرِيَرْكِيَّةٌ وبَطْرِكِيَّةٌ	Patriarchate.
بَطَش يبطِش ب	To assault.
بَطْشٌ	Power ; violence.
بِطَاقَةٌ	A marked ticket.
بطَل يَبطُل	To cease.
بطل وأبْطَل	To repeal, abolish.
بُطْلٌ وبطْلان	Vanity ; lie.
بطَلٌ ج أبْطَال	Hero.
بَاطِلٌ	False, vain, useless.
بَطَّالٌ	Lazy, idle ; useless.
بِطالَة	Idleness ; holidays.

إبْطَالٌ	Abolition, repeal.
بَطلَيْنوسٌ	Marine muscle.
بُطْمٌ	Terebinth.
بطَنَ وأَبْطَنَ	To line (clothes).
بَطْنٌ ج بُطونٌ	Belly, abdomen.
بطانَةٌ	Inner lining.
بَاطِنٌ ج بواطِنٌ	Inner, hidden.
باطناً	Internally, secretly.
بعَثَ يبْعَثُ إلى	To send.
بعَثَ	To raise the dead.
باعِثٌ	Cause, motive.
مَبعوثٌ	Sent. Envoy.
بعثرَ	To scatter, uncover.
بعد يبعد	To be far distant.
بَعَّدَ وأَبْعَدَ	To make distant.
تَبَاعَدَ عَن	To be far from.
إبتعدَ عَن	To go far from.
إستَبعَدَ	To regard improbable.
بُعْدٌ	Distance ; interval.
بَعْدُ	Then ; afterwards ; after.
بعيدٌ	Distant ; far.
بعيرٌ ج بعْوانٌ	Camel.
بعزق	To scatter, dissipate.
بَعضٌ	Portion, part ; some.
بعوضٌ	Gnats, mosquitoes.
بعوضةٌ	A gnat or mosquito.
بعْلٌ ج بعولٌ	Husband, wife.
بَعْلٌ	Unwatered land.
بَغَتَ يَبغَتُ وبَاغَتَ	To take by surprise.
بغْتة ج بغْتات	Surprise.
بغتَةً	Suddenly, unexpectedly.
بوغاز ج بوَاغيزُ	Strait.
أبغَضَ	To hate, detest.
بُغْضٌ	Hatred ; enmity.
بغْضةٌ وبغْضاء	Violent hatred.
مُبْغِضٌ	One who hates.
بغلٌ ج بِغال وأبغال	Mule.
بَغالٌ	Muleteer.

بَغْمَةٌ	Necklace.
بَغَى يَبْغِي	To seek ; desire.
بَغَى عَلَى	To be unjust ; oppress.
يَنْبَغِي أَنْ	It is desirable.
بَغْيٌ	Injustice ; aggression.
بِغَاءٌ وَٱبْتِغَاءٌ	Wish, desire.
بُغْيَةٌ وَبَغِيَّةٌ	Anything wished for or sought.
بَاغٍ ج بُغَاةٌ	Unjust aggressor.
بُقْجَةٌ ج بُقَجٌ	Bundle of clothes.
بَقْدُونَسٌ	Parsley.
بَقَرٌ ج أَبْقَارٌ	Oxen.
بَقَرَةٌ ج بَقَرَاتٌ	Cow.
بَقْسٌ	Box-tree.
بَقِعَ يَبْقَعُ بَقَعًا	To be spotted.
بَقَعٌ	Spots, stains.
بُقْعَةٌ ج بُقَعٌ وَبِقَاعٌ	Piece of land.
بَقْلٌ ج بُقُولٌ	Vegetables, herbs.
بَقَّالٌ	Green-grocer.
بَقَّمٌ	Logwood.
بَقِيَ يَبْقَى	To remain ; continue.
أَبْقَى وَٱسْتَبْقَى	To preserve.
تَبَقَّى	To be left.
بَقَاءٌ	Continuance, uration.
بَقِيَّةٌ ج بَقَايَا	Remainder.
بَاقٍ ج بَاقُونَ	Remaining.
ٱلْبَاقِي	The Everlasting (God).
بَاقِيَةٌ	Vetch.
أَبْقَى	More enduring.
بَكَّتَ	To reprove, scold.
بَكَّرَ وَبَاكَرَ	To come early.
بِكْرٌ ج أَبْكَارٌ	First-born ; virgin.
بُكْرَةٌ	Dawn ; to-morrow.
بَكْرَةٌ ج بَكَرٌ	Pulley.
بَكَارَةٌ	Virginity.
بَاكِرًا	Early.
بَاكُورَةٌ	First fruits.
بَكِمَ يَبْكَمُ	To be dumb.
أَبْكَمَ	To cause to be silent.

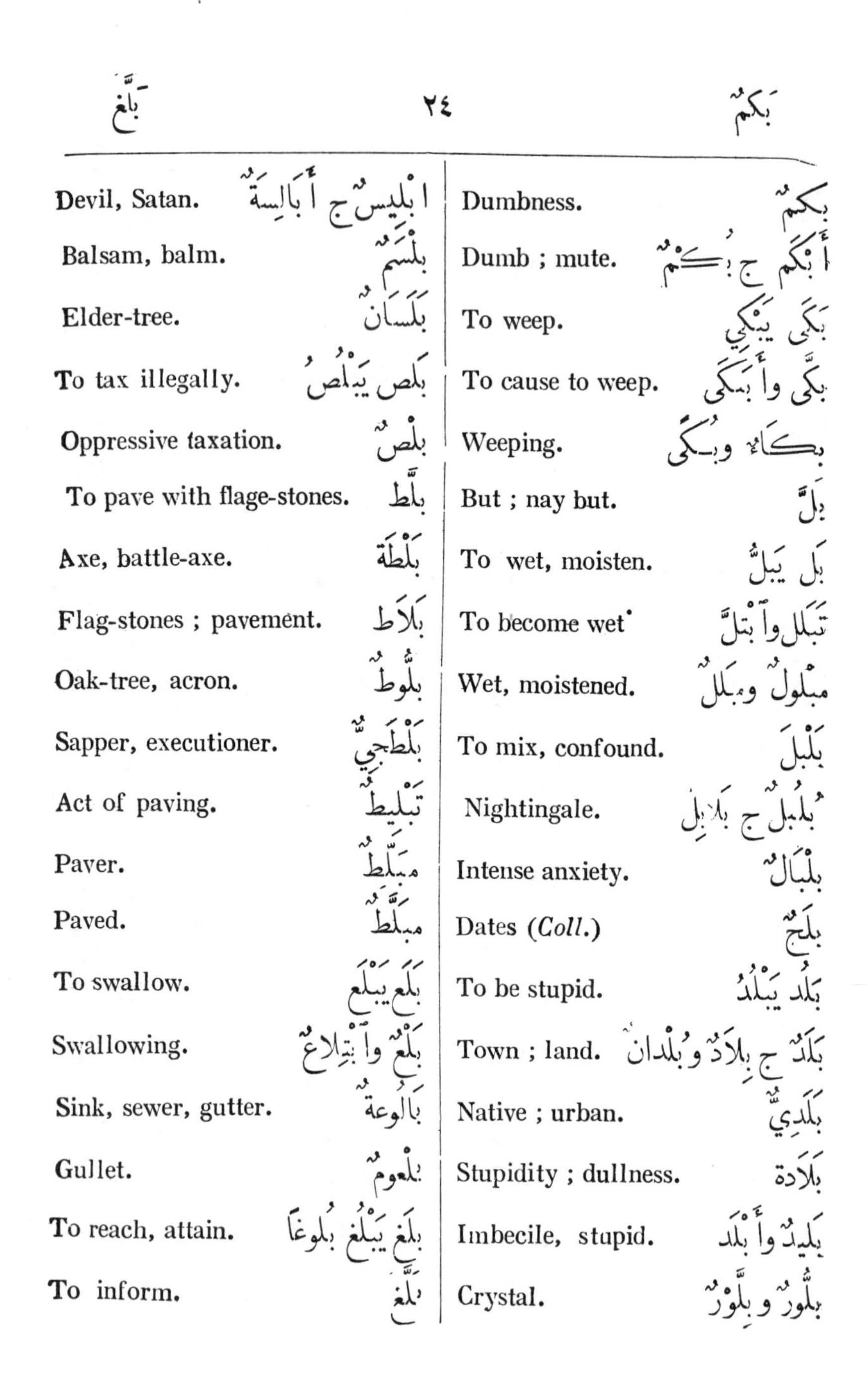

Dumbness. بَكَمٌ

Dumb ; mute. أَبْكَم ج بُكْمٌ

To weep. بَكَى يَبْكِي

To cause to weep. بَكَّى وأَبْكَى

Weeping. بُكَاءٌ وبُكًى

But ; nay but. بَلْ

To wet, moisten. بَلَّ يَبُلُّ

To become wet. تَبَلَّلَ وٱبْتَلَّ

Wet, moistened. مَبْلُولٌ ومُبَلَّلٌ

To mix, confound. بَلْبَلَ

Nightingale. بُلْبُلٌ ج بَلَابِل

Intense anxiety. بَلْبَالٌ

Dates (*Coll.*) بَلَحٌ

To be stupid. بَلُدَ يَبْلُدُ

Town ; land. بَلَدٌ ج بِلَادٌ وبُلْدَانٌ

Native ; urban. بَلَدِيٌّ

Stupidity ; dullness. بَلَادَة

Imbecile, stupid. بَلِيدٌ وأَبْلَد

Crystal. بِلَّورٌ وبِلَّوْرٌ

Devil, Satan. إِبْلِيسٌ ج أَبَالِسَة

Balsam, balm. بَلَسَمٌ

Elder-tree. بَلَسَانٌ

To tax illegally. بَلَصَ يَبْلُصُ

Oppressive taxation. بَلْصٌ

To pave with flage-stones. بَلَّط

Axe, battle-axe. بَلْطَة

Flag-stones ; pavement. بَلَاط

Oak-tree, acron. بَلُّوطٌ

Sapper, executioner. بَلْطَجِيٌّ

Act of paving. تَبْلِيطٌ

Paver. مُبَلِّطٌ

Paved. مُبَلَّطٌ

To swallow. بَلَعَ يَبْلَعُ

Swallowing. بَلْعٌ وٱبْتِلَاعٌ

Sink, sewer, gutter. بَالُوعَة

Gullet. بُلْعُومٌ

To reach, attain. بَلَغَ يَبْلُغُ بُلُوغًا

To inform. بَلَّغ

بَالَغَ فِي To exaggerate.

بَالِغٌ Mature ; of full age.

بَلَاغ Message.

بَلَاغَة Elegance of style.

عِلْمُ ٱلْبَلَاغَةِ Rhetoric.

بُلُوغ Arrival, maturity.

بَلِيغ Eloquent efficacious.

مَبْلَغ ج مَبَالِغ Sum, amount.

مُبَالَغَة Exaggeration.

بَلْغَم ج بَلَاغِم Phlegm.

بَلْغَمِيّ Phlegmatic.

أَبْلَقُ م بَلْقَاء ج بُلْق Spotted.

بَلَان A thorny plant.

بَلَه و بَلَاهَة Stupidity, idiocy.

أَبْلَه م بَلْهَاء ج بُلْه Stupid ; simpleton, idiot.

بَلَا يَبْلُو To test, try ; afflict.

بَلِيَ يَبْلَى To decay.

بَالَى بِ To be attentive to.

بِلًى Decay ; rottenness.

بَلَى Yes, certainly.

بَلَاء Trial. Grief ; calamity.

بَلْوَى ج بَلَايَا Affliction.

بَالٍ Used up ; rotten.

بِمَ Wherewith ?

بِمَا أَنْ Because, inasmuch as

بُنّ Coffee-berries ; coffee.

بَنَان Fingers.

بَنَّجَ To drug, stupefy.

بَنْج Henbane, Hyoscyamus.

بَنْد ج بُنُود Section. Banner.

بَنَدُورَة Tomatoes.

بَنْدِيرَة Flag, banner.

بُنْدُقَة و بُنْدُق Hazel-nut.

بُنْدُقِيَّة Musket, gun.

بُنْدُوق ج بَنَادِيق Bastard.

بَنَفْسَج Violet (*plant*).

بَنَفْسَجِيّ Violet (*colour*).

بِنْصِر ج بَنَاصِر Ring-finger.

بَنْكٌ ج بُنُوكَةٌ	Seat. Bank.
بَنَى يَبْنِي	To construct, build.
تَبَنَّى	To adopt a son.
بِنَاءٌ وَبِنَايَةٌ	Building, edifice.
بِنَاءً عَلَى	In consequence of.
بَنَّاءٌ ج بَنَّاؤُونَ	Mason.
بُنْيَةٌ	Form ; constitution.
إِبْنٌ ج بَنُونَ وَأَبْنَاءٌ	Son, boy.
إِبْنَةٌ وَبِنْت ج بَنَاتٌ	Daughter.
إِبْنُ ٱلسَّبِيلِ	Traveller, wayfarer.
مَبْنِيٌّ	Built. Indeclinable.
بُهِتَ يُبْهَتُ	To be astonished ; faded.
بَهَتَ يُبْهِتُ	To astonish, perplex.
بُهْتَانٌ	Lie ; slander.
بَهَجَ وَأَبْهَجَ	To rejoice, cheer.
بَهِجَ وَٱبْتَهَجَ	To rejoice at.
بَهْجَةٌ	Joy, gladness ; beauty
مُبْهِجٌ	Cheering ; causing joy.
بَهَرَ يَبْهَرُ	To shine.
بَهَرَ	To be dazzled.
بَاهِرٌ	Beautiful, admirable.
بَاهِظٌ	Heavy, distressing.
اِبْتَهَلَ إِلَى	To supplicate.
إِبْتِهَالٌ	Supplication.
بَهْلَوَانٌ	Rope-dancer.
أَبْهَمَ وَٱسْتَبْهَمَ	To be doubtful.
بَهِيمَةٌ ج بَهَائِمُ	Brute, beast.
إِبْهَامٌ	Doubt ; ambiguity.
إِبْهَامٌ ج أَبَاهِمُ	Thumb.
مُبْهَمٌ	Ambiguous ; doubtful.
بَهَا يَبْهُو	To be beautiful.
بَاهَى	To rival in beauty.
بَهَاءٌ	Beauty, brilliancy.
بَهِيٌّ	Beautiful splendid.
بَابٌ ج أَبْوَابٌ	Door. Chapter.
أَلْبَابُ ٱلْعَالِي	The Sublime Porte.
بَوَّابٌ	Door-keeper.
بَوَّابَةٌ	Large door, gate.

باحَ يبُوح	To be known.
باحَ ب	To divulge.
أَباحَ	To allow.
إستَبَاح	To consider lawful.
إِبَاحَة	Revealing, licence.
مُباحٌ	Permissable; lawful.
باخَ يَبُوخ	To abate ; fade.
بارَ يَبور	To perish.
بورٌ	Uncultivated land.
بَوَارٌ	Destruction, ruin.
بُورَق	Borax ; natron.
بَاز ج بِيزَانٌ	Falcon, hawk.
باسَ يَبُوس بَوْساً	To kiss.
بُوسطَةٌ	Post ; mail.
بُوسْطَجيٌّ	Postman.
باعٌ ج ابْوَاعٌ	A fathom.
طَوِيل ٱلبَاعِ	Generous. Able.
بوَّق	To blow a trumpet.
بوقٌ ج أَبْوَاقٌ	Trumpet; shell.
بائِكَةٌ ج بَوَائِك	Storehouse.
بالَ يَبُولُ	To micturate. Melt ; flow.
بالٌ	Condition ; mind ; thought.
خَطَر بِبَال	To occur to mind
بَالَةٌ	Bale.
بَوْلٌ	Urine.
بُولَادٌ (فولاَذ)	Steel.
بُومَة	An owl.
بُوليصَةٌ ج بَوَالص	Bill ; order ; receipt.
بَانٌ	The Egyptian willow.
بَوْنٌ	Distance ; difference.
بَاتَ يَبِيت	To pass the night.
بَيت ج بيُوتٌ وَأَبْيَاتٌ	House, room. Verse of poetry.
بَيْت ٱلْمَاء بيْتُ ٱلخَلَاء بَيْتُ ٱلفَضَاء	Water-closet ; latrine ; privy.
بيتُ ٱلْمَال	Public treasury.
بَيت ٱلعنْكَبوت	Cobweb.
بيتُ ٱلمقدِس	Jerusalem.

أَلْبَيْتُ الْحَرَام	The Kaaba in Mecca.
مَبِيت	House, night's lodging.
بَادَ يَبِيد	To perish, vanish.
أَبَادَ	To destroy, annihilate.
بَيْدَاء ج بِيدٌ	Desert.
بَيَّادِيٌّ بَيَّادَة	Foot-soldier.
بَيْدَ أَنْ	But, although.
بَيْدَرٌ	Thrashing-floor.
بِيرٌ	Well of water.
بَيْرَقٌ بَيَارِق	Banner.
بَاضَ يَبِيض	To lay eggs.
بَيَّضَ	To whiten, bleach.
إِبْيَضَّ	To become white.
بَيْضٌ ج بُيُوضٌ	Eggs.
بَيْضَة	An egg. Testicle.
بَيْضِيٌّ	Oval, ovate ; elliptical.
بَيَاضٌ	Whiteness.
أَبْيَضُ م بَيْضَاء ج بِيضٌ	White.
مُبَيِّضٌ	Tinner; white-washer.
بَيْطَرَ	To shoe a horse.
بَاعَ يَبِيع	To sell.
بَايَعَ مُبَايَعَة	To swear fealty.
إِبْتَاعَ مِنْ	To buy from.
بَيْعٌ	Selling, sale.
بِيعَةٌ ج بِيَعٌ	Church, synagogue.
بَائِعٌ ج بَاعَة	Seller.
بَيَّاع	Seller.
مَبِيع	Sale ; place of sale.
بَيْكٌ و بَك	Bey.
بِيكَارٌ	Pair of compasses.
بَيْلَسَانٌ	Elder (tree).
بِيمَارِسْتَان	Hospital.
بَانَ يَبِين	To be distinct, separate.
بَيَّنَ	To render clear ; explain.
بَايَنَ	To quit, abandon.
تَبَيَّنَ	To be clear, lucid.
بَيْنَ	Between, among.
بَيْنَ بَيْنَ	Middling.

بَيْنَا وبَيْنَمَا	Whilst, while.
بَيَان	Explanation.
عِلْمُ ٱلْبَيَان	A branch of Rhetoric.
بَائِنٌ و بَيِّنٌ	Distinct, evident.
بَيِّنَةٌ ج بَيِّنَاتٌ	Evidence.
تَبَايُن	Difference ; contrast.
مُبِينٌ و بَيِّن	Clear, evident.

ت

ت	As a numeral sign=400
تَاللّٰه	I swear by God.
تَابُوت ج تَوَابِيت	Chest. Coffin.
تَارَةً	Once ; sometimes.
تَوْأَمَةٌ ج تَوَائِمُ	Twin.
تَوْأَمٌ	Twins ; double.
أَلتَوْأَمَان	The sign of Gemini.
تَبَّ يَتِبُّ	To suffer loss.
إِسْتَتَبَّ	To be established.
تَبًّا لَهُ	Evil be to him !
تِبْرٌ	Native gold.
تَبِعَ يَتْبَعُ واتَّبَعَ	To follow.
أَتْبَعَ	To cause to follow.
تَابَعَ مُتَابَعَةً عَلَى	To follow.
تَتَبَّعَ	To follow up.
تَتَابَعَ	To follow consecutively.
تَبَعٌ ج أَتْبَاعٌ	Follower.
مُتَتَابِعٌ	Successive.
تُبْغٌ	Tobacco.
تَبَّلَ وتَابَلَ	To season (a dish).

تَوَابِلُ	Condiments.
مُتَبَّلٌ	Seasoned (dish.)
تِبْنٌ	Straw.
تَتَرٌ	Tartars (*coll.*)
تَتَرِيٌّ	A Tartar.
تَتْرَى	One after another.
تُتُنٌ	Tobacco
تَجَرَ يَتْجُرُ وتَاجَرَ	To trade.
تِجَارَةٌ	Commerce, trade.
تَاجِرٌ ج تُجَّارٌ	Merchant.
مَتْجَرٌ ج مَتَاجِر	Commerce.
تُجَاهَ	In front of, opposite to.
تَحْتَ	Under, below, beneath.
تَحْتَانِيٌّ	Inferior, placed below.
أَتْحَفَ بِ	To present with.
تُحْفَةٌ	Precious object, gift.
تَخْتٌ ج تُخُوتٌ	Bench ; bedstead.
تَخْتَرَوَان	Palanquin.
تَخْتُ الْمُلْكِ	Capital of a kingdom.
تَخَمَ يَتْخَمُ تَخْماً	To confine, limit.
تَاخَمَ	Adjoin, border upon.
أَتْخَمَ	To cause indigestion.
تَخْمٌ ج تُخُومٌ	Boundary.
مُتَاخِمٌ	Adjoining.
تُخَمَةٌ	Indigestion.
تَرَّبَ	To cover with earth.
تُرَابٌ ج أَتْرِبَةٌ	Earth, dust.
تُرْبَةٌ ج تُرَبٌ	Cemetery. Soil.
أُتْرُجٌّ وأُتْرُنْجٌ	Citron.
تَرْجَمَ	To translate.
تَرْجَمَةٌ	Translation.
تُرْجُمَانٌ	Dragoman, interpreter.
مُتَرْجِمٌ	Translator, interpreter.
مُتَرْجَمٌ	Translated, interpreted.
تَرَحٌ ج أَتْرَاحٌ	Sorrow, grief.
تُرْسٌ ج أَتْرَاسٌ	Shield.
مِتْرَاسٌ ج مَتَارِيس	Bulwark.
تَرْسَانَةٌ وتَرْسَخَانَةٌ	Arsenal.

Channel, canal.	تَرعَة ج تُرَع
Luxury ; ease.	تَرَفٌ وتُرفَة
Collar-bone, clavicle.	تَرقوة
To abandon, allow.	تَرَك يَتْرُك
To leave to, bequeath.	تَرَك ل
Abandoning leaving.	تَرْك
Turk.	تُرْك ج أتراك
A turk ; Turkish.	تُرْكِيّ
Estate of one dead.	تَرِكَة وتَرْكَة
Abandoned, omitted.	مَتْروك
Lupine.	تُرْمُس
Theriac ; antidote.	تِرْياق
Nine.	تِسْعَة م تِسْع
A ninth (part).	تُسْع
Ninth (ord. num.)	تاسِع
Ninety, ninetieth.	تِسْعون
October.	تِشْرين الأوّل
November.	تِشْرين الثاني
Come !	تَعَال

To become tired.	تَعِب يَتْعَب
To give trouble ; tire.	أتْعَب
Fatigue, toil.	تَعَب ج أتْعاب
Tired, fatigued.	تَعِب
Toilsome, fatiguing.	مُتْعِب
Fatigued.	مُتْعَب
To stumble	تَعِس يَتْعَس
Misfortune.	تَعْس وتَعاسة
Unhappy, unlucky.	تَعِس
Apple.	تُفّاح
An apple, apple-tree.	تُفّاحة
To spit.	تَفَل يَتْفِل
Spittle, saliva.	تَفْل
Spittoon.	مَتْفَلة
To be mean, foolish.	تَفِه يَتْفَه
Insipidity.	تَفاهة
To arrange skilfully.	أتْقَن
Perfection (of a work).	تَقانة
Skilful elaboration.	إتْقان

مُتْقَن Skilfully made.

تَقِيٌّ Pious.

تَقْوَى Piety.

تَلٌّ ج تِلَالٌ Small hill.

تَلِفَ يَتْلَفُ تَلَفًا To perish.

أَتْلَفَ To ruin.

تَلَفٌ Destruction.

مُتْلِفٌ Destroyer, waster.

مِتْلَافٌ Squanderer.

تِلْكَ That (*fem.*)

تَلَمٌ ج اتْلَامٌ Furrow, rut.

تَلْمَذَ To be a pupil.

تِلْمِيذٌ ج تَلَامِيذُ Disciple, pupil.

تَلَا يَتْلُو تُلُوًّا To follow ; succeed.

تَلَا يَتْلُو تِلَاوَةً To read ; recite.

تِلَاوَة Reading, recitation.

تَالٍ Following, next.

تَمَّ يَتِمُّ To be complete.

تَمَّمَ وأَتَمَّ To complete, finish.

تَمَامٌ Completion, end.

تَمَامًا وبِالتَّمَامِ Completely.

تَمِيمَةٌ ج تَمَائِمُ Talisman, amulet

تَامٌّ م تَامَّةٌ Perfect, complete.

تَتِمَّةٌ Complement.

تَمْتَامٌ Stammerer.

تَمْرٌ ج تُمُورٌ Ripe dates.

تَمْرٌ هِنْدِيٌّ Tamarind (*fruit*).

تَمُوز وتَمُّوز July.

تِمْسَاحٌ ج تَمَاسِيحُ Crocodile.

تِنِّينٌ ج تَنَانِين Dragon.

تَنْبَكُ Persian tobacco.

تِنْبَلٌ ج تَنَابِلُ Idler, lazy.

تَنُّورٌ ج تَنَانِيرُ Oven-pit.

تَنَكٌ Tin.

أَتْهَمَ وٱتَّهَمَ To suspect, accuse.

تُهْمَةٌ Suspicion. Accusation.

تَابَ يَتُوبُ To repent.

تَوْبَةٌ Repentence ; penitence.

تَائِبٌ Repentant, penitent.

تُوتٌ White mulberry.

تُوتٌ شَامِيٌّ Black mulberry.

تُوتُ ٱلْعُلَّيْقِ Blackberry.

تُوتِيَاءُ Zinc.

تَوَّجَ To crown.

تَتَوَّجَ To be crowned.

تَاجٌ ج تِيجَانٌ Crown, diadem.

تَوْرَاةٌ Pentateuch. Bible.

تَارَةً One time.

تَاقَ يَتُوقُ إِلَى To long for, desire.

تَوْقٌ وَتَوَقَانٌ Passion, desire.

تَائِقٌ Yearning, desiring.

تَاهَ يَتُوهُ To lose one's way.

تَيَّارٌ A strong, deep current.

تَاحَ وَأُتَاحَ لِ To be appointed, decreed to.

تَيْسٌ ج تُيُوسٌ He-goat.

تِينٌ Figs ; fig-trees.

تِينَةٌ A fig, a fig tree.

تَاهَ يَتِيهُ To be proud. Wander.

تِيهٌ Desert. Pride.

تَائِهٌ Lost, wandering. Proud.

ث

ث As a numeral sign = 500

تَثَاءَبَ تَثَاؤُبًا To yawn.

ثَأْرٌ وَثَارٌ ج اثَارٌ Revenge.

ثُؤْلُولٌ ج ثَآلِيلُ Wart.

ثَبَتَ يَثْبُتُ To stand firm.

ثَبَتَ عِنْدَ To be certain, assured.

To prove.	ثَبَّتَ وَأَثْبَتَ
Firmness. Reality.	ثَبَاتٌ وَثُبُوتٌ
Firm ; certain sure.	ثَابِتٌ
Fixed star.	ثَابِتَةٌ ج ثَوَابِتُ
Firm ; proved.	مُثْبَتٌ وَثَابِتٌ
To persevere in.	ثَابَرَ عَلَى مُثَابَرَةً
Assiduous, persevering.	مُثَابِرٌ
To be thick.	ثَخُنَ يَثْخُنُ
To make slaughter.	أَثْخَنَ
Thickness; hardness.	ثُخْنٌ وَثُخُونَةٌ
Thick, firm.	ثَخِينٌ ج ثِخَانٌ
Breast (mamma).	ثَدْيٌ ج ثُدِيٌّ
Omentum, caul.	ثَرْبٌ ج ثُرُوبٌ
Bread with broth.	ثَرِيد
To abound in wealth.	ثَرِيَ وَأَثْرَى
Wealth, riches.	ثَرَاءٌ وَثَرْوَةٌ
The Pleiades.	ثُرَيَّا
Moisture ; earth.	ثَرًى ج أَثْرَاءٌ
Large serpent.	ثُعْبَان ج ثَعَابِينُ
Fox.	ثَعْلَبٌ ج ثَعَالِبُ
Alopecia, falling of hair.	دَاءُ الثَّعْلَبِ
To make a breach.	ثَغَرَ يَثْغَرُ
Frontier. Mouth.	ثَغْرٌ ج ثُغُورٌ
Opening ; breach.	ثُغْرَةٌ ج ثُغُورٌ
Sediment, dregs.	ثُفْلٌ
To pierce.	ثَقَبَ يَثْقُبُ ثَقْبًا
To be pierced.	تَثَقَّبَ وَانْثَقَبَ
Hole.	ثَقْبٌ ج ثُقُوبٌ
Penetrating.	ثَاقِبٌ
Gimlet, drill.	مِثْقَبٌ ج مَثَاقِبُ
Pierced, perforated.	مَثْقُوبٌ
To be skilful.	ثَقِفَ يَثْقَفُ
Sagacity, intelligence.	ثَقَافَةٌ
Well-made; educated.	مُثَقَّفٌ
To be heavy.	ثَقُلَ يَثْقُلُ
To make heavy.	ثَقَّلَ
To burden, annoy.	ثَقُلَ عَلَى
To deem heavy	إِسْتَثْقَلَ

ثِقْلٌ ج أَثْقَالٌ	Weight, burden.
أَلثَّقَلَانِ	Mankind and geni.
ثَقِيلٌ ج ثُقَلَاءُ وَثِقَالٌ	Heavy.
مُثَقَّلٌ	Overburdened.
مِثْقَالٌ ج مَثَاقِيلُ	$1\frac{3}{7}$ dirhems.
ثَاكِلٌ وَثَكْلَى	Mother bereft of children.
ثَلَبَ يَثْلِبُ	To blame, censure.
ثَلْبٌ	Censure, reproach.
مَثْلَبَةٌ ج مَثَالِبُ	Fault, vice.
ثَلَّثَ	To make three.
أَثْلَثَ	To become three.
ثُلْثٌ وَثُلُثٌ	Third part, third.
ثَالِثٌ	Third.
ثَالِثًا	Thirdly.
ثَلَاثًا	Thrice, three times.
اَلثُّلَاثَاءُ وَٱلثَّلَثَاءُ	Tuesday.
ثَلَاثَةٌ اوْ ثَلٰثَةٌ م ثَلَاثٌ	Three.
ثُلَاثِيٌّ	Triliteral.
ثَلَاثُونَ وَثَلٰثُونَ	Thirty.
مُثَلَّثٌ	Triangular ; triangle.
ثَالُوثٌ	Trinity.
عِلْمُ ٱلْمُثَلَّثَاتِ	Trigonometry.
ثَلَجَ يَثْلُجُ وَأَثْلَجَ	To snow.
ثَلْجٌ ج ثُلُوجٌ	Snow.
ثَلِجٌ	Icy cold.
ثَلَمَ يَثْلِمُ ثَلْمًا وَثَلَّمَ	To blunt.
ثَلِمَ وَتَثَلَّمَ وَٱنْثَلَمَ	To be blunted.
ثَلْمٌ	Furrow ; breach.
ثَمَّ	Yonder ; there.
ثُمَّ وَثُمَّتْ	Then ; moreover.
إِثْمِدٌ	Antimony.
ثَمَرَ يَثْمُرُ وَأَثْمَرَ	To bear fruit.
ثَمَرٌ ج أَثْمَارٌ وَثِمَارٌ	Fruit.
ثَمَرَةٌ ج ثَمَرٌ وَثَمَرَاتٌ	A fruit.
مُثْمِرٌ	Productive, fruitful.
ثَمَلٌ	Intoxication.
ثَمَّنَ	To value, estimate.
ثَمَنٌ ج أَثْمَانٌ	Price, value.

ثُمْنٌ ج أَثْمَانٌ	Eighth part.
ثَامِنٌ	Eighth.
ثَمَانِيَةٌ م ثَمَانٍ	Eight.
ثَمَانُونَ	Eighty.
ثَمِينٌ وَمُثْمِنٌ	Costly, precious.
تَثْمِينٌ	Valuation, estimation.
مُثَمِّنٌ	Estimator appraiser.
مُثَمَّنٌ	Octagon. Estimated.
ثَنَى يَثْنِي ثَنْياً	To fold, double.
ثَنَى عَنْ	To dissuade.
ثَنَّى	To make two.
أَثْنَى عَلَى	To praise a person.
إِنْثَنَى	To be bent, folded.
إِنْثَنَى عَنْ	To desist from.
إِسْتَثْنَى مِنْ	To exclude.
ثَنَاءٌ ج أَثْنِيَةٌ	Praise, eulogy.
ثَانٍ م ثَانِيَةٌ	Second.
ثَانِياً وَثَانِيَةً	Secondly.
في إِثْنَاء ج ثَوَانٍ	Second, (time).
ثَانِيَةً ذَلِكَ	Meanwhile.
إِثْنَانِ م ثِنْتَانِ وَٱثْنَتَانِ	Two.
يَوْمُ ٱلإِثْنَيْنِ	Monday.
إِسْتِثْنَاءٌ	Exception, exclusion.
إِسْتِثْنَائِيٌّ	Exceptional.
مُثَنًّى	Put in the dual, (noun).
أَلْمُثَنَّى	The dual.
مُسْتَثْنًى	Excpeted, excluded.
ثَوَّبَ	To reward, recompense.
أَثَابَ إِثَابَةً	To reward.
ثَوْبٌ ج ثِيَابٌ وَأَثْوَابٌ	Garment.
ثَوَابٌ	Reward, recompense.
ثَارَ يَثُورُ	To rise up ; break out.
ثَوَّرَ وَأَثَارَ	To stir up ; rouse.
ثَوْرٌ ج أَثْوَارٌ وَثِيرَانٌ	Bull, ox.
ثَوْرَةٌ	Excitement. Mutiny.
ثُومٌ	Garlic.
ثَوَى يَثْوِي	To abide. To die.
مَثْوًى ج مَثَاوٍ	Abode.
ثَيِّبٌ ج ثَيِّبَاتٌ	Woman freed from her husband

ج

ج	As a numeral sign = 3.
جَاثَلِيقٌ	Primate of Christians.
جَاشٌ	Agitation, commotion.
جَبَّ يَجُبُّ	To lop ; cut off.
جُبٌّ ج أَجْبَابٌ	A deep well.
جُبَّةٌ ج جُبَبٌ	A long coat.
جَبَرَ يَجْبُرُ	To set a broken bone. To repair.
جَبَرَ عَلَى	To force, compel.
جَبَّرَ	To set a broken bone.
أَجْبَرَ عَلَى	To constrain, force.
تَجَبَّرَ عَلَى	To be haughty.
جَبْرٌ	Compulsion.
أَلْجَبْرُ	Algebra.
جَبِيرَةٌ ج جَبَائِرُ	Bandage ; splint.
جَبَّارٌ ج جَبَابِرَةٌ	Strong, Proud.
أَلْجَبَّارُ	God. Orion.
مُجَبِّرٌ	Bone-setter.
مَجْبُورٌ	Set (bone) ; constrained.
جِبْرِيلُ	The Angel Gabriel.
جِبْسٌ	Gypsum.
جَبَلَ يَجْبُلُ	To form, knead.
جَبَلٌ ج أَجْبَالٌ وَجِبَالٌ	Mountain.
جِبِلَّةٌ وَجِبْلَةٌ	Natural temper.
جَبَلِيٌّ	Mountainous.
جِبِلِّيٌّ	Natural, inborn.
مَجْبُولٌ	Kneaded ; formed.
جَبُنَ يَجْبُنُ	To be timid, cowardly.
تَجَبَّنَ	To become curdled.
جُبْنٌ وَجَبَانَةٌ	Cowardice.
جُبْنٌ وَجُبُنٌ	Cheese.
جَبِينٌ	Brow forehead.
جَبَانٌ ج جُبَنَاءُ	Coward.
جَبَّانَةٌ	Burying-ground.
جَبْهَةٌ	Brow, forehead.
جَبَا يَجْبُو وَيَجْبِي	To gather taxes.
إِجْتَبَى	To choose.

جِبَايَةٌ ج جِبَايَاتٌ — Tribute, tax.

جَابٍ — Tax-gatherer.

جُثَّةٌ ج جُثَثٌ — Corpse ; body.

جَثَا يَجْثُو جُثُوًّا — To kneel.

جَحَدَ يَجْحَدُ — To deny ; disbelieve.

جَاحِدٌ — Denying. An apostate.

جُحُودٌ — Unbelief ; denial.

جُحْرٌ ج أَجْحَارٌ وَأَجْحِرَةٌ — Den, hole.

جَحْشٌ ج جِحَاشٌ — Foal of an ass.

جَحَظَ ـَ جُحُوظًا — To protrude (eye).

جَحَظَ إِلَى — To look sharply at.

أَجْحَفَ بِ — To injure ; oppress.

إِجْحَافٌ — Damage ; injury.

جَحِيمٌ — Large fire ; hell.

جَدَّ يَجِدُّ — To exert oneself.

جَدَّ جِدَّةً — To be new.

جَدَّدَ — To renew ; restore.

تَجَدَّدَ — To be renewed, restored.

إِسْتَجَدَّ — To become new.

جَدٌّ — Fortune, success.

جِدٌّ — Exertion, seriousness.

جِدًّا — Much ; very ; seriously.

جَدٌّ ج جُدُودٌ — Grandfather.

جَدَّةٌ ج جَدَّاتٌ — Grandmother.

جَدِيدٌ ج جُدُدٌ — New, recent.

جَدْبٌ — Drought ; dearth.

أَجْدَبُ م جَدْبَاءُ — Sterile, bare.

مَجْذُوبٌ — Imbecile, idiot.

جَدَثٌ ج أَجْدَاثٌ — Grave.

جِدَارٌ ج جُدُرٌ — Wall, enclosure.

جَدَرِيٌّ — Small-box.

جَدِيرٌ بِ — Fit, worthy of.

أَجْدَرُ — More worthy, fitted.

جَدَعَ يَجْدَعُ — To cut off, main.

جَدْعٌ — Mutilation.

أَجْدَعُ — Maimed, mutilated.

جَدَفَ — To row.

جَدَفَ عَلَى — To blaspheme.

Blasphemy. تَجْدِيفٌ ج تَجَادِيفُ

Oar, paddle. مِجْدَافٌ ج مَجَادِيفُ

To twist. جَدَلَ يَجْدُلُ جَدْلاً

To braid the hair. جَدَّلَ

To contend, dispute. جَادَلَ

Contention, dispute. جِدَالٌ وَمُجَادَلَةٌ

Brook. List. جَدْوَلٌ ج جَدَاوِلُ

Plaited, twisted. مَجْدُولٌ

To be useful, profitable. اجدى

Gift. Benefit. جَدْوَى

Kid. Capricorn. جَدْيٌ ج جِدَاءٌ

To draw; attract. جَذَبَ يَجْذِبُ

To be drawn, attracted. إِنْجَذَبَ

Power of attraction. قُوَّةٌ جَاذِبَةٌ

To lop, cut off. جَذَرَ يَجْذِرُ

Root, origin. Root of number. جَذْرٌ ج جُذُورٌ

Lad, youth. جَذَعٌ وَجُذْعَانٌ

Trunk of tree. جِذْعٌ

To row (a boat). جَذَفَ يَجْذِفُ

Oar. مِجْذَافٌ مَجَاذِيفُ

To cut off. جَذَمَ يَجْذِمُ وَجَذَمَ

Leprosy. جُذَامٌ

Leper. أَجْذَمُ ج جَذْمَى

To draw, drag. جَرَّ يَجُرُّ جَرًّا

To be pulled, drawn. إِنْجَرَّ

To chew the cud. إِجْتَرَّ

And so on, et cetera. هَلُمَّ جَرًّا

Prepositions. حُرُوفُ ٱلْجَرِّ

Mechanics. جَرُّ ٱلأَثْقَالِ

Earthen jar. جَرَّةٌ ج جِرَارٌ

Preposition and case governed by it. جَارٌّ وَمَجْرُورٌ

Large army. جَيْشٌ جَرَّارٌ

Sin, crime. جَرِيرَةٌ ج جَرَائِرُ

Milky-way. أَلْمَجَرَّةُ

To be bold. جَرُؤَ يَجْرُؤُ جَرَاءَةً

To embolden, encourage. جَرَّأَ

To bare, venture. إِجْتَرَأَ

Boldness, courage. جُرْأَةٌ وَجَرَاءَةٌ

جَرِبَ يَجْرَبُ	To have the itch.
جَرَّبَ	To put to the test, try.
جَرَبٌ	Itch, scabies.
جِرَابٌ ج أَجْرِبَةٌ	Leathern sack.
أَجْرَبُ	Suffering from itch.
جَرِيبٌ ج أَجْرِبَةٌ	A corn-measure.
تَجْرِبَةٌ ج تَجَارِبُ	Trial, experiment; temptation.
مُجَرَّبٌ	Tried, tested.
جُرْثُومَةٌ ج جَرَاثِيمُ	Root; germ.
جَرْجِيرٌ	Cress, water-cress.
جَرَحَ يَجْرَحُ	To wound, hurt.
جُرْحٌ ج جُرُوحٌ	Wound, cut.
جِرَاحَةٌ ج جِرَاحٌ	Wound.
عِلْمُ ٱلْجِرَاحَةِ	Surgery.
جَرَّاحٌ وَجِرَاحِيٌّ	Surgeon.
جَرِيحٌ ج جَرْحَى	Wounded.
جَارِحَةٌ ج جَوَارِحُ	Beast of prey.
مَجْرُوحٌ ج مَجَارِيحُ	Wounded.
مُجَرَّحٌ	Covered with wounds.
جَرَّدَ	To strip, abstract.
تَجَرَّدَ	To be stripped, bared.
جَرَادٌ	Locusts.
جَرِيدٌ	Branch of palm-tree.
أَجْرَدُ م جَرْدَاءُ	Naked, hairless.
مُجَرَّدٌ	Separated; bare, naked.
مُجَرَّدًا لِ	Solely for.
مُجَرَّدَاتٌ	Abstractions.
جُرَذٌ ج جِرْذَانٌ	Field-rat.
جُرْزَةٌ	Bundle of sticks.
جَرَسٌ ج أَجْرَاسٌ	Bell.
جَرَشَ يَجْرُشُ	To bruise; bray.
جَارُوشٌ ج جَوَارِيشُ	Hand-mill.
جَرَعَ يَجْرَعُ وَٱجْتَرَعَ	To swallow.
جُرْعَةٌ	Draught of water.
جَرَفَ يَجْرُفُ	To sweep away.
مِجْرَفَةٌ	Shovel; hoe.
جَرَمَ وَأَجْرَمَ	To commit a crime.
تَجَرَّمَ	To impute a crime falsely.

جُرْمٌ ج جُرُومٌ وَأَجْرَامٌ Sin, crime.
جُرْمٌ ج أَجْرَامٌ Body, bulk.
الأَجْرَامُ الفَلَكِيَّةُ The celestial bodies.
جُرْمٌ ج جُرُومٌ Boat, lighter.
لَا جَرَمَ Verily, truly.
جَرِيمَةٌ ج جَرَائِمُ Sin, guilt, crime.
مُجْرِمٌ Criminal, guilty.
جُرْنٌ ج أَجْرَانٌ Mortar, basin.
جَرْوٌ ج أَجْرِيَةٌ Cub, whelp.
جَرَى يَجْرِي جَرْيًا وَجَرَيَانًا To flow.
جَرَّى وَأَجْرَى To cause to flow.
أَجْرَى To carry out, execute.
جَارَى فِي To agree with.
جِرَايَةٌ Rations of a soldier.
جَارٍ Running ; current.
جَارِيَةٌ Slave-girl, girl.
إِجْرَاءٌ Execution of an order.
مَجْرًى ج مَجَارٍ Course ; duct.
جَزَّ يَجُزُّ To shear, cut, mow.

جَزَّةٌ Fleece, shorn wool.
جَزَّازٌ Shearer.
مِجَزٌّ Shears, scissors.
مَجْزُوزٌ Shorn, cut.
جَزَّأَ To divide into portions.
تَجَزَّأَ To be divided into parts.
جُزْءٌ ج أَجْزَاءٌ Part, portion.
جُزْئِيٌّ Partial, particular.
جُزْئِيَّةٌ Particular proposition.
جُزْئِيَّاتٌ Details, parts ; trifles.
أَجْزَائِيٌّ Apothecary, druggist.
أَجْزَائِيَّةٌ Pharmacy.
مُتَجَزِّئٌ Divided into parts.
جَزَرَ يَجْزُرُ To slaughter, kill.
جَزَرَ يَجْزُرُ جَزْرًا To ebb (sea).
جَزْرٌ Slaughter. Ebb.
جَزَرٌ Carrots.
جَزَّارٌ Butcher ; slaughterer.
جَزِيرَةٌ ج جَزَائِرُ وَجُزُرٌ Island.

شِبْهُ جَزِيرَةٍ	Peninsula.
أَلْجَزَائِر	Algiers.
مَجْزَرٌ ج مَجَازِر	Slaughter-house.
جَزِعَ يَجْزَعُ	To grow impatient.
جَزَعٌ وَجُزُوعٌ	Impatience, grief.
جَزِعٌ وَجَزُوعٌ	Impatient.
جِزَافٌ وَمُجَازَفَةٌ وَجِزَافًا	At random, by conjecture.
جَزُلَ يَجْزُلُ جَزَالَةً	To abound.
أَجْزَلَ	To give largely.
جَزِيلٌ	Abundant ; much.
جَزِيلُ ٱلْاِحْتِرَامِ	Very venerable.
جَزَمَ يَجْزِمُ جَزْمًا	To decide ; make binding.
جَزْمَةٌ ج جَزْمَات	Boot.
جَازِمٌ ج جَوَازِمُ	Decisive.
جَزَى يَجْزِي	To recompense.
جَازَى	To reward.
تَجَازَى	To be rewarded or punished.
جَزَاءٌ وَمُجَازَاةٌ	Requital, reward.
جِزْيَةٌ	Tax on a tributary ; land tax.
جَسَّ يَجُسُّ وَٱجْتَسَّ	To touch.
جَسَّ وَتَجَسَّسَ	To spy out.
جَاسُوسٌ ج جَوَاسِيسُ	Spy.
تَجَسَّدَ	To assume a body.
جَسَدٌ ج أَجْسَادٌ	Body, flesh.
جَسَدِيٌّ وَجُسْدَانِيٌّ	Corporeal.
تَجَسُّدٌ	Incarnation.
جَسَرَ يَجْسُرُ	To dare venture.
تَجَاسَرَ	To venture boldly.
جِسْرٌ ج أَجْسُرٌ	Bridge. Dike.
جَسَارَةٌ	Courage, audacity.
جَسُورٌ	Bold, courageous.
تَجَاسُرٌ	Courage, audacity.
جَسُمَ جَسَامَةً	To be large.
تَجَسَّمَ	To assume a form.
جِسْمٌ ج أَجْسَامٌ	Body.
جُسْمَانِيٌّ	Bodily ; material.
جَسَامَةٌ	Importance.

جَسِيمٌ Large. Important.
مُجَسَّمٌ Solid, corporeal, bulky.
جَشَأَ وَتَجَشَّأَ To belch, eruct.
جُشَاءٌ Eructation.
جَشِمَ وَتَجَشَّمَ To undertake a difficult task.
جِصٌّ Gypsum ; mortar.
جَعْبَةٌ ج جِعَابٌ Quiver.
جَعُدَ يَجْعُدُ To be curly (hair).
تَجَعَّدَ To be curly, wrinkled.
جُعَيْدِيٌّ Buffoon ; low fellow.
جَعَلَ يَجْعَلُ To put, place, make.
جَعَلَ يَبْكِي He began to weep.
جَعَالَةٌ وَجُعْلٌ Pay, wages; bribe.
جَفَّ يَجِفُّ جَفَافاً To become dry.
جَفَّفَ To dry cause to dry.
تَجَفَّفَ To become dry.
جَافٌّ وَجَفِيفٌ Dry, withered,
جَفَلَ وَأَجْفَلَ To be frightened, shy.
جَفَّلَ To put to flight ; frighten.

جَفْنٌ ج جُفُونٌ وَأَجْفَانٌ Eyelid.
جَفَا يَجْفُو جَفَاءً To treat rudely.
جَافَى To shun, turn away from.
جَفْوَةٌ وجَفَاءٌ Harshness.
جَافٍ Thick, coarse, rude.
جَلَّ يَجِلُّ جَلَالاً To be great.
جَلَّ وَتَجَالَّ عَنْ To disdain.
اجَلَّ To honour, magnify.
جُلٌّ ج أَجْلَالٌ Pack-saddle.
جُلُّ الأَمْرِ The gist of a matter.
جَلَالٌ Splendour, majesty.
جَلَالَاتِيٌّ Maker of pack-saddles.
جَلَالَةٌ Human greatness ; majesty.
جَلِيلٌ ج أَجِلَّاءُ Great.
مَجَلَّةٌ Book ; review.
جَلَبَ يَجْلُبُ To gather ; bring.
إِنْجَلَبَ To be led, imported.
جَلْبٌ Importation, import.
جَلَبٌ Camlour, noise, tumult.

جَلَبٌ	Imported slaves, cattle.
جُلْبَةٌ	Scab. Hunger, distress.
جَلَبَةٌ	Clamour, tumult.
جَلَّابٌ	Cattle or slave-dealer.
جُلَابٌ	Julep, raisin-water.
مَجْلُوبٌ	Drawn ; imported.
جُلْجُلٌ ج جَلَاجِلُ	Little bell.
جَلَحَةٌ	Baldness on the temples.
أَجْلَحُ	Bald on the temples.
جَلَخَ وَجَلَّخَ	To whet (a razor).
جَلْخٌ	Grindstone.
جَلَدَ يَجْلِدُ جَلْداً	To scourge.
جَلِدَ يَجْلَدُ جَلَداً	To be frozen.
جَلَّدَ	To bind a book.
تَجَلَّدَ	To bear patiently.
جَلَدٌ	Endurance. Firmament.
جِلْدٌ ج جُلُودٌ	Skin, hide, leather.
جَلَادَةٌ وَجُلُودَةٌ	Endurance.
جَلَّادٌ	Executioner.
جَلِيدٌ	Hoar-frost, ice.
مُجَلِّدٌ	Book-binder.
مُجَلَّدٌ	Bound in leather, book.
جَلَسَ يَجْلِسُ	To sit, sit up.
جَالَسَ	To sit in company with.
أَجْلَسَ	To cause to sit.
جَلْسَةٌ	A single sitting ; session.
جَالِسٌ	Sitting. Straight.
جُلُوسٌ	Act of sitting.
جَلِيسٌ ج جُلَسَاءُ	Companion.
مَجْلِسٌ ج مَجَالِسُ	Council.
مَجْلِسُ ٱلْوُزَرَاءِ	Council of ministers.
أَلْمَجْلِسُ ٱلِابْتِدَائِيُّ	Court of the First Instance.
مَجْلِسُ ٱلِاسْتِئْنَافِ	Court of Appeal.
أَلْمَجْلِسُ ٱلْمُخْتَلَطُ	Mixed Tribunal.
مَجْلِسٌ حَرْبِيٌّ	Council of war.
جَلَفَ يَجْلِفُ جَلْفاً	To tear, scrape.
جُوَالِقُ ج جَوَالِيقُ	Large sack.
مَنْجَلِيقٌ وَمَنْجَنِيقٌ	Catapult.

جَلَا يَجْلُو	To polish ; remove.
جَلَا لِ	To become evident.
جَلَا عَنْ	To depart.
أَجْلَى	To emigrate.
تَجَلَّى لِ	To appear.
إِنْجَلَى	To be disclosed.
جَلَاءٌ	Clearness. Emigration.
جَلِيٌّ	Clear, evident, manifest.
جليا	Clearly, evidently.
اَلتَّجَلِّي (عيد)	Transfiguration.
مَجْلُوٌّ وَمَجْلِيٌّ	Polished, planed.
جَلَى يَجْلِي جَلْيًا	To polish.
جَمٌّ غَفِيرٌ	Great number, crowd.
جُمْجُمَةٌ ج جَمَاجِم	Skull.
جَمَحَ يَجْمَحُ	To be restive, run-away (horse).
جَامِحٌ وَجَمُوحٌ	Refractory.
جَمَدَ يَجْمُدُ	To congeal, harden.
جَامِدٌ ج جَوَامِد	Underived word.
اَلْجَوَامِد	The mineral kingdom
جَمَادٌ	Mineral, solid.
جُمَادَى الْاُولَى / » الْآخِرَة	The fifth and sixth months of the Mohammedan year.
جَمْرَةٌ ج جَمْرٌ	Live coal. Tribe.
جَمْرَةٌ	Carbuncle (*disease*).
مِجْمَرَةٌ ج مَجَامِر	Censer ; fire-pan.
جُمَّيْز وَجُمَّيْزَى	Sycamore.
جَامُوسٌ ج جَوَامِيس	Buffalo.
جَمَعَ يَجْمَعُ	To gather, add.
جَمَعَ بَيْنَ	To bring together.
أَجْمَعُوا عَلَى	To agree upon.
تَجَمَّعَ وَاجْتَمَعَ	To assemble, be gathered.
جَمْعٌ ج جُمُوع	Assembly ; plural.
اَلْجَمْعُ السَّالِم	Whole plural.
جَمْعُ التَّكْسِير	Broken plural.
جُمْعَةٌ ج جُمَع	Week.
اَلْجُمْعَة	Friday.
جَمَاعَةٌ	Party ; community.
جَامِعٌ	Collector ; comprehensive.

جَامِعٌ ج جَوَامِعُ — Mosque.

جَمِيع — All, the whole of.

جَمِيعاً — All; altogether.

جَمْعِيَّةٌ — Company ; committee.

أَجْمَعُ ج أَجْمَعُونَ — All, whole.

إِجْمَاعٌ — Unanimity.

إِجْتِمَاعٌ — Assembly, gathering.

مَجْمَعٌ ج مَجَامِعُ — Confluence. Society of learned men.

مَجْمُوعٌ ج مَجَامِيعُ — United, total.

جَامَكِيَّةٌ — Pay, salary.

جَمَّلَ — To embellish, adorn.

جَامَلَ — To treat with affability.

جَمَلٌ ج جِمَالٌ — Camel.

جُمْلَةٌ ج جُمَلٌ — Sum, total. Sentence, phrase, paragraph.

بِالْجُمْلَةِ — In the aggregate.

جَمَالٌ — Beauty, grace.

جَمَّالٌ — Camel-driver.

جَمِيلٌ — Handsome, good deed.

بِالإِجْمَالِ — Generally speaking.

مُجْمَلٌ — Sum, total; summary.

جُمْهُورٌ ج جَمَاهِيرُ — Multitude.

جُمْهُورِيٌّ — Republican.

جُمْهُورِيَّةٌ — Republic.

جَنَّ يَجُنُّ — To be dark (night).

جُنَّ — To become mad.

جَنَّنَ وَأَجَنَّ — To madden.

جِنٌّ وَجَانٌ وَجِنَّةٌ — Demons, genii.

جَنَّةٌ ج جَنَّاتٌ — Garden, paradise.

جَنَانٌ ج أَجْنَانٌ — Heart, mind.

جُنُونٌ — Madness, insanity.

جَنِينٌ ج أَجِنَّةٌ — Embryo, fœtus.

جُنَيْنَةٌ — Small garden.

مِجَنٌّ ج مَجَانٌّ — Shield.

مَجْنُونٌ ج مَجَانِينُ — Mad, insane.

تَجَنَّبَ وَاجْتَنَبَ — To shun, avoid.

جَنْبٌ ج جُنُوبٌ — Side, flank.

ذَاتُ الْجَنْبِ — Pleurisy.

جَانِبٌ ج جَوَانِبُ — Flank, part.

Mild, gentle.	لَيِّنُ ٱلْجَانِبِ
Title of respect.	جَنَابٌ
South ; south wind.	جَنُوبٌ
Southern.	جَنُوبِيٌّ
Foreign.	أَجْنَبِيٌّ ج أَجَانِبُ
Act of avoiding.	إِجْتِنَابٌ وَتَجَنُّبٌ
To incline towards.	جَنَحَ يَجْنَحُ
Wing.	جَنَاحٌ ج أَجْنِحَة
Sin, crime, guilt.	جُنَاحٌ
To levy troops.	جَنَّدَ
To be enlisted, enrolled.	تَجَنَّدَ
Army.	جُنْدٌ ج جُنُودٌ
A soldier.	جُنْدِيٌّ
Grasshopper.	جُنْدُبٌ ج جَنَادِبُ
To throw a man down.	جَنْدَلَ
A kind of plum.	جنريك
Funeral, corps.	جَنَازَةٌ ج جَنَائِزُ
Funeral rites.	جُنَازٌ ج جَنَانِيزُ
Verdigris.	جِنْزَارٌ
To make similar.	جَنَّسَ
To appear similar.	جَانَسَ
Genus, kind, race, sex ; nationality.	جِنْسٌ ج أَجْنَاسٌ
Generic noun.	إِسْمُ جِنْسٍ
Nationality.	جِنْسِيَّة
Of the same kind.	مُجَانِس
To act unjustly.	جَنَفَ وَأَجْنَفَ
Wrong, injustice.	جَنَفٌ
Coarse linen.	جِنْفَاصٌ وَجَنْفَيْصٌ
Catapult.	مَنْجَنِيقٌ ج مَجَانِقُ وَمَجَانِيقُ
To gather (fruit).	جَنَى ـِ وَٱجْتَنَى
To commit a crime.	جَنَى جِنَايَةً
To accuse falsely.	تَجَنَّي على
A gatherer. Criminal.	جَانٍ
Crime ; sin.	جِنَايَة
To toil.	جَهِدَ
To weary, fatigue.	جَهَّدَ
To struggle.	جَاهَدَ مُجَاهَدَةً وَجِهَاداً
To strive after.	إِجْتَهَدَ فِي

جُهْدٌ — Exertion, effort.

أَفْرَغَ جُهْدَهُ — He did his best.

جِهادٌ — Combat, struggle.

جِهَادِيٌّ — Military.

إِجْتِهَادٌ — Diligence, effort.

مُجَاهِدٌ — Champion.

جَهَرَ بِ — To publish.

جَهِرَ يَجْهَرُ — To be dazzled.

جَاهَرَ بِ — To declare publicly.

تَجَاهَرَ — To appear in public.

جَهْراً وَجِهَاراً — Publicly, openly.

أَجْهَرُ م جَهْرَاءُ — Day-blind.

مِجْهَرٌ — Microscope.

جَهَّزَ — To equip, fit out.

تَجَهَّزَ — To get ready.

جَهَازٌ ج أَجْهِزَةٌ — Trousseau. Requisites, apparatus.

تَجْهِيزٌ — Equipment, expedition.

جَهِلَ يَجْهَلُ — To be ignorant.

جَهَّلَ — To impute ignorance.

تَجَاهَلَ — To affect ignorance.

إِسْتَجْهَلَ — To deem one ignorant.

جَهْلٌ وَجَهَالَةٌ — Ignorance. Folly.

جَاهِلٌ — Ignorant, fool.

أَلْجَاهِلِيَّةُ — Pre-islamic age.

مَجْهُولٌ — Unknown. Passive verb.

جَهَنَّمُ — Hell.

جَهَنَّمِيٌّ — Hellish, infernal.

جَوٌّ — Sky, atmosphere.

جَابَ يَجُوبُ — To travel.

جَاوَبَ — To answer, reply.

أَجَابَ — To answer, respond.

إِسْتَجَابَ — To answer ; listen to.

جَوَابٌ ج أَجْوِبَةٌ — Answer reply.

إِجَابَةٌ وَٱسْتِجَابَةٌ — Compliance.

مُجِيبٌ وَمُسْتَجِيبٌ — Answerer.

مُسْتَجَابٌ — Answered (prayer).

جُوخٌ ج أَجْوَاخٌ — Broadcloth.

جَوَّاخٌ — Cloth-maker or dealer.

جادَ يَجُود جُودَةً To excel.

جادَ جوداً To give abundantly.

جَوَّدَ To make good.

جُودٌ Liberality, generosity.

جَوْدَةٌ Goodness, excellence.

جَوَادٌ ج أَجْوادٌ Generous.

جَوادٌ ج جِيَاد Fleet (horse).

جَيِّدٌ ج جِيادٌ Good, excellent.

جَيِّداً Very well.

جارَ يَجُورُ عَلَى To oppress.

جَاوَرَ To be contiguous.

أَجَارَ إِجَارَةً To save ; protect.

تَجَاوَرَ To be neighbours.

إِستَجَارَ To seek protection.

جَارٌ ج جِيرَانٌ Neighbour.

جَوْرٌ Oppression, tyranny.

جُوَارٌ Neighbourhood, vicinity.

مُجَاوِرٌ Neighbour ; contiguous.

مُجِيرٌ Protector, defender.

جَوْرَبٌ ج جوَارِب Stocking.

جَازَ يَجُوزُ To pass, travel.

جَازَ جَوَازًا To be allowable.

جَوَّزَ To allow ; permit.

جَاوَزَ مُجَاوَزَةً To exceed.

أَجَازَ إِجَازَةً To allow ; permit.

تَجَاوَزَ To exceed the bounds.

تَجَاوَزَ عَنْ To overlook.

إِجْتَازَ بِ To pass by.

جَوْزٌ Nut, nut-tree. Walnut.

جَوْزٌ هِنْدِيٌّ Cocoa-nut.

جَوْزَ الطِّيبِ Nutmeg.

الْجَوْزَاءُ Twins. Orion.

جائِزٌ Passing ; lawful.

جَوَازٌ Lawfulness ; passage.

جَائِزَةٌ ج جَوَائِزِ Present, prize.

إِجَازَةٌ Permission ; licence.

مَجَاز Passage. Figurative.

مجازِيٌّ Metaphoric.

جَوْشَنٌ ج جَوَاشِنُ — Coat of mail.

جَاعَ يَجُوعُ — To be hungry.

جَوَّعَ وَأَجَاعَ — To starve.

جُوعٌ — Hunger.

جَائِعٌ ج جِيَاعٌ — Hungry.

مَجَاعَةٌ — Famine ; hunger.

جَوَّفَ — To hollow.

جَوْفٌ ج أَجْوَافٌ — Cavity. Belly.

اجْوَف — Empty, hollow.

تَجْوِيفٌ ج تَجَاوِيف — Cavity.

مُجَوَّفٌ — Hollow, empty.

جَوْقَةٌ ج جَوْقَاتٌ — Crowd.

جَالَ يَجُولُ — To travel.

جَائِلٌ — Travelling roaming.

جَوَلَانٌ — Act of travelling about.

مَجَالٌ — Range ; sphere of action.

جَامٌ ج جَامَاتٌ — Vessel, tray.

جَاهٌ — Honour,rank, dignity

جَوْهَرٌ ج جَوَاهِر — Jewels, pearls, Essence, nature element.

أَلْجَوْهَر أَلْفَرْدُ — Atom ; monad.

جَوْهَرَةٌ — A jewel, pearl.

جَوْهَرِيٌّ — Jeweller. Essential.

جَوَّانِيٌّ — Interior, inward.

جَاءَ يَجِيءُ — To come, arrive.

جَاءَ بِ — To bring.

مَجِيءٌ — Act of coming, arrival.

جَيْبٌ ج جُيُوبٌ — Pocket, Sinus.

جِيدٌ ج أَجْيَادٌ وَجُيُودٌ — Neck.

جِيرٌ — Gypsum ; quicklime.

جَيَّشَ — To collect an army.

جَأْشٌ وجَاشٌ — The soul.

جَيْشٌ ج جُيُوشٌ — Army.

جِيفَةٌ ج جِيَفٌ — Corpse, carcass.

جِيلٌ ج أَجْيَالٌ — Race ; generation.

ح

ح As a numeral sign = 8.

حَبَّ يُحِبُّ حِبًّا وَحُبًّا To love.

حَبَّبَ إِلَى To make lovable.

أَحَبَّ To love ; like.

تَحَبَّبَ To show love.

إِسْتَحَبَّ عَلَى To prefer.

حَبٌّ ج حُبُوبٌ Grain ; seed ; berry; pill ; pustule.

حُبٌّ وَمَحَبَّةٌ Love, friendship.

حَبَّةٌ ج حَبَّاتٌ A grain.

حَبِيبٌ ج احبَّاء Lover ; beloved.

حبًّا وَكَرَامَةً With all my heart.

أَحَبُّ Dearer ; preferable.

مُحِبٌّ Lover ; friend.

مَحْبُوبٌ Beloved ; liked.

حَبَّذَا . يا حَبَّذَا Well done.

حَبِرَ يَحْبَرُ حُبُوراً To be glad.

حَبْرٌ ج أَحْبَارٌ Learned, good man.

الْحَبْرُ الأَعْظَمُ High priest, the Pope.

حِبْرٌ Ink.

حُبُورٌ Joy, gladness, happiness.

مَحْبَرَةٌ ج مَحَابِرُ Inkstand.

حَبَسَ يَحْبِسُ To imprison.

حَبَسَ عَنْ To restrain.

حَبْسٌ ج حُبُوسٌ Prison.

حَبْسٌ وَٱحْتِبَاسٌ Imprisonment.

إِحْتِبَاسٌ Retention.

مَحْبُوسٌ Imprisoned ; arrested.

حُبَشٌ وَحَبَشَةٌ The Abyssinians.

حَبَشِيٌّ An Abyssinian.

بِلَادُ ٱلْحَبَشِ وٱلْحَبَشَةِ Abyssinia.

حَبَطَ يَحْبَطُ To fail ; perish.

حُبُوطٌ Failure.

حَبَقٌ Basil, penny-royal.

حَبَكَ يَحْبُكُ To weave ; unite.

مَحْبُوكٌ Well woven ; strong.

حَبِلَتْ تَحْبَلُ To conceive (woman).

تَحَبَّلَ To be entangled.

حَبْلٌ ج حِبَالٌ Rope, cable.

حَبْلُ ٱلْوَرِيدِ Jugular vein.

حَبَل Pregnancy, conception.

أُحْبُولَةٌ ج حَبَائِل Net, snare.

حُبْلَى ج حَبَالَى Pregnant (woman).

حَبَّالٌ Rope-maker.

حَبَا يَحْبُو To creep, crawl.

حَابَى To bepartial to.

مُحَابَاةٌ Partiality, favour.

مُحَاب Partial.

حَتَّ يَحُتُّ حَتًّا To rub off.

حَتَّةٌ ج حَتَتٌ Bit of anything.

حَتَّى Until, to, as far as, even.

حَتَّى أَنْ So that.

حَتْفٌ ج حتوفٌ Death.

حتفَ أَنْفِهِ Natural death.

حَتَمَ يَحْتِمُ To decide, decree.

حَتَمَ ب To decide ; order.

حَتَمَ عَلَى To compel.

حَتْمٌ ج حُتُومٌ Final decision.

مَحْتُومٌ Decided, fixed.

حَثَّ يَحُثُّ To exhort, instigate.

حَثٌّ وَإِحْثَاثٌ Instigation.

حَجَّ يَحِجُّ To go as a pilgrim to Mecca.

حَجَّهُ To overcome in argument.

حَاجَّ To dispute, contend with.

إِحْتَجَّ ب To offer as a proof.

إِحْتَجَّ عَلَى To argue against.

حَجٌّ وَحِجَّةٌ Pilgrimage to Mecca.

حُجَّةٌ ج حُجَجٌ Proof ; title, deed. Pretext, excuse.

ذُو ٱلْحِجَّةِ The last month of the Mohammedan year.

حَاجٌّ ج حُجَّاجٌ Pilgrim to Mecca.

حَجَبَ يَحْجُبُ To hide, cover.

حَجَبَ عَنْ To prevent.

إِحْتَجَبَ To conceal one's self.

Partition; veil. حِجَابٌ ج حُجُبٌ

Diaphragm. أَلْحِجَابُ ٱلْحَاجِزُ

Chamberlain. Door-keeper. حَاجِبٌ ج حُجَّابٌ

Eye-brow. حَاجِبٌ ج حَوَاجِبُ

To prevent, restrain. حَجَرَ يَحْجُرُ

To be turned into stone. تَحَجَّرَ

Prevention, prohibition. حَجْرٌ

Stone. حَجَرٌ ج أَحْجَارٌ وَحِجَارَةٌ

Nitrate of silver. حَجَرُ جَهَنَّمَ

Chamber; sepulchre. حُجْرَةٌ

Stone-cutter. حَجَّارٌ ج حَجَّارُونَ

Larynx. حَنْجَرَةٌ ج حَنَاجِرُ

To prevent, hinder. حَجَزَ يَحْجُزُ

To separate. حَجَزَ بَيْنَ

To sequester goods. حَجَزَ عَلَى

Prevention, restraint. حَجْزٌ

Arabia Petrœa, Hijas. أَلْحِجَازُ

A barrier. حَاجِزٌ ج حَوَاجِزُ

Hindered, prevented. مَحْجُوزٌ

To hop, leap. حَجَلَ يَحْجِلُ

Partridge. حَجَلٌ ج حِجْلَانٌ

Having white foot, or feet, (horse). مُحَجَّلٌ

To cup, scarify. حَجَمَ يَحْجُمُ

To be cupped. إِحْتَجَمَ

Bulk; size. حَجْمٌ ج حُجُومٌ

Art of cupping, cupping. حِجَامَةٌ

Cupper. حَجَّامٌ

Cupping instrument. مِحْجَمٌ

To propose riddles. تَحَاجَى

Intelligence. حِجًى ج أَحْجَاءٌ

Enigma; riddle. أُحْجِيَّةٌ ج أَحَاجِيُّ

To confine, define. حَدَّ يَحُدُّ

To go into mourning. حَدَّ حِدَادًا

To confine; define; sharpen. حَدَّدَ

To look sharply. أَحَدَّ ٱلنَّظَرَ

To be limited; defined. تَحَدَّدَ

To be excited. إِحْتَدَّ

Limit, boundary. حَدٌّ ج حُدُودٌ

حِدَّةٌ Impetuosity ; acerbity.

حَادٌّ Sharp, pointed ; pungent.

زَاوِيَةٌ حَادَّةٌ Acute angle.

حِدَادٌ Mourning.

حَدَّادٌ Blacksmith.

حَدِيدٌ Iron.

حَدِيدَةٌ A piece of iron.

تَحْدِيدٌ Demarcation.

مَحْدُودٌ Limited ; bounded.

حِدَأَةٌ ج حِدَاءٌ Kite (hawk).

تَحَدَّبَ To become convex.

إِحْدَوْدَبَ To be hump-backed.

أَحْدَبُ م حَدْبَاءُ Hump-backed.

مُحَدَّبٌ Convex ; bulging.

حَدَثَ يَحْدُثُ To happen, occur.

حَدَّثَ To tell ; relate.

حَادَثَ مُحَادَثَةٌ To converse.

أَحْدَثَ To cause to exist.

تَحَادَثَ To converse together.

حَادِثَةٌ ج حَوَادِثُ Event.

حَدَاثَةٌ Newness, youth.

حَدِيثٌ New, recent.

حَدِيثٌ ج أَحَادِيثُ Story, tale. Mohammedan tradition.

اُحْدُوثَةٌ ج أَحَادِيثُ Tale.

مُحَادَثَةٌ Conversation.

إِنْحَدَرَ To descend.

حُدُورٌ وَانْحِدَارٌ Descent.

حَدَسَ يَحْدِسُ فِي To surmise.

حَدْسٌ Conjecture; guess.

حَدَسِيَّاتٌ Hypotheses.

أَحْدَقَ بِ To surround, enclose.

حَدَّقَ إِلَى To look sharply at.

حَدَقَةٌ The pupil of the eye.

حَدِيقَةٌ ج حَدَائِقُ Garden.

حَدْمٌ وَحَدَمٌ Glow (of a fire).

مُحْتَدِمٌ Growing with heat.

حَادٍ ج حُدَاةٌ Camel-driver.

The eleventh. حَادِي عَشَرَ

To be cautious. حَذِرَ يَحْذَرُ

To warn. حَذَّرَ

To be cautious. تَحَذَّرَ وَٱحْتَذَرَ

Caution ; distrust. حِذْرٌ وَحَذَرٌ

Cautious. حَذِرٌ ج حَذِرُون

Take care ! حَذَارِ

A thing to be avoided. مَحْذُورٌ

To cut off ; drop. حَذَفَ يَحْذِفُ

To throw at. حَذَفَ بِ

Elision ; suppression. حَذْفٌ

Cut off ; suppressed. مَحْذُوفٌ

To be skilful. حَذَقَ يَحْذَقُ

Sharpness, skill. حِذْقٌ

Sharp ; clever. حَاذِقٌ ج حُذَّاقٌ

To imitate, emulate. حَذَا يَحْذُو حَذْواً

To be opposite to. حَاذَى

Opposite to ; vis-à-vis. حِذَاءَ

Shoe, sandal. حِذَاءٌ ج أَحْذِيَةٌ

Placed opposite ; vis-a-vis. مُحَاذٍ

To be hot. حَرَّ يَحِرُّ

To set free, free (a slave). حَرَّرَ

To be set free, freed. تَحَرَّرَ

Heat. حَرٌّ

Freeman ; noble. حُرٌّ ج أَحْرَارٌ

Heat warmth. حَرَارَةٌ

Liberty, freedom. حُرِّيَّةٌ

Silk ; silk-stuff. حَرِيرٌ

Letter, note. تَحْرِيرٌ ج تَحَارِيرُ

Hot, burning ; fervent. حَارٌّ

Liberated ; set free. مُحَرَّرٌ

Heated (with anger, etc.) مَحْرُورٌ

To fight. حَارَبَ مُحَارَبَةً

To fight one another. تَحَارَبَ

War, battle. حَرْبٌ ج حُرُوبٌ

Enemy's territory. دَارُ ٱلْحَرْبِ

Chameleon. حِرْبَاءٌ ج حَرَابِيُّ

Lance ; bayonet. حَرْبَةٌ ج حِرَابٌ

مِحْرَابٌ	Place of prayer.
حَرَثَ يَحْرُثُ حَرْثًا	To till.
حِرَاثَةٌ	Agriculture.
حَارِثٌ وَحَرَّاثٌ	Ploughman.
مِحْرَثٌ وَمِحْرَاثٌ	A plough.
حَرِجَ يَحْرَجُ	To be in difficulty.
حَرِجَ عَلَى	To be forbidden.
حَرِجٌ	Narrow. Forbidden.
لَا حَرَجَ	No blame or sin.
حَرَاجٌ	Auction.
حَرِدَ يَحْرَدُ	To be angry.
حَرَدٌ	Anger, grudge, hatred.
حِرْذَوْنٌ ج حَرَاذِينَ	Lizard.
حَرَزَ يَحْرُزُ	To guard carefully.
أَحْرَزَ	To guard. Obtain.
تَحَرَّزَ وَٱحْتَرَزَ	To guard against.
حِرْزٌ	Caution ; amulet.
حَرِيز	Fortified ; valued.
حَرَسَ يَحْرُسُ	To guard, watch.
تَحَرَّسَ وَٱحْتَرَسَ	To be cautioned.
حِرَاسَةٌ	Watch, guard.
حَارِسٌ ج حُرَّاسٌ	Watchman, guard.
حَرَّشَ بَيْنَ	To excite discord.
تَحَرَّشَ بِ	To meddle with.
حُرْشٌ ج أَحْرَاشٌ	Wood, thicket.
حَرَصَ يَحْرِصُ	To covet eagerly.
حِرْصٌ	Greed, cupidity.
حَرِيصٌ ج حُرَصَاءُ	Covetous.
حَرَّضَ عَلَى	To incite, instigate.
حَرَفَ يَحْرِفُ عَنْ	To turn from.
حَرَّفَ	To falsify, garble.
إِنْحَرَفَ عَنْ	To deviate from.
اِحْتَرَفَ	To earn sustenance.
حَرْفٌ ج حِرَفٌ	Edge, border.
حَرْفٌ ج حُرُوفٌ وَأَحْرُفٌ	Letter, particle (in grammer).
حَرْفِيٌّ	Literal.
حِرْفَةٌ ج حِرَفٌ	Trade, craft.

حَرَافَة	Pungency.
حِرِّيف	Sharp, pungent.
مُحَرَّف	Falsified.
مُنْحَرِف	Oblique ; trapezium
حَرَقَ يَحْرُقُ وَأَحْرَقَ	To burn.
اِحْتَرَقَ وَتَحَرَّقَ	To be burned.
حُرْقَة	Heat, burning pain.
حَرِيق	Heat, conflagration.
حَرَّاقَة ج حَرَّاقَات	Blister ; tinder.
حَرْقَفَة ج حَرَاقِف	Hip-bone.
حَرَكَ يَحْرُكُ	To be in motion.
حَرَّكَ	To move a thing
تَحَرَّكَ	To be moved.
حَرِك	Brisk, nimble.
حَرَكَة ج حَرَكَات	Motion ; gesture.
(َ ُ ِ)	Vowel-point.
حَرَاك	Motion.
حَارِك	Withers of a horse.
تَحْرِيك	Act of moving.

حَرَمَ يَحْرِمُ	To refuse, forbid.
حَرُمَ يَحْرُمُ	To be unlawful.
حَرَّمَ	To forbid.
تَحَرَّمَ	To be forbidden.
إِحْتَرَمَ	To honour, venerate.
إِسْتَحْرَمَ	To hold as unlawful.
حِرْم	Excommunication.
حَرَم	Sacred (territory).
اَلْحَرَم	Sacred territory at Mecca.
اَلْحَرَمَان	Mecca and Medina.
حُرْمَة ج حُرَم	Sacredness. Wife.
حَرَام	Unlawful, sacred.
اَلْمَسْجِدُ ٱلْحَرَام	El Kaaba.
اَلشَّهْرُ ٱلْحَرَام . مُحَرَّم	The month.
حَرَامِيّ ج حَرَامِيَة	Robber, thief.
حَرِيم	Women of a household.
مُحَرَّم	Unlawful ; first month of the Moslem year.
مَحْرُوم	Denied, refused. Excommunicated.
مُحْتَرَم	Venerable, respected.

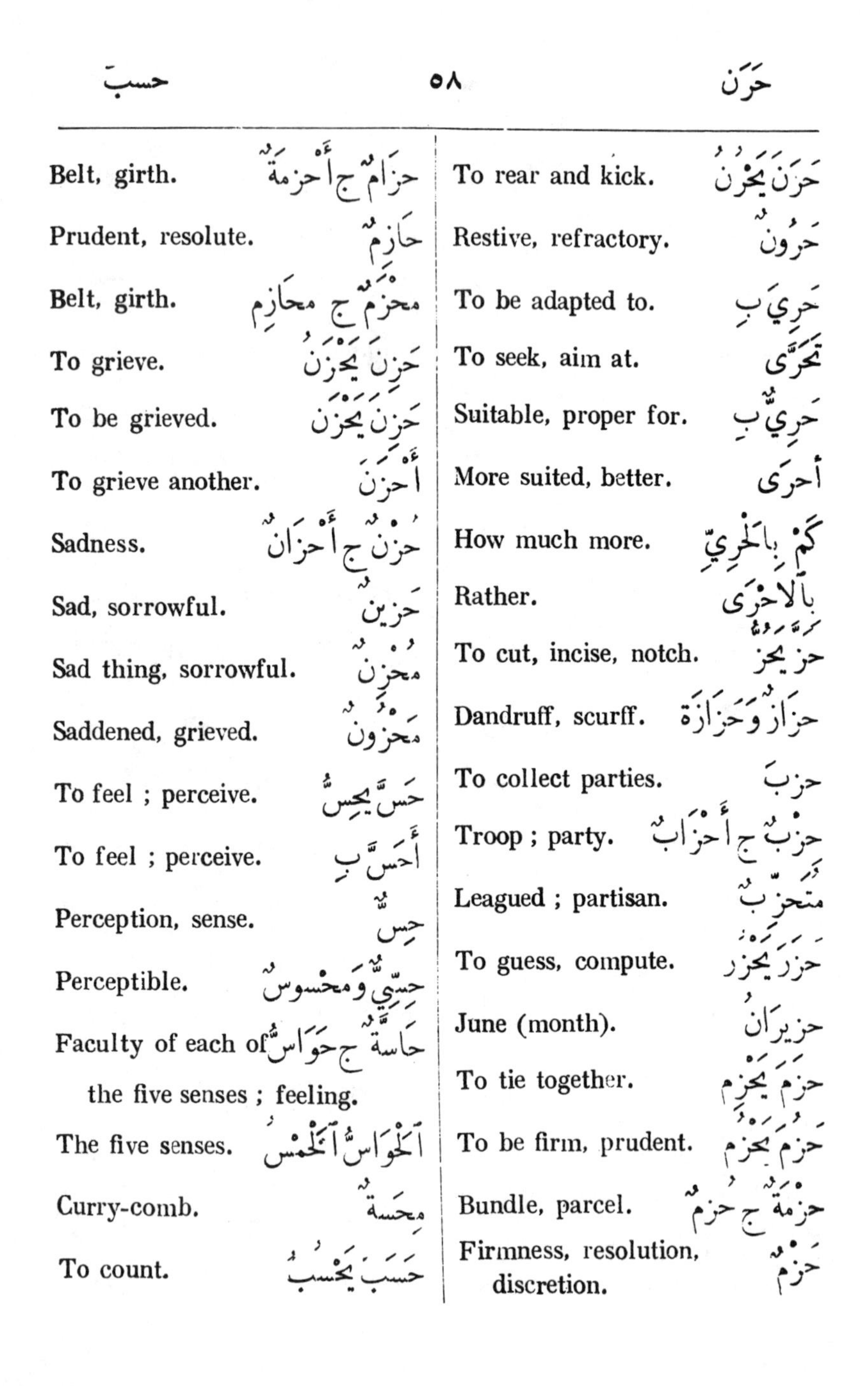

To rear and kick.	حَرَنَ يَحْرُنُ
Restive, refractory.	حَرُونٌ
To be adapted to.	حَرِيَ بِ
To seek, aim at.	تَحَرَّى
Suitable, proper for.	حَرِيٌّ بِ
More suited, better.	أَحْرَى
How much more.	كَمْ بِالْحَرِيِّ
Rather.	بِالأَحْرَى
To cut, incise, notch.	حَزَّ يَحُزُّ
Dandruff, scurf.	حَزَازٌ وَحَزَازَة
To collect parties.	حَزَبَ
Troop ; party.	حِزْبٌ ج أَحْزَابٌ
Leagued ; partisan.	مُتَحَزِّبٌ
To guess, compute.	حَزَرَ يَحْزِرُ
June (month).	حُزَيرَانُ
To tie together.	حَزَمَ يَحْزِمُ
To be firm, prudent.	حَزُمَ يَحْزُمُ
Bundle, parcel.	حُزْمَةٌ ج حُزَمٌ
Firmness, resolution, discretion.	حَزْمٌ
Belt, girth.	حِزَامٌ ج أَحْزِمَةٌ
Prudent, resolute.	حَازِمٌ
Belt, girth.	مِحْزَمٌ ج مَحَازِم
To grieve.	حَزِنَ يَحْزَنُ
To be grieved.	حَزَنَ يَحْزُنُ
To grieve another.	أَحْزَنَ
Sadness.	حُزْنٌ ج أَحْزَانٌ
Sad, sorrowful.	حَزِينٌ
Sad thing, sorrowful.	مُحْزِنٌ
Saddened, grieved.	مَحْزُونٌ
To feel ; perceive.	حَسَّ يَحِسُّ
To feel ; perceive.	أَحَسَّ بِ
Perception, sense.	حِسٌّ
Perceptible.	حِسِّيٌّ وَمَحْسُوسٌ
Faculty of each of the five senses ; feeling.	حَاسَّةٌ ج حَوَاسُّ
The five senses.	اَلْحَوَاسُّ اَلْخَمْسُ
Curry-comb.	مِحَسَّةٌ
To count.	حَسَبَ يَحْسُبُ

حَسِبَ يَحْسِبُ	To suppose, consider.
حَاسَبَ	To account with.
تَحَاسَبَ	To settle an account.
حَسْبُ	Sufficient ; sufficiency.
بِحَسَبِ	According to.
حَسَبٌ	Honour ; pedigree.
حِسَابٌ	Account, calculation.
عِلْمُ ٱلْحِسَابِ	Arithmetic.
حَسِيبٌ ج حُسَبَاءُ	Noble
مَحْسُوبٌ	Counted, calculated.
حَسَدَ يَحْسُدُ	To envy.
حَسَدٌ	Envy, grudge.
حَاسِدٌ وَحَسُودٌ ج حُسَّادٌ	Envious.
مَحْسُودٌ	Envied ; object of envy.
حَسَرَ يَحْسُرُ عَلَى	To grieve for.
تَحَسَّرَ عَلَى	To feel regret.
حَسْرَةٌ ج حَسَرَاتٌ	Grief.
يا حَسْرَتِي . وَاحَسْرَتَاه	Alas !
حَسَكٌ	Hatred. Thistle.
حَسَمَ يَحْسِمُ	To cut off ; stop.
حُسَامٌ	Sharp sword.
حَسُنَ يَحْسُنُ	To be handsome.
حَسَّنَ	To embellish, adorn.
حَاسَنَ	To treat well.
احْسَنَ	To do a thing well.
أَحْسَنَ إِلَى	To confer a benefit.
إِسْتَحْسَنَ	To approve.
حُسْنٌ ج مَحَاسِن	Beauty ; good.
حَسَنٌ ج حِسَانٌ	Beautiful ; good.
حَسَنَةٌ ج حَسَنَاتٌ	Good deed.
حَسُّونٌ	Goldfinch.
احْسَنَ	More beautiful, better.
مَا أَحْسَنَ	How beautiful.
إِحْسَانٌ	Benefit, beneficence.
مَحَاسِن	Good deeds or qualities.
حَشَّ يَحُشُّ حَشًّا	To cut hay.
حَشَّاشٌ	Smoker of hashish.
حَشِيشٌ	Grass; hay. Hashish.

حَشَدَ يَحْشُدُ	To assemble, v. t.
إِحْتَشَدَ	To be assembled.
حَشْدٌ	Troop, assembly.
مَحَاشِد	Places of assembling.
حَشَرَ يَحْشُرُ حَشْرًا	To assemble.
يَوْمُ ٱلْحَشْرِ	Day of Judgment.
مَحْشَرٌ ج مَحَاشِر	Place of gathering.
حَشَرَةٌ ج حَشَرَاتٌ	Insect.
إِحْتَشَمَ	To stand in awe. or shame.
حَشَمٌ	Attendants, retinue.
حِشْمَةٌ	Reverence ; modesty.
اِحْتِشَامٌ	Reverence ; modesty.
حَشَا يَحْشُو	To stuff, cram.
إِحْتَشَى وَانْحَشَى	To be filled.
حَشًا ج أَحْشَاءٌ	Viscera, bowels.
حَشْوٌ	Stuffing, wadding.
تَحَاشَى عَنْ	To abstain, disdain.
حَاشَا	Except. God forbid!
حَاشِيَةٌ ج حَوَاشٍ	Annotation. Followers.
حِصَّةٌ ج حِصَصٌ	Part, share.
حَصْبٌ	Stones, firewood.
حَصْبَةٌ	Measles.
حَصَدَ يَحْصُدُ	To mow, reap.
حَاصِدٌ وَحَصَّادٌ	Mower, reaper.
حَصَادٌ	Harvest, harvest-time.
حَصِيدٌ وَمَحْصُودٌ	Mown, reaped.
حَصَرَ يَحْصُرُ	To confine, restrict.
حَاصَرَ مُحَاصَرَةً	To besiege.
حَصْرٌ	Restriction ; confinement.
بِالْحَصْرِ	Strictly speaking.
حِصَارٌ وَمُحَاصَرَةٌ	Siege, blockade.
حُصُرِيٌّ	Maker or seller of mats.
حَصِيرٌ وَحَصِيرَةٌ ج حَصَائِرُ	Mat.
مُحَاصِرٌ	Besieger ; blockader.
مَحْصُورٌ	Besieged ; restricted.
حِصْرِمٌ	Green grapes.
حَصَافَةٌ	Sound judgment.
حَصَلَ ـ لِ	To happen to one.

To obtain, acquire.	حَصَلَ عَلَى
To be obtained.	تَحَصَّلَ
Result.	حَاصِلٌ ج حَوَاصِلُ
The result ; in short.	الحَاصِلُ
Acquisition.	تَحْصِيلٌ
Result, produce.	مَحْصُولٌ ج مَحَاصِيل
To be fortified.	حَصُنَ يَحْصُنُ
To fortify.	حَصَّنَ
To be entrenched.	تَحَصَّنَ
Fortress.	حِصْنٌ ج حُصُونٌ
Horse.	حِصَانٌ ج حُصُنٌ وَأَحْصِنَةٌ
Strongly fortified.	حَصِينٌ
Fox.	أَبُو ٱلْحُصَيْنِ
To count, number.	احْصَى
Small pebbles.	حَصًى
Small pebble.	حَصَاةٌ
Innumerable.	غَيْرُ مُحْصًى
To instigate, incite.	حَضَّ يَحُضُّ
Foot of a mountain.	حَضِيضٌ
To be present.	حَضَرَ يَحْضُرُ
To come.	حَضَرَ إِلَى
To bring.	حَضَّرَ وَأَحْضَرَ
To be ready.	تَحَضَّرَ
To cause to come.	إِسْتَحْضَرَ
Towns, cultivated land.	حَضَرٌ
Presence. Highness.	حَضْرَةٌ
Present, ready.	حَاضِرٌ
Present tense.	أَلْحَاضِرُ
Approach of death.	مُحْتَضَرٌ
To embrace.	حَضَنَ يَحْضُنُ
Bosom.	حِضْنٌ ج حُضُونٌ
Nursing ; incubation.	حِضَانَةٌ
To fall, go down.	حَطَّ يَحُطُّ
To put down.	حط
To descend, fall.	انْحَطَ
Falling.	إِنْحِطَاطٌ
Railway station.	مَحَطٌّ وَمَحَطَّةٌ
Fallen, depressed.	مُنْحَط

مَحْطُوطٌ	Placed, laid, deposited.
إِحْتَطَبَ	To collect fire-wood.
حَطَبٌ	Fuel, wood.
حَطَّابٌ	Wood-cutter.
حَطَمَ يَحْطِمُ وَحَطَّمَ	To break.
تَحَطَّمَ وَٱنْحَطَمَ	To crumble.
حِطْمَةٌ وَحُطَامٌ	Piece, fragment.
حُطَامُ ٱلدُّنْيَا	Goods or vanities of this world.
حَظَّ يَحَظُّ	To be fortunate.
حَظٌّ ج حُظُوظٌ	Happiness.
مَحْظُوظٌ	Happy.
حَظَرَ يَحْظُرُ عَلَى	To forbid.
حَظِيرَةٌ ج حَظَائِرُ	Enclosure.
مَحْظُورَاتٌ	Prohibited things.
حَظِيَ يَحْظَى بِ	To obtain.
حَفَّ بِ	To encompass.
خُبْزٌ حَافٌّ	Dry bread.
حَافَّةٌ	Edge, rim, border.
مِحَفَّةٌ	Kind of litter.
مَحْفُوفٌ	Surrounded.
حَفِيدٌ ج حَفَدَةٌ	Grandson.
حَفَرَ يَحْفِرُ وَٱحْتَفَرَ	To dig.
حُفْرَةٌ ج حُفَرٌ	Ditch, pit.
حَافِرٌ ج حَوَافِرُ	Hoof.
حَفَّارٌ	Grave-digger.
مَحْفُورٌ	Dug, dug out.
حَفِظَ يَحْفَظُ	To guard, keep.
حَافَظَ عَلَى	To be careful of.
تَحَفَّظَ	To be watchful.
حِفْظٌ	Guard ; careful watch.
حِفَاظٌ	Truss.
(أَلْقُوَّةُ) ٱلْحَافِظَةُ	Memory.
مُحَافِظٌ	Guardian, keeper.
مُحَافَظَةٌ	Guardianship.
مَحْفُوظٌ	Guarded, preserved.
حَفَلَ يَحْفِلُ	To gather, assemble.
إِحْتَفَلَ لَهُ	To receive with houour.
إِحْتَفَلَ بِ	To give attention to.

Large assembly ; care. حَفْلٌ

Entirely full (hall &c.) حَافِلٌ

Celebration ; pomp. إِحْتِفَالٌ

Assembly. مَحْفِلٌ ج مَحَافِلُ

Place of assembly. مُحْتَفَلٌ

Handful. حَفْنَةٌ ج حُفُنَاتٌ

To go bare-foot. حَفِيَ يَحْفَى

To show joy and honour. حَفِيَ وَاحْتَفَى بِ

Bare-footedness. حَفَاءٌ وَحُفُوَّةٌ

Bare-foot ; unshod. حَافٍ

To be true, right. حَقَّ يَحُقُّ

To verify, confirm. حَقَّقَ

To assure one's self. تَحَقَّقَ

To deserve ; fall due. إِسْتَحَقَّ

Right ; truth ; obligation, worth ; true ; truthful. حَقٌّ ج حُقُوقٌ

Duty. حَقٌّ عَلَى

Worthy of. حَقٌّ بِ

Truly, indeed. حَقًّا وَبِالْحَقِّ

Socket. حُقٌّ ج حِقَاقٌ

Case, casket. حُقَّةٌ ج حُقَقٌ

Reality, truth. ssence. حَقِيقَةٌ ج حَقَائِقُ

Truly. حَقِيقَةً وَفِي ٱلْحَقِيقَةِ

Real ; proper (sense). حَقِيقِيٌّ

More worthy of. أَحَقُّ بِ

Merit. إِسْتِحْقَاقٌ ج إِسْتِحْقَاقَاتٌ

Verification. تَحْقِيقٌ

Verified, confirmed. مُحَقَّقٌ

Worthy of, deserving. مُسْتَحِقٌّ

A long time. حُقْبٌ ج أَحْقَابٌ

Saddle-bag. حَقِيبَةٌ

To bear spite. حَقَدَ يَحْقِدُ

Hatred, grudge, spite. حِقْدٌ

Spiteful. حَاقِدٌ وَحَقُودٌ

To despise. حَقَرَ يَحْقِرُ وَاحْتَقَرَ

To be contemptible. حَقُرَ يَحْقُرُ

Contempt ; vileness. حَقَارَةٌ

Despised ; mean ; paltry. حَقِيرٌ

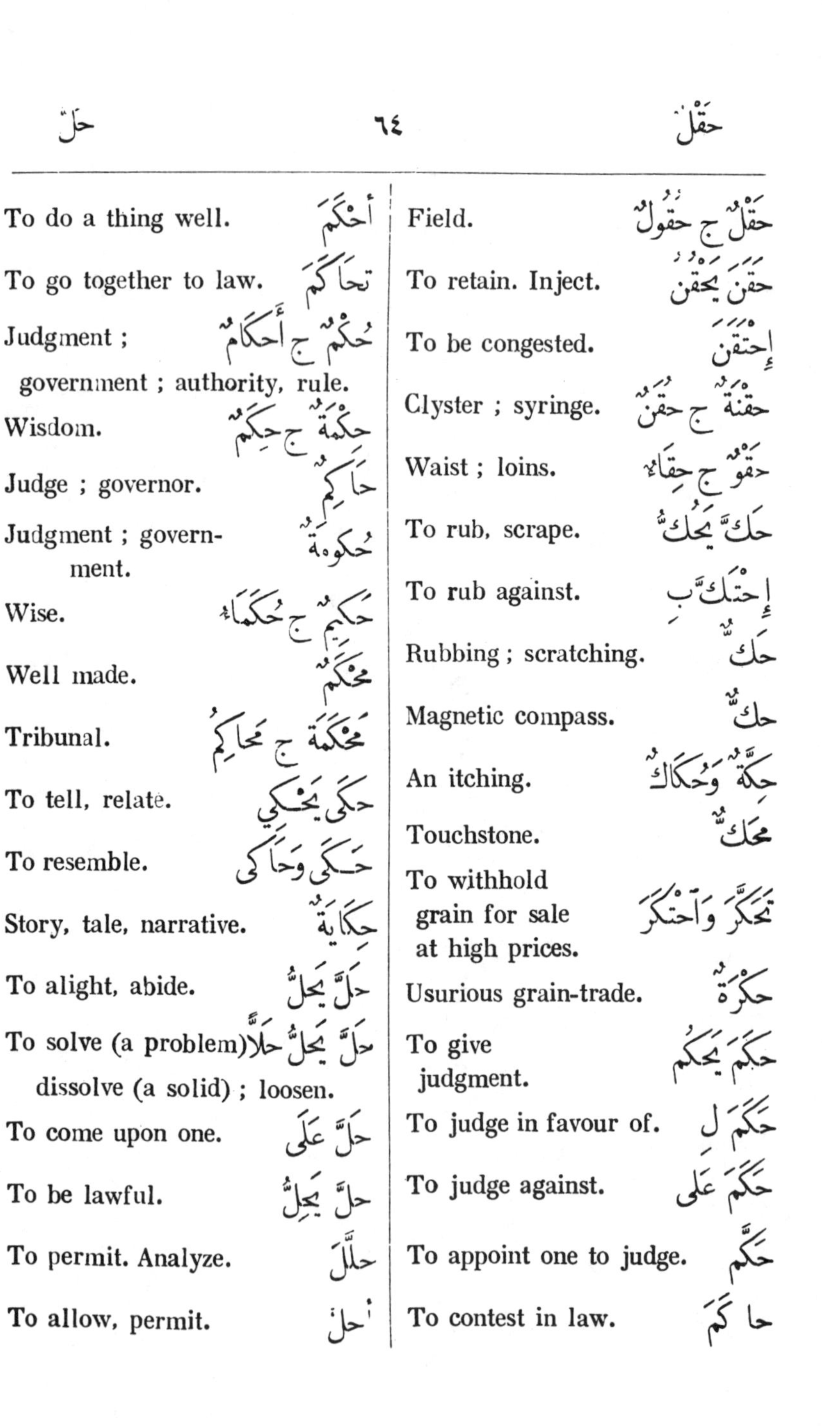

Field. حَقْلٌ ج حُقُولٌ

To retain. Inject. حَقَنَ يَحْقُنُ

To be congested. إِحْتَقَنَ

Clyster ; syringe. حُقْنَةٌ ج حُقَنٌ

Waist ; loins. حَقْوٌ ج حِقَاءٌ

To rub, scrape. حَكَّ يَحُكُّ

To rub against. إِحْتَكَّ بِ

Rubbing ; scratching. حَكٌّ

Magnetic compass. حُكٌّ

An itching. حِكَّةٌ وَحُكَاكٌ

Touchstone. مِحَكٌّ

To withhold grain for sale at high prices. تَحَكَّرَ وَٱحْتَكَرَ

Usurious grain-trade. حُكْرَةٌ

To give judgment. حَكَمَ يَحْكُمُ

To judge in favour of. حَكَمَ لِ

To judge against. حَكَمَ عَلَى

To appoint one to judge. حَكَّمَ

To contest in law. حَاكَمَ

To do a thing well. أَحْكَمَ

To go together to law. تَحَاكَمَ

Judgment ; government ; authority, rule. حُكْمٌ ج أَحْكَامٌ

Wisdom. حِكْمَةٌ ج حِكَمٌ

Judge ; governor. حَاكِمٌ

Judgment ; government. حُكُومَةٌ

Wise. حَكِيمٌ ج حُكَمَاءُ

Well made. مُحْكَمٌ

Tribunal. مَحْكَمَةٌ ج مَحَاكِمُ

To tell, relate. حَكَى يَحْكِي

To resemble. حَكَى وَحَاكَى

Story, tale, narrative. حِكَايَةٌ

To alight, abide. حَلَّ يَحُلُّ

To solve (a problem) dissolve (a solid) ; loosen. حَلَّ يَحُلُّ حَلًّا

To come upon one. حَلَّ عَلَى

To be lawful. حَلَّ يَحِلُّ

To permit. Analyze. حَلَّلَ

To allow, permit. أَحَلَّ

To deem lawful. إِسْتَحَلَّ
A solving, dissolving. حَلٌّ
Lawful. حِلٌّ
Garment. حُلَّةٌ ج حُلَلٌ
Lawful ; right. حَلَالٌ
An alighting, abiding. حُلُولٌ
Husband ; wife. حَلِيلٌ م حَلِيلَةٌ
Deeming lawful. إِسْتِحْلَالٌ
Dissolving ; analysis. تَحْلِيلٌ
Place ; quarter. مَحَلٌّ ج مَحَالّ
Inn ; stopping-place. مَحَلَّةٌ
To milk. حَلَبَ يَحْلُبُ
To flow ; exude. تَحَلَّبَ وَٱنْحَلَبَ
Aleppo. حَلَبُ
Fenugreek. حُلْبَةٌ
Milkman. حالِبٌ وَحلابٌ
Fresh milk. حَلِيبٌ
Emulsion. مستحْلَبٌ
Assafoetida. حِلْتِيتٌ

To card cotton. حَلَجَ يَحْلِجُ
Carding of cotton. حِلَاجَةٌ
Cotton-carder. حَلَّاجٌ
Instrument for carding. مِحْلَجٌ
Snail. حَلَزُونٌ
Spiral. حَلَزُونِيٌّ
To swear. حَلَفَ يَحْلِفُ
To make swear. حَلَّفَ وَٱسْتَحْلَفَ
To be in league with. حَالَفَ
To confederate. تَحَالَفَ
Oath ; league. حِلْفٌ
Confederate. حَلِيفٌ ج حُلَفَاءُ
Alliance. تَحَالُفٌ وَمُحَالَفَةٌ
To shave. حَلَقَ يَحْلِقُ
Throat, palate. حَلْقٌ ج حُلُوقٌ
Guttural letters. حُرُوفُ ٱلْحَلْقِ
Circle ; link, ear-ring. حَلَقَةٌ
Barber. حَلَّاقٌ
Barber's trade. حِلَاقَةٌ

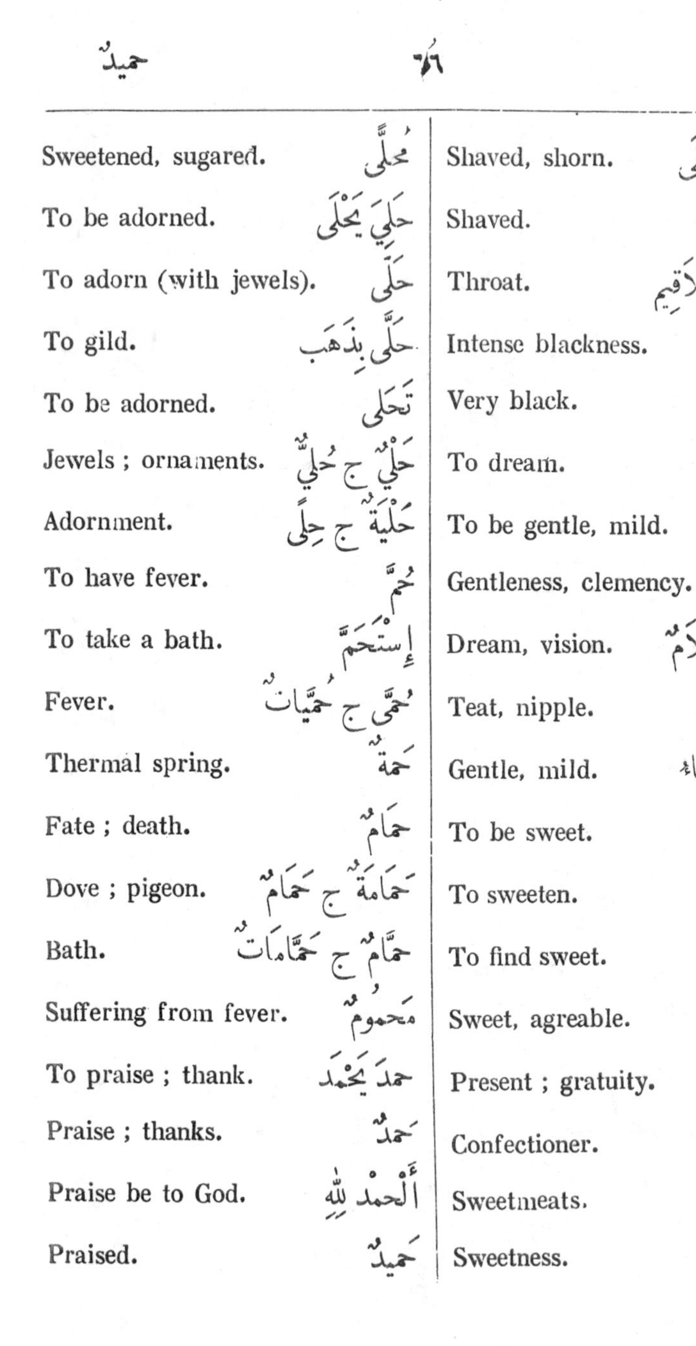

حَلِيقٌ ج حَلْقَى	Shaved, shorn.
مَحْلُوقٌ	Shaved.
حُلْقُومٌ ج حَلَاقِيمُ	Throat.
حَلَكٌ	Intense blackness.
حَالِكٌ	Very black.
حَلَمَ يَحْلُمُ	To dream.
حَلُمَ يَحْلُمُ	To be gentle, mild.
حِلْمٌ	Gentleness, clemency.
حُلْمٌ ج أَحْلَامٌ	Dream, vision.
حَلَمَةٌ	Teat, nipple.
حَلِيمٌ ج حُلَمَاءُ	Gentle, mild.
حَلَا يَحْلُو	To be sweet.
حَلَّى تَحْلِيَةً	To sweeten.
إِسْتَحْلَى	To find sweet.
حُلْوٌ	Sweet, agreable.
حُلْوَانٌ	Present ; gratuity.
حَلَوَانِيٌّ	Confectioner.
حَلْوَى	Sweetmeats.
حَلَاوَةٌ	Sweetness.
مُحَلًّى	Sweetened, sugared.
حَلِيَ يَحْلَى	To be adorned.
حَلَّى	To adorn (with jewels).
حَلَّى بِذَهَبٍ	To gild.
تَحَلَّى	To be adorned.
حَلْيٌ ج حُلِيٌّ	Jewels ; ornaments.
حِلْيَةٌ ج حِلًى	Adornment.
حُمَّ	To have fever.
إِسْتَحَمَّ	To take a bath.
حُمَّى ج حُمَّيَاتٌ	Fever.
حَمَّةٌ	Thermal spring.
حِمَامٌ	Fate ; death.
حَمَامَةٌ ج حَمَامٌ	Dove ; pigeon.
حَمَّامٌ ج حَمَّامَاتٌ	Bath.
مَحْمُومٌ	Suffering from fever.
حَمِدَ يَحْمَدُ	To praise ; thank.
حَمْدٌ	Praise ; thanks.
أَلْحَمْدُ لِلّٰهِ	Praise be to God.
حَمِيدٌ	Praised.

Praised, praiseworthy.	مَحْمُودٌ
To dye red ; redden.	حَمَّرَ
To become red; blush.	إِحْمَرَّ
Bitumen.	حُمَّرٌ
Redness. Erysipelas.	حُمْرَةٌ
Ass, donkey.	حِمَارٌ ج حَمِيرٌ
Wild ass.	حِمَارُ ٱلْوَحْشِ
Ass-driver.	حَمَّارٌ ج حمارَةٌ
Red.	أَحْمَرُ م حَمْرَاءُ ج حُمْرٌ
Rubefacient.	مُحَمِّرٌ
To be hard in religion, etc.	حَمِسَ يَحْمَسُ
To irritate.	حَمَّسَ وَأَحْمَسَ
Bravery energy.	حَمَاسَةٌ
To roast, toast.	حَمَّصَ
To be roasted.	تَحَمَّصَ
Hems (city).	حِمْصُ
Chick-peas.	حِمِّصٌ
To be sour, acid.	حَمِضَ يَحْمَضُ
Acid ; sour.	حَامِضٌ
Acidity ; sourness.	حُمُوضَةٌ
Sorrel (plant).	حُمَاضٌ وَحُمَّيْضٌ
Acidulated, acid, sour.	مُحَمَّضٌ
To be foolish.	حَمِقَ يَحْمُقُ
Stupidity, folly.	حُمْقٌ وَحَمَاقَةٌ
Chicken-pox.	حُمَاقٌ
Stupid, foolish.	أَحْمَقُ
To carry, lift.	حَمَلَ يَحْمِلُ
To conceive (woman).	حَمَلَتْ
To attack, charge.	حَمَلَ على
To bear fruit.	حَمَلَ يَحْمِلُ
To overflow (river).	حَمَلَ ٱلنَّهْرُ
To burden, load.	حَمَّلَ
To suffer patiently.	تَحَمَّلَ
To bear, suffer.	إِحْتَمَلَ
To be possible.	إِحْتَمَلَ أَنْ
Carrying. Pregnancy.	حَمْلٌ
Burden, load.	حِمْلٌ ج أَحْمَالٌ
Lamb.	حَمَلٌ ج حُمْلَانٌ

أَلْحَمَلُ	Sign of the Ram (Aries).
حَمْلَةٌ	Attack ; charge in battle.
حَمَّالٌ	Porter.
إِحْتِمَالٌ	Patience ; endurance.
مَحْمِلٌ ج مَحَامِلُ	Litter.
مَحْمُولٌ	Borne ; suffered.
مُحْتَمَلٌ	Bearable. Possible.
حَمُوٌ ج أَحْمَاءٌ	Father-in-law.
حَمَاةٌ ج حَمَوَاتٌ	Mother-in-law.
حَمَى يَحْمِي	To protect, defend.
حَمِيَ يَحْمَى	To be very hot.
أَحْمَى إِحْمَاءً	To make hot.
حَامَى عَنْ	To defend.
إِحْتَمَى	To protect one's self.
حِمًى ج أَحْمَاءٌ	Interdicted place.
حِمْيَةٌ	Care of diet.
حَمِيَّةٌ	Anger, rage. Disdain.
حُمَةٌ	Venom, sting.
حَامٍ	Protector. Hot.
حَامِيَةٌ	Guard, garrison.
حِمَايَةٌ	Protection. Protégé,
مُحْمًى	Heated.
مُحَامٍ	Protector ; advocate.
حَنَّ يَحِنُّ إِلَى	To yearn.
تَحَنَّنَ عَلَى	To have compassion.
حَنَانٌ وَحَنُونٌ	Compassionate, tender.
حَنَّأَ	To dye with *Henna*.
حِنَاءٌ	The plant *henna*.
حَانُوتٌ ج حَوَانِيتُ	Shop.
حَنِثَ يَحْنَثُ	To break an oath.
حِنْثٌ	Perjury. Sin, crime.
حَانِثٌ	A perjurer.
حَنَشٌ ج أَحْنَاشٌ	Snake.
حَنَطَ وَأَحْنَطَ	To embalm.
حِنْطَةٌ	Wheat.
حَنْظَلٌ	Colocynth.
حَنَفِيَّةٌ	Tap.
حَنِقَ يَحْنَقُ	To be enraged.

حَنَق Violent anger ; spite.

حنكَ وَأَحْنَكَ To make wise.

حَنَكٌ ج احْنَاكٌ Palate.

مُحَنَّكٌ Experienced.

حَنَى يَحْنِي To bend, incline.

تَحَنَّى وَانْحَنَى To be bent.

حُنُوٌّ Tenderness, compassion.

حَانِيَةٌ Wine-house, tavern.

مُنْحَنٍ Bent, crooked ; inclined.

حُوتٌ ج حِيتَانٌ Large fish. Whale.

أَحْوَجَ To compel.

إحتاجَ To want, need, require.

حَاجَةٌ ج حاجَات وَحَوَائِج Want ; need ; necessity ; object ; desire.

إحْتِيَاجٌ Want ; having need.

مُحْتَاجٌ إلى In want or need of.

اسْتَحْوَذَ على To overcome.

حوذِيٌّ Coachman, cabman.

حَارَ يَحَارُ To be bewildered.

حاوَرَ To converse, debate.

حَوْرٌ Leather. Poplar tree.

حَوَارِيٌّ Disciple of a prophet.

حَارَةٌ A quarter of a town.

مَحَارَةٌ Panier. Oyster.

مِحْوَرٌ ج مَحَاوِر Pivot.

مُحَاوَرَة Conversation ; debate.

حاز يحوز To get ; possess.

إنْحَازَ عَنْ To drow aside from.

إنْحازَ إِلَى To turn to and join.

حيِّز Space occupied by a body

حَوَّش To gather, collect.

إنْحاشَ To be taken in.

حَوْشٌ ج احْوَاشٌ Fold ; court.

حَوَشٌ Mixed people ; rabble.

حِيَاصَةٌ Saddle-girth, girdle.

حَوْصلَة Stomach of a bird.

حَوْضٌ ج أَحْوَاضٌ Reservoir, tank.

حَوَّطَ To surround ; enclose.

احاطَ ب To invest, surround.

Wall.	حَائِطٌ ج حِيطَانٌ
Investment. Caution.	إِحتِيَاطٌ
Circumference.	مُحِيطٌ
The ocean.	أَلْبَحْرُ ٱلْمُحِيطُ
Edge, border.	حَافَةٌ ج حَافَاتٌ
To surround.	حَاقَ يَحُوقُ بِ
To strike out, erase.	حوَّقَ
To weave.	حَاكَ يَحُوكُ
Weaver.	حَائِكٌ ج حَاكَةٌ
The art of weaving.	حِيَاكَةٌ
To be changed.	حَالَ وَتَحَوَّلَ
To come between.	حالَ بَيْنَ
To change, alter.	حوَّلَ إِلَى
To attempt.	حَاوَلَ
To use stratagem.	احْتَالَ
To be changed. Absurd.	إِسْتَحَالَ
State, condition.	حَالٌ ج أَحوَالٌ
Immediately.	حالاً وَفِي ٱلْحَال
As soon as.	حَالَمَا

State, condition.	حَالَةٌ ج حَالَاتٌ
Power. Year.	حَوْلٌ ج احْوَالٌ
All around, around.	حوْلَ
Squint.	حَوَلٌ
Transfer of a debt.	حَوَالَةٌ
Stratagem ; means.	حِيلَةٌ ج حِيَلٌ
Mechanics.	عِلْمُ ٱلْحِيَلِ
In front of, opposite to.	حِيَالَ
Squint-eyed.	أَحْوَلُ م حولاءُ
More cunning, crafty.	أَحْيَلُ
Transferring.	تَحوِيلٌ
Absurd, unreasonable.	مُحَالٌ
Undoubtedly.	لَا مَحَالَةَ
Cunning, sly, wily.	مُحْتَالٌ
Impossible ; absurd.	مستَحِيلٌ
To run around ; hover.	حامَ يَحُوم
Wine-shop.	حَانَةٌ وَحَانُوتٌ
Eve (mother of mankind).	حَوَّاءُ
To possess ; contain.	حَوَى يَحْوِي

إِحْتَوَى عَلَى To comprise.

حَاوٍ Snake-charmer. Containing.

حَيْثُ Where, where there.

حَيْثُمَا Wherever.

مِنْ حَيْثُ In respect of, since.

بِحَيْثُ انْ So that.

حَادَ يَحِيدُ To deviate ; turn aside.

حَايَدَ مُحَايَدَةً To avoid, shun.

حَارَ يَحَارُ To be bewildered.

حيَّرَ To bewilder, perplex.

تَحَيَّرَ فِي To be perplexed.

حَيْرَةٌ وَتَحَيُّرٌ Perplexity.

حَارَةٌ ج حَارَاتٌ Street ; quarter.

حَائِرٌ Confused, perplexed.

مُتَحَيِّرَةٌ ج مُتَحَيِّرَاتٌ Planet.

حَيِّزٌ Space occupied by a body.

حَاضَتْ تَحِيضُ To menstruate.

حَيْضٌ Menstruation ; menses.

حَافَ يَحِيفُ To be unjust.

حَيْفٌ Injustice, oppression.

حَاقَ يَحِيقُ بِ To surround, befall.

حَيْلٌ Strength, power, might.

حَانَ يَحِينُ To draw near (time).

حَانٌ وَحَانَةٌ Wine-house, tavern.

حِينٌ ج أَحْيَانٌ Time, season.

لِلْحِين Instantaneously ; at once.

أَحْيَانًا From time to time.

حِينَئِذٍ Then ; at that time.

حَيِيَ يَحْيَا حَيَاةً To live.

حَيِيَ حَيَاءً مِنْ To be ashamed of.

حَيَّا تَحِيَّةً To salute, greet.

أَحْيَا To bring to life.

إِسْتَحْيَا To spare one's life.

إِسْتَحْيَا وَٱسْتَحَى To be ashamed.

حَيَّ Come ! come quickly !

حَيَاءٌ Shame ; modesty.

حَيَاةٌ أَوْ حَيَوةٌ Life ; life-time.

حَيٌّ ج أَحْيَاءٌ Alive. Tribe. Quarter of a town.

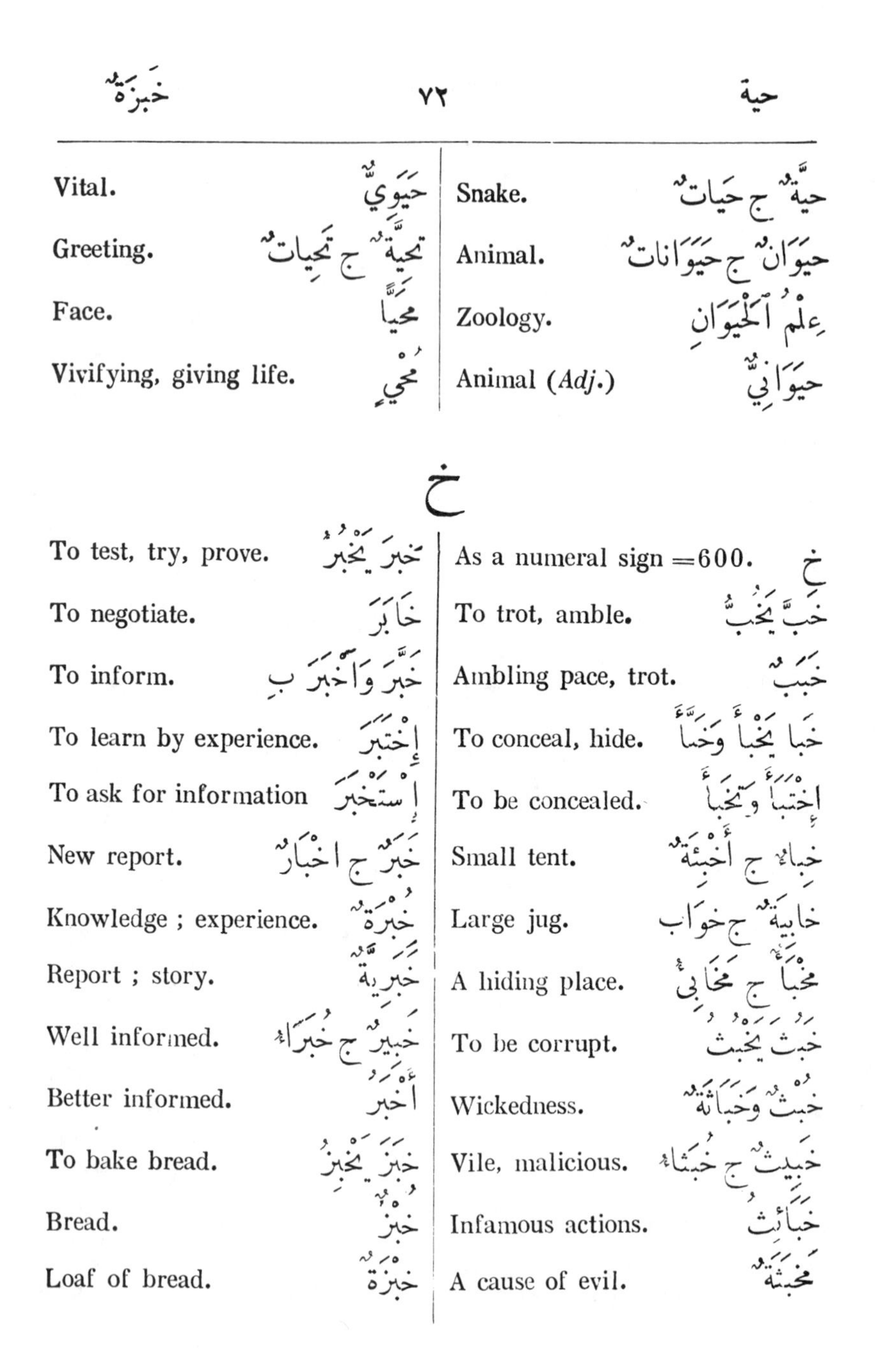

حَيَّةٌ ج حَيَّاتٌ	Snake.
حَيَوَانٌ ج حَيَوَانَاتٌ	Animal.
عِلْمُ ٱلْحَيَوَانِ	Zoology.
حَيَوَانِيٌّ	Animal (*Adj.*)
حَيَوِيٌّ	Vital.
تَحِيَّةٌ ج تَحِيَّاتٌ	Greeting.
مُحَيًّا	Face.
مُحْيِي	Vivifying, giving life.

خ

خ	As a numeral sign =600.
خَبَّ يَخُبُّ	To trot, amble.
خَبَبٌ	Ambling pace, trot.
خَبَا يَخْبَأُ وَخَبَّأَ	To conceal, hide.
إِخْتَبَأَ وَتَخَبَّأَ	To be concealed.
خِبَاءٌ ج أَخْبِيَةٌ	Small tent.
خَابِيَةٌ ج خَوَابٍ	Large jug.
مَخْبَأٌ ج مَخَابِئُ	A hiding place.
خَبُثَ يَخْبُثُ	To be corrupt.
خُبْثٌ وَخَبَاثَةٌ	Wickedness.
خَبِيثٌ ج خُبَثَاءُ	Vile, malicious.
خَبَائِثُ	Infamous actions.
مَخْبَثَةٌ	A cause of evil.
خَبَرَ يَخْبُرُ	To test, try, prove.
خَابَرَ	To negotiate.
خَبَّرَ وَأَخْبَرَ بِ	To inform.
إِخْتَبَرَ	To learn by experience.
إِسْتَخْبَرَ	To ask for information
خَبَرٌ ج أَخْبَارٌ	New report.
خُبْرَةٌ	Knowledge ; experience.
خَبَرِيَّةٌ	Report ; story.
خَبِيرٌ ج خُبَرَاءُ	Well informed.
أَخْبَرُ	Better informed.
خَبَزَ يَخْبِزُ	To bake bread.
خُبْزٌ	Bread.
خُبْزَةٌ	Loaf of bread.

Baker's trade. خِبَازَةٌ

Baker. خَبَّازٌ م خَبَّازَةٌ

Mallow (plant). خُبَازَى وَخُبَّيْزَةٌ

Any thing baked. مَخْبُوزٌ وَخَبِيزٌ

To mix ; bungle. خَبَصَ يَخْبِصُ

Rash bungler. خَبَّاصٌ

To strike. خَبَطَ يَخْبِطُ

At random. خَبْطُ عَشْوَاءَ

To be or make insane. خَبَلَ يَخْبُلُ

Mad, insane. خَبِلٌ وَأَخْبَلُ وَمُخَبَّلٌ

Fatigued ; weakened. مَخْبُولٌ

Tent of wool. خِبَاءٌ ج أَخْبِيَةٌ

Large jug, jar. خَابِيَةٌ ج خَوَابٍ

To cheat. خَتَلَ يَخْتِلُ وَخَاتَلَ

Fraud, deceit. مُخَاتَلَةٌ

To seal, stamp. خَتَمَ يَخْتِمُ

To conclude, terminate. خَتَمَ

Seal-ring, signet. خَاتِمٌ ج خَوَاتِمُ

End, conclusion. خَاتِمَةٌ

End, conclusion. خِتَامٌ ج خُتُمٌ

Sealed ; closed. مَخْتُومٌ

To circumcise. خَتَنَ يَخْتِنُ

To be circumcised. إِخْتَتَنَ

Any relation on side of wife. خَتَنٌ

Noble lady. خَاتُونٌ ج خَوَاتِينُ

Circumcision. خِتَانٌ وَخِتَانَةٌ

To coagulate. خَثَرَ يَخْثُرُ وَتَخَثَّرَ

To thicken. خَثَّرَ وَأَخْثَرَ

Sediment, dregs. خُثَارَةٌ

Coagulated ; thickened. خَاثِرٌ

To be ashamed, blush. خَجِلَ يَخْجَلُ

To put to shame. خَجَّلَ وَأَخْجَلَ

Shame, confusion. خَجَلٌ

Modest, bashful. خَجْلَانٌ وَمَخْجُولٌ

Cheek. خَدٌّ ج خُدُودٌ

Furrow, pit. خَدٌّ وَأُخْدُودٌ

Furrow, track. خُدَّةٌ ج خُدَدٌ

Small cushion. خُدَيْدِيَةٌ

مِخَدَّةٌ	Cushion, pillow.
خَدِرَ يَخْدَرُ	To be benumbed.
خَدَّرَ	To benumb.
خِدْرٌ ج خُدُورٌ	Curtain, veil.
خَدَرٌ	Numbness ; stupefaction.
مُخَدِّرٌ	Sedative, anæsthetic.
مُخَدَّرَةٌ	Girl kept in seclusion.
خَدَشَ يَخْدِشُ خَدْشاً	To scratch.
خَدَعَ يَخْدَعُ وَخَادَعَ	To deceive.
خُدْعَةٌ	Deceit, guile.
إِنْخَدَعَ	To be deceived.
خَدِيعَةٌ ج خَدَائِعُ	Deceit.
خَادِعٌ	Impostor ; deceitful.
خَدَّاعٌ	Impostor, great cheat.
مُخْدَعٌ ج مَخَادِعُ	Chamber.
مَخْدُوعٌ	Deceived, deluded.
خَدَمَ يَخْدُمُ خِدْمَةً	To serve.
إِسْتَخْدَمَ	To employ.
خِدْمَةٌ	Service ; official duty.
خَادِمٌ ج خَدَمٌ وَخُدَّامٌ	Servant.
خِدْنٌ ج أَخْدَانٌ	Friend.
خُدَيْوِيٌّ	Prince, viceroy.
خَذَلَ يَخْذُلُ خَذْلاً	To forsake.
إِنْخَذَلَ	To be forsaken.
مَخْذُولٌ	Forsaken, unaided.
خَرَّ يَخِرُّ	To gurgle, rumble.
خَرَّ لِ	To prostrate one's self.
خَرِيرٌ	Gurgling, murmur.
خَرِئَ يَخْرَأُ	To ease the bowels.
خُرْءٌ وَخِرَاءٌ	Excrement.
خَرِبَ يَخْرَبُ	To be ruined.
خَرَّبَ يُخَرِّبُ	To demolish, ruin.
تَخَرَّبَ	To be destroyed.
خِرْبَةٌ ج خِرَبٌ	A ruin, waste.
خَرَابٌ	Devastation ; ruin.
خَرُّوبٌ وَخُرْنُوبٌ	Carob-tree.
تَخْرِيبٌ	Devastation, destruction.
خَرْبَشَ	To scratch a writing.

خَرْبَقٌ	Hellebore.
خَرَجَ يَخْرُجُ	To get out ; emerge.
أَخْرَجَ	To take out ; expel.
تَخَرَّجَ	To be well trained.
إِسْتَخْرَجَ	To draw out, extract.
خَرْجٌ	Expenditure.
خُرْجٌ ج أَخْرَاجٌ	Saddle-bags.
خَارِجٌ	Exterior, quotient.
اَلْأُمُورُ ٱلْخَارِجِيَّةُ	Fareign affairs.
خَرَاجٌ	Land-tax ; tribute, tax.
خُرَاجٌ ج خُرَاجَاتٌ	Abscess.
مَخْرَجٌ	Outlet ; issue.
مُخَرَّجٌ	Skilful, well-trained.
خَرْخَرَ	To rattle, snore.
خُرْدُقٌ	Small shot.
خَرْدَلٌ	Mustard.
خَرَزَ يَخْرِزُ	To pierce ; bore.
خَرَزٌ	Small shells, beads.
خَرَزَاتُ ٱلظَّهْرِ	Vertebræ of the back.
مِخْرَزٌ ج مَخَارِزُ	Awl.
خَرِسَ يَخْرَسُ	To be dumb.
خَرَسٌ	Dumbness.
أَخْرَسُ	Dumb.
خُرْصٌ ج خِرْصَانٌ	Ear-ring.
خَرَطَ يَخْرُطُ	To turn on a lathe.
إِخْتَرَطَ	To unsheathe a sword.
خِرَاطَةٌ	Trade of a turner.
خُرَاطَةٌ	Shavings of a lathe.
خَرَّاطٌ	Turner. Liar.
مِخْرَطَةٌ ج مَخَارِطُ	Lathe.
مَخْرُوطٌ	Cone.
مَخْرُوطِيٌّ	Conical.
خُرْطُومٌ ج خَرَاطِيمُ	Snout.
إِخْتَرَعَ	To invent, devise.
خِرْوَعٌ	Castor-oil-plant.
إِخْتِرَاعٌ ج إِخْتِرَاعَاتٌ	Invention.
خَرِفَ يَخْرَفُ	To dote from old age.
خَرَفٌ وَخَرَافَةٌ	Dotage.

Doting, idiotic. خَرِفٌ وَخِرْفَانٌ

Fictitious tale, fable. خُرَافَةٌ

Lamb, sheep. خَرُوفٌ ج خِرَافٌ

Autumn. خَرِيفٌ

To pierce. خَرَقَ يَخْرُقُ خَرْقًا

To be pierced. إِنْخَرَقَ

To traverse. إِخْتَرَقَ

Rent, hole. خَرْقٌ ج خُرُوقٌ

Stupid, awkward. خَرِقٌ وَاخْرَقُ

Rag, tatter. خِرْقَةٌ ج خِرَقٌ

Unusual. خَارِقٌ ج خَوَارِقُ

To slit. Fail. خَرَمَ يَخْرِمُ

To embroider. خَرَّمَ

To be torn, slit, pierced. إِنْخَرَمَ

Bore. خُرْمٌ ج خُرُومٌ

Acromion (anatomy). اَلْأَخْرَمُ

Embroidery. تَخْرِيمٌ

Embroidered, chased. مُخَرَّمٌ

To scratch. خَرْمَشَ

See. خَرُّوبٌ خُرْنُوبٌ

Silk-stuff. خَزٌّ ج خُزُوزٌ

Caspian Sea. بَحْرُ الْخَزَرِ

Ratan, Bamboo. خَيْزُرَانٌ

A fable. خُزَعْبَلَةٌ ج خُزَعْبَلَاتٌ

Earthenware, pottery. خَزَفٌ

Potter. خَزَفِيٌّ وَخَزَّافٌ

To penetrate; tear. خَزَقَ يَخْزُقُ

To impale. خَوْزَقَ

To cut off. خَزَلَ يَخْزِلُ خَزْلًا

To pierce the nose. خَزَمَ يَخْزِمُ

Nose-ring. خِزَامٌ

Lavender. Hyacinth. خُزَامَى

To store, hoard. خَزَنَ يَخْزُنُ

Treasury. خَزْنَةٌ وَخِزَانَةٌ

Treasure. خَزْنَةٌ وَخَزِينَةٌ ج خَزَائِنُ

Library. خِزَانَةُ الْكُتُبِ

Armoury. خِزَانَةُ السِّلَاحِ

Treasurer. خَازِنٌ ج خَزَنَةٌ

Magazine. مَخْزَنٌ ج مَخَازِنُ

To subdue. خَزَا يَخْزُو خَزْواً

To be despised. خَزِيَ يَخْزَى

To be ashamed of. خَزِيَ مِنْ

Shame, disgrace. خِزْيٌ

Shameful thing. خِزْيَةٌ

To be mean. خَسَّ يَخِسُّ خَسَاسَةً

Lettuce. خَسٌّ

Vile, mean (miserly). خَسِيسٌ

To lose. خَسِرَ يَخْسَرُ

To cause loss, damage. خَسَّرَ

Loss. خسرٌ وخسارةٌ وَخسْرانٌ

Losing, loser. خَاسِرٌ

To sink into the earth and vanish. Be eclipsed. خَسَفَ يَخْسِفُ

To be eclipsed. إِنْخَسَفَ

Eclipse. خُسُوفٌ

Eclipsed. مَخْسُوفٌ

To enter, penetrate. خَشَّ يَخُشُّ

Timber-wood. خَشَبٌ

A piece of wood. خَشَبَةٌ

Coarse ; hard. خَشِبٌ

Wood-seller. خَشَّابٌ

To rustle ; clink. خَشْخَشَ

Poppy. خَشْخَاشٌ

Charnel-house. خَشْخَاشَةٌ

Refuse. خُشَارٌ وَخُشَارَةٌ

Te be submissive. خَشَعَ يَخْشَعُ

To humble one's self. تَخَشَّعَ

Lowliness ; humility. خُشُوعٌ

Humble. خَاشِعٌ ج خاشِعُونَ

Young gazelle. خِشْفٌ وَخِشْفَةٌ

Bat (animal). خُشَّافٌ

Nose. خَشْمٌ . خَيْشُومٌ ج خَيَاشِيمُ

To be rough. خَشُنَ يَخْشُنُ

To treat one harshly. خاشَنَ

Roughness. خُشْنَةٌ وَخُشُونَةٌ

Rough. خَشِنٌ ج خِشَانٌ

To fear, dread. خشي يخشى
Fear. خشية وخشيان
For fear that. خشية أن
Fearful. خاش وخشيان
To distinguish by خص يخص ب
To be special to. خص خصوصاً
To assign. خصص ب
To be one's property. إختص ب
Hut, booth. خص ج خصاص
Special to. خاص ل وب
Quality, property. خاصة ج خواص
Particularly. خاصة
The notables. الخاصة والخواص
Particular property. خاصية
Especially. على الخصوص وخصوصاً
Special, particular. خصوصي
To be fertile. خصب يخصب
Fertility. خصب
Fertile. خصب ومخصب

To abridge إختصر
Waist. خصر ج خصور
Side; flank. خاصرة ج خواصر
Abridgment. إختصار
In short; briefly. بالإختصار
Whip, staff. مخصرة ج مخاصر
Abridged; compend. مختصر
Habit, quality. خصلة ج خصال
Lock of hair. Bunch. خصلة ج خصل
To dispute, contend with. خاصم
Adversary. خصم ج خصوم
Adversary. خصيم ج خصماء
Dispute, quarrel. خصام
To geld, castrate. خصى يخصي
Eunuch. خصي ج خصيان
Testicle. خصية ج خصى
To stir (water). خض وخضخض
To dye. خضب يخضب
To be dyed. تخضب واختضب

Dye, colour.	خِضَابٌ
To be green.	خَضِرَ يَخْضَرُ
To become green.	خْضَرَّ
Greenness. Vegetables.	خُضْرَةٌ ج خُضَرٌ
Green.	أَخْضَرُ م خَضْرَاءُ ج خُضْرٌ
Fruits ; herbs.	خِضْرَاوَاتٌ
To submit ; obey.	خَضَعَ يَخْضَعُ
To subdue.	خَضَّعَ وَأَخْضَعَ
To humble one's self.	تَخَضَّعَ
Submissive.	خَاضِعٌ وَخَضُوعٌ
Submission.	خُضُوعٌ
To trace ; write.	خَطَّ يَخُطُّ
To mark with lines.	خَطَّطَ
Line, streak.	خَطٌّ ج خُطُوطٌ
Equator.	خَطُّ ٱلْاِسْتِوَاءِ
Equinoctial line.	خَطُّ ٱلْاِعْتِدَالِ
Meridian.	خَطُّ نِصْفِ ٱلنَّهَارِ
Imperial edict.	خَطٌّ شَرِيفٌ
Affair. Line of action.	خُطَّةٌ
To err, sin.	خَطِئَ يَخْطَأُ
To charge with mistake.	خَطَّأَ
To err, transgress ; miss one's aim.	أَخْطَأَ
Error ; sin, mistake.	خَطَأٌ وَخَطَاءٌ
Sin.	خَطِيئَةٌ ج خَطَايَا
Sinner.	خَاطِئٌ ج خَطَأَةٌ وَخُطَاةٌ
Erring, missing.	مُخْطِئٌ
To make a speech.	خَطَبَ يَخْطُبُ
To betroth, ask in marrigae.	خَطَبَ يَخْطُبُ
To talk or converse with.	خَاطَبَ
Calamity.	خَطْبٌ ج خُطُوبٌ
Address, speech.	خُطْبَةٌ وَخِطَابٌ
Betrothal.	خِطْبَةٌ
Preacher.	خَطِيبٌ ج خُطَبَاءُ
Second person, (*Gram.*)	مُخَاطَبٌ
To occur to his mind.	خَطَرَ لَهُ
To expose to danger.	خَاطَرَ بِ
Danger, risk.	خَطَرٌ ج أَخْطَارٌ
Thought, idea.	خَاطِرٌ ج خَوَاطِرُ

إِخْطَارٌ	Admonition, warning.
خَطِيرٌ	Great ; important.
مُخْطِرٌ وَخَطِرٌ	Dangerous.
مَخَاطِرُ	Risks, dangers, perils.
خَطَفَ يَخْطَفُ	To seize, abduct.
إِخْتَطَفَ	To snatch away, rob.
خَطْفٌ	Robbery ; abduction.
خَاطِفٌ	Seizing with violence.
خُطَّافٌ ج خَطَاطِيفُ	Swallow (bird).
خَطَمَ يَخْطِمُ	To muzzle.
خِطْمِيٌّ	Marsh-mallow.
خَطَا يَخْطُو	To step, walk.
تَخَطَّى	To pass beyond.
خُطْوَةٌ ج خُطُوَاتٌ	Step, pace.
خَطِيَّةٌ	Sin, transgression.
خَفَّ يَخِفُّ	To be light (in weight).
خَفَّفَ	To make light, ease.
إِسْتَخَفَّ	To make light of.
خُفٌّ ج اخْفَافٌ	Boot, shoe.
خِفَّةٌ	Lightness ; agility.
خَفِيفٌ	Light (in weight) ; quick.
إِسْتِخْفَافٌ	Slighting, despising.
تَخْفِيفٌ	Alleviating, lightening.
خَفَرَ يَخْفُرُ	To protect, guard.
خَفَرٌ	Sentry, guard.
خَفِيرٌ ج خُفَرَاءُ	Sentry, escort.
خُفَّاشٌ ج خَفَافِيشُ	Bat (animal).
خَفَضَ يَخْفِضُ	To depress, lower.
خَفَّضَ	To let down, lower.
إِنْخَفَضَ	To become low.
خَفْضٌ	Abasement.
خَفَقَ يَخْفِقُ	To beat. Flutter.
أَخْفَقَ	To fail, miss.
خَفَقَانٌ	Palpitation.
خَفِيَ يَخْفَى خَفَاءً	To be hidden.
خَفِيَ خُفْيَةً	To go out of sight.
اخْفَى إِخْفَاءً	To conceal.
تَخَفَّى	To be concealed.

إِخْتَفَى مِنْ	To disappear.
خَفًا وَخَفَاءٌ	Secret ; unperceived.
خَفًا ج خَفَايَا	Cocealed, secret.
خُفْيَةً	Secretly ; in secret.
خَاقَانٌ ج خَوَاقِينُ	King.
خَلَلَ	To become vinegar.
اخَلَّ ب	To be remiss in, neglect.
تَخَلَّلَ فِي	To penetrate, enter.
اخْتَلَّ	To be shaky, faulty.
خَلٌّ	Vinegar. Slit, rent.
خِلٌّ ج أَخْلَالٌ	Intimate friend.
خَلَلٌ	Defect ; injury.
خلةٌ ج خلالٌ	Quality, habit.
خَلِيل ج أَخلاء وَخلانٌ	Friend.
إِخْتِلَالٌ	Mental disorder ; fault.
مُخِلٌّ	Leading to disorder.
مِخْلَبٌ ج مَخَالِبُ	Claw, talon.
خَلَجَ يَخْلُجُ خَلْجاً	To quiver.
خَالَجَ	To contend with.
إِخْتَلَجَ	To tremble, quiver.
خَلِيجٌ ج خُلْجَانٌ	Bay, gulf; canal.
تَخَلْخَلَ	To be displaced.
خَلْخَالٌ ج خَلَاخِيلُ	Ankle-ring.
خَلَدَ يَخْلُدُ	To be eternal.
خُلُودٌ	Eternity ; immortality.
خُلْدٌ ج مَنَاجِذ	Mole (animal).
خَالِدٌ وَمُخلدٌ	Everlasting.
خَلَسَ يَخْلِسُ وَٱخْتَلَسَ	To steal.
إِخْتِلَاسٌ	Theft, robbery.
مُخْتَلِسٌ وخَالِسٌ	Thief, robber.
خَلَصَ يَخْلُص	To be pure. Escape.
خَلَّصَ	To deliver, rescue, save.
أَخْلَصَ	To be sincere.
تَخَلَّص	To be saved ; escape.
خَلَاصٌ	Rescue ; salvation.
خُلَاصَةٌ	Essence ; extract.
خَالِصٌ	Pure, unmixed ; free.
إِخْلَاصٌ وَخلوصٌ	Sincerity.

مُخْلِصٌ	Sincere.
اَلْمُخَلِّصُ	The Saviour.
خَلَطَ يَخْلِطُ	To mix, mingle.
خَلَّطَ	To confuse, disorder.
خَالَطَ وَتَخَالَطَ	To associate with.
إِخْتَلَطَ	To be mixed, mingled.
خِلْطٌ ج أَخْلَاطٌ	Mixture.
خُلْطَةٌ	Social intercourse.
خَلَعَ يَخْلَعُ	To cast off, strip. Depose ; unhinge ; dislocate.
خَلَّعَ	To disjoint, pull to pieces.
إِنْخَلَعَ	To be removed ; dislocated.
خَلْعٌ	Dislocation. Deposition.
خِلْعَةٌ ج خِلَع	Robe of honour.
خَلَاعَةٌ	Disorderly life. Vice.
مُخَلَّعٌ	Unhinged ; feeble, weak.
خَلَفَ يَخْلُفُ	To succeed ; replace.
خَلَفَ	To leave behind.
خَالَفَ مُخَالَفَةً وَخِلَافًا	To oppose.
اخْلَفَ اَلْوَعْدَ	To break one's promise.
تَخَلَّفَ عَنْ	To remain behind.
تَخَالَفَ وَاخْتَلَفَ	To disagree.
خَلْفَ	Behind, after.
خَلَفٌ	Successor, descendant.
خُلْفَةٌ واخْتِلَافٌ	Difference.
خلَافٌ	Disagreement.
خِلَافًا لذلكَ	Contrary to that.
خِلَافَةٌ	Caliphate. Succession.
خَلِيفَةٌ ج خُلَفَاء	Successor. Caliph.
مُخَالَفَةٌ	Opposition.
مُخْتَلِفٌ	Varied, different.
خَلَقَ يَخْلُقُ خَلْقًا	To create.
خَلُقَ يَخْلُقُ	To be worn out.
خَلُقَ بِ وَلِ	To be adapted to.
إِخْتَلَقَ	To invent, forge lies.
تَخَلَّقَ بِ	To affect, feign.
خَلْقٌ	Creation ; creatures. Mankind.
خِلْقَةٌ ج خِلَق	Natural shape.
خُلُقٌ ج اخلَاقٌ	Inbron quality.

خِلْقِيٌّ	Congenital.
خَالِقٌ وَخَلَّاقٌ	Creator (God).
خَلِيقٌ ج خُلَقَاءُ بِ	Fit, suitable.
خَلِيقَةٌ ج خَلَائِقُ	Creature.
أَلْمَخْلُوقَاتُ	Created things.
خَلَا يَخْلُو	To be vacant ; alone.
خَلَا مِنْ وَعَنْ	To be free from.
خَلَا بِ	To meet privately.
خَلَّى	To leave, let alone.
اخْلَاهُ	To vacate a place.
تَخَلَّى عَنْ	To withdraw from.
تَخَلَّى لِ	To confine himself to.
خَلَاءٌ	Empty space ; solitude.
بَيْتُ ٱلْخَلَاءِ	Water-closet.
خَلَا وَمَا خَلَا	Except.
خُلُوٌّ	Emptiness.
خَلْوَةٌ	Privacy, solitude.
عَلَى خَلْوَةٍ	Aside, apart.
خَلِيَّةٌ ج خَلَايَا	Bee-hive ; cell.
خَالٍ	Empty, vacant. Free.
أَلْقُرُونُ ٱلْخَالِيَةُ	Past ages.
مِخْلَاةٌ	Feed-bag (for animals).
خَمَّ يَخِمُّ	To be putrid.
خَمَّ يَخُمُّ خَمًّا	To examine a country.
خُمٌّ	Hen-coop.
خَمَدَ يَخْمُدُ	To subside ; abate.
خَامِدٌ	Silent ; dead.
خُمُودٌ	Abatement, subsidence.
خَمَرَ يَخْمُرُ	To veil, conceal.
خَمَّرَ	To conceal. Leaven.
خَامَرَ	To be mixed with.
تَخَمَّرَ	To veil the head, face.
إِخْتَمَرَ	To ferment ; rise (dough).
خَمْرٌ وَخَمْرَةٌ	Wine.
خِمَارٌ ج خُمُرٌ	Covering ; veil.
خَمِيرٌ وَخَمِيرَةٌ	Leaven.
خَمَّارٌ	Wine-merchant.
خَمَّارَةٌ	Wine-shop.

Fermented.	مُخَمَّرٌ
To be the fifth.	خَمَسَ يَخْمُسُ
To make pentagonal.	خَمَّسَ
The fifth part.	خُمْسٌ ج أَخْمَاسٌ
Five.	خَمْسَةٌ م خَمْسٌ
Fifth.	خَامِسٌ
Fifty, fiftieth.	خَمْسُونَ
Thursday.	يَوْمُ ٱلْخَمِيسِ
Pentagon. Pentagonal.	مُخَمَّسٌ
To scratch.	خَمَشَ يَخْمِشُ
Hollow of the foot.	أَلْأَخْمَصُ
To limp.	خَمَعَ يَخْمَعُ
Nap of cloth.	خَمْلٌ
To be obscure (man).	خَمَلَ يَخْمُلُ
Villi of stomach.	خَمَلُ ٱلْمِعْدَةِ
Velvet.	مُخْمَلٌ
To surmise.	خَمَنَ يَخْمُنُ وخَمَّنَ
By supposition.	عَلَى ٱلتَّخْمِينِ
To snuffle.	خَنَّ يَخِنُّ خَنِينًا
Nasal twang.	خُنَّةٌ
Sunffles (disease).	خُنَانٌ
To be effeminate.	خَنِثَ يَخْنَثُ
Hermaphrodite.	خُنْثَى
Poniard.	خَنْجَرٌ ج خَنَاجِرُ
Trench, moat.	خَنْدَقٌ ج خَنَادِقُ
Canals of the Nile.	خَنَادِلُ
Hog, pig.	خِنْزِيرٌ ج خَنَازِيرُ
Wild boar.	خِنْزِيرٌ بَرِّيٌّ
Scrofula.	دَآءُ ٱلْخَنَازِيرِ
The stars.	أَلْخُنَّسُ
Satan.	أَلْخَنَّاسُ
Fern (plant).	خِنْشَارٌ
Sucking, pig.	خِنَّوْصٌ ج خَنَانِيص
The little finger.	خِنْصِرٌ ج خَنَاصِر
Black beetle	خُنْفُسَاءُ ج خَنَافِس
To strangle.	خَنَقَ يَخْنُقُ
To be strangled.	إِخْتَنَقَ وٱنْخَنَقَ
Quinsy (disease).	خُنَّاقٌ

خنقٌ وَمَخْنوقٌ	Strangled.
الخَنَى	Foul words.
إِخْتِنَاقٌ	Suffocation ; asphyxia.
(خَوَاجَه خَوَاجَاتٌ	(Mister, Mr.
(خوجَه ج خوجَات	(Teacher.
خَوْخٌ	Plum ; peach.
خُوذَةٌ ج خُوَذٌ	Helmet.
خارَ يَخُورُ	To bellow.
خارَ خَؤُوراً	To fail (strength).
خُوَارٌ	Bellowing of cattle.
خُورِيٌّ ج خَوَارِنَةٌ	Curate, person.
خاسَ يَخُوسُ	To be unsaleable.
خوصٌ	Leaves of the plam-tree.
أَخْوَصُ	Having a deformed eye.
خَاضَ يَخُوضُ	To wade ; ford.
مَخَاضَةٌ ج مَخَاوِضُ	Ford.
خافَ يَخَافُ	To fear, be afraid of.
خوَّفَ وَأَخَافَ	To frighten.
خوفٌ وَمَخَافة وَخِيفَةٌ	Fear, fright.
خَائفٌ	Timid, fearing.
تَخْوِيفٌ	Intimidation.
مخوّفٌ	Fearful, perilous.
مخيفٌ	Terrible, inspiring fear.
مَخَافَةٌ ج مَخاوِفُ	Cause of fear.
خَوَّلَ	To bestow upon.
خَالٌ ج أَخْوَالٌ	Maternal uncle.
خَالٌ ج خِيلانٌ	Mole on the face.
خَالَةٌ ج خَالَاتٌ	Maternal aunt.
خَوْلِيٌّ ج خَوَلٌ	Steward.
خَامٌ	Calico.
خانَ يَخونُ	To be unfaithful.
خوَّنَ	To accuse of treachery.
خانٌ ج خَانَاتٌ	Inn (Prince).
خَوْنٌ وَخِيانَةٌ	Deceit, treachery.
خِوَانٌ ج أَخْوِنَةٌ	Table for food.
خَائِنٌ	Unfaithful, traitor.
خَؤُونٌ وَخَوَّانٌ	Treacherous.
خَوَى يَخْوِي	To be waste, empty.

Empty, hollow ; void. خاوٍ

To be disappointed. خَابَ يَخِيبُ

To disappoint. خيَّبَ وَاخاب

Failure, disappointment. خَيْبَةٌ

Frustrated. خَائِبٌ

To deem better ; prefer. خيَّرَ عَلَى

To give one a choice. خيَّرَ

To choose, select, prefer. إِخْتَار

A good thing. خَيْرٌ ج خِيَارٌ

Better than. خَيْرٌ مِنْ

The best of men. خَيْرُ النَّاسِ

Good, benevolent. خَيْرِيٌّ

Choice. Cucumber. خِيَارٌ

Good, liberal. خَيِّرٌ

Better ; preferable. خَيْرٌ (اخيَرُ)

Choice, election. اخْتِيَارٌ

Voluntary. اخْتِيَارِيٌّ

Free to choose. مُخَيَّرٌ

Preferred. مُخْتَارٌ

Zinc. خَارصِينِي

Coarse canvas. خَيْشٌ

Large sack. خَيْشَةٌ ج خَيْشَاتٌ

To sew. خَاطَ يَخِيطُ وَخَيَّطَ

Thread. خَيْطٌ ج خُيُوطٌ وَخِيطَانٌ

Needle-work, sewing. خِيَاطَةٌ

Tailor. خَيَّاط

Sewn, stitched. مَخِيطٌ وَمَخْيُوطٌ

To conceive; imagine. خَالَ يَخَالُ

To seem to. خُيِّلَ لِ وَإِلَى

To imagine, fancy. تَخَيَّلَ

Horse ; cavalry. خَيْلٌ ج خُيُول

Spectre, phantom. خَيَالٌ ج اخْيِلَةٌ

Imaginary ideal. خَيَالِيٌّ

Faculty of imagination. اَلْمُخَيِّلَةُ

Horseman. خَيَّالٌ ج خَيَّالَةٌ

To pitch a tent ; abide. خَيَّمَ

Unbleached cloth. خَامٌ

Tent ; booth. خَيْمَةٌ ج خِيَامٌ

د

د As a numerical sign=4.
دَابٌ State, condition ; habit.
دَبَّ يَدِبُّ To crawl, creep.
دبٌّ ج أَدْبَابٌ Bear (animal).
دَابَّةٌ ج دَوَابُّ Animal ; beast.
دُوَيْبَّةٌ Little animal ; reptile.
دِيبَاجٌ Silk brocade.
دِيبَاجَةٌ Introduction, preface.
دَبْدَبَ To tread, crawl.
دَبَّرَ To plan ; manage well.
أَدْبَرَ To go back, retreat.
تَدَبَّرَ To regard attentively.
دُبْرٌ ج أَدْبَارٌ Back, hind part.
تَدْبِيرٌ ج تَدَابِيرُ Management.
مُدْبِرٌ One who turns back.
مُدَبِّرٌ Administrator ; director.

دِبْسٌ Thick juice of grapes.
دَبُّوسٌ ج دَبَابِيس Mace. Pin.
دَبَغَ يَدْبُغُ To tan (leather).
دِبَاغَةٌ Trade of a tanner.
دَبَّاغٌ Tanner.
مَدْبَغَةٌ ج مَدَابِغ Tannery.
مَدْبُوغٌ Tanned.
دَبِقَ يَدْبَقُ ب To adhere to.
دِبْقٌ Glue, bird-lime.
دَثَرَ يَدْثُرُ To be effaced.
دَثَّرَ To cover with a blanket.
إِنْدَثَرَ To be destroyed.
دَاثِرٌ That which perishes.
دُجَاجٌ Poultry.
دُجَاجَةٌ A hen.
دُجَاجُ ٱلْهِنْدِ Turkey.

Woodcock. دُجَاجُ ٱلأَرْضِ

Partridge. دُجَاجُ ٱلْبَرِّ

Completely armed. مُدَجَّجٌ

To lie ; cheat. دجَلَ يَدْجُلُ

Liar ; imposter ; quack. دَجَّالٌ

Tigris (river). دِجْلَة

To be cloudy, dark. To become tame. دَجَنَ يَدْجُنُ

To abide. دَجَنَ دُجُونًا بِ

Darkness. دُجْنَةٌ ج دُجَنٌ

Tame animal. دَاجِنٌ ج دَوَاجِنُ

Darkness. دجًى

To drive away. دَحَرَ يَدْحَرُ

To roll down (*tran*). دَحْرَجَ

To be rolled. تَدَحْرَجَ

Lucern. دُحَيْرِجَةٌ

Whitlow. دَاحِسٌ

To force into. دَحَشَ يَدْحَشُ

To rebut, refute. أَدْحَضَ

To be refuted, rebutted. إِنْدَحَضَ

To enter. دَخَلَ يَدْخُلُ

To be included. دخلَ تَحتَ وَفِي

To cause to enter. أَدْخَلَ

To intermeddle. تَدَاخَلَ فِي

Income, revenue. دَخْلٌ

I beseech you. دَخْلَكَ وَدَخِيلَكَ

Interior, inside. دَاخِلٌ

Home Secretary. وَزِيرُ ٱلدَّاخِلِيَّةِ

Stranger. Guest. دَخِيلٌ ج دُخَلَاءُ

Door ; access. مَدْخَلٌ ج مَدَاخِلُ

Revenue. مَدْخُولٌ ج مَدَاخِيل

To smoke. دَخَنَ وَدَخَّنَ وَأَدْخَنَ

Millet. دُخْنٌ

Smoke. Tobacco. دُخَّانٌ

Chimney. مَدْخَنَةٌ ج مَدَاخِنُ

To flow copiously. دَرَّ يَدِرُّ

Copious flow of milk. دَرٌّ

How exquisite ! لِلّٰهِ دَرُّهُ

Pearl. Parrot. دُرَّةٌ ج دُرَّات

مِدْرَارٌ	Copious flow.
دَرَّبَ	To guide, direct.
تَدَرَّبَ	To be practised in.
دَرْبٌ ج دُرُوبٌ	Path ; way.
تَدْرِيبٌ	Training ; drill.
مُدَرَّبٌ	Trained ; excercised.
دَرَبْزِينٌ وَدَرَابِزُون	Balustrade.
دَرَجَ يَدْرُجُ	To proceed gradually.
أَدْرَجَ وَدَرَّجَ فِي	To introduce.
تَدَرَّجَ	To proceed by degrees.
دَرْجٌ ج أَدْرَاجٌ	Roll of Paper.
دُرْجٌ ج أَدْرَاجٌ	Box, case.
دَرْجٌ ج ادرَاجٌ وَدِرَاجٌ	Road, path.
دَرَجَةٌ ج دَرَجَاتٌ	Step; degree.
تَدْرِيجاً وَبِٱلتَّدْرِيجِ	Gradually.
دَارِجٌ	Common, current.
دُرَّاجٌ	Francolin.
انْدَرَجَ	To lie unconscious.
دَرْدَارٌ	Elm.
دَرَزَ يَدْرُزُ	To sew, stitch.
دَرْزٌ ج دُرُوزٌ	Seam.
دُرْزِيٌّ ج دُرُوزٌ	Druze.
دَرَسَ يَدْرُسُ	To efface.
دَرَسَ يَدْرِسُ	To read, study.
دَرَسَ	To tread out corn, thresh.
دَرَسَ عَلَى	To study or read under a teacher.
دَرَّسَ	To teach, lecture.
إِنْدَرَسَ	To be effaced.
دَرْسٌ ج دُرُوسٌ	Lesson. study.
دِرَاسٌ وَدِرَاسَةٌ	Threshing.
مَدْرَسَةٌ ج مَدَارِسُ	School.
مُدَرِّسٌ	Teacher, professor.
إِدَّرَعَ وَتَدَرَّعَ	To put on a coat of mail.
دِرْعٌ ج دُرُوعٌ	Coat of mail.
مُدَرَّعٌ	Armoured.
دَوْرَقٌ ج دَوَارِقُ	Water jug.
دُرَاقِنٌ وَدُرَّاقٌ	Peach.
دَرَّكَ	To make responsible for.

To overtake. دَارَكَ

To reach ; comprehend. أَدْرَكَ

To overtake ; rectify. تَدَارَكَ

To seek to obviate. إِسْتَدْرَكَ

Comprehension. إِدْرَاكٌ

To be filthy. دَرِنَ يَدْرَنُ

Dirt. Tubercle. دَرَنٌ ج أَدْرَانٌ

Polluted, dirty. دِرْنٌ

Drachm ; money. دِرْهَمٌ ج دَرَاهِم

Dervish. دَرْوِيشٌ ج دَرَاوِيشُ

To know. دَرَى يَدْرِي

To treat kindly, cajole. دَارَى

To acquaint, inform. أَدْرَى بِ

Knowledge. دِرَايَةٌ

To hide, insert. دَسَّ يَدُسُّ

To plot against. دَسَّ عَلَى

To be hidden, concealed. إِنْدَسَّ

Spy. دَاسُوسٌ ج دَوَاسِيسُ

Intrigue. دَسِيسَةٌ ج دَسَائِسُ

A game. Copper pot. دَسْتٌ ج دُسُوتٌ

Rule, regulation. دُسْتُورٌ

Town, village. دَسْكَرَةٌ ج دَسَاكِرُ

To be fatty. دَسِمَ يَدْسَمُ

Fat, grease. دَسَمٌ وَدُسُومَةٌ

To dismiss ; leave. دَشَّرَ

Let ! (*imp. from.* وَدَعَ) دَعْ

To sport, jest with. دَعَبَ وَدَاعَبَ

Wickedness. دَعَرٌ وَدَعَارَةٌ

To tread under foot. دَعَسَ يَدْعَسُ

A track, foot-print. دَعْسَةٌ

To rup. دَعَكَ يَدْعَكُ

To contend with. دَاعَكَ مُدَاعَكَةً

To prop. دَعَمَ يَدْعَمُ دَعْماً

Support, prop. دِعَامَةٌ ج دَعَائِمُ

To call ; pray. دَعَا يَدْعُو

To invite. دَعَا دَعْوَةً

To pray for. دَعَا لِ

To invoke a curse upon. دَعَا عَلَى

إِدَّعَى بِ	To claim ; pretend.
إِدَّعَى على	To claim against.
إِسْتَدْعَى	To call, invite.
دُعَاءٌ ج ادْعِيَةٌ	Call ; prayer.
دَعْوَةٌ	Invocation ; invitation. Imprecation.
دعْوَى ج دَعَاوٍ	Claim ; law-suit.
دَاعٍ ج دُعَاةٌ	Calling. Preacher.
دَاعِيَةٌ ج دَوَاعٍ	Cause ; motive.
إِدِّعَاءٌ	Claim, pretention.
مُدَّعٍ	Pretender ; plaintiff.
مُدَّعًى عَلَيْهِ	Defendant.
دَغْدَغَ دَغْدَغَةً	To tickle.
دَغَشٌ	Darkness ; nightfall.
دَغَلٌ ج أَدْغَالٌ	Corruption. Thicket.
دَفٌّ ج دفوفٌ	Tambourine.
دَفَّةٌ	Side. Rudder.
دَفِئَ يَدْفَأُ	To be warm.
دَفَّأَ وَأَدْفَأَ	To warm.
تَدَفَّأَ	To warm one's self.
دِفْءٌ	Heat, warmth.
دَفْتَرٌ ج دفَاتِرُ	Register. Account-book.
دَفْتَرْدَارٌ	Minister of Finances.
دَفَرَ يَدْفُرُ	To push back.
دِفْرَان	Juniper tree.
دَفَشَ يَدْفِش	To push.
دَفَعَ يَدْفَعُ	To push back, repel.
دَفَعَ إِلَى وَلِ	To hand over to.
دَافَعَ	To contend with. Defer.
دَافَعَ عَنْ	To protect, defend.
إِنْدَفَعَ	To be thrust back.
دَفْعٌ	Pushing back. Payment.
قُوَّةٌ دَافِعَةٌ	Expulsive force.
مِدْفَعٌ ج مَدَافِعُ	Cannon.
دَفَقَ يَدْفُقُ	To pour forth (water).
تَدَفَّقَ وَانْدَفَقَ	To be poured out.
مُتَدَفِّقٌ	Overflowing.
دِفْلٌ وَدِفْلَى	Oleander.
دَفَنَ يَدْفِنُ	To bury ; conceal.

إِنْدَفَنَ	To be buried.
دَفْنٌ	Burying, burial.
دَفِينَةٌ ج دَفَائِنُ	Buried treasure.
مدْفَنٌ ج مَدَافِنُ	Tomb.
دقَّ يَدِقُّ	To be fine, thin.
دَقَّ يَدُقُّ	To crush ; knock.
دق ٱلْجرَس	To ring the bell.
دَقَّقَ	To be precise.
دَقَّقَ ٱلنظَرَ	To examine minutely.
دقّةٌ	Exactness, accuracy.
مدَقٌّ وَمِدَقَّةٌ	Pestle.
دَقِيقٌ ج أَدِقَّةٌ وَدِقَاقٌ	Fine : thin. Fine flour.
دقِيقَةٌ ج دقائِقُ	Minute (time).
تَدْقِيقٌ	Exactness, precision.
مُدَقِّقٌ	Exact, precise.
دَكَّ يَدُكُّ	To demolish. To charge a gun.
دَكَّةٌ	Wide bench, seat.
مِدَكٌّ	Ramrod.
مَدْكُوكٌ	Loaded (gun).
دَكِنَ يَدْكَنُ	To be blackish.
دُكْنَةٌ	Blackish colour.
دُكَّانٌ ج دَكَاكِينُ	Shop.
دُكَّنْجِيٌّ	Shop-keeper.
أَدْكَنُ م دَكْنَاءُ	Blackish.
دَلَّ يَدُلُّ على	To point out, show.
دَلَّلَ	To spoil (a child).
دلَّلَ عَلَى	To sell at auction.
تَدَلَّلَ	To be coquettish.
إِسْتَدَلَّ عَلَى	To seek, or to find a proof.
دَلَالٌ	Coquetry.
دَلَّالٌ	Broker, auctioneer.
دَلِيلٌ ج أَدِلَّةٌ	Sign, proof.
دَلِيلٌ ج أَدِلَّاءُ	Guide.
دُلْبٌ	Plane-tree.
دُولَابٌ ج دَوَالِيبُ	Water-wheel.
دَلَسٌ وَدُلْسَةٌ	Deceit.
دَلَعَ لِسَانَهُ	To loll the tongue.
دَلَفَ يَدْلِفُ دُلْفًا	To leak.

Dolphin. دُلْفِينٌ ج دَلَافِينُ

To pour out (a liquid). دَلَقَ يَدْلُقُ

To rub. دَلَكَ يَدْلُكُ دَلْكًا ب

Rubbing stone. مَدْلَكٌ وَمَدْلَكَةٌ

To be very dark. ادْلَهَمَّ

Very black. مُدْلَهِمٌّ

To draw a bucket. دَلَا يَدْلُو

To let down. دَلَّى وَأَدْلَى

To be let down. تَدَلَّى

Bucket. دَلْوٌ ج دِلَاءٌ

Aquarius. الدَّلْوُ

Grape-vine. دَالِيَةٌ ج دَوَالٍ

Blood. دَمٌ

Bloody. دَمَوِيٌّ

To be gentle. دَمُثَ يَدْمُثُ

Mild, soft. دَمْثٌ وَدَمِيثٌ

Gentleness, delicacy. دَمَاثَةٌ

To be joined. دَمَجَ يَدْمُجُ وَٱنْدَمَجَ

Compact. مُدْمَجٌ وَمُنْدَمِجٌ

To murmur against. دَمْدَمَ عَلَى

To perish utterly. دَمَرَ يَدْمُرُ

To annihilate, destroy. دَمَرَ وَدَمَّرَ

Destruction, annihilation. دَمَارٌ

Palmyra. تَدْمُرُ

To be dense, (darkness). دَمَسَ يَدْمُسُ

To conceal, bury. دَمَسَ يَدْمُسُ

Dark, (night). دَامِسٌ

Damascus. دِمَشْقُ

To shed tears, (eyes). دَمَعَ يَدْمَعُ

Tears. دَمْعٌ ج دُمُوعٌ وَأَدْمُعٌ

A tear, a drop. دَمْعَةٌ

To mark by branding. دَمَغَ يَدْمَغُ

Mark, brand. دَمْغَةٌ

Brain. دِمَاغٌ ج أَدْمِغَةٌ

To manure land. دَمَلَ يَدْمُلُ

To be healed. دَمَلَ يَدْمُلُ وَٱنْدَمَلَ

Pustule, boil. دُمَّلٌ ج دَمَامِلُ

Manure. دَمَالٌ

Bracelet. دُمْلُجٌ ج دَمَالِجُ
To manure land. دَمَنَ وَدَمَّنَ
To be permanent. دَمِنَ يَدْمَنُ
To persevere in, cleave to. أَدْمَنَ
Constant practice. إِدْمَانٌ
Addicted to. مُدْمِنٌ
To bleed, flow (blood). دَمِيَ يَدْمَى
To cause to bleed. دَمَّى وَأَدْمَى
Blood. دَمٌ ج دِمَاءٌ
Bloody. دَمِيٌّ وَدَمَوِيٌّ
Large wine-jar. دَنٌّ ج دِنَانٌ
To be low, vile. دَنَا يَدْنَأُ
Meanness; weakness. دَنَاءَةٌ
Low; worthless. دَنِيءٌ ج أَدْنِيَاءُ
A gold coin. دِينَارٌ ج دَنَانِيرُ
To be defiled. دَنِسَ يَدْنَسُ
To stain, pollute. دَنَّسَ
To be defiled. تَدَنَّسَ
Filth, pollution. دَنَسٌ ج أَدْنَاسٌ

Soiled, foul. دَنِسٌ ج أَدْنَاسٌ
To be near death. أَدْنَفَ
To perish with cold. دَنِقَ يَدْنَقُ
Small coin. دَانِقٌ ج دَوَانِقُ
To approach. دَنَا يَدْنُو
Nearness; proximity. دَنَاوَةٌ
Meanness, baseness. دَنَايَةٌ
Vile. Near. دَنِيءٌ ج أَدْنِيَاءُ
Anything base. دَنِيَّةٌ ج دَنَايَا
The (present) world. دُنْيَا
Worldly. دُنْيَوِيٌّ
Nearer. Viler, worse. أَدْنَى
Time; age. دَهْرٌ ج دُهُورٌ
For ever and ever. دَهْرُ ٱلدَّاهِرِينَ
To be bewildered. دَهِشَ يَدْهَشُ
To perplex. دَهَّشَ وَأَدْهَشَ
Astounded. دَهِشٌ وَمَدْهُوشٌ
Confusion; perplexity. دَهْشَةٌ
Vestibule. دِهْلِيزٌ ج دَهَالِيزُ

To scatter.	دَهَكَ يَدْهَكُ دَهْكاً
To come unexpectedly.	دَهِمَ يَدْهَمُ
Blackness.	دُهْمَةٌ
Black (horse).	أَدْهَمُ
To anoint, paint.	دَهَنَ يَدْهِن
To beguile ; coax.	داهَنَ
To be anointed.	تَدَهَّنَ
Oil, grease.	دُهْنٌ ج أَدْهَانٌ
Paint. Ointment.	دِهَانٌ ودَهُونٌ
Painter.	دَهَّانٌ
Dissimulation ; flattery.	مُدَاهَنَةٌ
Painted.	مُدَهَّنٌ وَمَدْهُونٌ
To be sly, subtle.	دهِي يَدْهَى
Cunning, craft.	دَهَاءٌ
Calamity.	دَاهِيَةٌ ج دَوَاهٍ
Sagacious, cunning.	داهٍ وَدَاهِيَةٌ
To throw down.	دَهْوَرَ
To tumble down.	تَدَهْوَرَ
Illness, disease.	دَاءٌ ج أَدْوَاءٌ
Gout.	دَاءُ ٱلْمُلُوكِ
Hydrophobia.	دَاءُ ٱلْكَلَبِ
Elephantiasis.	دَاءُ ٱلْفِيل
To be giddy, sea sick.	دَاخَ يَدُوخُ
To subdue, conquer.	دوَّخَ
Giddiness.	دَوْخَةٌ
A worm.	دُودَةٌ ج دِيدَانٌ وَدُودٌ
Silk-worm.	دُودَةُ ٱلْقَزِّ
David.	دَاوُدُ
To revolve, circulate.	دَارَ يَدُورُ
To set going; administer.	اَدَارَ
To be round.	تَدَوَّرَ وَٱسْتَدَارَ
House.	دَارٌ ج دُورٌ ودِيَارٌ
The world to come.	دَارُ ٱلْبَقَاءِ
The world that is.	دَارُ ٱلْفَنَاءِ
The two worlds (of time and eternity).	اَلدَّارَانِ
Turn ; age, period.	دَوْرٌ ج أَدْوَارٌ
Rotation, circulation.	دَوَرَانٌ
Sparrow.	دُورِيٌّ

By turns, alternately.	مُدَاوَلَةٌ
Used, employed commonly.	مُتَدَاوَلٌ
To continue ; endure.	دَامَ يَدُومُ
As long as it stands.	مَادَامَ قَائِمًا
To persist in.	دَاوَمَ عَلَى
To prolong.	أَدَامَ
To continue.	إِسْتَدَامَ
Continuance.	دَوَامٌ وَدَيْمُومَةٌ
The ban palm.	دَوْمٌ
Continually ; for ever.	عَلَى ٱلدَّوَامِ
Spinning-top.	دُوَّامَةٌ
Continuing, lasting.	دَائِمٌ
Always.	دَائِمًا
Wine.	مُدَامٌ وَمُدَامَةٌ
Perseverance.	مُدَاوَمَةٌ
To write out.	دَوَّن
Beneath. Before, behind.	دُونَ
Except.	دُونَ أَنْ

Revolving ; roaming.	دَائِرٌ
Circle; or bit of a planet. Calamity. Department.	دَائِرَةٌ ج دَوَائِرُ
Encyclopedia.	دَائِرَةُ ٱلْعُلُومِ
Giddiness.	دُوَارٌ
Convent.	دَيْرٌ ج أَدْيِرَةٌ
Administration.	إِدَارَةٌ
Circular form.	إِسْتِدَارَةٌ
Pivot, axis.	مَدَارٌ
Round, circular.	مُدَوَّرٌ وَمُسْتَدِيرٌ
Inspector ; director.	مُدِيرٌ
Territory of a Mudir.	مُدِيرِيَّةٌ
To tread, trample.	دَاسَ يَدُوسُ
To be trodden upon.	إِنْدَاسَ
Shoe, sandal.	مَدَاسٌ
To alternate.	دَاوَلَ مُدَاوَلَةً
To do by turns.	تَدَاوَلَ
Dynasty ; empire.	دَوْلَةٌ ج دُوَلٌ
Vine, grapes.	دَوَالِيٌّ

بِدُونِ وَمِنْ دُونِ	Without.
دُونٌ	Low, mean, vile, bad.
دُونَكَ	Take it !
دِيوَانٌ ج دَوَاوِينُ	Court of justice ; tribunal Poems.
مُدَوَّنٌ	Inserted, registered.
دَاوَى	To treat medically.
دَوَاءٌ ج أَدْوِيَةٌ	Medicine, remedy.
دَوَاةٌ وَدَوَايَةٌ	Inkstand.
دَوِيٌّ	Hum, buzz; rustling.
مُدَاوَةٌ	Treatment, cure.
مُدَاو	Physician.
دِيكٌ ج دُيُوكٌ	Cock.
دَانَ يَدِينُ	To borrow ; lend.
دَانَ دِيناً	To judge, requite. Follow a religion.
دانَ لِ	To submit, yield to.
دَيَّنَ وَأَدَانَ	To lend money.
تَدَيَّنَ وَٱسْتَدَانَ مِنْ	To borrow.
تَدَيَّنَ بِ	To follow a religion.
دَيْنٌ ج دُيُونٌ	Debt, loan.
دِيْنٌ ج اَدْيَانٌ . دِيَانَةٌ ج دِيَانَاتٌ	Religion ; belief.
يَوْمُ ٱلدِّينِ	The Judgment Day.
دَيْنُونَةٌ	Judgment.
دَائِنٌ	Debtor ; creditor.
دَيَّانٌ	Judge.
مَدِينَةٌ	City. (*see* مدن)
مَدْيُونٌ ج مَدْيُونون	Debtor.

ذ

ذ As a numeral sign=700.

ذا ج اولاء This, this one.

ذَاكَ ج اولئِكَ That, that one.

ذلِك ج اوْلاَئِكَ That, that one.

لمَاذا What? مَاذاَ Why?

كذا Thus, like this.

هذَا مث هذَانِ ج هؤُلاَءِ This.

هـكَذا Thus, like this.

ذِئْبٌ ج ذ ئَابٌ Wolf.

ذبَّ يَذُبُّ عَنْ To repel; defend.

ذُبَابٌ ج ذِبَّانٌ Fly.

ذُبَابَةٌ A fly.

ذبَحَ يَذْبَحُ To slaughter, slay.

تَذابَحَ To kill one another.

ذَبْحٌ Act of slaughtering.

ذبحَة Angina, croup.

ذبيحٌ Slaughtered.

ذَبِيحَةٌ ج ذَبائِحُ Sacrifice.

مذْبَحٌ ج مَذابِحُ Alter.

مذبُوحٌ Slaughtered, immolated.

ذَبْذَبَ To swing to and fro.

مُذَبْذبٌ وَمتَذَبْذِبٌ Wavering.

ذَبَلَ يَذْبُلُ ذُبولاً To wither.

أَذْبَلَ To cause to wither, dry up.

ذابِلٌ Withered, withering.

ذَخَرَ يَذْخَرُ وَآذخَرَ To treasure up.

ذُخْرٌ ج أَذْخَارٌ وَذَخِيرَةٌ ج ذَخائِرُ Treasure; stores.

ذَرَّ يَذُرُّ ذَرًّا To scatter, sprinkle.

ذَرٌّ Young or small ants.

ذَرَّةٌ An atom.

ذُرِّيَةٌ ج ذَرارِيُّ Descendants.

ذَرَّاحٌ ج ذَرَارِيح — Spanish fly.
ذَرْذَرَ — To scatter, strew.
ذَرْعٌ — Power, capacity.
ضَاقَ ذَرْعًا — To be unable.
ذِرَاعٌ ج أَذْرُعٌ — Arm ; cubit.
ذَرِيعٌ — Sudden, rapid.
ذَرَفَ يَذْرِفُ — To flow; shed (tears).
ذَرَى يَذْرِي — To winnow ; scatter.
ذَرَّى وَأَذْرَى — To winnow.
ذَرَّى وَاسْتَذْرَى — To seek shelter.
ذُرَةٌ — A kind of millet.
ذُرَةٌ صَفْرَاءُ — Maize.
ذَرًى — Dispersed dust. Shelter.
ذَرْوَةٌ ج ذُرًى — Summit.
مِذْرًى — Winnowing fork.
ذَعَرَ يَذْعَرُ وَأَذْعَرَ — To frighten.
ذَعِرَ وَٱنْذَعَرَ — To be terrified.
ذُعْرٌ — Fright, terror.
ذَعَرٌ — Bewilderment.

مَذْعُورٌ — Bewildered ; frightened.
ذَعِنَ يَذْعَنُ وَأَذْعَنَ لِ — To obey.
اذْعَنَ بِ — To confess, submit.
إِذْعَانٌ — Submission.
مُذْعِنٌ — Obedient, submissive.
ذَفَرٌ — Strong odour.
ذَقْنٌ ج ذُقُونٌ — Chin ; beard.
ذَكَرَ يَذْكُرُ — To remember.
ذَكَّرَ — To mention, relate.
ذَكَّرَ وَأَذْكَرَ — To remind of
ذَاكَرَ فِي — To confer with.
تَذَكَّرَ — To remember, think of.
تَذَاكَرَ فِي — To confer together.
ذِكْرٌ — Memory ; praise. Mention.
ذَكَرٌ ج ذُكُورٌ — Male. Male organ.
ذِكْرَى — Remembrance.
ذَاكِرَةٌ — Faculty of memory.
تَذْكِرَةٌ ج تَذَاكِرُ — Permit, passport.
تَذْكَارٌ — Remembrance.

تَذَكُّرٌ Frequent remembrance.
مُذَاكَرَةٌ Conference.
مُذَكَّرٌ Masculine, (word).
مَذْكُورٌ Mentioned. Praised.
ذَكِيَ يَذْكَى To be quick, (in intellect).
ذَكَاءٌ Quick understanding.
ذَكِيٌّ ج أَذْكِيَاء Intelligent.
أَذْكَى Quicker in perception.
ذَلَّ يَذِلُّ To be low ; submissive.
ذَلَّلَ وَأَذَلَّ To humble, humiliate.
ذَلَّلَ To render tractable.
تَذَلَّلَ To humble one's self.
ذُلٌّ Submissiveness.
ذُلٌّ وَمَذَلَّةٌ Humiliation.
ذَلِيلٌ ج أَذِلَّاء Low, abject.
ذَلِكَ This ; that. (*see* ذَا)
ذَمَّ يَذُمُّ To blame, censure.
ذَمٌّ وَمَذَمَّةٌ Blame, rebuke.
ذِمَّةٌ ج ذِمَمٌ Covenant ; security.

أَهْلُ ٱلذِّمَّةِ Protected tributaries.
ذِمَّةٌ Conscience ; moral sense.
ذَمِيمٌ Blamed ; censured.
مَذَمَّةٌ Blameworthy action.
مَذْمُومٌ Blamed ; censured.
تَذَمَّرَ عَلَى To murmur against.
أَذْنَبَ To be guilty.
ذَنْبٌ ج ذُنُوبٌ Crime guilt.
ذَنَبٌ ج أَذْنَابٌ Tail, extremity.
نَجْمٌ ذُو ذَنَب Comet.
مُذْنِبٌ Guilty ; criminal.
ذَهَبَ يَذْهَبُ To go, depart.
ذَهَبَ إِلَى To think, believe.
ذَهَّبَ وَأَذْهَبَ To gild.
أَذْهَبَ To cause to disappear.
ذَهَبٌ Gold.
ذَهَبِيٌّ Golden, of gold.
ذَهَبِيَّةٌ Nile-boat.
ذَاهِبٌ Going ; passing.

ذَهَابٌ	Departure.
مذَهَّبٌ	Gilt.
مَذْهبٌ ج مَذَاهِبُ	Way. Creed.
تَمَذْهَبَ	To embrace a creed.
ماء ٱلذهَبِ	Gold powder.
ذَهِلَ يَذْهَلُ عَنْ	To forget, neglect.
ذَهَلَ وَٱنْذَهَلَ	To be astonished.
أَذْهلَ عَنْ	To cause to forget.
إِنْذِهَالٌ	Astonishment.
مُنْذَهِلٌ	Astonished, bewildered.
ذِهْنٌ ج أَذْهَانٌ	Mind, intellect.
ذِهْنِيٌّ	Intellectual, subjective.
ذُو ج ذَوُو	Master, possessor.
ذَاتٌ	Essence; person, self.
ذاتَ ٱلْيمينِ	To the right.
ذَاتَ يَوْمٍ	On a certain day.
بذَاتِهِ	In person.
في ذَاتِهِ	In itself.
ذَاتِيٌّ	Essential, personal.
مَحَبَّة ٱلذاتِ	Selfishness.
ذَابَ يذُوبُ	To dissolve, melt.
ذوَّب وَاذابَ	To cause to melt.
ذَائِبٌ	Melting, in a fluid state.
مِذْوَدٌ ج مَذَاوِد	Manager.
ذَاقَ يذُوقُ	To taste; try.
أَذَاقَ	To give to taste.
ذَوْقٌ	Taste, sense of taste.
ذَوقٌ سَلِيمٌ	Sound taste.
مَذَاقٌ	Flavour.
ذَاكَ	That, yonder. (*See* اذا)
ذَوَى يَذْوِي	To wither, (plant).
ذِي وَهذي	This, (*fem. of* ذا)
ذَاعَ يذِيعُ	To be public, (news).
اذَاع وَب	To make public.
إِذَاعَة	Publication.
ذَيلَ	To add an appendix.
ذَيْلٌ ج ذُيُولٌ	Tail, skirt. Fringes. Appendix.
تَذْييل	Appendix, supplement.

ر

ر As a numeral sign=200.

راتينج Resin.

رأس يرأس To be a chief.

رأس To make one a leader.

ترأس To become a chief.

رأس ج رؤوس Head ; peak ; cape ; chief, leader ; principal part.

رأسا Directly ; completely.

على الرأس والعين Most willingly.

رأس المال Capital ; stock.

رآسة ورياسة Headship, authority.

رئيس ج رؤساء President, chief.

الأعضاء الرئيسة The vital organs.

مرؤوس Under authority.

رأف يرأف To show pity.

رأفة Compassion, pity, mercy.

رؤوف ورئف Compassionate.

رئم ج آرام White antelope.

رأى يرى To see, perceive ; judge.

رأى رؤيا To have a vision.

راءى مراءاة To dissemble.

يا ترى Do you suppose ?

أرى إراءة To show.

ترأى وتراءى ل To appear to.

إرتأى To consider.

رأي ج آراء Opinion ; view.

راية Military banner.

رياء Hypocrisy.

رئة ج رئات Lung.

ذات الرئة Inflammation of lung.

رؤيا ج رؤى Dream, vision.

رؤية ج رؤى Act of seeing.

مِرْآةٌ ج مَرَايَا	Mirror.
مُرَاءٍ	Hypocrite.
مُرَاءَاةٌ	Hypocrisy.
رَبٌّ ج أَرْبَابٌ	Lord, master.
أَلرَّبُّ	The Lord.
رُبٌّ ج رِبَابٌ	Syrup.
رُبَّ وَرُبَّمَا	Often. Seldom.
رَبَّانِيٌّ	Divine. Rabbi.
رَبَابٌ	A kind of violoncello.
رُبَّانٌ	Captain of ship ; chief.
رَبِحَ يَرْبَحُ رِبْحًا	To gain.
رَبَّحَ	To cause one to gain.
رِبْحٌ ج أَرْبَاحٌ	Profit, gain.
رِيبَاسٌ	A kind of sorrel (plant).
تَرَبَّصَ	To wait, expect.
رُوْبَاصٌ	Pure, refined, (silver).
رَبَضَ يَرْبِضُ	To lie in wait.
رَبَضٌ ج أَرْبَاضٌ	Suburb.
مَرْبِضٌ ج مَرَابِضُ	Enclosure.
رَبَطَ يَرْبُطُ	To tie, bind, fasten.
تَرَابَطَ	To agree upon.
إِرْتَبَطَ	To be tied.
رَبْطَةٌ ج رَبْطَاتٌ	Bundle, parcel.
رَابِطُ ٱلدَّرْبِ	Highway-robber.
رِبَاطٌ ج رُبُطٌ	Bond, rope.
رَابِطَةٌ	Connective, copula.
مِرْبَطٌ ج مَرَابِطُ	Stable.
مِرْبَطٌ	Cord, rope ; halter.
رَبَعَ بِ	Pasture freely in.
رَبَّعَ	To square.
تَرَبَّعَ	To sit cross-legged.
رُبْعٌ ج ارْبَاعٌ	Fourth part.
رَبْعَةٌ	Medium in stature.
رَابِعٌ رَابِعَةٌ	Fourth.
رُبَاعِيٌّ	Quadrilateral.
رَبِيعٌ	Spring-time.
رَبِيعُ ٱلأَوَّلُ	The third month of the Mohammedan year.

The fourth month.	رَبِيعُ ٱلْآخِرُ
Four.	أَرْبَعَةٌ م أَرْبَعُ
Quadrupeds.	ذَوَاتُ ٱلْأَرْبَعِ
Wednesday.	ٱلْأَرْبَعَاءُ
Forty.	أَرْبَعُونَ
Square form or number.	مُرَبَّعٌ
Of medium stature.	مَرْبُوعٌ
Jerboa.	يَرْبُوعٌ ج يَرَابِيعُ
To entangle, bind.	رَبَقَ يَرْبُقُ رَبْقًا
Loop, noose.	رِبْقٌ وَرِبْقَةٌ
To mix, confuse.	رَبَكَ يَرْبُكُ
To be entangled.	رَبِكَ وَٱرْتَبَكَ
Confused, entangled.	مُرْتَبِكٌ
Captain of a ship.	رُبَّانٌ
To increase ; grow.	رَبَا يَرْبُو
To nourish ; train up.	رَبَّى
To take usury.	رَابَى مُرَابَاةً
To increase *v. t.*	أَرْبَى
To be brought up.	تَرَبَّى
Usury, interest.	رِبًا وَرِبَاءٌ
Asthma, panting.	رَبْوٌ
Hill, height.	رَبْوَةٌ ج رُبًى
Ten thousand.	رَبْوَةٌ ج رَبْوَاتٌ
Hill, height.	رَابِيَةٌ ج رَوَابٍ
Education, training.	تَرْبِيَةٌ
Groin.	ارْبِيَّةٌ
Usurer.	مُرَابٍ
Educator, trainer.	مُرَبٍّ
Educated, trained up.	مُرَبًّى
To set in order.	رَتَّبَ
To be arranged.	تَرَتَّبَ
To result from.	تَرَتَّبَ عَلَى
Rank, position.	رُتْبَةٌ ج رُتَبٌ
Salary, pension.	رَاتِبٌ
Arrangement, order.	تَرْتِيبٌ
Grade, rank.	مَرْتَبَةٌ ج مَرَاتِبُ
To live in abundance.	رَتَعَ يَرْتَعُ
To repair.	رَتَقَ يَرْتُقُ رَتْقًا

رَتَلَ	To sing.
رُتَيْلَاءُ ج رُتَيْلَاوَاتٌ	Large spider.
تَرْتِيلٌ ج تَرَاتِيلُ	Singing, chanting.
رَثَّ يَرِثُّ	To be ragged.
رَثٌّ	Worn out. Rags.
رَثَاثَةٌ	Squalor, raggedness.
رَثَى يَرْثِي	To bewail (the dead).
رَثَى لِ	To sympathize with, pity.
رِثَاءٌ	Elegy.
مَرْثِيَةٌ وَمَرْثَاةٌ ج مَرَاثٍ	Elegy.
رَجَّ يَرُجُّ	To move, shake.
إِرْتِجَاجٌ	Agitation, trembling.
أَرْجَأَ	To put off, defer.
رَجَبٌ	The seventh month of the Moslem year.
رَجَحَ يَرْجُحُ	To over-weigh.
رَجَّحَ عَلَى	To prefer.
تَرَجَّحَ	To be more probable.
رَاجِحٌ	Outweighing, preferable.
أَرْجَحُ	Preferable, more probable.
أُرْجُوحَةٌ	Swing.
تَرْجِيحٌ	Preference, probability.
رَجَزٌ	A poetical metre.
أُرْجُوزَةٌ	Poem of رَجَز metre.
رَجَسَ يَرْجُسُ	To defile one's self.
رِجْسٌ وَرَجَسٌ وَرَجَاسَةٌ	Pollution.
رَجِسٌ	Dirty, foul.
رَجَعَ يَرْجِعُ	To return.
رجعَ إِلَى	To have recourse to.
رَجَعَ عَنْ	To renounce.
رَجَّعَ	To restore.
رَاجَعَ	To review.
أَرْجَعَ	To restore.
إِسْتَرْجَعَ	To reclaim.
رُجُوعٌ	Return.
مُرَاجَعَةٌ	Review, repetition.
رَجَفَ يَرْجُفُ	To quake, tremble.
أَرْجَفَ	To shake, agitate.
إِرْتَجَفَ	To tremble.

رَجْفَةٌ	Trembling, shaking.
أَرَاجِيفُ	Seditious rumours.
رَجَل يَرْجَلُ	To go on foot.
تَرَجَلَ	To dismount.
إِرْتَجَلَ	To speak extempore.
رِجْلٌ ج أَرْجُلٌ	Foot, leg.
رَجُلٌ ج رِجَالٌ	A man.
رَجِلٌ وَرَاجِلٌ	Pedestrain.
رُجُولِيَّةٌ	Manliness ; virility.
إِرْتِجَالٌ	Extemporizing.
مِرْجَلٌ ج مَرَاجِلُ	Caldron.
مُرْتَجَلٌ	Improvised (speech).
رَجَمَ يَرْجُمُ	To stone ; kill.
رَجَمَ بِالْغَيْبِ	To guess.
إِرْتَجَمَ	To be heaped up.
رَجَمٌ ج رِجَامٌ	Heap of stones.
رُجْمَةٌ ج رُجَمٌ	Tomb-stone.
رَجِيمٌ	Stoned, killed. Cursed.
مَرْجَانٌ	Coral.
رَجَا يَرْجُو	To hope, expect.
تَرَجَّى وَٱرْتَجَى	To hope for.
تَرَجَّى	To beg, entreat.
أَرْجَى	To put off, defer.
رَجَاءٌ	Hope.
رَحِبَ يَرْحَبُ	To be spacious (place).
رَحَّبَ وَأَرْحَبَ	To make wide.
رَحَّبَ وَتَرَحَّبَ بِ	To welcome.
رَحْبٌ وَرَحِيبٌ	Ample, spacious.
تَرْحَابٌ	Welcome.
مَرْحَبًا بِكَ	Welcome !
رَحَضَ يَرْحَضُ	wash.
مِرْحَاضٌ ج مَرَاحِيضُ	Wash-tub, water, closet.
رُحَاقٌ وَرَحِيقٌ	Choice wine.
رَحَلَ يَرْحَلُ وَٱرْتَحَلَ	To depart, migrate.
رَحْلٌ ج رِحَالٌ	Pack-saddle.
رِحْلَةٌ وَٱرْتِحَالٌ	Journey.
رَحِيلٌ وَٱرْتِحَالٌ	Migration.
رَاحِلٌ ج رُحَّلٌ	Traveller.

رَحَّالٌ وَرَحَّالَةٌ Great traveller.

مَرْحَلَةٌ ج مَرَاحِلُ Day's journey.

رَحِمَ يَرْحَمُ To pity, to be merciful.

تَرَحَّمَ عَلَى To have, or pray for, pity for one.

إِسْتَرْحَمَ To implore pity.

رَحِمٌ ج أَرْحَامٌ Uterus, womb.

رَحْمَةٌ Pity, compassion.

رَحِيمٌ ج رُحَمَاءُ Compassion.

اَلرَّحْمٰنُ اَلرَّحِيمُ The Merciful.

مَرْحَمَةٌ ج مَرَاحِمُ Act of mercy.

مَرْحُومٌ Deceased (person).

رَحًى ج أَرْحَاءٌ Mill-stone.

رخ A fabulons bird.

رَخْتٌ ج رُخُوتٌ Saddle.

رَخُصَ يَرْخُصُ To be cheap.

رَخُصَ رَخَاصَةً To be soft, supple.

رَخَّصَ To lower the price.

رَخَّصَ لِ To allow, permit.

إِسْتَرْخَصَ To consider a thing cheap. To ask leave.

رَخْصٌ م رَخْصَةٌ Soft, tender.

رُخْصٌ Cheapness of price.

رَخِيصٌ Cheap. Soft, tender.

رَخَّمَ يَرْخُمُ To be soft (voice).

رُخَامٌ Marble.

رَخِيمٌ وَرَخَمٌ Soft (voice).

تَرْخِيمٌ Elision of last letter of a word.

رَخِيَ يَرْخَى To be soft, flaccid.

أَرْخَى To loosen, let down.

تَرَاخَى To flag, be slow.

إِرْتَخَى وَاسْتَرْخَى To become lax.

رَخَاءٌ Relaxation; abundance.

رَخْوٌ Lax, soft, loose.

رَخَاوَةٌ Softness, slackness.

رَخِيُّ ٱلْبَالِ Free from care.

إِرْتِخَاءٌ وَٱسْتِرْخَاءٌ Relaxation.

رَدَّ يَرُدُّ To return, send back, turn away. Refer.

رَدَّدَ To ponder; repeat.

تَرَدَّدَ إِلَى To frequent (a place).

تَرَدَّدَ فِي	To waver ; hesitate.
إِرْتَدَّ	To go back, retreat, revert.
إِرْتَدَّ إِلَى	To be converted to.
إِرْتَدَّ عَنْ	To depart from.
اِسْتَرَدَّ	To reclaim ; revoke.
رَدٌّ	Repulse. Return. Reply.
إِرْتِدَادٌ إِلَى	Conversion to.
إِرْتِدَادٌ عَنْ	Apostasy.
اِسْتِرْدَادٌ	Reclamation, recovery.
تَرَدُّدٌ	Frequenting. Wavering.
مَرَدٌّ	Setting aside, repelling.
مُرْتَدٌّ	Convert ; apostate.
مُتَرَدِّدٌ	Vacillating, hesitating.
مَرْدُودٌ	Rejected ; refuted.
مَرْدُودَةٌ	Divorced woman.
رَدَاءَةٌ وَرَدَاوَةٌ	Evil, malice.
رَدِيءٌ ج أَرْدِيَاءُ	Bad, wicked.
أَرْدَأُ	Worse, more wicked.
أَرْدَبٌّ	Corn measure.
رَدَعَ يَرْدَعُ عَنْ	Restrain, prevent.
إِرْتَدَعَ عَنْ	To be restrained.
رَدَفَ يَرْدُفُ	To follow.
تَرَادَفَ	To be synonymous, (words).
رَدِيفٌ	The reserves, (soldiers).
مُتَرَادِفٌ	Synonymous (words).
رَدَمَ يَرْدِمُ	To stop, fill up.
إِرْتَدَمَ	To be stopped up.
رَدْمٌ	Ruins of a wall, debris.
رَدَنَ يَرْدِنُ	To spin. Purr (cat).
رِدْنٌ ج أَرْدَانٌ	Sleeve.
الأُرْدُنُّ	The Jordan.
مِرْدَنٌ ج مَرَادِنُ	Spindle.
رَدْهَةٌ ج رِدَاهٌ	A large hall.
رَدِيَ يَرْدَى رَدًى	To perish.
تَرَدَّى	To put on a mantle.
رِدَاءٌ ج أَرْدِيَةٌ	Mantle, cloak.
مُتَرَدٍّ	Enveloped in a mantle.
رَذَلَ يَرْذُلُ	To be mean, base.

To reject.	رَذَلَ يَرْذُلُ رَذْلاً
Ignoble, base.	رَذِيلٌ ج رُذَلاَءُ
Vileness.	رَذَالَةٌ ج رَذَالاَتٌ
Vice.	رَذِيلَةٌ ج رذَائِلُ
Rice.	رُزٌّ (for أُرُزٌّ)
Iron peg.	رَزَّةٌ ج رَزَّاتٌ
To diminish. Afflict.	رَزَأَ يَرْزَأُ
Misfortune.	رَزِيئَةٌ ج رَزَايَا
Iron rod.	إِرْزَبَّةٌ وَمِرْزَبَةٌ
Satrap.	مَرْزُبَانٌ ج مَرَازِبَةٌ
To fall from fatigue.	رَزَحَ يَرْزَحُ
Extreme fatigue.	رُزُوحٌ
Fatigued, exhausted.	رَازِحٌ
District.	رُزْدَاقٌ ج رُزْدَاقَاتٌ
To grant, bestow.	رَزَقَ يَرْزُقُ
To receive means of life.	إِرْتَزَقَ
To seek means of life.	إِسْتَرْزَقَ
Means of living.	رِزْقٌ ج أَرْزَاقٌ
God.	اَلرَّازِقُ وَاَلرَّزَّاقُ
Blessed with worldly goods.	مَرْزُوقٌ
To wrap up a package.	رَزَمَ يَرْزِمُ
Package, bale.	رِزْمَةٌ ج رِزَمٌ
To be grave, dignified.	رَزُنَ يَرْزُنُ
Gravity, dignity.	رَزَانَةٌ
Weighty, grave, calm.	رَزِينٌ
Almanac.	رُزْنَامَةٌ
To settle down. (liquid).	رَسَبَ يَرْسُبُ
Sediment.	رُسُوبٌ وَرُسَابَةٌ
Theatre.	مَرْسَحٌ ج مَرَاسِحُ
To be firm, stable.	رَسَخَ يَرْسَخُ
Firm, stable.	رَاسِخٌ ج رَاسِخُونَ
Well instructed.	رَاسِخٌ فِي ٱلْعِلْمِ
The ankle, wrist.	رُسْغٌ ج أَرْسَاغٌ
To correspond about.	رَاسَلَ
To dismiss, send.	أَرْسَلَ
To hang loose, (hair).	إِسْتَرْسَلَ
Message, letter, epistle. Mission.	رِسَالَةٌ ج رَسَائِلُ
Messenger, apostle.	رَسُولٌ ج رُسُلٌ

One sent, missionary.	مُرْسَلٌ
Correspondent.	مُرَاسِلٌ
Correspondence.	مُرَاسَلَةٌ
To trace ; design.	رَسَمَ يَرْسُمُ عَلَى
To prescribe, enjoin.	رَسَمَ لِ
To ordain to a sacred office.	رَسَمَ رِسَامَةً
Trace ; sign. Tax.	رَسْمٌ ج رُسُومٌ
Official, authoritative.	رَسْمِيٌّ
Marked. Ordained.	مَرْسُومٌ
Halter.	رَسَنٌ ج أَرْسُنٌ وَأَرْسَانٌ
To be firm.	رَسَا يَرْسُو
To cast anchor.	أَرْسَى إِرْسَاءً
At anchor, (ship).	رَاسٍ
Port. Anchorage.	مَرْسًى ج مَرَاسٍ
Anchor.	مِرْسَاةٌ ج مَرَاسٍ
To sprinkle.	رَشَّ يَرُشُّ
Watering-pot.	مِرَشَّةٌ ج مِرَشَّاتٌ
To exude, ooze.	رَشَحَ يَرْشَحُ رَشْحًا
To train, bring up.	رَشَّحَ لِ
To be trained for.	تَرَاشَحَ لِ
Cold in the heat.	رَشْحٌ
Trained. Candidate.	مُرَشَّحٌ
To direct, guide.	أَرْشَدَ
To ask for guidance.	إِسْتَرْشَدَ
Rectitude. Maturity.	رُشْدٌ
Cress, pepperwort.	رَشَادٌ
Follower of right way.	رَاشِدٌ وَرَشِيدٌ
To sip. suck.	رَشَفَ يَرْشُفُ
To hurl (a weapon).	رَشَقَ يَرْشُقُ
Fine, elegant form.	رَشِيقٌ
Elegance of from.	رَشَاقَةٌ
Window.	رَوْشَنٌ ج رَوَاشِنُ
To bribe.	رَشَا يَرْشُو رَشْوًا
To receive a bribe.	إِرْتَشَى
To ask for a bribe.	إِسْتَرْشَى
Bribe.	رَشْوَةٌ ج رُشًى
To press, squeeze.	رَصَّ يَرُصُّ
To overlay with lead.	رَصَّصَ

Lead.	رَصَاصٌ
Piece of lead ; bullet.	رَصَاصَةٌ
Lead-colour.	رَصَاصِيٌّ
Firm, compact.	مَرْصُوصٌ
To watch for.	رَصَدَ يَرْصُدُ
To lie in wait for.	رَصَدَ لِ
To observe, watch.	تَرَصَّدَ
Watching, observation.	رَصْدٌ
Balance of account.	رَصِيدٌ
Observatory.	مَرْصَدٌ ج مَرَاصِدُ
Highway, lurking-place.	مِرْصَادٌ
To set with jewels	رَصَّعَ
Inlaid with gold-work.	مُرَصَّعٌ
To pave.	رَصَفَ يَرْصُفُ رَصْفًا
Firmness, solidity.	رَصَافَةٌ
Firm. Paved road.	رَصِيفٌ
To be solid, grave.	رَصُنَ يَرْصُنُ
Gravity, sedateness.	رَصَانَةٌ
Firm, dignified, grave.	رَصِينٌ
To pound, bruise.	رَضَّ يَرُضُّ
To be bruised.	تَرَضَّضَ وَارْتَضَّ
Bruise, contusion.	رَضٌّ وَرَضَّةٌ
Saliva.	رُضَابٌ
To submit.	رَضَخَ يَرْضَخُ رَضْخًا لِ
To nurse (infant).	رَضِعَ يَرْضَعُ
To nurse, (mother).	أَرْضَعَ
Infant at the breast.	رَضِيعٌ
Act of nursing a child.	إِرْضَاعٌ
Wet-nurse.	مُرْضِعَةٌ ج مُرْضِعَاتٌ
To be pleased.	رَضِيَ يَرْضَى
To consent to.	رَضِيَ بِ
To satisfy, conciliate.	رَاضَى
To satisfy, please.	أَرْضَى إِرْضَاءً
To be content with.	إِرْتَضَى
Satisfaction.	رِضًى وَرِضْوَانٌ
Satisfied, content.	رَاضٍ ج رَاضُونَ
Comfortable life.	عِيشَةٌ رَاضِيَةٌ
Mutual agreement.	تَرَاضٍ

مُرْضٍ Satisfying, pleasing.

رَطَبَ يَرْطَبُ To be moist, damp.

رَطَّبَ To moisten; cool.

تَرَطَّبَ To be moistened.

رُطَبٌ Fresh, ripe dates.

رُطُوبَةٌ Moisture; humidity.

رَطْلٌ ج أَرْطَالٌ 449.28 grammes.

إِرْتَطَمَ To stick in mire.

رَعَاعُ The rabble, dregs of men.

رَعَبَ يَرْعَبُ To frighten.

رَعَّبَ وَأَرْعَبَ To terrify.

إِرْتَعَبَ To be frightened.

رُعْبٌ وَرُعُبٌ Fright, fear.

رَاعِبٌ وَمُرْعِبٌ Causing fear.

رَعَدَ يَرْعُدُ To thunder.

إِرْتَعَدَ To tremble, be afraid.

رَعْدٌ ج رُعُودٌ Thunder.

رَعَشَ يَرْعَشُ وَآرْتَعَشَ To tremble.

أَرْعَشَ To cause to tremble.

رَعْشٌ A trembling, shaking.

رَعِفَ يَرْعَفُ To bleed, (nose).

رُعَافٌ Bleeding from the nose.

رَعْنٌ Sun-stroke.

رَعْنٌ وَرُعُونَةٌ Stupidity

رَعَى يَرْعَى To graze; tend (cattle). Rule (subjects). Have regard to.

رَاعَى To have regard for.

إِرْتَعَى وَتَرَعَّى To pasture, graze.

رِعَايَةٌ Guarding; pasturing.

رَعِيَّةٌ ج رَعَايَا Subjects (of a ruler).

رَاعٍ ج رُعَاةٌ Shepherd. Pastor.

مَرْعًى ج مَرَاعٍ Pasturage, pasture.

مَرْعِيٌّ Observed, regarded.

مُرَاعَاةً لِ Out of regard for.

رَغِبَ يَرْغَبُ فِي To desire, long for.

رَغِبَ عَنْ To have no desire for, refrain from.

رَغِبَ إِلَى To implore, entreat.

رَغَّبَ To inspire with desire.

رَغْبَةٌ Strong desire, eagerness.

رَغِيبَةٌ ج رَغَائِبُ A desired object.

رَغْدٌ وَرَغِيدٌ Comfortable, easy.

رَغِيفٌ ج أَرْغِفَةٌ Loaf (of bread).

أَرْغَمَ To humiliate, vex ; force.

رَغْماً عَنْهُ In spite of him.

رَغَا يَرْغُو To effervesce, froth.

رَغْوَةٌ Foam, froth, cream.

رَفَّ يَرِفُّ To shine ; flutter.

رَفٌّ ج رُفُوفٌ Flock. Shelf.

رَفَأَ يَرْفَأُ To mend (a garment).

رَفَأَ بَيْنَ To make peace between.

رَفَاءٌ Peace, concord, accord.

مَرْفَأٌ Harbour for ships.

رَفَتَ يَرْفُتُ To refuse, reject.

رَفْتِيَّةٌ Permit (for goods).

رَفَخَ To rise, swell (dough).

رَفَدَ يَرْفِدُ To aid. Dress (a wound).

إِسْتَرْفَدَ To ask help.

رِفْدٌ ج أَرْفَادٌ Assistance.

رِفَادَةٌ Cushion ; bandage.

رَفْرَفَ To flap the wings.

رَفَسَ يَرْفِسُ To kick.

رَفْسَةٌ A kick.

رَفَشَ يَرْفُشُ رَفْشاً To shovel.

رَفْشٌ Winnowing-shovel.

رَفَضَ يَرْفُضُ To leave, reject.

إِرْفَضَّ To be separated, disperse.

رَافِضٌ ج رَفَضَةٌ One who rejects.

مُتَرَفِّضٌ A fanatic.

مَرْفُوضٌ Rejected.

رَفَعَ يَرْفَعُ To raise ; take away.

رُفِعَ يُرْفَعُ To be exalted.

رَفَعَ إِلَى To present to ; inform.

رَافَعَ إِلَى To cite before a judge.

تَرَافَعَ To bring a cause together before a judge.

إِرْتَفَعَ To rise high ; carried off.

رَفْعٌ Act of raising, elevating.

High rank, dignity.	رِفْعَةٌ
High, elevated.	رَفِيعٌ
Elevation, height.	إِرْتِفَاعٌ
Carnival.	مَرْفَعٌ ج مَرَافِعُ
Raised up. Carried off.	مَرْفُوعٌ
To be gentle towards.	رَفِقَ يَرْفُقُ ب
To accompany one.	رَافَقَ
To treat with kindness.	تَرَفَّقَ ب
To be companions.	تَرَافَقَ
Kindness, compassion.	رِفْقٌ
Company.	رِفْقَةٌ ج رُفَقٌ
Companion.	رَفِيقٌ ج رُفَقَاءُ
Elbow.	مِرْفَقٌ وَمَرْفِقٌ ج مَرَافِقُ
Water-closet	مُرْتَفَقٌ
To live in luxury.	رَفِهَ يَرْفَهُ
To be comfortable, (life).	رَفُهَ يَرْفُهُ
Good living.	رَفَاهَةٌ وَرَفَاهِيَةٌ
To be thin, fine.	رَقَّ يَرِقُّ
To pity one.	رَقَّ لَهُ
To become a slave.	رَقَّ رِقًّا
To make thin, fine.	رقق وأَرَقَّ
To enslave.	إِسْتَرَقَّ
Slavery.	رِقٌّ
Parchment ; paper.	رِقٌّ ج رُقُوقٌ
Fineness. Compassion.	رِقَّةٌ
Tender-heartedness.	رِقَّةُ ٱلْقَلْبِ
Thin bread.	رُقَاقٌ ج رِقَاقٌ
Thin. Slave.	رَقِيقٌ ج رِقَاقٌ
Not rich.	رَقِيقُ ٱلْحَالِ
To watch, observe.	رَقَبَ يَرْقُبُ
To guard, keep. Observe.	رَاقَبَ
To expect, look for.	تَرَقَّبَ
Neck. Slave.	رَقَبَةٌ ج رِقَابٌ
Guardian.	رَقِيبٌ ج رُقَبَاءُ
Watch-tower.	مَرْقَبٌ ج مَرَاقِبُ
Telescope.	مِرْقَبٌ
To sleep.	رَقَدَ يَرْقُدُ
To put to sleep.	أَرْقَدَ

Sleep. رُقَاد

Bed ; dormitory. مَرْقَدٌ ج مَرَاقِدُ

To variegate. رَقَشَ يَرْقُشُ وَرَقَّشَ

To be embellished. تَرَقَّشَ

Variegated. أَرْقَشُ رَقْشَاءُ ج رُقْشٌ

To dance. رَقَصَ يَرْقُصُ رَقْصاً

To cause to dance. رَقَّصَ وَأَرْقَصَ

Dancing, leaping. رَقْصٌ

Dancer. Pendulum. رَقَّاصٌ

To be spotted. تَرَقَّطَ

Spotted. أَرْقَطُ م رَقْطَاءُ ج رُقْطٌ

To patch. رَقَعَ يَرْقَعُ وَرَقَّعَ

To be foolish. رَقُعَ يَرْقُعُ رَقَاعَةً

Patch scrap. رُقْعَةٌ ج رِقَاعٌ

Folly, stupidity. رَقَاعَة

Firmament. رَقِيعٌ

Patched, mended. مُرَقَّعٌ

To write. رَقَمَ يَرْقُمُ رَقْماً

To mark with stripes. رَقَّمَ وَرَقَمَ

Numerical sign. رَقْمٌ ج أَرْقَامٌ

Indian numerals. الرَّقْمُ الهِنْدِيُّ

Written. Embroidered. مَرْقُومٌ

Clavicle. collar-bone. تَرْقُوَةٌ

To ascend, rise. رَقِيَ يَرْقَى

To use magic. رَقَى يَرْقِي رُقْيَةً

To raise high, elevate. رَقَّى

To rise high. تَرَقَّى وَارْتَقَى فِي وَإِلى

Magic, incantation. رُقْيَةٌ

Charmer, magician. رَاقٍ ج رُقَاةٌ

Rising, progress. تَرَقٍّ وَارْتِقَاءٌ

Ladder, stairs. مَرْقًى وَمِرْقَاةٌ ج مَرَاقٍ

To be weak. رَكَّ يَرِكُّ رَكَاكَةً

To make a foundation. رَكَّ يَرُكُّ

Rubble used in masonry. رَكَّةٌ

Weak. رَكِيكٌ ج رِكَاكٌ

Pressed. مَرْكُوكٌ

To ride ; embark. رَكِبَ يَرْكَبُ

To follow one's fancy. رَكِبَ هَوَاهُ

To brave danger. رَكِبَ ٱللَّيْلَ
To compose, mix. رَكَّبَ
To be constructed, mixed. تَرَكَّبَ
To commit a crime. إِرْتَكَبَ
Band of horsemen. رَكْبٌ
Knee. رُكْبَةٌ ج رُكَبٌ
Stirrup. رِكَابٌ ج رُكُبٌ
Rider. Passenger. رَاكِبٌ ج رُكَّابٌ
Composition, structure. تَرْكِيبٌ
Ship, vessel. مَرْكَبٌ ج مَرَاكِبُ
Carriage. مَرْكَبَةٌ
Shoes. مَرْكُوبٌ ج مَرَاكِيبُ
Compound. Joined. مُرَكَّبٌ
To be still, motionless. رَكَدَ يَرْكُدُ
Still, stagnant. رَاكِدٌ
To fix in (the ground). رَكَزَ يَرْكِزُ
Prop, buttress. رَكِيزَةٌ ج رَكَائِزُ
Centre. مَرْكَزٌ ج مَرَاكِزُ
To run. رَكَضَ يَرْكُضُ رَكْضًا
To vie with in running. رَاكَضَ
Good runner. رَكُوضٌ
To bow (in prayer); kneel. رَكَعَ يَرْكَعُ
To cause one to bow. رَكَّعَ وَارْكَعَ
Bowing in (prayer). رَكْعَةٌ ج رَكَعَاتٌ
To heap up. رَكَمَ يَرْكُمُ رَكْمًا
To be heaped up. تَرَاكَمَ وَٱرْتَكَمَ
Heap, pile. رَكْمٌ وَرُكَامٌ
To rely upon. رَكَنَ يَرْكُنُ إِلَى
To trust in. أَرْكَنَ إِلى
To take to fight. أَرْكَنَ إِلَى ٱلفِرَارِ
Support, prop. رُكْنٌ ج أَرْكَانٌ
The elements (of things). الاركانُ
Firmness; gravity. رُكُونَةٌ وَرَكَانَةٌ
To rely upon. تَرَكَّى وَٱرْتَكَى عَلَى
Small vessel. رَكْوَةٌ ج رَكْوَةٌ
Well. رَكِيَّةٌ ج رَكَايَا
To mend, restore. رَمَّ يَرُمُّ وَرَمَّمَ
To become decayed. رَمَّ وَأَرَمَّ

To be repaired by degrees.	تَرَمَّمَ
Altogether.	بِرُمَّتِهِ
Decayed bones.	رِمَّةٌ ج رِمَمٌ
Decayed (bone).	رَمِيمٌ
Lance, spear.	رُمْحٌ ج رِمَاحٌ
Lancer, spearman.	رَامِحٌ
To have sore eyes.	رَمِدَ يَرْمَدُ
Ophthalmia.	رَمَدٌ
Ashes.	رَمَادٌ
Having ophthalmia.	رَمْدَانُ
Grey, ash-coloured.	رَمَادِيٌّ
To indicate by a sign.	رَمَزَ يَرْمُزُ
To be intelligent.	رَمُزَ يَرْمُزُ رَمَازَةً
Sign. Allegory.	رَمْزٌ ج رُمُوزٌ
Model, specimen.	رَامُوزٌ ج رَوَامِيزُ
Alluded to.	مَرْمُوزٌ إِلَيْهِ
To conceal; bury.	رَمَسَ يَرْمُسُ
Tomb, grave.	رَمْسٌ ج رُمُوسٌ
Lupine (herb).	تُرْمُسٌ
To be very hot.	رَمِضَ يَرْمَضُ
Intense heat.	رَمْضَاءُ
The ninth month of the Moslem year.	رَمَضَانُ
To glance furtively.	رَمَقَ يَرْمُقُ
The last breath of life.	رَمَقٌ
To put sand into.	رَمَلَ
To become sandy.	أَرْمَلَ
To become a widow or widower.	أَرْمَلَ وَتَرَمَّلَ
Sand.	رَمْلٌ ج رِمَالٌ وَأَرْمَالٌ
Hour-glass.	سَاعَةٌ رَمْلِيَّةٌ
Widower; widow.	أَرْمَلٌ ج أَرَامِلُ أَرْمَلَةٌ
Pomegranate.	رُمَّانٌ
The Armenians.	أَلأَرْمَنُ
Armenian.	أَرْمَنِيٌّ
To throw; hit; accuse.	رَمَى يَرْمِي
To be thrown.	إِرْتَمَى آرْتِمَاءً
Throw, hit.	رَمْيَةٌ ج رَمَيَاتٌ
Archer, slinger.	رَامٍ ج رُمَاةٌ
Sagittarius (of the Zodiac).	الرَّامِي

مِرمىً ج مرامٍ Instrument for throwing (projectile, arrow).

مِرْماةٌ ج مرامٍ Arrow, missile.

رَنَّ يرِن رَنيناً To twang, ring.

رنينٌ وَرَنَّةٌ Sound, tone, echo.

أَرْنَبٌ ج أَرَانِبُ Hare.

رنحَ To make giddy, (wine).

ترنَّحَ To stagger.

رَوْنَقٌ Lustre, brilliancy.

رَنِمَ يَرْنَمُ ورنَّمَ وَتَرَنَّمَ To sing.

تَرْنيمةٌ Poem. Hymn.

تَرَنُّمٌ Singing, psalmody.

رهِبَ يرْهَبُ رَهْبَةً To fear, dread.

رهَّبَ وَأَرْهَبَ To frighten.

ترَهَّبَ To become a monk.

رَهْبَةٌ Fear.

رَهْبَنَةٌ ورهْبَانِيةٌ Monachism.

راهِبٌ ج رُهبَانٌ Monk.

راهِبَةٌ ج راهِبَاتٌ Nun.

رَهِيبٌ Fearful, awful.

رهجٌ Dust. Excitement.

إِرْتَهَطَ To assemble, congregate.

رهْطٌ ج أَرْهُطٌ Company of men.

رَهُفَ يرْهُفُ To be thin, sharp.

رَهِيفٌ وَمرْهَفٌ Thin, slender.

راهَقَ To approach puberty.

مراهِقٌ Boy at puberty.

مَرْهمٌ ج مَرَاهِمُ Ointment.

رَهَنَ يَرْهَنُ رهْناً To be firm.

رَهَنَ عِنْدَ To pledge with.

رَاهَنَ To bet, lay a wager.

تَرَاهَنَ To bet together.

إِرْتَهَنَ To receive a pledge.

إِسْتَرْهَنَ To require a pledge.

رَهْنٌ ج رِهَانٌ Pledge, mortgage.

رَاهِنٌ Fixed, stable, durable.

رهينٌ وَمُرْتَهَنٌ ومرْهُونٌ Pledged.

رَهِينَةٌ ج رَهَائِن Pledge, security.

Ambling-horse. رَهْوَانٌ

To curdle, (milk.) رَابَ يَرُوبُ

Curdled ; churned. رَائِبٌ وَمُرَوَّبٌ

Ferment of; milk. رَوْبَةٌ

To void excrement, (horse). رَاثَ يَرُوثُ رَوْثًا

To be current. رَاجَ يَرُوجُ

To put in circulation· رَوَّجَ

Currency. Good market. رَوَاجٌ

Selling well. Current. رَائِجٌ

To go, depart. رَاحَ يَرُوحُ

To give rest. أَرَاحَ إِرَاحَةً

To be pleased. إِرْتَاحَ

To rest. إِسْتَرَاحَ

Wine. Mirth. رَاحٌ

Rest ease, quietude. رَاحَةٌ

Palm of the hand. رَاحَةٌ رَاحَاتٌ

Water-closet. بَيْتُ ٱلرَّاحَةِ

Breath, spirit. رُوحٌ ج أَرْوَاحٌ

The Holy Spirit. رُوحُ ٱلْقُدُسِ

Long-suffering. طَوِيلُ ٱلرُّوحِ

Spiritual, incorporeal. رُوحَانِيٌّ

Wind. Odour. رِيحٌ ج رِيَاحٌ

Whitlow. رِيحُ ٱلشَّوْكَةِ

Odour. Puff of wind. رِيحَةٌ

Myrtle. رَيْحَانٌ ج رَيَاحِينُ

Odour. رَائِحَةٌ ج رَوَائِحُ

Generous, liberal. أَرْيَحِيٌّ

Cattle-fold. مُرَاحٌ

Fan. مِرْوَحٌ وَمِرْوَحَةٌ ج مَرَاوِحُ

Water-closet. مُسْتَرَاحٌ

To ask for. Seek (food). رَادَ يَرُودُ

To beguile, seduce ; entice. رَاوَدَ

To wish, desire. أَرَادَ

To mean, intend. أَرَادَ بِ

Slowly, gently. رُوَيْدًا

Will ; volition. إِرَادَةٌ

Voluntary. إِرَادِي

Desired. Purpose · meaning. مُرَادٌ

رَوَّضَ	To train, discipline.
رَوْضٌ	Garden, flower-bed.
رَوْضَةٌ ج رِيَاضٌ	Meadow.
رِيَاضَةٌ	Exercise, training.
عِلْمُ ٱلرِّيَاضَاتِ	Mathematics.
رَاعَ يَرُوعُ وَٱرْتَاعَ	To fear.
رَاعَ وَروَّعَ وَارَاعَ	To frighten.
رَوْعٌ وَرَوْعَةٌ	Fear, fright.
رَاغَ يَرُوغُ رَوْغًا	To act slyly.
رَاوَغَ	To employ a ruse.
مُرَاوَغَةٌ	Ruse, trick.
رَاقَ يَرُوقُ	To be clear, limpid.
رَوَّقَ	To render clear, clarify.
أَرَاقَ	To pour out or forth.
اترَوَّقَ	To breakfast.
رِوَاقٌ ج أَرْوِقَةٌ	Tent, portico.
رَائِقٌ	Clear, limpid, pure.
رَامَ يَرُومُ	To desire strongly.
رُومٌ ج أَرْوَامٌ	Roman. Greek.
بَحْرُ ٱلرُّوم	Mediterranean Sea.
رُومِيَّةٌ ج رَوَامِيُّ	Rafter.
مَرَام	Desire, purpose.
رَوَنْدٌ وَرَوَانْدٌ	Rhubarb.
رَوَى يَرْوِي رِوَايَةً	To report, quote.
رَوِيَ يَرْوى	To quench one's thirst.
تَروَّى	To consider attentively.
أَرْوَى إِرْوَاءً	To quench thirst.
رِوَايَةٌ	Narration, tale.
رَاوٍ ج رُوَاةٌ وَرَاوُون	Narrator.
رِيٌّ	Rain ; irrigation.
رَيَّانٌ	Well watered.
مَرْوِيٌّ	Well watered. Cited.
رَابَ يَرِيبُ	To make doubtful.
أَرَابَ	To trouble, disquiet.
إِرْتَابَ	To have doubts.
رَيْبٌ وَرَيْبَةٌ ج رِيَبٌ	Doubt.
ارْتِيَابٌ	Doubt, hesitation.
مُرِيبٌ	Causing, doubt.

رَيْثَمَا As long as ; while.

رِيشٌ ج رِيَاش Feathers.

رِيشَةٌ A feather.

رِيَاشٌ Furniture, goods.

رَيْعَانٌ The best part.

رِيفٌ ج أَرْيَافٌ A fertile land along the banks of a river.

رِيفُ الْبَحرِ Sea-coast.

رَاقَ يَرِيقُ To pour out.

أَرَاقَ To pour out a liquid.

رِيقٌ Saliva.

على الرِّيق Before breakfast.

رَالَ يَرِيلُ رَيلاً To droll (child).

رِيَالٌ Saliva. Dollar.

رِيمٌ White gazelle or antelope.

رَايَة ج رَايَاتٌ Flag ; standard.

ز

ز As a numeral sign=7.

زِوِبرٌ وَزِوْبِرٌ Nap of cloth.

زِئْبَقٌ Mercury, quicksilver.

زَأَرَ يَزْأَرُ وَزَئِرَ To roar (lion).

زَائِرٌ Roaring ; angry ; enemy.

زَوَانٌ Tares, (seed and plant).

زَبَبٌ Hairiness, Down.

زَبِيبٌ Raisins, dried figs.

أَزَبُّ م زَبَّاءُ Hairy.

عامٌ أَزَبُّ Fertile year.

زَبَدَ يَزْبُدُ To churn (butter).

زَبَدَ وازْبَدَ To foam, froth.

زَبَدٌ Foam, froth.

زُبدٌ وزُبْدَةٌ Butter.

زُبْدَةٌ	Cream.
زَبَادٌ	A kind of perfume ; civet.
مُزْبِدٌ	Foaming. Enraged.
زَبُورٌ ج زُبُرٌ	Psalms of David.
زِبِّيرٌ	Powerful man.
زَبَرْجَدٌ	Chrysolite.
زَوْبَعَةٌ ج زَوَابِعُ	A whirlwind.
زَبَلَ يَزْبِلُ وَزَبَّلَ	To manure.
زِبْلٌ وَزِبْلَةٌ	Manure.
زُبَالَةٌ	Dirt ; sweepings.
زَبَّالٌ	Manure-gatherer.
زِنْبِيلٌ ج زَنَابِيل	Basket, pannier.
مَزْبَلَةٌ ج مَزَابِلُ	Dung-hill.
زَبُونٌ ج زَبَائِنُ	Customer.
زَجَّ يَزُجُّ زَجًّا	To thrust with a lance.
زُجٌّ ج زِجَاجٌ	Point of a spear.
زُجَاجٌ	Glass ; glass vessels.
زُجَاجَةٌ	Piece, or cup, of glass.
زَجَّاجٌ	Glass-manufacturer
زُجَاجِيٌّ	Glass-merchant.
أَزَجُّ م زَجَّاء	Having long eyebrows.
زَجَرَ يَزْجُرُ	To forbid. Rebuke.
إِنْزَجَرَ	To be forbidden.
زَجَلٌ	Play. Uproar.
حَمَامُ ٱلزَّاجِلِ	Carrier-pigeons.
زَحَّ يَزُحُّ	To remove a thing.
زَحَرَ يَزْحِرُ	To strain in breathing.
زَحِيرٌ	Straining. Dysentery.
زَحْزَحَ عَنْ	To remove a thing.
زَحَفَ يَزْحَفُ	To march. Creep.
زَحْفٌ	Marching. An army.
ٱلزَّحَافَةُ وَٱلزَّحَّافَاتُ	Reptiles.
زَحَلَ يَزْحَلُ عَنْ	To depart ; retire.
زَحَّلَ وَأَزْحَلَ	To move a thing.
زُحَلُ	The planet Saturn.
زَحَمَ يَزْحَمُ وَزَاحَمَ	To crowd ; press.
تَزَاحَمَ وَٱزْدَحَمَ	To be crowded.
زَحْمَةٌ وَزِحَامٌ	Pressure ; throng.

زَاخِرٌ Full ; copious.

زَخِيرَةٌ ج زَخَائِرُ Munitions of war.

زَخْرَفَ زَخْرَفَةً To adorn.

زُخْرُفٌ ج زَخَارِفُ Vain show.

مُزَخْرَفٌ Adorned with tinsel.

زَخْمَةٌ Whip of thong. Strap.

زَرَّ يَزُرُّ زَرًّا وَزَرَّرَ To button.

زِرٌّ ج أَزْرَارٌ Button. Knob.

زَرَبَ يَزْرُبُ To make a sheep-fold.

زَرِبَ يَزْرَبُ زَرَبًا To flow ; leak.

زِرَابَةٌ Payment for stabling.

زَرِيبَةٌ ج زَرَائِبُ Flod for cattle ; lurking place.

زَارُوبٌ ج زَوَارِيبُ Narrow street.

مِزْرَابٌ ج مَزَارِيبُ Water-course.

زَرِدَ يَزْرَدُ وَازْدَرَدَ To swallow.

زَرَدٌ ج زُرُودٌ Coat of mail.

زَرَدَةٌ Ring, or link of a chain.

زُرْدِى A kind of pudding.

زُرْزُورٌ ج زَرَازِيرُ Starling.

زَرَعَ يَزْرَعُ To sow ; plant.

زَارَعَ مُزَارَعة To sow in shares.

زَرْعٌ ج زُرُوعٌ Seed. Off-spring.

زَارِعٌ ج زُرَّاعٌ Husbandman.

زِرَاعَةٌ Seed. Agriculture.

مَزْرَعَةٌ ج مَزَارِعُ Plantation.

زَرَافَةٌ ج زَرَافى Giraffe.

زَرَقَ يَزْرُقُ To thrust ; dung, (bird).

إِزْرَقَّ آزْرِقَاقًا To become blue.

زُرْقَةٌ Blue (colour).

أَلزَّرْقَاءُ Sky ; heavens.

زُرَيْقٌ A black singing bird.

زُرَيْقَاءُ A kind of bread-salad.

أَزْرَقُ م زَرْقَاءُ ج زُرْقٌ Blue.

عَدُوٌّ ازْرَقُ Bitter enemy.

مِزْرَاقٌ ج مَزَارِيقُ Short spear.

زَرَكَ يَزْرُكُ To press, vex.

زَرْكَةٌ Crowd, throng.

زَرْكَشَ To embroider.

زَرْكَشٌ Brocade of silk.

زِرْنِيخٌ Arsenic.

زَرَى يَزْرِي عَلَى To reproach.

ازْدَرَى إِزْدِرَاءً ب To despise.

زَرِيٌّ Contemptible.

مُزْدَرٍ Despiser.

زَعْبَرَ زَعْبَرَةً To cheat by tricks.

مُزَعْبِرٌ Juggler.

زَعْتَرٌ (see صَعْتَر) Thyme.

زَعَجَ يَزْعَجُ وَأَزْعَجَ To disturb.

إِنْزَعَجَ To be troubled.

زَعَجٌ وَانْزِعَاجٌ Agitation; trouble.

زُعْرُورٌ Medlar (tree and fruit).

أَزْعَرُ ج زُعْرَانٌ Thin haired. Thief.

زَعْزَعَ To shake; move.

تَزَعْزَعَ To be shaken; moved.

زَعْزَعٌ ج زَعَازِعُ Violent wind.

مُتَزَعْزِعٌ Inconstant; unstable.

زُعَافٌ Quick in killing.

زَعْفَرَانٌ Saffron.

زَعَقَ يَزْعَقُ To cry out, shout.

زَعَقَ ب وَأَزْعَقَ To frighten.

زَاعِقَةٌ (see صَاعِقَة) Thunderbolt.

زَعِلَ يَزْعَلُ To be angry; bored.

زَعْلَانُ Angry, bored.

زَعَمَ يَزْعَمُ زَعْمًا To assert.

زُعْمٌ وَزَعْمَةٌ Assertion.

زَعَامَةٌ Honour. Authority.

زَعِيمٌ Chief. Spokesman.

زِعْنِفَةٌ ج زَعَانِفُ Fin.

زَغَبٌ Down; fine hair, feathers.

زَغْبَرٌ وَزَغَبَرٌ Nap of cloth.

زَغَلَ يَزْغَلُ زَغْلًا To adulterate.

زُغْلُولٌ ج زَغَالِيلُ Young pigeon.

زَفَّ يَزِفُّ To lead a bride home.

زِفَّةٌ Procession of joy.

زَفَتَ To cover with pitch.

زِفْتٌ Pitch.

Covered with pitch.	مزفّت
To expire breath.	زفر يزفر
Deep sigh.	زفرة ج زفرات
Expiration. Deep sigh.	زفير
Oleaster.	زيزفون
Water-skin.	زقّ ج زقاق
Street, lane.	زقاق ج ازقة
A sack made of hair.	زكيبة
A wine-skin.	زكرة ج زكر
To tickle.	زكزك
To have a cold in the head.	زكم
A cold in the head; catarrh.	زكام وزكمة
To consider.	زكن يزكن
To be pure.	زكا يزكو
To give alms. Justify.	زكى
To be justified.	تزكى
Alms.	زكوة (زكاة) ج زكا
Pure; just.	زكيّ ج أزكياء
To stumble; slip.	زلّ يزلّ زلًّا
A slip; fault.	زلل
A fault, fall.	زلة ج زلات
Clear, pure, cool (water). (White of an egg).	زلال
Tortoise.	(زلحفة زلاحف)
To shake.	زلزل زلزلة وزلزالًا
Earth-quake.	زلزلة ج زلازل
To strip one's self.	(تزلط)
Throat.	زلعوم ج زلاعيم
To exaggerate.	زلّف
To bring near.	أزلف
Nearness.	زلفة وزلفى
To slip, glide.	زلق يزلق زلقًا
Slippery (place).	زلق ومزلقة
Diarrhœa.	زلق الامعاء
A kind of fish.	زليق
Arrow for devining.	زلم ج أزلام
Man. Footman.	(زلمة ج زلم)
To tighten. Strap.	زمّ يزمّ زمًّا
Halter. Shoe-strap.	زمام ج ازمة

To shout ; roar. زَمْجَرَ زَمْجَرَةً

To play on a reed. زَمَّرَ يُزَمِّرُ

Musical reed. زَمْرٌ ج زُمُورٌ

Group ; party. زُمْرَةٌ ج زُمَرٌ

A piper. زَمَّارٌ

A pipe. زَمَّارَةٌ ومِزْمَارٌ ج مَزَامِيرُ

Epiglottis. لِسَانُ ٱلْمِزْمَار

Psalm. مَزْمُورٌ ج مَزَامِيرُ

Emerald. زُمُرُّدٌ

To be about to happen. أَزْمَعَ

About to happen. مُزْمِعٌ

Beast of burden. زَامِلَةٌ ج زَوَامِلُ

Comrade ; companion. زَمِيلٌ ج زُمَلَاءُ

Chisel. إِزْمِيلٌ ج أَزَامِيلُ

To continue a long time. أَزْمَنَ

Time. زَمَنٌ وزَمَانٌ ج أَزْمِنَةٌ

Temporal ; transient. زَمَنِيٌّ

Chronic disease. مُزْمِنٌ (مَرَضٌ)

To be inflamed. زَمْهَرَ وازْمَهَرَّ

Intense cold. زَمْهَرِيرٌ

To scorn ; frown. تَزَنْبَرَ عَلَى

Wasp ; hornet. زُنْبُورٌ ج زَنَابِيرُ

Spring of a watch. زُنْبُرُكٌ

Lily. Iris, (flower and plant). زَنْبَقٌ

The black races. زِنْجٌ ج زُنُوجٌ

A black ; negro. زِنْجِيٌّ

Ginger. زَنْجَبِيلٌ

To bind with a chain. زَنْجَرَ

Verdigris. زِنْجَارٌ

Chain. زِنْجِيرٌ (جِنْزِيرٌ) ج زَنَاجِير

Book-keeping. حِسَابُ ٱلزِّنْجِير

Cinnabar. زُنْجُفْرٌ وزِنْجَفْرٌ

To become rancid. زَنِخَ يَزْنَخُ

Ulna (bone). زَنْدٌ ج زِنَادٌ

Steel for atriking fire. زِنَادٌ

To disbelive religion. تَزَنْدَقَ

Unbeliever. زِنْدِيقٌ ج زَنَادِقَة

To gird one's self. تَزَنَّرَ

زُنَّارٌ ج زَنَانِيرُ Girdle.

زَنْزَلَخْتٌ (أَزْدَرَخْتٌ) Melia (tree).

زِنَاقٌ Necklace. Shackle.

زَنَى يَزْنِي To commit adultery.

زَانٍ ج زُنَاةٌ Adulterer.

(زَهْبٌ وزُهْبَةٌ) Munition.

زَهِدَ يَزْهَدُ (فِي وعَنْ) To renounce.

تَزَهَّدَ To become an ascetic.

زُهْدٌ Indifference.

زَاهِدٌ ج زُهَّادٌ Ascetic; indifferent.

زَهِيدٌ Little. Insignificant.

زَهَرَ يَزْهَرُ زُهُوراً To shine.

أَزْهَرَ To blossom; flourish.

زَهْرَةٌ ج أَزْهَارٌ Flower.

زَهْرُ ٱلنَّرْدِ Dice.

أَلزُّهْرَةُ The planet Venus.

أَلْجَامِعُ ٱلأَزْهَرُ A Mosque in Cairo.

أَزْهَرِيٌّ A graduate of الأَزْهَر

مُزْهِرٌ In blossom; flourishing.

مِزْهَرٌ ج مَزَاهِرُ Lute. Timbrel.

زَهَقَ يَزْهَقُ زُهُوقاً To vanish.

زَهَا يَزْهُو زَهْواً وازْهَى To blossom.

زَهَا ٱلدُّنْيَا Pomp of this world.

زُهَاءٌ Quantity; number.

زُهَاءَ مِئَةٍ About a hundred.

زَاهٍ Beautiful; bright.

زَوَّجَ To give in marriage.

تَزَوَّجَ To marry a woman.

زَاجٌ Copperas; vitriol.

زَوْجٌ ج أَزْوَاجٌ Husband. Pair.

زَوْجَانِ Pair, couple.

زَوْجَةٌ ج زَوجَاتٌ Wife.

زَوَاجٌ وزِيجَةٌ Marriage.

مُزَوَّجٌ ومُتَزَوِّجٌ Married.

مُزْدَوِجٌ Double; doubled.

زَاحَ يَزُوحُ To leave its place.

أَزَاحَ To move from its place.

زَوَّدَ To provide food for journey.

تَزَوَّدَ	To take provisions.
زَادٌ	Food for the journey.
مِزْوَدٌ ج مَزَاوِدُ	Sack for food.
مَزَادٌ ج مَزَاوِدُ	Water-skin.
زَارَ يَزُورُ زِيَارَةً وَمَزَاراً	To visit.
زَوَّرَ	To falsify ; forge.
زُورٌ	Falsehood.
زَائِرٌ ج زُوَّارٌ	Visitor. Pilgrim.
أَلزَّوْرَاءُ	Baghdad.
زِيَارَة	Visit. Pilgrimage.
ازْوَر	Crooked.
تَزْوِيرٌ	Falsification ; forgery.
مَزَارٌ ج مَزَارَاتٌ	Shrine.
مُزَوِّرٌ	Falsifier ; counterfeiter.
مُزَوَّرٌ	Falsified ; conterfeited.
زَوْرَقٌ ج زَوَارِق	Small boat.
زَاغَ يَزُوغُ زَوْغاً	To deviate.
زُوفَاءُ وَزُوفَى	Hyssop (plant).
زَوَّقَ تَزْوِيقاً	To embellish.
مُزَوَّقٌ	Embellished, decorated.
زَالَ يَزُولُ	To pass away ; cease.
مَا زَالَ وَلَا يَزَالُ	To continue.
زَوَّلَ وَأَزَالَ	To remove.
زَاوَلَ مُزَاوَلَةً	To strive, prevail.
زَوَالٌ	Disappearance. Cessation.
زَائِلٌ	Vanishing ; transient.
زُومٌ	Juice.
إِنْزَوَى	To be apart ; removed.
زُوَانٌ	Tares.
زَاوِيَةٌ ج زَوَايَا	Angle, corner.
زَاوِيَةٌ حَادَّةٌ	Acute angle.
زَاوِيَةٌ مُنْفَرِجَةٌ	Obtuse angle.
زَاوِيَةٌ قَائِمَةٌ	Right anlge.
زِيبَقٌ وَزِئْبَق	Quicksilver.
زَيَّتَ	To oil.
زَيْتٌ ج زُيُوت	Oil.
زَيْتُونٌ	Olive (tree and fruit).
زَيْتُونِيٌّ	Olive-coloured.

زِيجٌ Astronomical tables. Plumb-line.

زَاحَ يَزِيحُ To depart ; deviate.

أَزَاحَ To move away ; remove.

زِيحٌ ج أَزْيَاحٌ Line.

زَادَ يَزِيدُ To increase, (*v. t. & i.*)

زَادَ عَنْ وعَلَى To exceed.

زَايَدَ To bid higher.

تَزَايَدَ To increase gradually.

إِزْدَادَ To be increased.

زِيَادَةٌ ج زِيَادَاتٌ An increase.

زَائِدٌ In excess ; superfluous.

أَزْيَدُ More ; more abundant.

مَزَادٌ ج مَزَادَاتٌ Auction.

مَزِيدٌ ج مَزِيدَاتٌ Increased.

زِيرٌ ج أَزْيَارٌ Large water-jar.

زِيرٌ A kind of cricket.

زَاغَ يَزِيغُ زَيَغَانًا وزَيْغًا To deviate.

أَزَاغَ To cause to deviate.

زَاغٌ ج زِيغَانٌ A kind of crow.

زَافَ يَزِيفُ To be counterfeit.

زَيَّفَ To counterfeit money.

زَائِفٌ ج زُيُوفٌ Counterfeit.

زَانَ يَزِينُ وَزَيَّنَ To adorn.

تَزَيَّنَ تَزَيُّنًا وَازْدَانَ To be adorned.

زِينَةٌ ج زِيَنٌ Ornament ; finery.

مُزَيِّنٌ Barber ; hair-dresser.

تزيا ب To assume the costume, or habits of others.

زِيٌّ ج أَزْيَاءٌ Form. Costume.

س

س	As a numeral sign=60.
سَائِرٌ	Remaining ; the rest ; all.
سَأَلَ يَسْأَلُ	To ask; request.
تَسَآلَ وَتَسَوَّلَ	To beg (alms).
سُؤَالٌ	Question, request.
سَائِلٌ	Questioner. Beggar.
مَسْأَلَةٌ ج مَسَائِلُ	Question; request.
مَسْؤُولٌ	Questioned. Responsible.
مَسْؤُولِيَّةٌ	Responsibility.
سَئِمَ يَسْأَمُ مِن	To loathe.
سَبَّ يَسُبُّ	To revile, defame.
سَبَّبَ	To cause, occasion.
تَسَبَّبَ	To be caused.
تَسَبَّبَ بِ	To live by.
سَبٌّ	Abuse, invective.
سَبَبٌ ج أَسْبَابٌ	Cause, reason ; means ; means of living.
سَبَبِيَّة	Causality.
سَبَّابَةٌ	Forefinger, index.
مُسَبَّبٌ وَمُتَسَبِّبٌ عَنْ	Caused.
مُتَسَبِّبٌ	Trader.
سَبْتٌ ج سُبُوتٌ	Sabbath. Saturday.
سُبَاتٌ	Heavy sleep, lethargy.
سَبَحَ يَسْبَحُ سِبَاحَةٌ	To swim, float.
سَبَّحَ	To praise, magnify God.
سُبْحَانَ اللهِ	Praise be to God !
سُبْحَةٌ ج سُبَحٌ وسُبُحَاتٌ	Rosary.
سِبَاحَةٌ	Swimming floating.
سَابِحَاتٌ	Ships. Stars.
سَوَابِحُ	Fleet horses

Hymn. تَسْبِحَةٌ ج تَسَابِيحُ

Act of praising God. تَسْبِيحٌ

Rosary. مِسْبَحَةٌ ج مَسَابِحُ

Salty, marshy (sod). سَبِخٌ

Salty, marsh. سَبْخَةٌ ج سِبَاخٌ

To probe. Try, test. سَبَرَ يَسْبُرُ

Probing, sounding. سَبْرٌ

Surgeon's probe. مِسْبَرٌ ج مَسَابِرُ

Tribe Jewish). سِبْطٌ ج أَسْبَاطٌ

February (month). شُبَاطُ

To make (in) seven. سَبَّعَ

To become seven. أَسْبَعَ

Seven. سَبْعَةٌ م سَبْعٌ

Seventh part. سُبْعٌ ج أَسْبَاعٌ

Beast of prey. سَبُعٌ ج سِبَاعٌ

Seventh. سَابِعٌ

Composed of seven. سُبَاعِيٌّ

Seventy ; seventieth. سَبْعُونَ

Week. أُسْبُوعٌ ج أَسَابِيعُ

Heptagon. مُسَبَّعٌ

To give abundantly. أَسْبَغَ عَلَى

To go before, precede. سَبَقَ يَسْبُقُ

To go hastily to one. سَبَقَ إِلَى

To try to precede. سَابَقَ سِبَاقًا

To contend for precedence. تَسَابَقَ

Previous, former. سَابِقٌ

Formerly, before, of old. سَابِقًا

Antecedent. سَابِقَةٌ ج سَوَابِقُ

Racing ; a race. سِبَاقٌ وَمُسَابَقَةٌ

To melt metals ; cast into a mould. سَبَكَ يَسْبُكُ سَبْكًا

Melted; moulded. سَبِيكٌ وَمَسْبُوكٌ

Ingot. سَبِيكَةٌ ج سَبَائِكُ

Foundery. مَسْبَكٌ ج مَسَابِكُ

To lower the veil ; let fall. أَسْبَلَ

To put forth ears, (grains). أَسْبَلَ الزَّرْعُ

Ears of grain. سَبَلٌ

Road, way ; manner; means. Public fountain. سَبِيلٌ ج سُبُلٌ

إِبْنُ ٱلسَّبِيلِ Traveller, wayfarer.
سَبَانِخُ وَاسْبَانَاخٌ Spinage.
سَبَى يَسْبِي To take prisoner, captivate.
سَبْيٌ وَسَبِيٌّ ج سَبَايَا Captives. Booty.
سِتَّةٌ م سِتٌّ Six.
(سِتٌّ ج سِتَّاتٌ) Lady.
سِتُّونَ Sixty ; sixtieth.
سَتَرَ يَسْتُرُ To cover, veil.
تَسَتَّرَ وَاسْتَتَرَ To be covered.
سِتْرٌ ج سُتُورٌ Veil, curtain, cover.
سِتَارٌ ج سُتُرٌ Veil, cover.
اَلسَّتَّارُ God who covers sins.
مُسْتَتِرٌ Concealed. Understood, (pronoun).
أَلْإِسْتَانَةُ Constantinople.
إِسْتٌ ج أَسْتَاهٌ Anus, podex.
سَجَدَ يَسْجُدُ To worship, adore.
سَاجِدٌ ج سُجَّدٌ Worshipper.
سَجَّادَةٌ Prayer-carpet.
سُجُودٌ Prostration, adoration.

مَسْجِدٌ ج مَسَاجِدُ Mosque.
سَجَسٌ Turbidness ; agitation.
سَجَعَ يَسْجَعُ To coo ; rhyme.
سَجْعٌ وَتَسْجِيعٌ Rhymed prose.
مُسَجَّعٌ وَمَسْجَعٌ Rhymed (prose).
سَجْفٌ ج سُجُوفٌ Curtain, veil.
سَجَّلَ To register, record.
سِجِلٌّ سِجِلَّاتٌ Record ; scroll.
سَجَمَ يَسْجُمُ وَٱنْسَجَمَ To flow, stream.
سَجَمَ يَسْجُمُ وَأَسْجَمَ To shed.
إِنْسِجَامٌ Flowing effusion.
سَجَنَ يَسْجُنُ سَجْنًا To imprison.
سِجْنٌ ج سُجُونٌ Prison.
سَجَّانٌ Jailor.
سَجِينٌ ج سُجَنَاءُ Imprisoned.
سَجِيَّةٌ ج سَجَايَا Natural disposition.
سَحَّ يَسُحُّ سَحًّا To flow.
سَحَبَ يَسْحَبُ سَحْبًا To drag, trail.
إِنْسَحَبَ To be dragged, drawn.

Cloud. سَحَابٌ وَسَحَابَةٌ ج سُحُبٌ

To scratch, rub off. سَحَجَ يَسْحَجُ

To be rubbed off. تَسَحَّجَ وَٱنْسَحَجَ

Dysentery. سَحْجٌ

To bewitch, fascinate. سَحَرَ يَسْحَرُ

To take a morning meal. تَسَحَّرَ

Magic, enchantment. سِحْرٌ

Early daybreak. سَحَرٌ ج أَسْحَارٌ

Sorcerer, magician. سَاحِرٌ ج سَحَرَةٌ

Wooden box. سَحَّارَةٌ

Meal before daybreak. سُحُورٌ

To pound, crush. سَحَقَ يَسْحَقُ

To be crushed. تَسَحَّقَ وَٱنْسَحَقَ

Bruised, powdered. مَسْحُوقٌ

Contrition. إِنْسِحَاقُ ٱلْقَلْبِ

Shore ; coast. سَاحِلٌ ج سَوَاحِلُ

To break, crush. سَحَنَ يَسْحَنُ

Aspect ; complexion. سَحْنَةٌ

Tanned leather. سِخْتِيَانٌ

To compel to labour without wages. سَخَرَ يَسْخَرُ وَسَخَّرَ

To laugh at, mock. سَخِرَ يَسْخَرُ مِنْ

Compulsory labour. سُخْرَةٌ

To be angry. سَخِطَ يَسْخَطُ وَتَسَخَّطَ

To provoke to anger. أَسْخَطَ

Anger, displeasure. سُخْطٌ وَسَخَطٌ

To be weak. سَخُفَ يَسْخُفُ سَخَافَةً

Shallowness, weakness. سَخَافَةٌ

To blacken with soot. سَخَّمَ

Soot, crock. سُخَامٌ

To be hot ; have fever. سَخَنَ يَسْخُنُ

To warm, heat. سَخَّنَ وَأَسْخَنَ

Heat. Fever ; illness. سُخُونَةٌ

Warm, hot. سُخْنٌ

Hot ; sick, ill. سَاخِنٌ ج سُخَّانٌ

So be liberal. سَخَا يَسْخُو وَسَخِيَ يَسْخَى

Generosity. سَخَاءٌ وَسَخَاوَةٌ

Generous, liberal. سَخِيٌّ ج أَسْخِيَاءُ

To close, stop up. سَدَّ يَسُدُّ سَدًّا

To take the place of. سَدَّ مَسَدًّا

Balance, pay an account. سَدَّدَ

To be stopped. إِنْسَدَّ وَٱسْتَدَّ

To collect a debt. إِسْتَدَّ

Barrier; dam. سَدٌّ ج أَسْدَادٌ

Vestibule, porch. سُدَّة

A stopper, a cork. سِدَادَةٌ

Right, true. سَدٌّ وَسَدِيدٌ

Stopped, corked. مَسْدُودٌ

Simplicity of mind. سَذَاجَة

A species of lotus. سِدْرٌ ج سُدُورٌ

To be the sixth. سَدَسَ يَسْدِسُ

To make six. سَدَّسَ

Sixth part. سُدْسٌ ج أَسْدَاسٌ

Sixth. سَادِسٌ

Consisting of six. سُدَاسِيٌّ

Hexagon. مُسَدَّسٌ

To let down. سَدَلَ يَسْدِلُ وَأَسْدَلَ

To be let down. تَسَدَّلَ وَٱنْسَدَلَ

Mist. Nebula. سَدِيمٌ

In vain, to no purpose. سُدًى

Warp (of cloth). سُدَاةٌ ج أَسْدِيَةٌ

Rue-plant. سَذَابٌ

To gladden, cheer. سَرَّ يَسُرُّ

To rejoice at. سُرَّ سُرُوراً بِ

To cheer, gladden. اسرَّ

To impart a secret. سَارَّ مُسَارَّةً

To keep secret, conceal. أَسَرَّ

To confide a secret to. اسرَّ إِلَى

Secret, mystery. سِرٌّ ج أَسْرَارٌ

Secretary. كَاتِمُ ٱلْأَسْرَار

Navel. سُرَّةٌ ج سُرَّاتٌ وَسُرُورٌ

Happy state of life. سَرَّاءُ

Mysterious, secret. سِرِّيٌّ

Joy, pleasure. سُرُورٌ وَمَسَرَّةٌ

Bed, cradle; throne. سَرِيرٌ ج أَسِرَّةٌ

Hidden thought. سَرِيرَةٌ ج سَرَائِرُ

Concubine.	سُرِّيَّة ج سَرَارِيّ
Joy, pleasure.	مَسَرَّة ج مَسَرَّات
Happy, pleased.	مَسْرُور
To drive to pasture.	سَرَّبَ
Troop, flock.	سِرْب ج أَسْرَاب
Aqueduct, canal.	سَرَب ج أَسْرَاب
Mirage.	سَرَاب
Shirt; dress.	سِرْبَال ج سَرَابِيل
To saddle (a horse).	سَرَجَ يَسْرِجُ
Saddle.	سَرْج ج سُرُوج
Dung, manure.	سِرْجِين
Lamp, torch.	سِرَاج ج سُرُج
Glow-worm.	سِرَاجُ ٱللَّيْلِ
Glanders. Saddlery.	سِرَاجَة
Saddler.	سَرَّاج وَسُرُوجِيّ
Sesame oil.	سِيرَج وَشِيرَج
Lamp-stand.	مِسْرَجَة ج مَسَارِج
To pasture at will.	سَرَحَ يَسْرَحُ
To send away; set free.	سَرَّحَ
Pasture.	مَسْرَح ج مَسَارِح
Comb.	مِسْرَح ج مَسَارِح
Cellar, vault.	سِرْدَاب ج سَرَادِيب
Strip of leather.	سَرِيدَة ج سَرَائِد
Awning.	سُرَادِق ج سُرَادِقَات
Sticking-paste. (for	سِرَاس (شِرَاس
Way, street, road.	سِرَاط وَصِرَاط
Crab. Cancer.	سَرَطَان
Cancer (of the Zodiac).	اَلسَّرَطَانُ
To hasten, hurry.	سَرُعَ يَسْرُعُ
To hasten to do.	أَسْرَعَ فِي
Quickness, haste, speed.	سُرْعَة
Quick, rapid, swift.	سَرِيع
To be extravagant, act immoderately.	أَسْرَفَ
Extravagance.	سَرَف وَإِسْرَاف
A spendthrift.	مُسْرِف
To steal, rob.	سَرَقَ يَسْرِقُ
To steal away.	إِنْسَرَقَ
Theft, robbery.	سِرْقَة وَسَرِقَة

Thing stolen.	سَرِقَةٌ وسَرَاقَةٌ
Thief.	سارِقٌ ج سُرَّاقٌ وسَرَقَةٌ
Great thief.	سَرَّاقٌ
Dung.	سَرْقِينٌ
Continuing endlessly.	سَرْمَدٌ
Eternal.	سَرْمَدِيٌّ
Cypress (tree).	سَرْوٌ
Liberal, noble.	سَرِيٌّ ج سَرَاةٌ
Trowsers.	سِرْوَالٌ ج سَرَاوِيلُ
To travel.	سرى يسري
To cause to travel.	أَسْرَى بِ
Night-journey.	سُرًى
Night-traveller.	سارٍ ج سُرَاةٌ
Column ; mast.	سارِيَةٌ ج سَوَارٍ
Palace.	سرايا ج سَرَايَاتٌ
The Syriac language.	السُّرْيَانِيَّةُ
To spread out.	سَطَحَ يَسْطَحُ وسطَّحَ
To be spread out.	تَسَطَّحَ
Surface ; terrace.	سَطْحٌ ج سُطُوحٌ
Flat, plane, even.	مُسَطَّحٌ
To write.	سَطَرَ يَسْطُرُ
Line ; row.	سَطْرٌ ج اسْطُرٌ وسُطُورٌ
Large knife.	سَاطُورٌ ج سَوَاطِيرُ
Fable, legend.	اسْطُورَةٌ ج أَسَاطِيرُ
Ruler (for lines). Sample.	مِسْطَرَةٌ
New wine.	مُسْطَارٌ
Authority, guardianship.	سَيْطَرَةٌ
To rise ; gleam.	سَطَعَ يَسْطَعُ
Pail, bucket.	سَطْلٌ
Ship of war. Fleet.	اسْطُولٌ
To stop up, bar.	سَطَمَ يَسْطِمُ
Cork, stopper ; bolt.	سِطَامٌ
Cylinder.	اسْطُوَانَةٌ ج اسَاطِينُ
Cylindrical.	اسْطُوَانِيٌّ
To attack ; assail.	سَطَا يَسْطُو عَلَى
Attack ; power.	سَطْوَةٌ ج سَطَوَاتٌ
Thyme (plant).	سَعْتَرٌ (أَوْ صعتر)
To be fortunate.	سَعِدَ يَسْعَدُ

To help, assist. سَاعَدَ

To make happy. أَسْعَدَ

Luck, success. سَعْدٌ ج سُعُودٌ

Monkey. سَعْدَانٌ ج سَعَادِينُ

Fore-arm. سَاعِدٌ ج سَوَاعِد

Happiness, felicity. سَعَادَةٌ

Your Excellency. سعادتُكَ

Fortunate. سعيدٌ ج سُعَدَاءُ

To light a fire. سعر يسعرُ

To fix, estimate a price. سَعَّرَ

To be fixed, (price). تَسَعَّرَ

To blaze, spread. إِسْتَعَرَ

Price. سِعْرٌ ج أَسْعَارٌ

Flame, blaze. Fire. سَعِيرٌ

Snuff. سَعُوطٌ

To assist. سَعَفَ يَسْعَفُ وأَسْعَفَ بِ

To assist, help. سَاعَفَ

Branches of palm-tree. سَعَفٌ

To cough. سَعَلَ يَسْعُلُ سُعَالًا

Cough. سُعَالٌ

To run. Seek. سَعَى يَسْعَى سَعْيًا

To calumniate. سَعَى بِ

Effort, exertion. سَعْيٌ

Messenger. سَاعٍ ج سُعَاةٌ

Effort ; enterprise. مَسْعًى ج مَسَاعٍ

Medicine (in powder). سَفُوفٌ

Bill of exchange. سُفْتَجَةٌ ج سَفَاتِجُ

To shed. سَفَحَ يَسْفَحُ سُفُوحًا وَسَفْحًا

To fornicate. سَافَحَ

Foot of a mountain. سَفْحٌ

Fornication. سِفَاحٌ

Roasting-fork. سَفُّودٌ ج سَفَافِيدُ

To travel. سَفَرَ يَسْفُرُ سَفْرًا

To send on a journey. سَفَّرَ

To depart, travel. سَافَرَ

To shine, (dawn). أَسْفَرَ

Written book. سِفْرٌ ج أَسْفَارٌ

Journey. سَفَرٌ ج أَسْفَارٌ

سَفْرَة ج سَفَرَات	A journey.
سُفْرَة	Table-cloth ; table.
مُسَافِر	Traveller.
سِفَارَة	Embassy.
سَفِير ج سُفَرَاء	Ambassador.
سَفَرْجَل ج سَفَارِج	Quince.
سَفْسَطَة وَسِفْسطَة	Sophism.
سَفْسَطِيّ	Sophistical ; sophist.
سَفَقَ يَسْفُق	To shut, slap.
سَفِيق	Thick, compact.
سَفِيقُ ٱلْوَجْهِ	Impudent, insolent.
سَفَكَ يَسْفُكُ سَفْكًا	To shed.
إِنْسَفَكَ	To be shed.
سَفَّاكٌ لِلدِّمَاءِ	Blood-shedder.
مَسْفُوك	Shed, (blood, &c.)
سَفُلَ يَسْفُلُ	To be low, sink.
سَفُلَ سَفَالَةً	To be mean.
سِفْل	The lowest part, bottom.
سُفْلِيّ	The lower part.
سَفَالَة	Baseness, vileness.
سَافِل ج سَفَلَة	Low, vile.
اسْفَلُ	The lowest part.
سَفِين وَإِسْفِين	Wedge.
سَفِينَة ج سُفُن	Ship, boat.
سَفَنْج وَسَفُنْج	Sponge.
سَفِهَ يَسْفَهُ سَفَهًا	To be foolish.
تَسَفَّهَ عَلَى	To revile.
سَفَهٌ وَسَفَاهَة	Stupidity.
سَفِيه ج سُفَهَاء	Stupid, foolish.
سَقَطَ يَسْقُطُ	To fall, fall down.
أَسْقَطَ	To cause to fall, let fall. Discount. Subtract.
تَسَاقَطَ	To fall by degrees.
سَقَط ج أَسْقَاط	Refuse. Defect.
سَقْطَة	Fall, slip, fault, error.
سَاقِط ج سُقَّاط	Low, worthless.
سُقَاطَة	Refuse, what is rejected.
سَقَاطَة	Door-latch.
سُقُوط	Falling, downfall.

إسْقَاطٌ Discount. Subtraction.

مسقَط الرَّأس Native place.

سَقَفَ يَسْقُفُ سَقْفاً وَسَقَّفَ To roof.

سَقْفٌ ج سقوفٌ Roof ; ceiling.

سَقِيفَةٌ ج سَقَائِفُ Porch, roof.

أُسْقُفٌ ج أَسَاقِفَةٌ Bishop.

اسقُفيةٌ Bishopric.

سَقْلَبِيٌّ ج سَقَالِبَةٌ A Slavonian.

سَقِمَ يَسْقَمُ To be weak, diseased.

أَسْقَمَ To make ill.

سُقْمٌ ج اسقامٌ Disease, illness.

سقيمٌ ج سُقَمَاءُ Diseased, weak.

سَقَمُونِيَا Scammony, (plant).

سَقَى يَسْقِي To give to drink, irrigate.

إسْتَقَى To draw water ; ask for water.

إسْتَسْقَى To be dropsical.

سَقْيٌ Giving to drink, watering.

سِقَاءٌ ج أَسْقِيَةٌ Water-skin.

سَقَّاءٌ ج سَقَّاؤُونَ Water-carrier.

سَاقٍ Cup-bearer.

سَاقِيَةٌ ج سَوَاقٍ Water-wheel. Irrigation-canal.

إسْتِسْقَاءٌ Dropsy.

مُسْتَسْقٍ Dropsical.

سكَّ آلنُّقُود To coin money.

سِكَّةٌ ج سِكَكٌ Ploughshare. Road, high road. Coined money.

سِكَّةُ حَدِيدٍ Railway.

سَكَبَ يَسْكُبُ To pour out ; melt.

سَكَبَ سُكُوبًا وَانْسَكَبَ To flow.

سَكْبٌ Melting, flowing.

سَكَتَ يَسْكُتُ To be silent, still.

سَكَّتَ وَأَسْكَتَ To silence, still.

سَكْتٌ وَسُكُوتٌ Silence ; pause.

سَكْتَةٌ Apoplexy. A pause.

سَكُوتٌ Silent, reserved.

سَكِرَ يَسْكَرُ To become intoxicated.

سَكَّرَ وَأَسْكَرَ To intoxicate.

سُكْرٌ Drunkenness.

سَكْرَةُ ٱلْمَوْتِ Agony of death.

سَكْرَةٌ Wooden lock to a door.

سُكَّرٌ Sugar.

سَكْرَانُ ج سُكَارَى Intoxicated.

سِكِّيرٌ Habitual drunkard.

سِكَافَة Trade of a shoemaker.

إِسْكَافٌ ج أَسَاكِفَةٌ Shoemaker.

أُسْكُفَّةٌ Threshold.

سَكَنَ يَسْكُنُ سُكُونًا To subside.

سَكَنَ سَكَنًا وفي To dwell in.

سَكَنَ إِلَى To rely upon, trust in.

سَكَّنَ To calm, pacify, quiet.

أَسْكَنَ To make to dwell.

سَكَنٌ Habitation.

سَاكِنٌ ج سُكَّانٌ An inhabitant.

سُكُونٌ Rest, quiescence.

سِكِّينٌ ج سَكَاكِينُ Knife.

سَكِينَة Quiet.

مَسْكَنٌ ج مَسَاكِنُ House. abode.

مَسْكَنَةٌ Poverty ; lowliness.

مَسْكُونٌ Inhabited; possessed.

أَلْمَسْكُونَةُ The world.

مِسْكِينٌ ج مَسَاكِينُ Poor ; lowly.

سَلَّ يَسُلُّ وَٱسْتَلَّ To draw a sword.

تَسَلَّلَ وَٱنْسَلَّ To slip away.

سَلٌّ وَسَلَّةٌ ج سِلَالٌ Basket.

دَاءُ ٱلسِّلِّ Consumption, (disease).

سُلَالَةٌ Offspring, progeny.

سَلِيلٌ Child ; male offspring.

مِسَلَّةٌ Large needle. Obelisk.

مَسْلُول Unsheathed. Phthisical.

سَلَأَ يَسْلَأُ To melt, clarify (butter).

سَلَبَ يَسْلُبُ وَٱسْتَلَبَ To rob. Seize.

سَلْبٌ Robbery. Negation.

مَسْلُوبٌ Robbed, plundered.

أُسْلُوبٌ ج أَسَالِيبُ Method, way.

سَلَّحَ بِ To arm equip.

تَسَلَّحَ To arm one's self.

Arms, weapons. سِلَاحٌ ج أَسْلِحَةٌ
Tortoise. سُلَحْفَاةٌ ج سَلَاحِفُ
To skin, flay. سَلَخَ يَسْلُخُ سَلْخًا
To be stripped off. اِنْسَلَخَ
End of (the month). سَلْخٌ وَمُنْسَلَخٌ
Slaughter-house. مَسْلَخٌ مَسَالِخُ
To be loose, docile. سَلِسَ يَسْلَسُ
Docility. سَلَسٌ وَسَلَاسَةٌ
Docile ; compliant. سَلِسٌ
To chain. سَلْسَلَ بِ
To trace a pedigree. سَلْسَلَ إِلَى
Chain. سِلْسِلَةٌ ج سَلَاسِلُ
Artificial fountain. سَلْسَبِيلٌ
A continued series. تَسَلْسُلٌ
To make one a ruler. سَلَّطَهُ
To overcome ; rule. تَسَلَّطَ عَلَى
Rule, dominion. سَلْطَةٌ وَتَسَلُّطٌ
Power, dominion. سَلْطَنَةٌ
Absolute power. سُلْطَانٌ

Sultan. سُلْطَانٌ ج سَلَاطِينُ
Imperial. سُلْطَانِيٌّ
High road. طَرِيقٌ سُلْطَانِيٌّ
Article for sale. سِلْعَةٌ ج سِلَعٌ
To pass away ; precede. سَلَفَ يَسْلُفُ
To give in advance. سَلَّفَ وَأَسْلَفَ
To borrow ; receive payment in advance. تَسَلَّفَ وَٱسْتَلَفَ
Payment in advance. سَلَفٌ
Predecessor. سَلَفٌ ج أَسْلَافٌ
Vanguard of army. سُلَافُ ٱلْعَسْكَرِ
Preceding ; former. سَالِفٌ
To boil. سَلَقَ يَسْلُقُ سَلْقًا
To scale or climb a wall. تَسَلَّقَ
Ulceration of eye-lids. سُلَاقٌ
Greyhound. سَلُوقِيٌّ
Natural trait. سَلِيقَةٌ ج سَلَائِقُ
Naturally, instinctively. بِٱلسَّلِيقَةِ
Boiled. مَسْلُوقٌ

سلكَ يسلُكُ — To travel, enter. Behave.
أَسْلَكَ — To make to enter.
سِلكٌ ج أَسْلاَكٌ — String ; wire.
سُلوكٌ — Conduct, behaviour.
عِلمُ ٱلسُّلُوك — Good manners.
سالك — Ordinary, usual, current.
مَسْلَك ج مَسَالِكُ — Path road.
سَلِمَ يَسلَمُ — To be sound, safe.
سلمَ مِنْ — To be free from.
سَلّمَ مِنْ — Tsave ; preser ove.
سلمَ بِ — To admit.
سلمَ لِ — To surrender, yield.
سلّمَ إِلى — To give over, hand to.
سلم عَلَى — To salute, greet.
سَالَم — To keep peace with.
اسْلَمَ — To deliver up.
أَسْلَمَ — To profess Islâm.
تَسلم — To take possession of.
إِسْتَسلمَ — To yield, surrender.

سِلْمٌ — Peace, reconciliation.
سُلمٌ ج سَلاَلِمُ — Ladder, stairs.
سَلاَمٌ وَسَلاَمَةٌ — Peace, well-being.
سَلاَمٌ — Greeting ; salutation.
سَالمٌ — Sound and safe.
أَلْجَمْعُ ٱلسالمُ — Sound plural.
سلِيمٌ ج سُلَمَاءُ — Sound, safe.
سُلَيْمَانِيٌّ — Corrosive sublimate.
أَسْلَمُ — More secure, safer.
الإِسْلاَمُ — Religion of Islâm.
تَسْلِيمٌ — Delivery ; surrender.
مسْلِمٌ ج مُسْلِمُونَ — Moslem.
مُسَلمٌ — Delivered ; conceded.
سُلاَ يَسلو — To forget.
سَلّى — To divert, cheer, amuse.
تَسلى — To be diverted.
سُلْوَةٌ وَتَسْلِيَة وَتسَلٍّ — Diversion.
سلْوَى — Quail. Consolation.
سُلْوَانٌ — Consolation.

To poison. سَمَّ يَسُمُّ سَمًّا

Hole. Poison. سُمٌّ ج سُمُومٌ

Arsenic ; ratsbane. سَمُّ ٱلْفَارِ

Poisonous. سَامٌّ

Hot wind. سَمُومٌ

Holes ; pores. مَسَامُّ

Poisoned. مَسْمُومٌ

Way ; manner. سَمْتٌ

Azimuth. أَلسَّمْتُ ج سُمُوتٌ

Zenith. سَمْتُ ٱلرَّأْسِ

To be ugly. سَمُجَ يَسْمُجُ سَمَاجَةً

Ugly, horrid ; foul. سَمْجٌ وَسَمِيجٌ

To grant, permit ; pardon. سَمَحَ يَسْمَحُ

To pardon, excuse. سَامَحَ

Kindness ; grace. سَمَاحٌ وَسَمَاحَةٌ

Allowed ; permitted. مَسْمُوحٌ بِهِ

Periosteum. سِمْحَاقٌ

To manure the soil. سَمَّدَ

Manure. سَمَادٌ

Semolino. سَمِيذٌ وَسَمِيدٌ

To be brownish. سَمُرَ يَسْمُرُ وَٱسْمَرَّ

To nail. سَمَرَ وَسَمَّرَ

To converse with. سَامَرَ وَتَسَامَرَ

Brownish colour. سُمْرَةٌ

Samaria (in Palestine). ٱلسَّامِرَةُ

Samaritan. سَامِرِيٌّ

Sable (animal). سَمُّورٌ

Brownish. أَسْمَرُ م سَمْرَاءُ ج سُمْرٌ

Nail. Foot-corn. مِسْمَارٌ ج مَسَامِيرُ

To act as a broker. سَمْسَرَ

Brokerage ; fee of a broker. سَمْسَرَةٌ

Broker. سِمْسَارٌ ج سَمَاسِرَةٌ

Sesame. سِمْسِمٌ

Sesamoid bone. سِمْسِمَانِيٌّ

To strap with thongs. سَمَّطَ

Thong. سِمْطٌ ج سُمُوطٌ

Table-cloth. سِمَاطٌ ج أَسْمِطَةٌ

To hear, listen. سَمِعَ يَسْمَعُ وَٱسْتَمَعَ

سَمِعَ ب	To hear of.
سَمِعَ لِ ومن	To accept, obey.
سَمْعٌ	Sense of hearing.
سَمْعاً وَطَاعَةً	You shall be obeyed.
سُمْعَةٌ	Report, fame.
سَمَاعِيٌّ	Irregular, traditional.
السَّمِيعُ	The hearer of all (God).
سُمَّاقٌ	Sumach, (tree and fruit).
سَمُكَ سَمَاكَةً	To become thick.
سَمَّكَ	To thicken, make thick.
سَمْكٌ وسَمَاكَةٌ	Depth, thickness.
سَمَكٌ ج اسْمَاكٌ	Fish.
سَمَكَةٌ	A fish.
سَمِيكٌ	Deep, thick.
سَمِنَ يَسْمَنُ سِمَناً	To grow fat.
سَمَّنَ	To butter; fatten.
سَمْنٌ	Clarified butter.
سَمَّانٌ	Seller of butter. Grocer.
(سُمْنَةٌ ج سُمَّنٌ وَسمَانِي)	Quail.
سَمِينٌ ج سِمَانٌ	Fat, corpulent.
سَمَا يَسْمُو	To be high ; rise high.
سَمَّى	Give a name ; name.
تَسَمَّى	To be named ; mentioned.
إِسْمٌ ج أَسْمَاءٌ	Name ; noun.
إِسْمُ ٱلْجَلَالَةِ	The name of God.
سُمُوٌّ	Height ; greatness.
سَمَاءٌ ج سَمَوَاتٌ	Heaven.
سَمَاوِيٌّ وَسَمَائِيٌّ	Heavenly.
سَامٍ ج سُمَاةٌ	High ; sublime.
أَمْرٌ سَامٍ	Grand vizierial order.
مُسَمًّى	Named, determined.
سَنَّ يَسُنُّ	To sharpen, whet.
سَنَّ سُنَّةً	To introduce a law.
اسَنَّ	To become aged.
سِنٌّ ج اسْنَانٌ	Tooth. Age in life.
طَعَنَ فِي ٱلسِّنِّ	To become old.
سُنَّةٌ ج سُنَنٌ	Law ; usage.
سِنَانٌ ج أَسِنَّة	Head of a spear.

سُنِّيٌّ ج سُنِّيَّةٌ — A Sunnite.
مِسَنٌّ — Whet-stone.
مُسِنٌّ — Advanced in age.
سُنْبُوقٌ — Skiff, small boat.
سُنْبُلَةٌ ج سَنَابِل — An ear of corn.
اَلسُّنْبُلَةُ — Virgo (of the Zodiac).
سُنْجَابٌ — Squirrel.
سِنْجَقٌ ج سَنَاجِقُ — Standard, flag.
سَنَحَ يَسْنَحُ — To occur to the mind.
سَنَحَ عَنْ — To dissuade.
سِنْخٌ ج اسْنَاخٌ — Socket of a tooth.
سَنَدَ يَسْنُدُ وَاسْتَنَدَ إِلى — To lean upon.
سَنَّدَ — To support firmly.
أَسْنَدَ إِلَى — To ascribe, trace up.
سَنَدٌ ج أَسْنَادٌ — Support; refuge.
سَنْدَانٌ ج سَنَادِينُ — Anvil.
سِنْدِيَانٌ — Evergreen oak; ilex.
مِسْنَدٌ ج مَسَانِدُ — Cushion, pillow.
مُسْتَنَدٌ — Supported, propped.
اَلْمُسْنَدُ — Predicate.
اَلْمُسْنَدُ إِلَيْهِ — Subject.
سَنْدَرُوسٌ — Sandarach.
سُنْدُسٌ — Silk brocade; fine silk.
سِنَّوْرٌ ج سَنَانِيرُ — Cat.
سَنْطٌ — Acacia (*Nilotica*).
سِنْطِيرٌ وَسَنْطُورٌ — A kind of harp.
سَنْكَرِيٌّ ج سَنَاكِرَةٌ — Tinker.
سَنَامٌ ج أَسْنِمَةٌ — Hump of camel.
مُسَنَّمٌ — Raised; convex.
تَسَنَّى — To ascend. Be easy.
سَنًى — Brightness, gleaming.
سَنَاءٌ — Sublimity; high rank.
سَنَا مَكَّةَ — Senna, (plant).
سَنَةٌ سِنُونٌ وَسَنَوَاتٌ — Year.
سَنِيٌّ — High, sublime, noble.
سَنَوِيٌّ — Annual, yearly.
سُنُونُو — Swallow.
أَسْهَبَ — To be lengthy, prolix.

To give largely. اسْهَبَ فِي ٱلْعَطَاءِ
Prolixity; amplification. اسْهَابٌ
Loquacious; diffuse. مُسْهِبٌ
To be sleepless. سَهِدَ يَسْهَدُ
To deprive of sleep. سَهَّدَ
Sleeplessness. سُهْدٌ وَسُهَادٌ
To keep awake. سَهِرَ يَسْهَرُ
Awake. سَاهِرٌ وَسَهْرَانُ
To be level; easy. سَهُلَ يَسْهُلُ
To smooth; facilitate. سَهَّلَ
To be level; become easy. تَسَهَّلَ
To be accommodating. تَسَاهَلَ
To regard as easy. إِسْتَسْهَلَ
Plain; level. سَهْلٌ ج سُهُولٌ
Gentle. سَهْلُ ٱلْخُلُقِ
Easy; smooth, soft. سَهْلٌ
Ease, facility. Evenness. سُهُولَةٌ
Canopus, (star). سُهَيْلٌ
Diarrhœa. إِسْهَالٌ

Purgative, laxative. مُسْهِلٌ
Arrow. سَهْمٌ ج سِهَامٌ
Lot, share. سَهْمٌ ج اسْهُمٌ
Sagittarius. سَهْمُ ٱلرَّامِي
To overlook, neglect. سَهَا يَسْهُو عَنْ
Oversight, forgetfulness. سَهْوٌ
Thoughtlessly. سَهْواً
Forgetful, negligent. سَاهٍ
To be evil, bad. سَاءَ يَسُوءُ
To treat badly; offend. سَاءَ سُوءًا
To be evil to; offend. أَسَاءَ إِلَى
To suspect evil. أَسَاءَ ٱلظَّنَّ
Evil. سُوءٌ ج أَسْوَاءٌ وَمَسَاوِئُ
Evil, bad. سَيِّئٌ م سَيِّئَةٌ
Sin; calamity. سَيِّئَةٌ ج سَيِّئَاتٌ
Teak-tree. سَاجٌ
See under. سيح سَاحَ يَسُوحُ
Court; yard. سَاحَةٌ ج سَاحَاتٌ
Traveller. سَائِحٌ ج سُيَّاحٌ

To rule. سَادَ يَسُودُ سِيَادَةً

To become black. إِسْوَدَّ

To blacken; write a rough draft. سَوَّدَ

To be blackened. تَسَوَّدَ

Dominion; honour. سُؤْدَدٌ وَسِيَادَةٌ

Black bile. Melancholy. سَوْدَاءُ

Sudan (country). بِلَادُ ٱلسُّودَانِ

Blackness. Large number. سَوَادٌ

Power, authority. سِيَادَةٌ

Master, lord. سَيِّدٌ ج سَادَةٌ

Black. أَسْوَدُ م سَوْدَاءُ ج سُودٌ

First copy, rough draft. مُسَوَّدَةٌ

Glass bottle. مُسَوَّدَةٌ ج مُسَوَّدَاتٌ

To wall in a town. سَوَّرَ

Wall, ramparts. سُورٌ ج أَسْوَارٌ

Chapter of Koran. سُورَةٌ ج سُوَرٌ

Syria. سُورِيَّة

Bracelet. سِوَارٌ وَأُسْوَارٌ ج أَسْوِرَةٌ

Surrounded with walls. مُسَوَّرٌ

To rule a people. To groom a horse. سَاسَ يَسُوسُ

To be moth-eaten. سَوَّسَ

Moth, worm. Liquorice. سُوسٌ

Political administration. سِيَاسَةٌ

Groom. سَائِسٌ ج سَاسَةٌ وَسُوَّاسٌ

Lily. سُوسَنٌ وَسُوسَانٌ

To whip. سَاطَ يَسُوطُ سَوْطًا

Whip, lash. سَوْطٌ ج سِيَاطٌ

Hour. Watch. سَاعَةٌ ج سَاعَاتٌ

Sun-dial. سَاعَةٌ شَمْسِيَّةٌ

Hour-glass. سَاعَةٌ رَمْلِيَّةٌ

Watch-maker. سَاعَاتِيٌّ

To be permitted, lawful. سَاغَ لَ

To allow, permit. سَوَّغَ لِ

Lawful, allowable. سَائِغٌ

To put off, defer. سَوَّفَ

Row, course. سَافٌ ج سَافَاتٌ

A particle which changes the *present* tense into a future; سَوْفَ
e.g. Thou shalt see. سَوْفَ تَرَى

مَسَافَةٌ	Distance.
سَاقَ يَسُوقُ	To drive, urge on.
سَاقَ إِلى	To lead to.
إِنْسَاقَ	To be driven, urged on.
سَاقٌ ج سُوقٌ وسِيقَانٌ	Leg. Stem (of a plant). Side of a triangle.
سُوقٌ ج أَسْوَاق	Market.
سَوِيق	Fine flour.
سِيَاقٌ	Logical connection.
سَائِقٌ	Driver, driving.
تَسَوَّكَ	To clean one's teeth.
سِوَاكٌ وَمِسْوَاك	Toothpick.
سَوَّلَ لِ	To deceive, incite to evil.
سَامَ يَسُومُ	To compel.
سَاوَمَ مُسَاوَمَةً	To bargain.
سِيمَةٌ وَسِيمَاء	Sign, mark.
سَوِيَ يَسْوَى وَسَاوى	To be worth.
سَوَّى تَسْوِيَةً	To adjust, rectify.
سَاوى وَاسْتَوى	To be equal.
إِسْتَوَى	To be ripe, well cooked.
إِسْتَوَى عَلَى	To sit upon.
سَوَاءٌ	Just, right. Same, alike.
عَلَى حَدٍّ سَوَاء	Alike, equally.
سَوِيَّةً وَسَوَاءً	Equally ; together.
لاَ سِيَّمَا	Chiefly, principally.
هُمَا سِيَّان	Equally, alike, (both).
خطُّ الإِستِوَاء	Equator.
مُسَاوَاةٌ	Equaliy. Moderation.
مسَاوٍ وَمُتَسَاوٍ	Equal.
مستَوٍ	Common gender.
سَيَّبَ	To set free.
سَائِبٌ	Left free, at liberty.
مُسَيَّبٌ	Unguarded ; free.
سَيَّجَ	To hedge in, enclose.
سِيَاجٌ ج سِيَاجَاتٌ	Hedge.
مسَيَّجٌ	Surrounded by a hedge.
سَاحَ يَسِيحُ	To travel. Flow.
سِيَاحة	Long journery.

Traveller.	سَائِحٌ ج سُيَّاحٌ
Great traveller.	سَيَّاحٌ
Area.	مَسَاحَةٌ
Land surveying.	عِلْمُ ٱلْمَسَاحَةِ
Large knife.	سِيخٌ ج أَسْيَاخٌ
To go ; travel.	سَارَ يَسِيرُ
To carry away.	سَارَ بِ
Journey. Thong.	سَيْرٌ ج سُيُورٌ
Conduct. Biography.	سِيرَةٌ ج سِيَرٌ
Current, customary.	سَائِرٌ
Planet.	سَيَّارَةٌ ج سَيَّارَاتٌ
Journey, road.	مَسِيرٌ
Sword.	سَيْفٌ ج سُيُوفٌ
To flow ; become liquid.	سَالَ يَسِيلُ
To liquify.	سَيَّلَ وَأَسَالَ
Stream ; torrent.	سَيْلٌ ج سُيُولٌ
Flow ; flux.	سَيَلَانٌ
Ceylon.	سِيلَانُ
Ruby ; carbuncle.	سَيْلَانٌ
Liquid, fluid.	سَائِلٌ ج سَوَائِلُ
Water-course.	مَسِيلٌ

ش

ش	As a numeral sign=300.
شَؤُمَ وَشَئِمَ	To be inauspicious.
تَشَاءَمَ	To take as a bad omen.
شُؤْمٌ	Evil omen, ill luck.
الشَّامُ	Syria. Damascus.
شَامِيٌّ	Syrian. Damascene.
شِئْمَةٌ	Nature, disposition.
مَشُومٌ	Inauspicious, unlucky.
شَأْنٌ	Thing ; state ; honour.
عَظِيمُ ٱلشَّأْنِ	Of great importance.
شَاهِينٌ ج شَوَاهِينُ	White falcon.
شَبَّ يَشِبُّ	To grow up, (youth).
شَبَّ يَشُبُّ	To blaze (fire, war).
شَبٌّ	Vitriol. Alum.
شَابٌّ ج شُبَّانٌ	Young man.
شَابَّةٌ ج شَابَّات	Young woman.
شَبَابٌ وَشَبِيبَةٌ	Youth.
شَبَّابَةٌ	A reed or musical pipe.
تَشَبَّثَ ب	To take firm hold.
شِبِثٌّ	Dill (plant).
شَبَحٌ ج أَشْبَاحٌ	Object of vision.
شُبْحَةٌ	A horse's shackle.
شِبْرٌ ج أَشْبَارٌ	Span.
شَبَّطَ	To scarify.
شُبَاطُ وَسُبَاطُ	February.
شَبِعَ يَشْبَعُ	To be satiated.
أَشْبَعَ	To satiate, satisfy.
شِبَعٌ	Satiety, satiation.
شَبْعَانُ	Satiated, satisfied.
شَبَكَ يَشْبُكُ	To entwine, entangle.

To be entangled. تَشَبَّكَ وَٱشْتَبَكَ

Fishing-net. شَبَكَةٌ ج شَبَكٌ

Window. شُبَّاكٌ ج شَبَابِيكُ

Cub of a lion. شِبْلٌ ج أَشْبَالٌ

Groomsman. شَبِينٌ م شَبِينَةٌ

To liken, compare. شَبَّهَ بِ

To resemble. شَابَهَ وَأَشْبَهَ

To imitate. تَشَبَّهَ بِ

To resemble one another. تَشَابَهَ

To be obscure. إِشْتَبَهَ

To be in doubt. إِشْتَبَهَ فِي

A similar person or thing. شِبْهٌ

Similarity ; likeness. شَبَهٌ

Point of resemblance. وَجْهُ ٱلشَّبَهِ

Doubt, suspicion. شُبْهَةٌ ج شُبُهَاتٌ

Resembling, like. شَبِيهٌ

Ambiguity ; doubt. اِشْتِبَاهٌ

Comparison ; metaphor. تَشْبِيهٌ

Doubtful, obscure. مُشْتَبَهٌ

Resemblance. مُشَابَهَةٌ

To be scattered. شَتَّ يَشِتُّ

To scatter. شَتَّ وَشَتَّتَ وَأَشَتَّ

To be dispersed. تَشَتَّتَ

Disunion. شَتٌّ وَشَتَاتٌ

Great is the difference ! شَتَّانَ

Various things. أَشْيَاءُ شَتَّى

Nursery-plant. شَتْلَةٌ

Plant-nursery. مَشْتَلٌ

To revile. شَتَمَ يَشْتُمُ شَتْمًا

Defamation. شَتِيمَةٌ ج شَتَائِمُ

Reviled. شَتِيمٌ وَمَشْتُومٌ

To pass the winter. شَتَا يَشْتُو وَشَتَّى

Winter ; rain. شِتَاءٌ

Pertaining to winter. شَتَوِيٌّ

Wintry ; rainy. شَاتٍ

Winter abode. مَشْتًى

To wound the head. شَجَّ يَشُجُّ

Wound in the head. شَجَّةٌ

To become woody. شَجَّرَ
To quarrel with. شَاجَرَ مُشَاجَرَةً
To abound in trees. شَجَرَ
To dispute, quarrel. تَشَاجَرَ
Tree; shrub, bush. شَجَرٌ ج أَشْجَارٌ
A tree. شَجَرَةٌ
Abounding in trees. شَجِرٌ وَمُشْجِرٌ
Dispute, contest. مُشَاجَرَةٌ
To be brave. شَجُعَ يَشْجُعُ شَجَاعَةً
To encourage, embolden. شَجَّعَ
To take courage. تَشْجِيعٌ
Courage, bravery. شَجَاعَةٌ
Brave, bold. شُجَاعٌ ج شُجْعَانٌ
To grieve. Coo. شَجُنَ يَشْجُنُ شَجْنًا
Grief. شَجَنٌ ج شُجُون
To cause anguish. شَجَا يَشْجُو
To be grieved. شَجِيَ يَشْجَى شَجًا
Anxiety, grief. شَجًا وَشَجْوٌ
Grieved, anxious, sad. شَجٍ وَشَجِيٌّ

To be niggardly. شَحَّ يَشُحُّ شَحًّا
To contend together. تَشَاحَّ
Avarice, covetousness. شِحٌّ
Avaricious. شَحِيحٌ ج شِحَاحٌ
Incontestable. لَا مُشَاحَّةَ فِي
To ask for alms, beg. شَحَذَ يَشْحَذُ
Mendicity. شِحَاذَةٌ
Importunate beggar. شَحَّاذٌ
Stye on the eyelid. شَحَّاذُ ٱلْعَيْن
To drag along. شَحَطَ يَشْحَطُ
Grease, lard, fat. شَحْمٌ ج شُحُومٌ
Lobe of the ear. شَحْمَةُ ٱلأُذُنِ
To fill, load. شَحَنَ يَشْحَنُ وأَشْحَنَ ب
To treat with enmity. شَاحَنَ
Freight, cargo. شَحْنٌ وَشَحْنَةٌ
Hatred, enmity. شَحْنَاءُ وَشِحْنَةٌ
Garrison. شِحْنَةٌ
Hatred, enmity. مُشَاحَنَةٌ
To micturate. شَخَّ يَشِخُّ شَخًّا

شِخَاخٌ Urine.

شخَرَ يشخِرُ شَخيراً To snore; snort.

شَخَصَ بِبَصَرِهِ إِلَى To gaze at.

شَخصَ مِنْ وَإِلَى To go from .. to ..

شَخصَ To distinguish.

تَشَخَّصَ To be distinct.

شَخْصٌ ج أَشْخَاصٌ Person, individual.

تَشخِيصٌ Diagnosis of (disease).

شَدَّ يَشُدُّ شَدًّا To strap, bind.

شَدَّدَ To bind fast, strengthen.

شَدَّدَ عَلَى To treat with severity.

تَشَدَّدَ وَاشْتَدَّ To be strengthened.

إِشْتَدَّ To be strong, intense.

شِدَّةٌ Violence, intensity.

شِدَّةٌ ج شَدَائِدُ Hardship, distress.

شَدَّةٌ Name of the sign (ّ).

شَدِيدٌ ج اشِدَّاء Violent, strong.

شَدِيدُ الْبَأْسِ Courageous, brave.

أَشَدُّ More intense, stronger.

أَشَدُّ سَوَاداً Blacker.

أَشَدُّ غَضَباً More or most angry.

إِشْتِدَادٌ Violence. Strength.

شِدْقٌ Cheek.

شَدْيَاقٌ ج شَدَايِقَة Deacon

مُتَشَدِّقٌ Diffuse in speech.

شَادِنٌ A young gazelle.

شَدَا يَشْدُو وَأَشْدَى To sing.

شَذَّ يَشُذُّ To be exceptional.

شَاذٌّ ج شَوَاذ Irregular, rare.

شُذُوذٌ Irregularity; rarity.

شَرٌّ ج شُرُورٌ Anything bad, evil.

شَرٌّ ج أَشْرَارٌ Wicked. Worse.

شَرَارَةٌ A spark.

شَرِيرٌ ج أَشْرَارٌ Bad, wicked.

شِرِّيرٌ ج شِرِّيرُونَ Very wicked.

أَلشِّرِّيرُ The Evil One, Satan.

شَرِبَ يَشْرَبُ To drink, swallow.

شَرِبَ الدُّخَّانَ To smoke tobacco.

To saturate. شَرَّبَ

To absorb, imbibe. تَشَرَّبَ

Act of drinking. شِرْبٌ

Draught. Water-jug. شَرْبَةٌ

Drink, beverage. شَرَابٌ ج أَشْرِبَةٌ

Syrup. شَرَابٌ

Tassel. شَرَّابَةٌ ج شَرَارِيبُ

Moustache. شَارِبٌ ج شَوَارِبُ

Addicted to drink. شِرِّيبٌ

Inclination. مَشْرَبٌ ج مَشَارِبُ

To entangle, confuse. شَرْبَكَ

A species of fir. شَرْبِينٌ

To baste. شَرَّجَ

Sesame-oil. شَيْرَجٌ وَسِيرَجٌ

To explain. شَرَحَ يَشْرَحُ

To dissect. شَرَّحَ

To be enlarged. Happy. إِنْشَرَحَ

Commentary. شَرْحٌ ج شُرُوحٌ

Commentator. شَارِحٌ ج شُرَّاحٌ

Long slice of meat. شَرِيحٌ وَشَرِيحَةٌ

Dissection. تَشْرِيحٌ

Anatomy. عِلْمُ ٱلتَّشْرِيحِ

Anatomist. مُشَرِّحٌ ج مُشَرِّحُونَ

Prime of youth. شَرْخٌ

To flee, take fright. شَرَدَ يَشْرُدُ

To depart from. شَرَدَ عَنْ

Roaming, fugitive. شَارِدٌ

Strange, unusual. شَوَارِدُ

Small number of men. شِرْذِمَةٌ

To be ill-natured. شَرِسَ يَشْرَسُ

Ill-natured. شَرِسٌ

Sticking-paste. شِرَاسٌ وَسِرَاسٌ

Extremity of a rib. شُرْسُوفٌ

Epigastric region. أَلْقِسْمُ ٱلشَّرَاسِيفِيُّ

Root. شِرْسٌ ج شُرُوسٌ

A fringe. شَرْشَرَةٌ ج شَرَاشِرُ

Bed-sheet. شَرْشَفٌ ج شَرَاشِفُ

To stipulate. شَرَطَ يَشْرُطُ وَٱشْتَرَطَ

To make incisions. شَرَطَ وَشَرَّطَ

To stipulate with. شَارَطَ وَتَشَارَطَ

Condition, stipulation, contract. شَرْطٌ ج شُرُوطٌ

Guard's-man. شَرْطِيٌّ ج شُرْطَةٌ

Wire ; tape. شَرِيطٌ ج شُرُط

Bistoury. مِشْرَط ج مَشَارِط

Stipulation. Betting. مُشَارَطَةٌ

To make a law. شَرَعَ يَشْرِعُ وَاشْتَرَعَ

To begin. شَرَعَ شُرُوعاً

He began to say. شَرَعَ يَقُولُ

To engage in an affair. شَرَعَ فِي

Divine or religious law. شَرْعٌ

Legitimate, legal. شَرْعِيٌّ

Main street. Legislator. شَارِعٌ ج شَوَارِعُ

A sail. شِرَاعٌ ج أَشْرِعَة

Law, statute. شَرِيعةٌ ج شَرَائِع

Jordan (river). أَلشَّرِيعةُ

Deuteronomy. تَثْنِيَةُ الاشْتِرَاعِ

Legislator. مُشْتَرِعٌ

To be noble. شَرُفَ يَشْرُف

To be high. شَرَفَ يَشْرُفُ شَرَفاً

To exalt, honour. شَرَّفَ

To be near to ; overtop. أَشْرَفَ عَلَى

To be honoured. تَشَرَّفَ

Elevated place. Eminence. شَرَفٌ ج أَشْرَافٌ

Honour, nobility ; height. شَرَفٌ

Battlement. شُرْفَةٌ ج شُرُفَاتٌ

Noble. شَرِيفٌ ج أَشْرَافٌ

An edict by the Sultan's own hand. أَلْخَطُّ الشَّرِيف

Projecting, overlooking. مُشْرِفٌ

To rise (sun). شَرَقَ يَشْرُقُ

To go eastward. شَرَّقَ

To rise, shine, beam. أَشْرَقَ

East ; Orient. شَرْق

Eastern ; Oriental. شَرْقِيٌّ

East ; Orient. Levant. مَشْرِقٌ ج مشَارِق

To share with. شَارَكَ مُشَارَكَةً

To take a partner. أَشْرَكَ فِي

To be a polytheist. أَشْرَكَ بِاللهِ
To share. اشارَكَ وَاشْتَرَكَ
Polytheism. شِرْكٌ
Snare. شَرَكٌ ج أَشْرَاكٌ
Company; partnership. شِرْكَةٌ
Shoe-string. شِرَاكٌ ج شُرُكٌ
Partner. شَرِيكٌ ج شُرَكَاءُ
Polytheist, idolater. مُشْرِكٌ
Associate. Subscriber. مُشْتَرِكٌ
Common to several. مُشْتَرَكٌ
To split, slit. شَرَمَ يَشْرُمُ شَرْماً
To be split. شَرِمَ وَتَشَرَّمَ وَانْشَرَمَ
Split, rent. شَرْمٌ ج شُرُومٌ
Cocoon. شَرْنَقَةٌ ج شَرَانِقُ
To be greedy for. شَرِهَ يَشْرَهُ إِلَى
Inordinate desire. شَرَهٌ وَشَرَاهَةٌ
Greedy. Glutton. شَرِهٌ وَشَرْهَانُ
Trowsers. شِرْوَالٌ وَسِرْوَالٌ
To buy. شَرَى يَشْرِي شِرَاءً وَشِرًى

To buy. إِشْتَرَى
Purchase. شِرَاءٌ وَشِرًى
Nettle-rash; urticaria. شَرًى
Artery. شَرْيَانٌ ج شَرَايِينُ
Buyer. شَارٍ وَمُشْتَرٍ ج شُرَاةٌ
Jupiter (planet). اَلْمُشْتَرِي
To look askance at. شَزَرَ يَشْزُرُ شَزْراً إِلَى
To be distant. شَسَعَ يَشْسَعُ شُسُوعاً
Very remote, distant. شَاسِعٌ
Water-closet. (شِشْمَةٌ)
Sample. (شِشْنَةٌ)
Fish-hook. شِصٌّ ج شُصُوصٌ
To go beyond bounds. شَطَّ فِي
Shore, bank. شَطٌّ ج شُطُوطٌ
Excess. Injustice. شَطَطٌ
Shore. Coast. شَاطِئٌ ج شَوَاطِئُ
To cut into strips. Deviate. شَطَبَ يَشْطُبُ
To divide, halve. شَطَرَ يَشْطُرُ
To balve with another. شَاطَرَ

Half ; part. شَطْرٌ ج شُطُورٌ

Wicked ; sharper. شَاطِرٌ ج شُطَّارٌ

Divided into halves. مَشْطُورٌ

Adjacent, neighbouring. مُشَاطِرٌ

Chess. شَطْرَنْجٌ

To wash ; rinse. شَطَفَ يَشْطُفُ شَطْفًا

To be rebellious. شَيْطَنَ وَتَشَيْطَنَ

Devilishness. شَيْطَنَةٌ

Satan, devil. شَيْطَانٌ ج شَيَاطِين

Splinter. Fibula. شَظِيَّةٌ ج شَظَايَا

To disperse. شَعَّ يَشِعُّ شَعَاعًا

To be dispersed. شَعَّ يَشِعُّ

To emit rays. أَشَعَّ

Sun-beam. شُعَاعٌ ج أَشِعَّةٌ وَشَعَاعٌ

To ramify. تَشَعَّبَ وَٱنْشَعَبَ

Mountain-pass. شِعْبٌ ج شِعَابٌ

People, nation. شَعْبٌ ج شُعُوبٌ

Branch. Portion. شُعْبَةٌ ج شُعَبٌ

The eighth lunar month. شَعْبَانُ

Ramified. مُشَعَّبٌ

To juggle. شَعْبَذَ

Juggler. مُشَعْبِذٌ

To be dishevelled. شَعِثَ وَتَشَعَّثَ

To know ; feel. شَعَرَ يَشْعُرُ بِ

To inform. أَشْعَرَهُ بِ

Poetry, verse. شِعْرٌ ج أَشْعَارٌ

Hair. شَعْرٌ ج شُعُورٌ

A hair. شَعْرَةٌ ج شَعَرَاتٌ

Poetical. شِعْرِيٌّ

Sirius, Dog-Star. أَلشِّعْرَى

Would that I knew ! لَيْتَ شِعْرِي

Hairy, shaggy. أَشْعَرُ ج شُعْرٌ

Rites. شِعَارٌ وَشَعَائِرُ

Trellis-work. شَعْرِيَّةٌ ج شَعْرِيَّاتٌ

Poet. شَاعِرٌ ج شُعَرَاءُ

Knowing, perceiving. شُعُورٌ

Barley. شَعِيرٌ

Sense (sight, &c.) مَشْعَرٌ ج مَشَاعِرُ

To kindle. شَعَلَ يَشْعَلُ وَشَعَّلَ وَاشْعَلَ

To be kindled. شَعَلَ وَٱشْتَعَلَ

To be enraged. إِشْتَعَلَ غَضَبًا

Firebrand, flame. شُعْلَةٌ ج شُعَلٌ

Burning wick. شَعِيلَةٌ ج شُعُلٌ

Conflagration. إِشْتِعَالٌ

Lamp ; torch. مِشْعَلٌ ج مَشَاعِلُ

Palm-Sunday. عِيدُ ٱلشَّعَانِينِ

To juggle. شَعْوَذَ

Jugglery. شَعْوَذَةٌ

Juggler. مُشَعْوِذٌ

To stir up discord, evil. شَغَبَ يَشْغَبُ

Discord, tumult ; revolt. شَغْبٌ

To inflame with love. شَغَفَ حُبًّا

To be smitten. شَغِفَ بِ

Passionate love. شَغَفٌ

Passionately taken up. مَشْغُوفٌ

To occupy. شَغَلَ يَشْغَلُ

To divert from. شَغَلَ عَنْ

To busy, occupy much. شَغَّلَ

To be occupied. To act. إِشْتَغَلَ

Occupation, work. شُغْلٌ ج أَشْغَالٌ

Busying affair. شَاغِلٌ ج شَوَاغِلُ

Occupation. إِشْتِغَال

Occupied ; busy. مَشْغُولٌ

To be very fine, transparent. شَفَّ يَشِفُّ

Thin, fine dress. شَفٌّ ج شُفُوفٌ

Transparent. شَفَّافٌ

Transparency. شُفُوفٌ

Edge, border. شُفْرٌ ج أَشْفَارٌ

Blade. شَفْرَةٌ ج شِفَارٌ

Border of a valley. شَفِيرُ ٱلْوَادِي

To plead, intercede. Couple, double. شَفَعَ يَشْفَعُ

To make double. شَفَّعَ

Right of pre-emption. شُفْعَةٌ

Intercession, mediation. شَفَاعَةٌ

Intercessor. شَافِعٌ وَشَفِيعٌ ج شُفَعَاءُ

To pity. شَفِقَ يَشْفَقُ وَأَشْفَقَ عَلَى

شَفَقٌ Evening twilight.

شَفَقَة Compassion ; tenderness.

شَفُوق وَشَفِيق Compasionate.

شَافَهَ To speak mouth to mouth.

شَفَةٌ ج شَفَاة وَشَفَهَاتٌ وَشَفَوَاتٌ Lip.

شَفَهِيٌّ وَشَفَوِيٌّ Labiat.

مُشَافَهَةً وَشِفَاهًا By word of mouth.

شَفَى يَشْفِي شِفَاءً مِنْ To cure, heal.

أَشْفَى عَلَى To be very near.

إِشْتَفَى To recover (one's health).

إِسْتَشْفَى To seek a cure.

شِفَاء Cure, recovery.

شَفًا Brink, edge, extremity.

شَافٍ Curing, healing.

جَوَابٌ شَافٍ A clear answer.

مُسْتَشْفًى وَدَارُ ٱلشِّفَاء Hospital.

شَقَّ يَشُقُّ شَقًّا To split, cleave.

شَقَّ مَشَقَّةً عَلَى To trouble, distress.

شَقَّ ٱلْعَصَا To rebel.

شَقَّقَ To split into pieces

إِنْشَقَّ To be split or separated.

شَقٌّ ج شُقُوقٌ Split, rent ; crack.

شَقٌّ وَمَشَقَّة Great hardship.

شِقٌّ Half, one side of a thing.

شُقَّةٌ ج شُقَقٌ Piece of cloth.

شَاقٌّ Troublesome, hard.

شِقَاق Separation, discord.

شَقِيقٌ ج أَشِقَّاء Full brother.

شَقَائِقُ ٱلنُّعْمَان Red anemone.

إِشْتِقَاقٌ Derivation of a word.

إِنْشِقَاقٌ Separation, division.

مَشَقَّةٌ ج مَشَاقٌّ Great hardship.

مُشْتَقٌّ Derived (word).

شُقْرَة Light red, sorrel colour.

أَشْقَرُ Of fair complexion, sorrel.

شِقِرَّاق The green wood pecker.

شَقْشَقَةُ ٱللِّسَان Verbosity.

شَقَعَ يَشْقَعُ شَقْعًا To pile up.

شَقَّفَ To split, cut into pieces.

شَقَفَةٌ ج شَقَفٌ Earthen pot ; piece.

شَقَلَ يَشْقُلُ شَقْلًا To lift up.

شَقِيَ يَشْقَى To be miserable.

شَقِيَ فِي To labour, toil.

شَاقَى To struggle with.

أَشْقَى To make miserable.

شَقًا وَشَقَاءٌ وَشَقَاوَةٌ Misery.

شَقِيٌّ ج أَشْقِيَاءُ Miserable.

شَكَّ يَشُكُّ وَتَشَكَّكَ فِي To doubt.

شَكَّ To pierce through.

شَكَّكَ فِي To throw into doubt.

شَكٌّ ج شُكُوكٌ Uncertainty, doubt.

شَكَّةٌ Thrust (of a lance, &c.)

شَاكُّ السِّلَاحِ Armed.

مَشْكُوكٌ فِيهِ Doubtful, uncertain.

شَكَرَ يَشْكُرُ وَتَشَكَّرَ لِ To thank.

شُكْرٌ وَشُكْرَانٌ ج شُكُورٌ Thanks.

شَاكِرٌ وَشَكُورٌ Thankful.

شَوْكَرَانٌ وَشَيْكَرَانٌ Hemlock.

شَكِسَ يَشْكُسُ To be stubborn.

شَكِسٌ وَشَكُسٌ Refractory.

شَكَلَ يَشْكُلُ واشْكَلَ عَلَى To be obscure.

شَكَلَ وَشَكَّلَ To tether, tie up.

شَاكَلَ To resemble.

تَشَكَّلَ To be fashioned, shaped.

تَشَاكَلَ To resemble one another.

إِشْتَكَلَ To be ambiguous.

إِسْتَشْكَلَ To deem dubious.

شَكْلٌ ج أَشْكَالٌ Likeness ; form. Fashion. Kind, sort. Vowel point.

شِكَالٌ ج شُكُلٌ Tether.

شَاكِلَةٌ ج شَوَاكِلُ Side. Way.

مُشَاكَلَةٌ وَتَشَاكُلٌ Resemblance.

مُشْكِلٌ ج مَشَاكِلُ Difficulty.

شَكِيمَةٌ Mouth-bit.

شَكَا يَشْكُو إِلَى To complain to.

To complain of pain. شَكَا أَلَمًا
To complain. تَشَكَّى وَٱشْتَكَى إِلَى
Complaint ; accusation. شَكَايَةٌ
Plaintiff. شَاكٍ وَمُشْتَكٍ
Accused. مَشْكُوٌّ وَمُشْتَكَى عَلَيْهِ
To be paralyzed. شَلَّ يَشَلُّ وَشَلَّ
To paralyze, disable. أَشَلَّ
Paralysis. شَلَلٌ
Cataract. شَلَّالٌ ج شَلَّالَاتٌ
To strip, undress. شَلَحَ يَشْلَحُ
To strip, plunder. شَلَّحَ
Mantle. مَشْلَحٌ
Body after decay. شِلْوٌ ج أَشْلَاءٌ
Darnel-grass. شَيْلَمٌ
To smell. شَمَّ يَشَمُّ شَمًّا
To make one smell. شَمَّمَ وَأَشَمَّ
Sense of smell. شَمٌّ
A fragrant, striped melon. شَمَّامٌ
To rejoice at the affliction of an enemy. شَمِتَ يَشْمَتُ شَمَاتَةً بِ
To disappoint. شَمَّتَ
To be high, lofty. شَمَخَ يَشْمَخُ
To be high ; be proud. تَشَامَخَ
High ; proud. شَامِخٌ ج شُمَّخٌ
Pride, haughtiness. تَشَامُخٌ
Proud, haughty. مُتَشَامِخٌ
To tuck up a garment. شَمَرَ يَشْمُرُ
To be ready for. تَشَمَّرَ وَٱنْشَمَرَ لِ
Fennel. شَمْرَةٌ وَشَمَارٌ
To abhor. شَمَزَ يَشْمُزُ مِنْ
To shrink from. اِشْمَأَزَّ ٱشْمِئْزَازًا
To be sunny. شَمِسَ يَشْمُسُ وَأَشْمَسَ
To be restive. شَمَسَ يَشْمُسُ
To expose in the sun. شَمَّسَ
Sun. شَمْسٌ ج شُمُوسٌ
Solar. شَمْسِيٌّ
Umbrella ; sun-shade. شَمْسِيَّةٌ
Deacon. شَمَّاسٌ ج شَمَامِسَةٌ
Restive, refractory. شَمُوسٌ

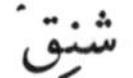

Exposed to the sun. مُشَمَّسٌ

Whiteness, hoariness. شَمَطٌ

Gray-haired, graizzled. أَشْمَطُ

To wax ; cover with wax. شَمَّعَ

Wax. شَمْعٌ ج شُمُوعٌ

Wax-candle. شَمَعَةٌ ج شَمَعَاتٌ

Waxed. Oil-cloth. مُشَمَّعٌ

Candlestick. شَمْعَدَانٌ

To shift to north. شَمَلَ يَشْمُلُ

To take the left side. شَمَلَ يَشْمُلُ

To include, contain. شَمِلَ يَشْمُلُ

To comprise, contain. إِشْتَمَلَ عَلَى

Union. شَمْلٌ

Comprehensive ; general. شَامِلٌ

Left side ; north. شِمَالٌ

Northern, northerly. شَمَالِيٌّ

Endowed. Included. مَشْمُولٌ

Beet (root). شَمَنْدَرٌ وَشُمُنْدُرٌ

To attack. شَنَّ وَأَشَنَّ ٱلْغَارَةَ عَلَى

To hate, detest. شَنَأَ وَشَنِئَ يَشْنَأُ

Hatred, detestation. شَنْءٌ

Hater, enemy. شَانِئٌ ج شُنَّاءٌ

Hated ; hateful. مَشْنُوءٌ

Moustache. شَنَبٌ ج اشْنَابٌ

A grain-measure. شُنْبُلٌ ج شَنَابِلُ

Spasmodic contraction. تَشَنُّجٌ

Nature, disposition. شِنْشِنَةٌ ج شَنَاشِنُ

To be bad. شَنُعَ يَشْنُعُ شَنَاعَةً

To disgrace, revile. شَنَعَ شَنْعًا

To accuse him of evil. شَنَّعَ عَلَيْهِ

To regard as foul. إِسْتَشْنَعَ

Infamy, ugliness. شُنْعَةٌ وَشَنَاعَةٌ

Foul, ugly. شَنِعٌ شَنِيعٌ وَأَشْنَعُ

To embellish. شَنَّفَ

Ear-ring. شَنْفٌ ج شُنُوفٌ

To hang. شَنَقَ يَشْنِقُ شَنْقًا

Hanging. شَنْقٌ

Longing, yearning. شَنِقٌ وَشَانِقٌ

Cord, rope. شِنَاقٌ ج أَشْنِقَة

Gibbet, gallows. مِشْنَقَةٌ ج مَشَانِقُ

Hanged. مَشْنُوق

Gray colour. شُبْهَةٌ وَشَهَبٌ

Meteor. شِهَابٌ ج شُهُبٌ

Gray. أَشْهَبُ م شَهْبَاء ج شُهْبٌ

Aleppo. اَلشَّهْبَاء

To witness, be present. شَهِدَ يَشْهَدُ

To witness against. شَهِدَ يَشْهَدُ عَلَى

To bear witness to. شَهِدَ بِ

To be an eye-witness; see. شَاهَدَ

Call to witness. أَشْهَدَ وَٱسْتَشْهَدَ

To die as a martyr. أُسْتُشْهِدَ

Honeycomb. شُهْدٌ ج شِهَادٌ

Eye-witness. شَاهِدٌ ج شُهُودٌ

Testimony. Diploma. شَهَادَةٌ

Martyrdom. شَهَادَةٌ وَٱسْتِشْهَادٌ

Witness. Martyr. شَهِيدٌ ج شُهَدَاء

Assembly. Aspect. مَشْهَدٌ

Vision, sight, scene. مُشَاهَدَة

To make public. شَهَرَ يَشْهَرُ

To make known, publish. أَشْهَرَ

To become known; be celebrated; notorious. إِشْتَهَرَ

Month. شَهْرٌ ج شُهُورٌ وَأَشْهُرٌ

Celebrity, fame, repute. شُهْرَة

Celebrated, notorious. شَهِيرٌ

Well-known. مَشْهُورٌ ج مَشَاهِيرُ

According to usage. عَلَى ٱلْمَشْهُور

To draw the breath. شَهَقَ يَشْهَقُ

A single cry. شَهْقَة

High, lofty. شَاهِقٌ ج شَوَاهِقُ

Inspiration and expiration in breathing. اَلشَّهِيقُ وَٱلزَّفِيرُ

A mixture of two colours. شَهَلٌ

To be sagacious. شَهُمَ يَشْهُمُ

Honourable. شَهْمٌ ج شِهَامٌ

Sagacity. Honour. شَهَامَة

Falcon. شَاهِينٌ ج شَوَاهِين

شَهَا يَشْهُو To crave for.

شَهَّى To excite a desire.

إِشْتَهَى To desire eagerly.

شَهْوَةٌ ج شَهَوَاتٌ Strong desire, appetite, passion, lust.

شَهِيٌّ وَمُشْتَهًى Desired, pleasant.

شَهَوَانِيٌّ Sensual.

أَشْهَى More desirable, delicious.

إِشْتِهَاءٌ Desire, craving.

مُشْتَهًى ج مُشْتَهَيَاتٌ Craved.

شَابَ يَشُوبُ شَوْبًا To mix.

شَائِبَةٌ ج شَوَائِب Blemish.

شُوحَةٌ A species of kite.

أَشَارَ إِلَى To point out or at.

أَشَارَ عَلَى بِ To counsel, advise.

شَاوَرَ وَاسْتَشَارَ To consult.

تَشَاوَرَ عَلَى To consult together.

مَشْوَرَةٌ وَمَشُورَةٌ Consultation.

أَهْلُ الشُّورَى Councillors.

مَجْلِسُ الشُّورَى Council.

إِشَارَةٌ Sign ; signal ; allusion.

إِسْمُ الإِشَارَةِ Demonstrative pronoun.

مُشَارٌ إِلَيْهِ Indicated, referred to.

مُشِيرٌ Councillor ; minister.

مُسْتَشَارٌ Councillor.

شَوْرَبَةٌ Soup.

شَوَّشَ To trouble, confuse.

تَشَوَّشَ To be confused ; sick.

شَاشٌ Thin muslin.

شَاوِيشٌ (جَاوِيشٌ) Sergeant.

شُوشَةٌ Hair of head.

تَشْوِيشٌ Confusion. Sickness.

مُشَوَّشٌ Confused. Ill.

أَشْوَصُ م شَوْصَاءُ Squint-eyed.

شَافَ يَشُوفُ شَوْفًا To see.

شَوَّفَ To show.

شَاقَ وَشَوَّقَ إِلَى To fill with longing.

تَشَوَّقَ وَاشْتَاقَ إِلَى To long for.

Strong desire. شَوْقٌ ج أَشْوَاق

Desirable, charming. شَائِقٌ

Ardently longing. مُشْتَاقٌ

To pierce with a thorn. شَاكَ وَشَوَّكَ

Thorns, prickles. شَوْكٌ ج أَشْوَاكٌ

A thorn, sting. شَوْكَةٌ

Shawl. شَالٌ ج شَالَاتٌ

Desert. شَوْلٌ ج أَشْوَالٌ

Large sack. شُوَالٌ ج شُوَالَاتٌ

The tenth lunar month. شَوَّالٌ

Watch-tower. Barn. شُونَةٌ ج شُوَن

To disfigure. شَوَّهَ

To be ugly, disfigured. تَشَوَّهَ

Deformity, ugliness. شَوَهٌ

Deformed ugly. أَشْوَهُ م شَوْهَاءُ

King ; Shah, (*Persian*). شَاهٌ

Royal, imperial. شَاهَانِيٌّ

Sheep, lamb. شَاةٌ ج شاءٌ وشِيَاهٌ

Ugly, deformed. Stupid. شَوٌّ

To roast, broil (meat). شَوَى يَشْوِي

To be roasted, grilled. إِنْشَوَى

Roasted, grilled. شَوِيٌّ وَمَشْوِيٌّ

Gridiron. مِشْوًى ومِشْوَاةٌ

To will, wish, desire. شَاءَ يَشَاءُ

Thing, something. شَيْءٌ ج أَشْيَاءُ

Gradually. شَيْئًا فشَيْئًا

A small thing ; a little. (شُوَيَّةٌ)

Will, wish, desire. مَشِيئَةٌ

To become gray. شَابَ يَشِيبُ

To make gray. أَشَابَ وَشَيَّبَ

Old age. شَيْبٌ وَمَشِيبٌ

White or hoary beard. شَيْبَةٌ

Hoary ; old. شَائِبٌ وَأَشْيَبُ

Cotton-prints. شِيتٌ

Artemesia ; wormwood. شِيحٌ

To grow old. شَاخَ يَشِيخُ وَشَيَّخَ

Old man, Sheikh. شَيْخٌ ج شُيُوخٌ

Religious Chief of the Moslems. شَيْخُ الإِسْلَامِ

شَيْخُوخَةٌ Old age.

مشيخَةٌ Republic. Senate.

شادَ يَشيدُ وَشَيَّد To build up.

مَشيدٌ و مُشَيَّدٌ High, elevated.

شَاطَ يَشيطُ To be slightly burnt.

إِسْتَشاطَ عَلَى To get angry.

شَيْطانٌ Satan, devil.

مُسْتَشيطٌ Inflamed by anger.

شَاع يشيعُ To be spread abroad.

شاعَ ب وَأَشَاعَ To publish.

شَيَّعَ To see a guest off.

شَايَعَ To escort, follow.

أَشاعَ ٱلْخَبَرَ To publish the news.

شيعَةٌ Party, sect ; the Shites.

شيعِيٌّ A Shite.

شَائِعٌ وَمُشاعٌ Public ; common.

مُشَايِعٌ ل Partisan of.

شَالَ يَشيلُ شَيْلاً To lift up, carry.

شيَالَةٌ To trade of a porter.

شَيَّالٌ A porter.

شَامَةٌ ج شَامَاتٌ Black spot ; mole.

أَلشّامُ Syria.

شيمَةٌ ج شِيَمٌ Character, nature.

كَرِيمُ ٱلشِّيَم Of noble qualities.

شانَ يَشينُ شَيْناً To disgrace.

شَيْنٌ A disgraceful thing.

شَايٌ Tea.

ص

ص As a numeral sign=90.

صَبَّ يَصُبُّ صَبًّا To pour out.

صَبَّ عَلَى To dart or rush upon.

صَبَّ يَصَبُّ صَبَابَةً To be in love.

أَصَبَّ To descend.

إِنْصَبَّ To be poured out. Incline.

صَبٌّ Longing lover.

صُبَّةٌ Catarrh of the nose.

صَبَابَةٌ Excessive love or desire.

صَبِيبٌ Poured forth.

مَصَبّ Mouth of a river.

صَابِئٌ ج صَابِئُونَ Sabian.

صَبُحَ يَصْبُحُ To be handsome.

صَبَّحَ To bid good morning.

أَصْبَحَ To rise in the morning.

أَصْبَحَ عَالِمًا He became learned.

أَصْبَحَ يَفْعَلُ To take to doing.

صُبْحٌ ج أَصْبَاحٌ Dawn. Morning.

صُبْحَةٌ Early part of forenoon.

صَبَاحٌ Morning.

صَبَاحَةٌ Beauty, comeliness.

صَبِيحَةٌ Morning.

مِصْبَاحٌ ج مَصَابِيحُ Lamp.

صَبَرَ يَصْبِرُ To be patient. Confine.

صَبَّرَ To ask one to be patient. Embalm Ballast.

تَصَبَّرَ وَاصْطَبَرَ To be patient.

صَبْرٌ Patience, endurance.

صَبِرٌ وَصَبْرٌ Aloe. Aloe-plant.

صَابِرٌ ج صَابِرُونَ Patient.

صَبَّارٌ وَصَبُورٌ Very patient.

صَبِّرٌ	Cactus.
صَابُورَةٌ	Ballast (of a ship).
صَابُورِيَّة	A kind of basket.
أُصْبُعٌ ج أَصَابِعُ	Finger, toe.
مُصَبَّعٌ	Gridiron.
صَبَغَ يَصْبُغُ	To dye, colour.
إِصْطَبَغَ	To be baptized ; dyed.
صِبْغٌ وَصِبَاغٌ	Dye ; paint.
صِبْغَةٌ	Dye. Religion. Baptism.
صَبَّاغٌ	Dyer.
صِبَاغَةٌ	Art of dyeing.
مَصْبَغَةٌ	A dye-house.
صَبَّنَ وَصَوْبَنَ	To wash with soap.
صَبَّانٌ	Soap-maker.
صَابُونٌ	Soap.
مَصْبَنَةٌ	Soap factory.
صَبَا ـُ إِلَى	To incline to, long for.
أَلصَّبَا	Light east-wind.
الصِّبَا	Youth, boyhood. Love.
صَبْوَةٌ	Youth.
صَبِيٌّ ج صُبْيَانٌ	Boy, youth.
صَبِيَّةٌ ج صَبَايَا	Young woman.
صَحَّ يَصِحُّ	To recover from disease. To be sound ; true.
صَحَّحَ تَصْحِيحاً	To cure a sick person. Correct ; render sound.
صِحَّةٌ	Health. Soundness. Truth.
صَحِيحٌ ج أَصِحَّاءُ	Healthy, sound. True.
إِصْحَاحٌ ج إِصْحَاحَاتٌ	Chapter.
تَصْحِيحٌ	Correction.
صَحِبَ يَصْحَبُ وَصَاحَبَ	To accompany.
تَصَحَّبَ لِ	To take the part of.
تَصَاحَبَ مَعْ	To associate with.
إِصْطَحَبَ	To associate together.
صُحْبَةٌ	Companionship.
صَاحِبٌ ج أَصْحَابٌ	Friend. Owner.
صَاحِبُ مَالٍ	Wealthy.
مَصْحُوبٌ	Accompanied.
صَحْرَاءُ ج صَحْرَاوَاتٌ	Desert.

To alter a word. صحّفَ تَصْحِيفاً

Large plate. صَحْفَةٌ ج صِحَافٌ

A written page. صَحِيفَةٌ ج صَحَائِفُ

The Koran. مُصْحَفٌ ج مَصَاحِفُ

Plate (for food). صَحْنٌ ج صحونٌ

Court (of a house). صَحْنُ الدَّارِ

To become clear (sky) صَحَا يَصْحُو وَصَحِيَ يَصْحَى

To recover consciousness after intoxication or sleep.

To rouse. أَصحى

Fair weather; clear sky. صَحْوٌ

Mental clearness. صَحْوَةٌ

Clear (sky); conscious. صَاحٍ

To shout, clamour. صخبَ

Clamourous. صخِبٌ وَصَخُوبٌ

Rock. صخرٌ وَصَخْرَةٌ ج صُخورٌ

Rocky; stony. صخِرٌ وَمُصْخِرٌ

To turn away from. صَدَّ يَصُدُّ عَنْ

To oppose; prevent. صَدَّ صَدًّا

Aversion; opposition. صَدٌّ

Subject in hand. صَدَدٌ

Pus; matter. صَدِيدٌ

To become rusty. صَدِئَ يَصْدَأُ

To confront; face. تصدَّى لِ

Rust. صَدَأٌ

To sing. صَدَحَ يَصْدُحُ

Singer. صَادِحٌ

To take place; occur. صَدَرَ ـُ

To proceed from. صَدَرَ مِنْ

To arise, result from. صَدَرَ عَنْ

To go to. صدرَ إِلَى

To begin (a book) with. صَدَّرَ بِ

To show forth; issue. أَصْدَرَ

Chest; bosom. صَدْرٌ ج صُدُورٌ

The first part. Chief.

Prime Minister. أَلصَّدْرُ الأَعْظَمُ

Vest. صدْرِيَّةٌ صَدَارَةٌ

The office of Prime Minister. صَدَارَةٌ

Going out. صَادِرٌ

(*opp. to* وارد coming in).

مَصْدَرٌ ج مَصَادِرُ Origin; source. Noun of action.

صُدِعَ وَصُدِّعَ To have a sprain.

صَدَّعَ To trouble; annoy.

إِنْصَدَعَ To be sprained.

صَدْعٌ ج صُدُوعٌ Fissure. Sprain.

صُدَاعٌ Headache.

صَدَغَ يَصْدَغُ إِلَى To incline to.

صُدْغٌ ج أَصْدَاغٌ Temple; temporal region.

صَدَفَ يَصْدُفُ To meet by chance.

صَادَفَ مُصَادَفَةً To encounter.

تَصَدَّفَ To happen by chance.

تَصَادَفَ To meet together.

صَدَفٌ Sea-shells.

صَدَفَةٌ ج صَدَفَاتٌ A see-shell.

صُدْفَةٌ ج صُدَفٌ Chance.

صَدَقَ يَصْدُقُ To say the truth.

يَصْدُقُ عَلَى It applies correctly to.

صَدَّقَ To believe. Verify.

صَادَقَ To treat as a friend.

صَادَقَ عَلَى To ratify, confirm.

تَصَدَّقَ To give alms, charity.

صِدْقٌ Truth; veracity; sincerity.

صَدَقَةٌ ج صَدَقَاتٌ Alms; charity.

صَدَاقٌ Dower given to a wife.

صَدَاقَةٌ True friendship.

صَادِقٌ True, sincere.

صَدِيقٌ ج أَصْدِقَاءُ True friend.

صِدِّيقٌ ج صِدِّيقُونَ Righteous.

أَصْدَقُ More, most, true.

تَصْدِيقٌ Belief; faith. Verification.

مُصَدِّقٌ Believer. Verifying. Confirming.

مُتَصَدِّقٌ One who gives alms.

صَيْدَلَةٌ An apothecary's trade.

صَيْدَلَانِيٌّ ج صَيَادِلَةٌ Druggist.

صَيْدَلِيَّةٌ A pharmacy.

صَدَمَ يَصْدِمُ To strike; repel.

صَادَمَ To dash against; thrust.

تَصَادَمَ وَٱصْطَدَمَ To collide.
صَدْمَةٌ Shock, collision.
أَصْدَى إِصْدَاءً To return an echo.
صَدًى ج أَصْدَاءٌ Echo ; sound.
صَرَّ يَصُرُّ صَرًّا To tie up.
صَرَّ يَصِرُّ Creak ; chirp ; tingle.
أَصَرَّ عَلَى To persist in.
صُرَّةٌ ج صُرَرٌ Parcel ; packet.
إِصْرَارٌ Persistence.
صَرِيرٌ Grating noise.
صَرُحَ يَصْرُحُ To be pure, clear.
صَرَّحَ To make clear proclaim.
صَرِيحٌ Pure, clear. Explicit.
صَرَاحَةٌ Clearness. Purity.
تَصْرِيحٌ Clear expression.
صَرَخَ يَصْرُخُ To cry out.
صَرْخَةٌ A loud cry.
صُرَاخٌ وَصَرِيخٌ Cries, screams.
صَارِخٌ Crying out.

صَرْصَرٌ Intense cold.
صُرْصُرٌ وَصُرْصُورٌ A cockroach.
رِيحٌ صَرْصَرٌ Violent, cold wind.
صِرَاطٌ Way ; path.
صَرَعَ يَصْرَعُ To strike down.
صُرِعَ To have a fit.
صَارَعَ وَتَصَارَعَ To wrestle.
إِنْصَرَعَ To be thrown down.
صَرْعٌ Epilepsy.
صَرِيعٌ وَمَصْرُوعٌ Epileptic.
مِصْرَاعٌ ج مَصَارِيعُ Hemistich.
Half of a folding door.
مُصَارِعٌ Wrestler, combatant.
صَرَفَ يَصْرِفُ To send away ;
change or spend (money).
صَرَفَ عَنْ To avert from.
صَرَفَهُ إِلَى To turn him to.
صَرَّفَ To conjugate, decline.
صَرَّفَ فِي To commit to.
تَصَرَّفَ To be inflected.

تَصَرَّفَ في	To carry out.
إِنْصَرَفَ	To depart; be inflected.
صَرْفٌ	Etymology.
صِرْفٌ	Pure, unmixed.
صُرُوفُ ٱلدَّهْرِ	Evils of fortune.
صِرَافَةٌ	Broker's trade ; brokerage.
صَرَّافٌ ج صَيَارِفَةٌ	Money-changer.
إِنْصِرَافٌ	Departing, going off.
تَصَرُّفٌ	Freedom of action.
تَصْرِيفٌ	Inflection of words.
تَصَارِيفُ الدَّهْرِ	Vicissitudes of time.
مَصْرُوفٌ مَصَارِيفُ	Expense.
مُتَصَرِّفٌ	Having free action. Inflected word. Governor.
مُتَصَرِّفِيَّةٌ	A governor's district.
مُتَصَرِّفٌ	A word capable of inflection.
صَرَمَ يَصْرِمُ	To cut off, sever.
تَصَرَّمَ وَٱنْصَرَمَ	To cease.
صَارِمٌ ج صَوارِمُ	Sharp severe.
صَرَامَةٌ	Severity.
(صُرْمَايَةٌ ج صَرَامِيُّ)	Shoe.
الْعَامُ ٱلْمُنْصَرِمُ	The past year.
صَارٍ وَصَارِيَةٌ ج صَوَارٍ	Mast.
مِصْطَبَةٌ ج مَصَاطِبُ	Platform.
صَعُبَ يَصْعُبُ	To be difficult.
صَعَّبَ وَتَصَعَّبَ	To make difficult.
إِسْتَصْعَبَ	To find difficult.
تَصَعَّبَ وَاسْتَصْعَبَ	To be difficult.
صَعْبٌ ج صِعَابٌ	Difficult, hard.
صُعُوبَةٌ	Difficulty.
مَصَاعِبُ	Difficulties, troubles.
صَعْتَرٌ (أَوْ سَعْتَرٌ)	Thyme.
صَعِدَ يَصْعَدُ صُعُوداً	To ascend.
صَعِدَ ب	To take or carry up.
أَصْعَدَ	To cause to ascend.
صَعْدَاءُ	Distress, calamity.
صُعَدَاءُ	Sighing, deep sigh.
مِنَ ٱلآنَ فَصَاعِداً	Henceforth.

صَعِيدٌ Earth. Elevated land.

صَعِيدُ مِصْرَ Upper Egypt.

مَصْعَدٌ ج مَصَاعِدُ Place of ascent.

صَعَقٌ Vehement sound, cry.

صَاعِقَةٌ ج صَوَاعِقُ Thunderbolt.

صُعْلُوكٌ ج صَعَالِيك Poor, pauper.

صَغُرَ يَصْغُرُ To be small.

صَغِرَ يَصْغَرُ To be base.

صَغَّرَ وَأَصْغَرَ To make small.

صَغَّرَ ٱلإِسْمَ To change a noun into the diminutive form.

تَصَاغَرَ To become small, or base.

إِسْتَصْغَرَ To esteem as little.

صِغَرٌ وصَغَارَةٌ Smallness.

صَاغِرٌ ج صَاغِرُونَ Adject.

صَغِيرٌ ج صِغَارٌ Little, small.

صَغِيرَةٌ ج صَغَائِرُ A small sin.

أَصْغَرُ Smaller, younger; least.

ٱلصُّغْرَى The minor proposition of a syllogism.

تَصْغِيرٌ Act of diminishing.

مُصَغَّرٌ Noun in the diminutive form.

صَغَا يَصْغُو إِلَى To incline to.

صَغَا وَأَصْغَى إِلَى To listen to.

إِصْغَاءٌ Attention, listening.

صَفَّ يَصُفُّ To set in a line.

إِصْطَفَّ To take position in line.

صَفٌّ ج صُفُوفٌ Row, line, class.

مَصَفٌّ ج مَصَافُّ Line of battle.

صَفَحَ ـَ To consider, examine.

صَفَحَ ـَ عَنْ To turn away from, leave. Pardon, forgive.

صَفَّحَ To cover with plates (metal).

صَفَّحَ بِٱلْيَدِ To clap the hands.

صَافَحَ مُصَافَحَةً وصِفَاحاً To take by the hands (in saluting).

تَصَفَّحَ To examine attentively.

صَفْحٌ Forgiveness.

ضَرَبَ عَنْهُ صَفْحاً To disregard.

صَفْحَةٌ ج صَفَحَاتٌ Page of a book.

صَفُوحٌ Generous, forgiving.

صَفِيحَة ج صَفَائِحُ Plate of metal.

مُصَافَحَة Grasp of the hand.

مُصَفَّح Broad, flat. Plated.

صَفَدَ يَصْفِدُ To shackle, fetter.

صَفَدٌ ج أَصْفَادٌ Bond, fetter.

صَفَرَ يَصْفِرُ صَفِيراً To whistle.

صَفِرَ يَصْفَرُ صَفَراً To be empty.

صَفَّرَ To make, or dye, yellow.

صَفَّرَ وأَصْفَرَ To make vacant.

أَصْفَرَ To become poor.

إِصْفَرَّ To become yellow, pale.

صُفْرٌ ج أَصْفَارٌ Empty.

صِفْرُ ٱلْيَدَيْنِ Having nothing.

صِفْرٌ وسِفْرٌ ج أَصْفَارٌ Zero.

صَفَرٌ Second month of lunar year.

صُفْرَةٌ Yellowness, paleness.

صَافُورَةٌ وَصُفَّيْرَةٌ Whistle.

صُفَارُ ٱلْبَيْضِ Yolk of an egg.

صُفَارِيَّةٌ Golden oriole.

أَصْفَرُ م صَفْرَاءُ ج صُفْرٌ Yellow.

صَفْرَاءُ (Yellow) bile.

مُصْفِرٌ A poor man, destitute.

صَفْصَفٌ Desert, plain.

صَفْصَافٌ Willow, osier.

صَفَعَ يَصْفَعُ صَفْعاً To slap.

صَفْعَةٌ A slap.

صَفَقَ يَصْفُقُ صَفْقاً To strike; flap.

صَفُقَ يَصْفُقُ صَفَاقَةً To be strong.

صَفَّقَ To clap the hands.

اِصْفَقَ عَلَى To agree upon.

تَصَافَقُوا They ratified a compact.

صَفَقٌ ج صُفُوقٌ Side, flank, face.

صَفْقَةٌ Contract, bargain.

صِفَاقٌ Fascia; aponeurosis.

صَفِيقٌ Thick, firm (texture).

صَفَنٌ ج أَصْفَانٌ Scrotum.

صَافِنٌ ج صَوَافِنُ Saphena vein.

صَفَا يَصْفُو To be clear.

To purify, filter. صفّى وأصفى

To be sincere. صافى وأصفى الودّ

To choose, select. إصطفى

Smooth stone. صفا ج أصفاء

Serenity of life, pleasure. صفاء

Clearness. صفو وصفاء وصفوة

Pure ; chosen. صفيّ ج أصفياء

Pure, lear, climpid. صافٍ

Strainer. مصفاة ج مصافٍ

Purified, filtered. مصفّى

Chosen. مصطفى

To strike. صقر يصقر

Hawk. صقر ج أصقر

Hell. صقر

A pickaxe. صاقور

To be covered with frost. صقع

To be cold, icy. صقع

Region, district. صقع ج اصقاع

Intenseness of cold. صقعة

Hoar-frost. صقيع

To polish, give lustre. صقل يصقل

Staging. صقالة ج صقائل

Polisher. صقال ج صياقلة

Polished. Sword. صقيل

Sclav. صقلبيّ ج صقالبة

To strike coin (money). صكّ يصكّ

To trip, stumble. صكّ يصكّ

To strike each other. إصطكّ

A legal deed. صكّ ج صكوك

Deadly serpent. صلّ ج أصلال

To crucify. صلب يصلب صلباً

To become hard, tough. صلب يصلب

To render hard. To make the sign of the cross. صلّب

To become hard, firm. تصلّب

Crucifixion. صلب وتصليب

The loins. صلب ج أصلاب

Hardness, firmness. صلابة

Cross. صليب ج صلبان

صليبيٌّ ج صَلِيبِيَّةٌ	Crusader.
مُصَالَبَةً	Crosswise.
مُصَلَّبٌ	Crossing at right angles.
مَصْلُوبٌ ج مَصَالِيبُ	Crucified.
صَلْت	Fair ; wide.
صَوْلَجَانٌ وَصَوْلَجَانَة	Sceptre.
صَلَحَ يَصْلُحُ	To be good, right.
صَلَحَ لِ	To be suitable, good for.
صَالَحَ مُصَالَحَةً	To make peace.
صَالَحَ عَلَى	To agree upon.
أَصْلَحَ	To repair, improve.
أَصْلَحَ بَيْنَ	To make peace between (two parties).
تَصَالَحَ وَٱصْطَلَحَ	To be reconciled.
إِصْطَلَحَ	To become better.
إِصْطَلَحَ عَلَى	To agree upon....
صُلْحٌ	Peace, reconciliation.
صَالِحٌ	Good ; fit ; just. (one's good, self-interest).
صَالِحَةٌ ج صَالِحَاتٌ	A good deed.
صَلَاحٌ	Goodness, virtue.
إِصْلَاحٌ	Reformation ; improvement.
إِصْطِلَاحٌ	Technical use.
إِصْطِلَاحِيٌّ	Conventional.
مُصْلِحٌ	Peacemaker, reformer.
مَصْلَحَةٌ ج مَصَالِحُ	Advantage. Department.
مُصَالَحَةٌ	Reconciliation.
صَلَدَ يَصْلُدُ صَلَداً	To be hard.
صَلْصَلَ وَتَصَلْصَلَ	To sound.
صِلْصَالٌ	Clay.
صَلَح	Baldness of the head.
صَلَعَةٌ وَصُلْعَةٌ	Bald spot.
أَصْلَعُ م صَلْعَاءُ ج صُلْعٌ	Bald.
صَلْعَمَ	*Abbreviation of the formula:* صَلَى ٱللهُ عَلَيْهِ وَسَلم
صَلَفَ يَصْلَفُ وَتَصَلَّفَ	To boast.
صَلَفٌ	Boasting.
صَلَّى صَلَاةً أَوْ صَلَوةً	To pray.
صَلَّى عَلَى	To pray for ; bless.
صَلَاةٌ ج صَلَوَاتٌ	Prayer. Mercy.

مُصَلًّى Place of prayer.

مُصَلٍّ One who prays.

صَلَى يَصْلِي To roast, broil.

أَصْلَى To put into the fire.

تَصَلَّى وَٱصْطَلَى بِالنَّارِ To warm one's self by the fire.

صِلَاءٌ Fuel ; fire.

صَمَّ يَصُمُّ صَمًّا To stop (a flask).

صَمَّ وَأَصَمَّ To become deaf.

صَمَّمَ عَلَى To determine upon.

صَمَمٌ Deafness.

صِمَامٌ Stopper, cork. Valve.

مِنْ صَمِيمِ ٱلْقَلْبِ Most sincerely.

أَصَمُّ م صَمَّاءُ ج صُمٌّ Deaf.

حَجَرٌ أَصَمُّ Hard stone.

جِذْرٌ أَصَمُّ A surd root.

صَمَتَ يَصْمُتُ صَمْتاً To be silent.

صَمَّتَ وَأَصْمَتَ To silence.

صَمْتٌ وَصُمَاتٌ وَصُمُوتٌ Silence.

مُصْمَتٌ Solid (not hollow).

صِمَاخٌ ج أَصْمِخَةٌ Canal of the ear.

صَمَدَ يَصْمُدُ صَمْداً To arrange ; adorn.

صَمَّدَ To lay up, save.

صَمَدٌ Solid ; not hollow.

أَلصَّمَدُ The Eternal (God).

صَوْمَعَةٌ ج صَوَامِعُ Cell of a recluse.

صَمَّغَ To gum, put gum into.

صَمْغٌ ج صُمُوغٌ Gum.

أَلصَّمْغُ ٱلْعَرَبِيُّ Gum Arabic.

أَصَنَّ To have a fetid odour.

صَنَّةٌ وَصُنَانٌ Stench.

صُنْبُورٌ Tube, pipe.

صَنَوْبَرٌ Pine tree.

صَنَوْبَرِيٌّ Cone-shaped.

صَنْجٌ ج صُنُوجٌ Cymbal.

صِنْدِيدٌ ج صَنَادِيدُ Valiant.

صُنْدُوقٌ ج صَنَادِيقُ Chest, trunk.

صَنْدَلٌ Sandal-wood.

صِنَّارَةٌ ج صَنَانِيرُ Fish-hook.

صَنَعَ يَصْنَعُ To make, construct.

صَنَّعَ To arrange skilfully.

صَانَعَ مُصَانَعَةً To coax, flatter.

تَصَنَّعَ To effect good manners.

إصْطَنَعَ To make ; have made.

صُنْعٌ Act of making ; deed.

صُنْعٌ Good deed ; benefit.

صَنْعَةٌ Work. Carft, trade.

صِنَاعَةٌ ج صِنَاعَاتٌ Craft, trade, industry. Art.

أَصْحَابُ ٱلْحِرَفَ Artisans.

صَانِعٌ ج صُنَّاعٌ Maker, artisan.

صِنَاعِيٌّ Artificial.

صَنِيعَةٌ ج صَنَائِعُ Deed. Good deed.

تَصَنُّعٌ Affectation.

مَصْنَعٌ وَمَصْنَعَةٌ ج مَصَانِعُ Factory.

مُصَنَّعٌ Affected ; artificial.

مَصْنُوعٌ Made. Fabricated.

صَنَّفَ To assort ; compose.

صِنْفٌ ج صُنُوفٌ Sort, kind.

مُصَنَّفٌ ج مُصَنَّفَاتٌ Literary work.

مُصَنِّفٌ Author.

صَنَمٌ ج أَصْنَامٌ Idol. Camel's hump.

صَهْ Hush ! Be silent !

صَهَبٌ وَصُهْبَةٌ A reddish colour.

أَصْهَبُ م صَهْبَاءُ ج صُهْبٌ Reddish.

يَوْمٌ أَصْهَبُ A very cold day.

اَلصَّهْبَاءُ (Red) wine.

صَهَرَ يَصْهَرُ To melt. Smite.

صَاهَرَ To become related. to by marriage.

صِهْرٌ ج أَصْهَارٌ Son-in-law, brother-in-law.

صِهْرِيجٌ ج صَهَارِيجُ Water-tank.

صَهَلَ يَصْهَلُ To neigh (horse).

صَهِيلٌ وَصُهَالٌ Neighing.

صَابَ ـُ وَأَصَابَ To hit the mark.

صَوَّبَ To approve. Point, aim.

أَصَابَ To attain one's pnrpose.

To be right. أَصَابَ فِي قَوْلِهِ

To do right. أَصَابَ فِي عَمَلِهِ

To assail, smite. أَصَابَ

To descend, (rain). أَنْصَابَ

To hold to be right. إِسْتَصْوَبَ

Side, course, direction. صَوْبٌ

Right, correct. صَائِبٌ وَمُصِيبٌ

What is right, correct. صَوَابٌ

Struck, stricken. مُصَابٌ

Affliction. مُصِيبَةٌ ج مَصَائِبُ

To make a noise. صَاتَ يَصُوتُ وَصَوَّتَ

Sound, voice. صَوْتٌ ج أَصْوَاتٌ

Reputation, fame. صِيتٌ

To fashion, shape, picture. صَوَّرَ

To imagine. صَوَّرَ لَهُ

To be formed. To imagine. تَصَوَّرَ

Tyre (city). Horn, trumpet. صُورٌ

Picture, form. صُورَةٌ ج صُوَرٌ

Imagination, idea. تَصَوُّرٌ

Sculptor. Painter. مُصَوِّرٌ

Young chick. صُوصٌ ج صِيصَانٌ

To measure grain. صَاعَ يَصُوعُ

A measure for grain. صَاعٌ

To form, fashion. صَاغَ يَصُوغُ صَوْغًا

Pure, unmixed. صَاغٌ

Money at its legal value. صَاغٌ

Grammatical form. صِيغَةٌ ج صِيَغٌ

Goldsmith. صَائِغٌ ج صَاغَةٌ وَصُيَّاغٌ

Goldsmith's art. صِيَاغَةٌ

Jewelry. مَصَاغٌ

To become a *Sûfi*. تَصَوَّفَ

Wool. صُوفٌ ج أَصْوَافٌ

A tuft of wool. صُوفَةٌ

Tinder, agaric. صُوفَانٌ

Religious mystic ; *Sûfi*. صُوفِيٌّ

To overpower, subdue. صَالَ يَصُولُ عَلَى

To clean wheat. صَوَّلَ ٱلْحِنْطَةَ

To soak, slake. صَوَّلَ

صَوْلَةٌ Power ; rule ; force.

صُوَالَةٌ Rubbish, refuse matter.

مِصْوَلٌ ج مَصَاوِلُ Implement for cleaning wheat ; trough.

صَوْلَجَانٌ Sceptre.

صَامَ يَصُومُ صَوْماً وَصِيَاماً To fast.

صَامَ عَنْ To abstain from.

صَوَّمَ To cause to fast.

صَوْمٌ وَصِيَامٌ Fast ; abstinence.

صَائِمٌ ج صُوَّامٌ وَصِيَّمٌ Fasting.

صَوْمَعَةٌ ج صَوَامِعُ Hermit's cell.

صَانَ يَصُونُ To keep, preserve, guard.

صَوَّنَ To enclose with a wall.

صَوْنٌ وَصِيَانَةٌ Act of preserving.

صَوَّانَةٌ ج صَوَّانٌ Flint, flint-stone.

مَصُونٌ Guarded, preserved.

صَاحَ يَصِيحُ To cry out ; crow, (cock).

صَاحَ بِ To call out to.

صَاحَ عَلَى To cry out against.

صِيَاحٌ Cry ; crowing of a cock.

صَيْحَةٌ Cry, shout.

صَيَّاحٌ Clamorous (man).

صَادَ يَصِيدُ وَتَصَيَّدَ وَاصْطَادَ To hunt; trap, snare ; catch fish

صَيْدٌ Hunting, fishing ; game.

صَيَّادٌ Hunter, fisherman.

صَيْدَاءُ Sidon (city).

مِصْيَدَةٌ ج مَصَايِدُ Trap, snare.

مَصِيدٌ Prey taken in hunting.

صَيْدَلَةٌ Pharmacy.

صَيْدَلَانِيٌّ Druggist.

صَارَ يَصِيرُ To become ; change into.

صَارَ لَهُ To happen to, befall.

صَارَ يَفْعَلُ To begin to do.

صَارَ مَصِيراً إِلَى To arrive at.

صَيَّرَ To cause to become.

صِيرَةٌ ج صِيَرٌ Fold (for sheep).

صَيْرُورَةٌ Act of becoming.

مَصِيرٌ Destination, end, result.

صَافَ يَصِيفُ To pass the summer.

صَيْفٌ Summer.

صَيْفِيٌّ Belonging to summer.

يَوْمٌ صَائِفٌ A hot day.

مَصِيفٌ Summer residence.

أَلصِّينُ China.

صِينِيٌّ Chinese, Chinese porcelain.

صِينِيَّةٌ Tray.

صِيوَانٌ Large tent. Pavilion.

صِيوَانُ ٱلأُذُن External ear.

ض

ض As a numeral sign=800.

ضَأضَأَ To shout in battle.

ضَوْضَى وَضَوْضَاءُ Shouts of war.

ضَئِيلٌ ج ضُؤَلَاءُ Thin ; small.

ضَأْنٌ Sheep, (*coll noun*).

ضَبَّ وَاضَبَّ على To grasp, keep.

ضَبٌّ ج ضِبَابٌ Lizard.

ضَبَابَةٌ ج ضَبَابٌ Mist ; thin cloud.

ضَبَطَ يَضْبطُ ضَبْطاً To guard. Do a thing well ; perfect.

ضَبَطَ عَلَى To withhold, restrain.

ضَبْطٌ Exactness, correctness.

ضَابِطٌ ج ضَوَابِطُ Rule ; canon.

ضَابِطٌ ج ضُبَّاطٌ Military officer.

ضَابِطُ ٱلْكُلِّ Almighty (God).

ضَابِطِيٌّ ج ضَابِطِيَّةٌ Policeman.

Written sentence, decision. (*law*). مَضْبَطَةٌ ج مَضَابِطُ

Well-regulated ; exact. مَضْبُوطٌ

Hyena. ضَبْعٌ وَضَبُعٌ ج ضِبَاعٌ

To cry, shout. ضَجَّ يَضِجُّ وَأَضَجَّ

To contend with. ضَاجَّ

Tumult, cry. ضَجَّةٌ وضَجِيجٌ

To be irritated, impatient, bored. ضَجِرَ يَضْجَرُ وَتَضَجَّرَ مِنْ

To bore, vex, distress. أَضْجَرَ

Uneasiness. ضَجَرٌ وَضُجْرَةٌ

Uneasy ; irritable. ضَجِرٌ وَمُتَضَجِّرٌ

Vexing, distressing. مُضْجِرٌ

To lie down. ضَجَعَ يَضْجَعُ وَاضَّجَعَ

To lie with (a woman). ضَاجَعَ

To make one to lie down. أَضْجَعَ

Bed-fellow. ضَجِيعٌ

Bed, bed-chamber. مَضْجَعٌ ج مَضَاجِعُ

To laugh. ضَحِكَ يَضْحَكُ ضَحِكاً

To laugh at. ضَحِكَ مِنْ وَعَلَى

To make one laugh. أَضْحَكَ

Pleasantry. ضُحْكَةٌ وَاضْحُوكَةٌ

Comic, causing laughter. مُضْحِكٌ

To appear. ضَحَا يَضْحُو ضَحْواً

To come in the morning. ضَحَّى

To sacrifice an animal. ضَحَّى بِ

To show, reveal. أَضْحَى وَضَحَّى عَنْ

He took to laughing. أَضْحَى يَضْحَكُ

ضَحَاءٌ وَضَحْوَةٌ وَضحىً وَضَحِيَّةٌ

Early morning after sunrise.

Sacrifice. ضَحِيَّةٌ ج ضَحَايَا

Suburb, region. ضَاحِيَةٌ ج ضَوَاحٍ

Bright ; cloudless. أَضْحَى م ضَحْيَاءُ

Day of sacrifice. يَوْمُ ٱلأَضْحَى

(tenth of the month. ذُو ٱلْحِجَّةِ)

To be large. ضَخُمَ يَضْخُمُ

Large bulk ; corpulence. ضَخَامَةٌ

Large ; heavy. ضَخْمٌ ج ضِخَامٌ

To overcome. ضَدَّ يَضُدُّ

ضادَّ مُضَادَّةً To oppose.

تَضَادَّ تَضَادًّا To disagree.

ضِدٌّ ج أَضْدَادٌ Contrary; enemy.

ضِدَّانِ Two opposites.

تَضَادٌّ Contrast ; opposition.

ضَرَّ يَضُرُّ وَأَضَرَّ بِ To injure.

تَضَرَّرَ To receive an injury.

إِضْطَرَّ إِلَى To force, compel.

اضْطُرَّ إِلَى To be forced.

ضُرٌّ وَضَرَرٌ Harm ; evil.

ضَرَّاءُ Adversity.

ضَرَّةُ ٱلْمَرْأَةِ ج ضَرَائِرُ A fellow-wife to a woman's husband.

ضَرُورَةٌ ج ضَرُورَاتٌ Necessity.

بالضَّرُورَةِ وَضَرُورَةً Necessarily.

ضَرُورِيٌّ Indispensable.

ضَرُورِيَّاتٌ Necessary things.

ضَرِيرٌ ج أَضِرَّاءُ Blind.

إِضْطِرَارٌ Necessity.

مُضِرٌّ Injurious, harmful.

مَضَرَّةٌ Injury ; means of harm.

ضَرَبَ يَضْرِبُ ضَرْبًا To strike.
Multiply, (*Arith*). Pitch (tent). Strike (money).

ضَرَبَ عَلَى To impose a tax.

ضَرَبَ عَنْهُ صَفْحًا To overlook.

ضَرَبَ إِلَى ٱلسَّوَادِ To incline to blackness.

ضَرَبَ فِي ٱلْبُوقِ To blow a trumpet.

ضَرَبَ فِي ٱلْأَرْضِ To travel.

ضَرَبَ مَثَلًا To give a parable.

أَضْرَبَ To be silent.

أَضْرَبَ عَنْ To quit, cease.

ضَارَبَ مُضَارَبَةً To speculate.

تَضَارَبَ To fight together.

إِضْطَرَبَ To be agitated.

إِضْطَرَبَ ٱلأَمْرُ To be confused.

ضَرْبٌ Multiplication. (*Arith*).

ضَرْبٌ ج ضُرُوبٌ Kind, form.

ضَرْبَةٌ ج ضَرَبَاتٌ	A blow, stroke.
ضَارِبٌ	Striking. Multiplier.
ضَرِيبَةٌ ج ضَرَائِبُ	Impost, tax.
إِضْطِرَابٌ	Agitation.
مَضْرَبٌ ج مَضَارِبُ	Large tent.
مَضْرُوبٌ	Struck. Multiplicand.
مُضَارِب	Sharer in traffic.
مُضْطَرِبٌ	Agitated, confused.
ضَرَجَ يَضْرِجُ ضَرْجًا	To smear.
ضَرَّجَ	To dye red. Adorn.
ضَرِيحٌ ج ضَرَائِحُ	Grave.
ضَرِسَ يَضْرَسُ	To be set on edge (teeth).
ضَارَسَ	To contend with.
ضِرْسٌ ج أَضْرَاسٌ	Molar tooth.
أَضْرَاسُ ٱلْعَقْلِ	Wisdom teeth.
مُضَرَّسٌ	Experienced man.
ضَرَعَ يَضْرَعُ إِلى	To beseech.
ضَارَعَ مُضَارَعَةً	To resemble.
تَضَرَّعَ إِلى	To beseech.
ضَرْعٌ ج ضُرُوعٌ	Udder.
تَضَرُّعٌ	Prayer with humility.
مضارِعٌ	Present-future tense of verbs; (*e.g.* يَضْرِبُ)
ضِرْغَامٌ	Lion. Brave man.
ضَرِمَ يَضْرَمُ وَأَضْطَرَمَ	To burn, blaze.
أَضْرَمَ	To kindle a fire.
إِضْطَرَمَ	To be kindled.
ضِرَامٌ	Firewood. Blazing.
مُضْطَرِمٌ	Blazing.
ضَارٍ ج ضَوَارٍ	Rapacious animal.
ضِعَةٌ	Humiliation, (*from* وَضَعَ).
ضَعْضَعَ ضَعْضَعَةً	To pull down, rase.
ضَعُفَ يَضْعُفُ	To be weak, feeble.
ضَعَّفَ يُضَعِّفُ وَضَاعَفَ	Te double.
أَضْعَفَ	To weaken , enfeeble.
تَضَاعَفَ	To be doubled.
ضُعْفٌ	Weakness, feebleness.
ضِعْفٌ ج أَضْعَافٌ	Double.

ضَعِيفٌ ج ضُعَفَاءُ Weak, feeble.

ضَغَثَ يَضْغَثُ To mix, confuse.

ضَغَطَ يَضْغَطُ ضَغْطاً To press, squeeze.

إِنْضَغَطَ To be pressed.

ضَغْطَةٌ Pressure. Compulsion.

ضَاغُوطٌ Night-mare.

ضَغِنَ يَضْغَنُ عَلَى To bear malice.

تَضَاغَنَ To bear malice or hatred against each other.

ضَغِنٌ Spiteful, malevolent.

ضِغْنٌ ج أَضْغَانٌ Hatred, malice.

ضَغِينَةٌ ج ضَغَائِنُ Malice, spite.

ضِفَّةٌ Side of a river.

ضِفْدَعٌ ج ضَفَادِعُ Frog.

ضَفَرَ يَضْفِرُ وَضَفْرٌ To braid, plait.

إِنْضَفَرَ To be braided, twisted.

ضَفِيرَةٌ ج ضَفَائِرُ Braid; tress.

ضَفَا يَضْفُو To be ample.

ضَلَّ يَضِلُّ To err; wander from.

أَضَلَّ إِضْلَالاً To lead into error.

ضَلٌّ وَضَلَالٌ وَضَلَالَةٌ Error.

ضَالٌّ ج ضَالُّونَ Strayed; erring.

ضَالَّةٌ A stray animal.

أُضْلُولَةٌ ج أَضَالِيلُ Error.

مُضِلٌّ Leading astray.

مَضَلَّةٌ Cause of error.

ضَلُعَ يَضْلُعُ ضَلَاعَةً To be strong.

تَضَلَّعَ To be full, strong.

ضِلْعٌ ج ضُلُوعٌ وَأَضْلَاعٌ وَأَضْلُعٌ (م) Rib. Side of a triangle, &c.

ضَلِيعٌ Strong, powerful; large.

مُضَلَّعٌ Ribbed; striped.

ضَمَّ يَضُمُّ ضَمًّا To join, add. To vocalize a letter with (ُ).

ضَمَّ عَلَى To grasp, seize.

إِنْضَمَّ To be joined, annexed.

ضَمٌّ وَضَمَّةٌ The vowel-point (ُ).

مَضْمُومٌ Collected, joined. Having the vowel-point.

إِضْمَحَلَّ To vanish.

To dress a wound. ضَمَدَ يَضْمِدُ وَضَمَّدَ
Dressing for a wound. ضِمَادٌ
Bandage. ضِمَادَةٌ
To be thin, emaciated. ضَمَرَ يَضْمُرُ
To conceal, hide. أَضْمَرَ
To resolve. أَضْمَرَ فِي نَفْسِهِ
To be shrivelled. تَضَمَّرَ وَٱنْضَمَرَ
Emaciation, atrophy. ضُمُورٌ
Secret thought. ضَمِيرٌ ج ضَمَائِرُ
Heart, Conscience. Pronoun.
Secret; understood. (*Gram*). مُضْمَرٌ
To stand surety. To farm or rent. ضَمِنَ يَضْمَنُ
To make one responsible for. To put in; inclose. ضَمَّنَ
To include, comprise. تَضَمَّنَ
Within. Inclosed. ضِمْنَ
Suretyship. Responsibility. ضَمَانٌ
Responsible for. ضَامِنٌ وَضَمِينٌ
Sense; meaning. مَضْمُونٌ ج مَضَامِينُ
Ensured; assured.

To be avaricious. ضَنَّ يَضِنُّ ضَنًّا
A prized thing. ضِنٌّ ج ضَنَائِنُ
Avaricious, stingy. ضَنِينٌ
To be larrow; feebne. ضَنُكَ يَضْنُكُ
Distress. Narrowness. ضَنْكٌ
To be sickly. ضَنِيَ يَضْنَى ضَنًى
To suffer, endure. ضَانَى مُضَانَاةً
To consume (disease). أَضْنَى
To be consumed slowly. إِنْضَنَى
Disease; weakness. ضَنًى
Sickly, emaciated. مُضْنًى
To overcome. ضَهَدَ يَضْهَدُ
To maltreat; persecute إِضْطَهَدَ
Presecution. إِضْطِهَادٌ
Persecutor. مُضْطَهِدٌ
To resemble. ضَاهَى مُضَاهَاةً
To shine; glitter. ضَاءَ يَضُوءُ
To illuminate. ضَوَّأَ تَضْوِئَةً
To shine. أَضَاءَ إِضَاءَةً

To seek light. إِسْتَضَاءَ

Light. ضِيَاءٌ وضَوْءٌ ج أَضْوَاءٌ

Light-giving ; brilliant. مُضِيءٌ

Tumult of war. ضَوْضَى وَضَوْضَاء

To injure. ضَارَ يَضِيرُ ضَيْراً

To suffer pain. تَضَوَّرَ

To be lost ; perish. ضَاعَ يَضِيعُ

To lose. Destroy. ضَيَّعَ وَأَضَاعَ

Lost. Neglected. ضَائِعٌ

Unmissed. ضَيَاعاً

Village. ضَيْعَةٌ ج ضِيَعٌ وَضِيَاعٌ

To be a guest. ضَافَ يَضِيفُ

To treat with hospitality. أَضَافَ

To join, add. To put a noun in the construct state. أَضَافَ إِلَى

To be joined. إِنْضَافَ إِلَى

To seek hospitality. إِسْتَضَافَ

Guest. ضَيْفٌ ج أَضْيَافٌ وَضُيُوفٌ

Entertainment. ضِيَافَةٌ

Annexation. إِضَافَةٌ

Two nouns in the construct state (e.g. كِتَابُ زَيْدٍ) أَلْمُضَافُ وَٱلْمُضَافُ إِلَيْهِ

Host. مُضِيفٌ

Hospitable. مِضْيَافٌ

To be narrow. ضَاقَ يَضِيقُ ضِيقاً

To be inabequate. ضَاقَ عَنْ

To make narrow. ضَيَّقَ

To annoy ; oppress. ضَايَقَ

To feel oppressed. تَضَايَقَ

Narrowness. Distress. ضِيقٌ

Poverty. Misery. ضِيقَةٌ

Narrow ; contracted. ضَيِّقٌ

Narrower. أَضْيَقُ

Narrowplace. مَضِيقٌ ج مَضَايِقُ

To oppress. ضَامَ يَضِيمُ ضَيْماً

Wrong ; injury. ضَيْمٌ

ط

ط — As a numeral sign=9.

طاطا — To bend down.

تطاطا — To be depressed, abased.

طبّب تطبيباً — To treat the sich.

طبّ — Medical treatment.

علم الطبّ — The science of medicine.

طبّيّ — Medical.

طبيب ج أطبّاء — Physician.

طبخ يطبخ طبخاً — To cook.

انطبخ — To be cooked.

طبخ — Cooking. Food cooked.

طبّاخ — Cook.

طباخة — Art of cookery.

طبيخ — Cooked food.

مطبخ ج مطابخ — Kitchen.

مطبوخ — Cooked.

طبرية — Tiberias.

طابور — Battalion.

طباشير — Chalk.

طبع يطبع — To stamp. Print.

طبّع — To break in (a horse).

تطبّع — To assume a character.

انطبع — To be imprinted.

طبع ج طباع — Natural disposition.

طباعة — Art of printing.

طبيعة ج طبائع — Nature.

طبيعيّ — Natural. Naturalist.

علم الطبيعيّات — Physics.

مطبعة ج مطابع — Printing-press.

مطبوع — Impressed, printed.

To fit, suit. طَابَقَ مُطَابَقَةً

To make to agree. طَبَّقَ وطَابَقَ بَيْنَ

To cover, close, shut. أَطْبَقَ

To agree upon. أَطْبَقَ عَلَى

To agree. تَطَابَقَ

To apply to something. إِنْطَبَقَ عَلَى

Suitable, conformable to. طِبْقٌ

Cover. Tray. طَبَقٌ ج أَطْبَاقٌ

Layer ; stratum. طَبَقَةٌ ج طَبَقَاتٌ
Class ; Grade. Stage.

A hard year سَنَةٌ مُطْبِقَةٌ

Conformable to. مُطَابِقٌ

Agreement, accord. مُطَابَقَةٌ

To beat the drum. طَبَّلَ

Drum. طَبْلٌ ج طُبُولٌ

Drummer. طَبَّالٌ

Pistol. طَبَنْجَةٌ ج طَبَنْجَاتٌ

To fry. طَجَنَ يَطْجُنُ طَجْناً

Frying-pan. طَاجِنٌ ج طَوَاجِنُ

To strain in breathing. طَحَرَ يَطْحِرُ

Straining. طَحَارٌ وَطَحِيرٌ

Spleen. طِحَالٌ ج طُحُلٌ

Water-moss. طُحْلُبٌ وَطِحْلِبٌ

To rush upon. طَحَمَ يَطْحَمُ عَلَى

Impetuous ; violent. طَحُومٌ

To grind (flour). طَحَنَ يَطْحَنُ طَحْناً

Miller. طَحَّانٌ

Mill. طَاحُونٌ وَطَاحُونَةٌ ج طَوَاحِينُ

Grinders, (teeth). طَوَاحِنُ

Flour. طَحِينٌ

Dregs of sesame-oil. طَحِينَةٌ

Mill-machine. مِطْحَنَةٌ

Mill. مِطْحَنَةٌ ج مَطَاحِنُ

All ; every one. طُرًّا

To happen to. طَرَأَ يَطْرَأُ عَلَى

To overwhelm with praise. اطْرَأَ

Fresh, juicy, moist. طَرِيٌّ

Unexpected calamity. طَارِئَةٌ

Exaggerated praise. إِطْرَاءٌ

To be joyful. طَرِبَ يَطْرَبُ طَرَباً

To sing, chant, trill. طَرَّبَ

To gladden. طَرَّبَ وَأَطْرَبَ

Mirth, glee. طَرَبٌ

One who feels merry. طَرِبٌ

Exciting mirth or delight. مُطْرِبٌ

Red cap, fez. طَرْبُوشٌ ج طَرَابِيشُ

To throw. Subtract. طَرَحَ يَطْرَحُ

Casting. Subtraction. طَرْحٌ

Abortion, miscarriage. طِرْحٌ

Veil worn by a female. طَرْحَةٌ

Sheet of paper. طَرْحِيَّةُ وَرَق

Cushion to sit on. طَرَّاحَةٌ

Cast down. طَرِيحَةٌ ج طَرْحَى

Place. مَطْرَحٌ ج مَطَارِح

Tarragon. طَرْخُونٌ (نَبَاتٌ)

To drive awry ; chase. طَرَدَ يَطْرُدُ

To attack, charge, assault. طَارَدَ

To be sent away. اِنْطَرَدَ

To follow regularly. اِطَّرَدَ

To digress. اِسْتَطْرَدَ اسْتِطْرَاداً

Bale of goods. طَرْدٌ ج طُرُودٌ

Attack ; charge ; pursuit. طِرَادٌ

Expelled, outcast. طَرِيدٌ

Chased game. طَرِيدَةٌ ج طَرَائِدُ

Having no exception. مُطَّرِدٌ

To embroider. طَرَّزَ

Form, shape, manner. طَرْزٌ

Mode, manner. طِرَازٌ

Embroiderer. طَرَّازٌ وَمُطَرِّزٌ

Embroidered. مُطَرَّزٌ

To be deaf. طَرِشَ يَطْرَشُ

To whitewash. (طَرَشَ يَطْرُشُ)

Deafness. طَرَشٌ

Lime for whitewashing. (طَرْشٌ)

Whitewasher. (طَرَّاشٌ)

Deaf. اطْرَشُ م طَرْشَاء ج طُرْشٌ

A high pointed cap. طَرْطُورٌ

To hurt the eye. طَرَفَ يَطْرِفُ

To go to an extreme. تَطَرَّفَ

The eye. طَرْفٌ

The eyelid. طَرْفُ ٱلْعَيْنِ

Side. End part. طَرَفٌ ج اطْرَافٌ

Limbs, extremities. ألاطْرَافُ

Choice subjects of conversation. أطْرَافُ ٱلْحَدِيثِ

The lower classes. أطْرَافُ ٱلنَّاسِ

Twinkling of an eye. طَرْفَةٌ

Tamarisk (tree). طَرْفَاءُ

To strike, knock. طَرَقَ يَطْرُقُ طَرْقاً

To be silent. أطْرَقَ

To find or seek a way. تطَرَّقَ إِلى

To take a way. إِسْتَطْرَقَ

Calamity; evil. طَارِقَةٌ ج طَوَارِقُ

Way; road, path. طَرِيقٌ ج طُرُقٌ

Way; manner. طَرِيقَةٌ ج طَرَائِقُ

Hammer. مِطْرَقَةٌ ج مَطَارِقُ

Beaten (road). مَطْرُوقٌ وَ مُسْتَطْرَقٌ

Cabin of a ship. طَارِمَةٌ

To soften, moisten. طَرَّى

To praise highly. أطْرَى إِطْرَاءً

Tender; fresh; juicy. طَرِي

طَسْتٌ وطَشْتٌ ج طُسُوتٌ وَطُشُوتٌ
Basin for washing.

To graft. Vaccinate. طَعَّمَ

To give food. أطْعَمَ

To be grafted, inoculated. تَطَعَّمَ

To taste. إِسْتَطْعَمَ

Taste; flavour. طَعْمٌ ج طُعُومٌ

Bait thrown to fish. طُعْم

Food. طَعَامٌ ج أطْعِمَةٌ

Food. Place of food. مَطْعَمٌ ج مَطَاعِمُ

Thrust, pierce. طَعَنَ يَطْعَنُ بِ

To defame. طَعَنَ فِي وَعَلَى

To become old. طَعَنَ فِي ٱلسِّنِّ

A thrust. طَعْنَةٌ

Plague. طَاعونٌ ج طَوَاعِينُ

طُغْرَاءُ ج طُغْرَاءَاتٌ The Turkish Imperial cypher.

طُغْمَةٌ A company ; order.

طَغَا يَطْغُو To overflow.

طَاغٍ ج طُغَاةٌ Highly wicked.

الطَّاغُوتُ Idol. Tempter.

أَطَفَّ عَلَى To look down upon.

طَفِيفٌ Small quantity.

أَطْفَأَ To put out (fire) ; allay.

انْطَفَأَ اَنْطِفَاءً To be extinguished.

طَفَحَ يَطْفَحُ To be full ; overflow.

طَفَّحَ واطْفَحَ To fill to overflowing.

طفْحانُ وَطَافِحٌ Ove flowing.

طَفَرَ يَطْفِرُ طَفْراً To jump, leap.

طَفْرَةٌ A leap. Eruption.

طَفِقَ يَفْعَلُ To commence to do.

أَطْفَلَ To have a child, (woman).

أَطْفَلَتِ ٱلشَّمْسُ To approach setting.

تَطَفَّلَ To intrude.

طَفَلٌ Time before sunset.

طِفْلٌ ج اطْفَالٌ Infant.

طُفُولِيَّةٌ Infancy. Chil dhood.

طُفَيْلِيٌّ Intruder.

طَفَا يَطْفُو To rise high, (water).

طَفَا فَوْقَ ٱلْمَاءِ To float.

طَفَاوَةٌ Scum.

طَقَّ يَطُقُّ To make a sound.

طَقْسٌ ج طُقُوسٌ Weather. Religious rite.

طَقْطَقَ طَقْطَقَةً To make a noise.

طَقْمٌ ج طُقُومَةٌ Suit of clothes. Set.

أَطَلَّ عَلَى To look down upon.

طَلٌّ Finest rain ; dew.

مَطَلٌّ Overlooking place.

طَلَبَ يَطْلُبُ To seek ; ask ; desire.

طَلَبَ إِلى To beseech ; pray.

طَالَبَ To demand ; claim.

تَطَلَّبَ To demand repeatedly.

طَلَبٌ وَطِلْبَةٌ Desire. Request.

طَالِبٌ ج طُلَّابٌ وَطَلَبَةٌ — Seeker.

طَالِبُ عِلْمٍ — A student.

مَطْلَبٌ ج مَطَالِبُ — Demand; desire.

مَطْلُوبٌ ج مَطَالِيبُ — Claim. Object sought or desired.

طَلَحَ يَطْلَحُ طَلَاحًا — To be wicked.

طَلْحٌ — A kind of thorny acacia.

طَالِحٌ ج طُلَّحٌ وَطَالِحُونَ — Wicked.

طَلَاحٌ — Wickedness.

طَلْحِيَّةٌ ج طَلَاحِيُّ — Sheet of paper.

طَلَسَ يَطْلِسُ — To blot. Obliterate.

أَطْلَسُ — Satin. Atlas.

طَيْلَسَانٌ ج طَيَالِسَةٌ — A particular robe worn by learned men.

طَلْسَمَ — To write a talisman.

طَلْسَمٌ ج طَلَاسِمُ — Talisman.

طَلَعَ يَطْلُعُ — To rise, (sun). Sprout.

طَلَعَ وَطَلِعَ يَطْلَعُ — To ascend.

طَالَعَ مُطَالَعَةً — To study; read.

أَطْلَعَ — To appear. Sprout.

أَطْلَعَ عَلَى — To inform.

تَطَلَّعَ إِلى — To look at, or for.

إِطَّلَعَ عَلَى — To know, see.

إِسْتَطْلَعَ — To examine.

طَلْعٌ — Spadix, spathe.

طَلْعَةٌ — Face. Aspect.

طَالِعٌ ج طَوَالِع — Star (of fortune).

طُلُوعٌ — Rising; appearance.

طَلِيعَةٌ ج طَلَائِعُ — Vanguard.

مَطْلَعٌ — First line of a poem.

طَلُقَ يَطْلُقُ — To be freed.

طَلُقَ يَطْلُقُ — To have a cheerful face.

طَلَّقَ — To divorce (his wife).

أَطْلَقَ — To free, liberate.

أَطْلَقَ ٱلْقَوْل — To generalize.

أَطْلَقَ لَهُ — To permit him.

أُطْلِقَ — To be applied; apply.

إِنْطَلَقَ — To go, depart.

طَلْقٌ — Pains of childbirth.

طَلْقُ ٱلْيَدَيْنِ	Liberal.
طَلْقُ ٱلْوَجْهِ	Cheerful.
طَلْقُ ٱللِّسَانِ	Eloquent.
طَلَاقٌ	Divorce.
طَالِقٌ وَطَالِقَةٌ	Divorced (woman).
عَلَى ٱلإِطْلَاقِ وَمطْلَقًا	Absolutely.
مُطْلَقٌ	Free. Absolute.
طُلْمَةٌ ج طُلْمٌ	Loaf of bread.
طلاوَةٌ	Beauty ; grace.
طَلَى يَطْلِي	To anoint ; cover with.
طِلَاءٌ	Ointment ; tar ; plaster.
مَطْلِيٌّ	Smeared, covered.
طامَّةٌ	Calamity.
طَمَّ يَطُمُّ طَمًّا	To cover up.
إِنْطَمَّ	To be filled, covered up.
طَمْثٌ	Menstruation ; menses.
طَمَحَ يَطْمَحُ إِلى	To gaze at.
طامِحٌ وطَمُوحٌ	Aspring. Proud.
طَمَرَ يَطْمِرُ	To bury, conceal.
مُطَمَّرٌ	Accumulated.
طَمَسَ يَطْمُسُ وَطَمَّسَ	To efface.
تَطَمَّسَ وَٱنْطَمَسَ	To be effaced.
طَمِيسٌ وَمَطْمُوسٌ	Obliterated.
طَمِعَ يَطْمَعُ فِي وَب	To covet, hope.
طَمَعٌ	Covetousness ; avidity.
طَمَعٌ ج أَطْمَاعٌ	A coveted object.
طَامِعٌ وَطَمِعٌ وَطَمَّاعٌ	Covetous.
مَطْمَعٌ ج مَطَامِعُ	Thing coveted.
طَمَّنَ	To tranquillize ; reassure.
إِطْمَأَنَّ	To be low, (land). To be free fro.n disquietude.
إِطْمَأَنَّ بِٱلْمَوْضِعِ	To abide, dwell.
إِطْمَأَنَّ إِلى	To trust implicitly.
طُمَأْنِينَةٌ وَٱطْمِئْنَانٌ	Tranquility.
مُطْمَئِنٌّ	Tranquil ; composed.
طَمَا يَطْمُو	To rise high, (water).
طَامٍ	High (water, sea).
طَنَّ يَطِنُّ طَنِينًا	To buzz ; ring.
طَنِينٌ	Humming ; ringing.

طَنَّانٌ Sonorous. Wide-spread.

أَطْنَبَ فِي To be eloquent ; exert one's self in.

طُنُبٌ ج أَطْنَابٌ Tent-rope.

إِطْنَابٌ Superfluity, prolixity.

مُطْنِبٌ An immoderate praiser.

مُطَنَّبٌ Made fast with ropes.

طُنْبُورٌ ج طَنَابِيرُ Tambour.

طَنْجَرَةٌ ج طَنَاجِرُ A cooking pan.

طَنْطَنَ طَنْطَنَةً To hum, ring.

طُنُفٌ ج أَطْنَافٌ Peak.

طَنْفَسَةٌ ج طَنَافِسُ A carpet.

طَهُرَ يَطْهُرُ To be clean, pure.

طَهَّرَ To cleanse. Circumcise.

تَطَهَّرَ To be cleansed, purified.

طَهَارَةٌ Purity. Holiness.

طَاهِرٌ ج أَطْهَارٌ Pure. Holy.

مَطْهَرٌ Purgatory.

مُطَهَّرٌ Purified.

طَاهٍ ج طُهَاةٌ A cook.

طُوبٌ Brick, canon.

طُوبْجِيٌّ Gunner ; artillery-man.

طُوبَى Blessedness.

طَاحَ يَطُوحُ To perish.

طَوَّحَ وَأَطَاحَ To mislead.

تَطَوَّحَ To wander ; perish.

طَوَائِحُ وَمَطَاوِحُ Adversities.

طَوْدٌ ج أَطْوَادٌ High mountain.

مُنْطَادٌ Lofty ; rising high.

طَوْراً بَعْدَ طَوْرٍ Time after time.

طَوْرٌ ج أَطْوَارٌ State, manner.

طُورٌ Mountain.

أَلطُّورُ Mount Sinai.

طَاسٌ ج طَاسَاتٌ Drinking-cup.

طَاوُوسٌ ج طَوَاوِيسُ Peacock.

طَوْشٌ Frivolity.

طَوَاشِي ج طَوَاشِيَةٌ Eunuch; gelding.

طَاعَ يَطُوعُ وَأَطَاعَ To obey.

طَاوَعَ مُطَاوَعَةً To consent; follow.

تَطَوَّعَ — To volunteer.
إِسْتَطَاعَ — To be able.
طَوْعٌ وطَائِعٌ — Obedient.
طَوْعاً — Voluntarily ; willingly.
طَاعةٌ — Obedience ; submission.
طْوَعُ — More submissive.
إِسْتِطَاعَةٌ — Ability ; power.
تَطَوُّعٌ — Voluntary action.
مُطَاعٌ — Obeyed. Accepted.
طَافَ يَطُوفُ حَوْلَ وفي — To go around. To travel. Circumambulate.
طَوَّفَ — To lead around.
أَطَافَ ب — To surround.
طَوْفٌ — Night-police. Raft.
طُوفَانٌ — Flood ; deluge.
طَائِفَةٌ ج طَوَائِفُ — Party, sect.
طَوَافٌ — Circumambulation.
مُطَوِّفٌ — A Mecca guide.
طَاقَ يَطُوقُ وأَطَاقَ — To be able.

طَوَّقَ — To put a collar on.
طَاقٌ ج طَاقَاتٌ — Window.
طَوْقٌ ج أَطْوَاقٌ — Collar.
طَاقَةٌ — Ability. Window.
إِطَاقَةٌ — Ability ; power.
طَالَ يَطُولُ طُولاً — To be long.
طَوَّلَ وأَطَالَ — To lengthen.
طَاوَلَ في — Defer, put off.
تطَاوَلَ عَلَى — To wrong.
إِسْتَطَالَ — To be long, extend.
طَالَمَا — During a long time.
طُولٌ — Length. Duration.
خطوطُ الطُّول — Longitude.
طَائِلٌ — Advantage ; benefit.
طَاوِلَةٌ — Table.
طَوِيلٌ ج طِوَالٌ — Long. Tall.
طَوِيلُ البَاعِ — Competent.
أَطْوَلُ — Longer.
تَطْوِيلٌ — Lengthening.

Parallelogram. مُسْتَطِيلٌ

To fold, fold up. طَوَى يَطْوِي طَيًّا

To suffer hunger. طَوِيَ يَطْوَى

To be folded up. إِنْطَوَى

Folding. Traversing. طَيٌّ

Within it. فِي طَيِّهِ

Hunger. طَوًى

Folded up. مَطْوِيٌّ

To be good. طَابَ يَطِيبُ طِيبًا

To be cheerful. طَابَتْ نَفْسُهُ

To perfume. طَيَّبَ

To be perfumed. تَطَيَّبَ

To find good. إِسْتَطَابَ وَاسْتَطْيَبَ

Perfume. طِيبٌ ج أَطْيَابٌ

Ball used in play. (طَابَةٌ)

Good. In good health طَيِّبٌ

Cheerful, happy. طَيِّبُ النَّفْسِ

A good thing. طَيِّبَةٌ ج طَيِّبَاتٌ

A tax on houses, &c. (طَابُو)

How good it is ! مَا أَطْيَبَهُ

Blessedness. طُوبَى

To fly, (bird). طَارَ يَطِيرُ طَيَرَانًا

To hasten to... طَارَ إِلَى

To make to fly. طَيَّرَ أَو أَطَارَ

To draw a bad omen. تَطَيَّرَ

To be dispersed. تَطَايَرَ تَطَايُرًا

Evil augury or omen. طِيَرَة

Flight (of birds, &c.) طَيَرَانٌ

Bird. طَائِرٌ ج طَيْرٌ وَطُيُورٌ

Paper-kite. طَيَّارَاتٌ

Spreading. مُسْتَطِيرٌ

To be light-headed. طَاشَ يَطِيشُ

To miss, (an arrow). طَاشَ عَنْ

Frivolity. طَيْشٌ وَطَيَشَانٌ

Light, fickle, frivolous. طَائِشٌ

Apparition ; spectre. طَيْفٌ

To plaster with clay. طَيَّنَ

Clay ; mortar. طِينٌ ج أَطْيَانٌ

A lump of clay. طِينَةٌ

Plasterer. طَيَّانٌ

ظ

ظ	As a numeral sign=900.
ظَبْيٌ م ظَبْيَةٌ ج ظِبَاءٌ	Gazelle.
ظَرَّفَ	To adorn, embellish.
إِسْتَظْرَفَ	To deem beautiful.
ظَرْفٌ ج ظُرُوفٌ	Vessel, receptacle. Adverbial noun of time or place.
ظَرِيفٌ ج ظُرَفَاءُ	Beautiful. Witty.
ظَعَنَ يَظْعَنُ ظَعْنًا	To travel.
ظَعُونٌ ج ظُعُنٌ	Camel.
ظَعِينَةٌ ج أَظْعَانٌ	Litter for woman.
ظَفَرَ يَظْفِرُ	To scratch with the nail.
ظَفِرَ بِ وعَلَى	To obtain. Overcome.
ظَفَّرَ وأَظْفَرَ	To give victory.
ظِفْرٌ ج أَظْفَارٌ	Nail; claw; hoof.
ظَفْرٌ وظَفَرَةٌ	Pterygium.
ظَفَرٌ	Success; victory.
مُظَفَّرٌ	Victorious; conqueror.
ظَلَّ يَظَلُّ	To continue.
ظَلَّ يَفْعَلُ	To continue to act.
ظَلَّلَ وأَظَلَّ	To cover; shade.
تَظَلَّلَ بِ	To be in the shade of.
إِسْتَظَلَّ بِ	To seek the shade.
ظِلٌّ ج أَظْلَالٌ	Shade; protection.
ظُلَّةٌ ج ظِلَلٌ	Cover. Cloud.
ظَلَالٌ وظِلَالٌ وظِلَالَةٌ	Cloud.
ظَلِيلٌ ومُظِلٌّ	Giving shade.
مُظِلٌّ ومُظَلَّلٌ	Shady. Cloudy.
مَظَلَّةٌ ج مَظَالُّ	Tent. Umbrella.
ظِلْفٌ ج ظُلُوفٌ وأَظْلَافٌ	Hoof.
ظَلَمَ يَظْلِمُ	To wrong; oppress.

ظَلِمَ يَظْلَمُ وَأَظْلَمَ To be dark.

ظَلَّمَ To accuse of injustice.

تَظَلَّمَ مِنْ To accuse of injustice.

انْظَلَمَ To suffer injustice.

ظُلْم Injustice ; oppression.

ظُلْمَةٌ ج ظُلُمَاتٌ Darkness.

بَحْرُ ٱلظُّلُمَاتِ Atlantic Ocean.

ظَالِمٌ ج ظَالِمُونَ وَظَلَمَةٌ Tyrant.

ظَلَامٌ وَظَلْمَاءُ Darkness.

ظَلَّامٌ وَظَلُومٌ Great tyrant.

مَظْلَمَةٌ ج مَظَالِمُ Wrong ; injustice.

مَظْلُومٌ وَظَلِيمٌ Wronged.

ظَلِمٌ Dark ; obscure.

ظَمِئَ يَظْمَأُ To be thirsty.

ظَمْءٌ ج أَظْمَاءٌ Thirst. Longing.

ظَمِئٌ وَظَمْآنُ Thirsty ; desirous.

ظَنَّ يَظُنُّ ظَنًّا To suppose.

ظَنَّ وَاظَّنَّ وَأَظَنَّ بِ To-suspect.

ظَنٌّ ج ظُنُونٌ Supposition

ظَنَّةٌ ج ظِنَنٌ Suspicion.

مَظَنَّةٌ Presumption.

مَظْنُونٌ Supposed.

مَظْنُونَاتٌ Probable propositions.

ظَهَرَ يَظْهَرُ ظُهُوراً To appear.

ظَهَرَ عَلَى To overcome, subdue.

ظَاهَرَ مُظَاهَرَةً To aid, assist.

أَظْهَرَ To show, manifest.

تَظَاهَرَ بِ To show forth.

إِسْتَظْهَرَ بِ To seek help or aid.

إِسْتَظْهَرَ عَلَى To overcome.

ظَهْرٌ ج ظُهُورٌ Back.

عَنْ ظَهْرِ ٱلْقَلْبِ From memory.

ظُهْرٌ ج أَظْهَارٌ Mid-day ; noon.

ظَاهِرٌ Clear ; evident. External.

فِي ٱلظَّاهِرِ Apparently.

ظَاهِرَةٌ ج ظَوَاهِرُ Phenomenon.

ظُهُورٌ Appearance.

ظَهِيرَةٌ Mid-day ; hour of noon.

إِظْهَارٌ Disclosure, manifestation.

ع

ع As a numeral sign=70.

عُبٌّ ج عِبَابٌ Covering of bosom.

عُبَابٌ Torrent, billows.

عَبَأَ يَعْبَأُ عَبْأً To care for.

عَبَاءٌ وَعَبَاءَةٌ ج أَعْبِئَةٌ Woollen cloak.

عَبِثَ يَعْبَثُ عَبَثًا To play.

عَبَثٌ Play, sport. Useless.

عَبَثًا To no purpose, in vain.

عَبَدَ يَعْبُدُ To worship, adore.

تَعَبَّدَ To take one as a slave.

تَعَبَّدَ لِ To devote one's self to ...

إِسْتَعْبَدَ To enslave.

عَبْدٌ ج عَبِيدٌ Servant, slave.

أَلْعِبَادُ Mankind.

عَابِدٌ ج عَبَدَةٌ وَعُبَّادٌ Worshipper.

عِبَادَة Religious worship.

عُبُودِيَّةٌ Slavery, servitude.

تَعَبُّدٌ Self-consecration to God.

مَعْبَدٌ ج مَعَابِدُ Place of worship.

مَعْبُودٌ Object of worship.

عَبَرَ يَعْبُرُ To pass; pass away.

عَبَّرَ To cause to pass over.

عَبَّرَ عَنْ To explain.

إِعْتَبَرَ To consider.

اعْتَبَرَ بِ To take warning from.

عِبْرٌ On the other side.

عَبْرَةٌ ج عَبَرَاتٌ Tear; sobbing.

عِبْرَةٌ ج عِبَرٌ Admonition.

عِبْرِيٌّ وَعِبْرَانِيٌّ Hebrew.

عابِر سَبِيل Awayfarer.

عِبَارَةٌ Expression. Style, diction.

هٰذَا عِبَارَةٌ عَنْ This means.

عُبُورٌ Act of passing over.

عَبِيرٌ Perfume.

إِعْتِبَارٌ Consideration, regard.

تَعْبِيرٌ Explanation.

مَعْبَرٌ ج مَعَابِرُ Ferry, passage.

مُعْتَبَرٌ Esteemed ; important.

عَبَسَ يَعْبِسُ To frown.

عَابِسٌ وَعَبُوسٌ Austere, stern.

عَبَّاسٌ Very stern. Lion.

عُبُوسٌ Frowning, sternness.

عَبَطَ يَعْبِطُ عَبْطًا To injure.

أَعْبَطَ وَاعْتَبَطَ To carry off in the flower of one's age, (death).

عَبْطٌ A pure lie.

إِعْتِبَاطٌ An act without reason.

عَبِقَ ـَ To be diffused, (perfume).

عَبَقَةٌ Sense of suffocation.

عَبْقَرِيٌّ Fine, excellent.

عَبَا يَعْبُو وَعَبَّى To pack (goods).

تَعَبَّى To be filled ; arranged.

عَتَّ يَعُتُّ To importune ; rebuke.

عَتَبَ يَعْتُبُ عَلَى To blame, censure.

عَاتَبَ مُعَاتَبَةً To blame, censure.

عَتَبَةٌ ج عَتَبَاتٌ Threshold.

عِتَابٌ وَمَعْتَبَةٌ ج مَعَاتِبُ Blame.

عَتُدَ يَعْتُدُ عَتَادًا To be ready.

عَتِيدٌ About to happen ; ready.

عَتِقَ يَعْتِقُ عِتْقًا To become old.

عَتَقَ يَعْتِقُ To set free.

عَتَّقَ To make old, let grow old.

أَعْتَقَ To set free, emancipate.

عِتْقٌ Antiquity, oldness.

عَتْقٌ وَعَتَاقٌ Emancipation.

عَاتِقٌ ج عَوَاتِقُ Shoulder.

عَتِيقٌ ج عِتَاقٌ Old. Emancipated.

مُعَتَّقٌ Kept long, made old.

Freed, emancipated. مَعْتُوقٌ

Shoulder-pole. عَتَلَةٌ

Porter. عَتَّالٌ ج عَتَّالَةٌ

Porterage. عِتَالَةٌ

To become dark. عَتَمَ يَعْتِمُ وَعَتَّمَ

Darkness of night. عَتْمٌ وَعَتَمَةٌ

Obscure, dark. مُعْتِمٌ وَمُعَتِّمٌ

To be idiotic. عَتِهَ عَتَاهَةً

Idiocy, stupidity. أعَتَهٌ وَعَتَاهَة

Idiot ; mad. مَعْتُوهٌ

To be proud, rebel. عَتَا يَعْتُو عُتُوًّا

Proud rebellious. عَاتٍ ج عُتَاةٌ

Moth-worm. عُثَّةٌ ج عُثٌّ

To stumble, trip. عَثَرَ يَعْثُرُ عَثْرًا

To stumble upon. عَثَرَ يَعْثُرُ عَلَى

To cause to stumble. عَثَّرَ وَأَعْثَرَ

A false step. عَثْرَةٌ ج عَثَرَاتٌ

Young bastard. Serpent. عُثْمَانُ

To do evil, mischief. عَثَا يَعْثُو عُثُوًّا

Acting corruptly. عَاثٍ ج عُثَاةٌ

To cry out. عَجَّ يَعُجُّ عَجًّا وَعَجِيجًا

To raise the dust, (wind). عَجَّجَ

Outcry, clamour. عَجٌّ وَعَجِيجٌ

Omelet. (عُجَّةٌ)

Dust, smoke. عَجَاجٌ وَعَجَاجَةٌ

عَجِبَ يَعْجَبُ عَجَبًا مِنْ وَلِ وَتَعَجَّبَ

To wonder at. وَٱسْتَعْجَبَ مِنْ

To cause to wonder. عَجَّبَ وَأَعْجَبَ

To please. أَعْجَبَ

To be vain, conceited. اعْجَبَ بِنَفْسِهِ

Pride, vanity, self-conceit. عُجْبٌ

Astonishment. عَجَبٌ

Very wonderful. عَجَبٌ وعُجَابٌ

O wonderful يَا لَلْعَجَبِ

Wonderful, extraordinary. عَجِيبٌ

عَجِيبَةٌ ج عَجَائِبُ وَأُعْجُوبَةٌ ج أَعَاجِيبُ

Wonderful thing, marvel.

More wonderful. أَعْجَبُ

Wonder, astonishment. تَعَجُّبٌ

Vain, self-conceited. مُعْجَبٌ بِنَفْسِهِ

Knot, knob. عُجْرَةٌ ج عُجَر

A kind of melon. عَجُّورٌ

To act haughtily. تَعَجْرَفَ عَلَى

Coarseness, rudeness. عَجْرَفَةٌ

To lack strength. عَجَزَ يَعْجِزُ عَجْزاً

To render unable. عَجَّزَ وَأَعْجَزَ

Weakness, impotence. عَجْزٌ
Second hemistich of a verse.

The posterior part. عَجُزٌ ج أَعْجَازٌ

Feeble. عَاجِزٌ ج عَوَاجِزُ

Old woman. عَجُوزٌ ج عَجَائِزُ

Miracle. مُعْجِزَةٌ ج مُعْجِزَاتٌ

To be lean. عَجِفَ يَعْجَفُ عَجَفاً

Very lean. أَعْجَفُ م عَجْفَاءُ ج عِجَافٌ

To hasten. عَجِلَ يَعْجَلُ وَاسْتَعْجَلَ

To press one on. عَجَّلَ وَاسْتَعْجَلَ

Haste. عَجَلٌ وَعَجَلَةٌ وَاسْتِعْجَالٌ

Calf. عِجْلٌ ج عُجُولٌ

Cart ; wheel. عَجَلَةٌ ج عَجَلٌ

Hasty, quick. عَجُولٌ

More hasty, expeditious. أَعْجَلُ

Hastened, accelerated. مُعَجَّلٌ

Foreigners. *sp*. Persians. عَجَمٌ

Persia. أَلْعَجَمُ وَبِلَادُ ٱلْعَجَمِ

Foreign origin of a word. عُجْمَةٌ

Foreigner. أَعْجَمِيٌّ ج أَعْجَامٌ

Marked with vowel-points (letters). Obscure. مُعْجَمٌ

To knead (dough). عَجَنَ يَعْجِنُ عَجْناً

The perinæum. عِجَانٌ

Kneaded ; dough. عَجِينٌ

Kneading-trough. مِعْجَنٌ ج مَعَاجِنُ

Pastry. مُعَجَّنَاتٌ

Electuary. مَعْجُونٌ ج مَعَاجِينُ

Pressed dates. عَجْوَةٌ

To number ; regard. عَدَّ يَعُدُّ

To prepare, make ready. أَعَدَّ

To be multiplied. تَعَدَّدَ

لا يُعْتَدُّ بِهِ	Of no account.
اِسْتَعَدَّ	To be ready, prepare.
عَدَدٌ ج أَعْدَادٌ	Number.
عُدَّةٌ ج عُدَدٌ	Implements.
عَدِيدٌ	Numerous.
إِسْتِعْدَادٌ	Preparation.
تَعْدَادٌ	Enumeration.
مُعَدٌّ	Reday, prepared.
مُعْتَدٌّ بِهِ	Important.
مَعْدُودٌ	Numbered, counted.
مُسْتَعِدٌّ	Reday, prepared.
عَدَسٌ	Lentils.
عَدَسَةٌ	Lens. A small pustule.
عَدَسِيٌّ	Lenticular.
عَدَلَ يَعْدِلُ عَدْلاً	To act justly.
عَدَلَ عُدُولاً عَنْ	To deviate.
عَدَلَ بَيْنَ	To act with equity.
عَدَّلَ	To make just, equal.
عَادَلَ مُعَادَلَةً	To be equal to.
تَعَدَّلَ	To be valued at.
تَعَادَلَ	To be equal, (two things).
إِنْعَدَلَ عَنْ	To turn aside from.
إِعْتَدَلَ	To become right.
عَدْلٌ	Equity, justice.
عَادِلٌ ج عُدُولٌ	Just, equable.
عَدَالَةٌ	Justice, equity.
عَدِيلٌ وَعِدْلٌ	Like, equal.
عَدِيلَةٌ	Bag, sack.
إِعْتِدَالٌ	Equality, equity. Moderation. Equinox.
إِعْتِدَالِيٌّ	Equinoctial.
مُعَادِلٌ	Equal, like.
مُعَادَلَةٌ	Equation. Equilibrium.
مُعَدَّلٌ	Average.
مُعْتَدِلٌ	Temperate, moderate.
عَدِمَ يَعْدَمُ عَدَماً	To lack, want.
أَعْدَمَ	To deprive of ; annihilate.
إِنْعَدَمَ	To cease to exist.
عَدَمٌ	Non-existence.

عَدِيمٌ ج عُدَمَاء Lacking.

مَعْدُومٌ Non-existent.

عَدَنَ وَعَدَّنَ To manure land.

عَدْنٌ Eden. Abode.

جَنَاتُ عَدْن Paradise.

مَعْدِنٌ ج مَعَادِنُ Mine. Metal, mineral. Origin, source.

مَعْدَنِيٌّ Mineral, metallic.

عَدَا يَعْدُو عَدْواً To run.

عَدَاهُ To pass beyond it.

عَدَّى To cause to go beyond.

عَادَى To treat with enmity.

أَعْدَى To infect (disease).

تَعَدَّى To pass the limit ; transgress. Be transitive (verb).

إِعْتَدَى عَلَى To be hostile toward.

عَدَا وَمَا عَدَا Except.

عِدًّى (قَوْمٌ) Hostile party.

عَدْوَى Infection or contagion.

عَدْوَانٌ Gross injustice.

عَدَاوَةٌ Hostility, enmity.

عَدُوٌّ ج أَعْدَاء وَأَعَادٍ وعِدى Enemy.

إِعْتِدَاء وَتَعَدٍّ Injustice.

مُعْدٍ Infectious, contagious.

مُتَعَدٍّ وَمُعْتَدٍ عَلَى Unjust.

مُتَعَدٍّ Transitive (verb).

عذب يَعْذُبُ عُذُوبَةً To be sweet.

عذَّب To punish, torment.

تَعَذَّب To be punished ; suffer.

عَذْبٌ Sweet, (water).

عَذَابٌ Punishment ; torment.

عُذُوبَةٌ Sweetness, agreableness.

عَذَرَ يَعْذِر To excuse.

تَعَذَّرَ وَأَعْتَذَر To apologize.

تَعَذَّرَ عَلَى To be impossible.

إِسْتَعْذَرَ To ask to be excused.

عُذْرٌ ج أَعْذَارٌ Excuse, apology.

عَذْرَاء ج عَذَارَى Virgin.

الْعَذْرَاء The sign Virgo.

عِذَارٌ ج عُذُرٌ	Halter. Cheek.
خلعَ ٱلْعِذَارَ	To throw off restraint.
إِعْتِذَارٌ	Excuse pretext.
تَعَذُّرٌ	Difficulty, impossibility.
مَعْذِرَةٌ ج مَعَاذِرُ	Excuse.
مَعْذُورٌ	Excused, excuseable.
عذلَ يَعْذِلُ عَذْلاً	To blame.
إِعْتَذَلَ وَتَعَذَّلَ	To blame one's self.
عَذْلٌ وَعَذَلٌ	Censure, blame.
عاذِلٌ ج عُذَّالٌ	One who blames.
عَذِيَةٌ (أَرْضٌ)	Salubrious, (land).
عَرَّبَ	To arabicize a foreign word.
أَعْرَبَ	To speak clearly.
تَعَرَّبَ وَٱسْتَعْرَبَ	To become an Arab.
أَلْعَرَبُ وَعُرْبَانُ	The Arabs.
أَلْعَرَبُ أَلْعَرْبَاءُ	The pure Arabs.
عَرَبَةٌ وَعَرَبَانَةٌ	Carriage, coach.
عَرَبِي	Arabic; An Arabian.
الْعَرَبِيَّةُ	The Arabic language.
عَرَبْجِيٌّ	Coachman.
إِعْرَابٌ	Syntax; parsing.
أَعْرَابِيٌّ ج أَعْرَابٌ	Bedouin.
مُعْرَبٌ	Declinable, capable of receiving all the vowel-points.
مُعَرَّبٌ	Arabicized.
عَرْبَسَ	To embroil, trouble.
عَرْبَنَ	To give a pledge.
عُرْبُونٌ ج عَرَابِينُ	Pledge.
عَرَجَ يَعْرُجُ فِي	To ascend, mount.
عُرِجَ بِهِ	To be taken up.
عَرِجَ عَرْجاً	To limp, be lame.
عَرَّجَ وَتَعَرَّجَ عَلَى	To halt, stop at.
إِنْعَرَجَ	To incline, decline.
عَرَجٌ وَعَرَجَانٌ	Lameness.
أَعْرَجُ م عَرْجَاءُ ج عُرْجٌ	Lame.
مُنْعَرَجٌ	Sloping, Bend.
عِرْزَالٌ ج عَرَازِيلُ	Booth.
عِرْسٌ ج أَعْرَاسٌ	Husband, wife.

Wedding.	عُرْسٌ ج أَعْرَاسٌ
Weasel.	إِبْنُ عِرْسٍ
Bridegroom.	عَرِيسٌ ج عُرْسٌ
Bride.	عَرُوسٌ ج عَرَائِسُ
Throne. Booth.	عَرْشٌ ج عُرُوشٌ
Grape-vine.	عَرِيشٌ ج عَرَائِشُ
Court of a house.	عَرْصَةٌ ج أَعْرَاصٌ
To happen.	عَرَضَ يَعْرِضُ
To offer.	عَرَضَ عَلَى
To be wide, broad.	عَرُضَ يَعْرُضُ
To make broad.	عَرَّضَ
To expose to.	عَرَّضَ لِ
To oppose ; contradict.	عَارَضَ
To turn away from.	أَعْرَضَ عَنْ
To be exposed.	تَعَرَّضَ وَٱعْتَرَضَ
To interfere in.	تَعَرَّضَ لِ
To review an army.	إِعْتَرَضَ ٱلْجُنْدَ
To be in the way of.	إِعْتَرَضَ دُونَ
To oppose, object to.	اعْتَرَضَ عَلَى

Breadth, width.	عَرْضٌ ج عُرُوضٌ
Latitude.	خُطُوطُ ٱلْعَرْضِ
Day of Judgment.	يَوْمُ ٱلْعَرْضِ
Petition.	عَرْضُحَالٍ ج عَرْضُحَالَاتٍ
Honour.	عِرْضٌ ج أَعْرَاضٌ
Accident.	عَرَضٌ ج اعْرَاضٌ
By chance, accidentally.	عَرَضاً
Accidental.	عَرَضِيٌّ
Cross-beam.	عَارِضَةٌ ج عَوَارِضُ
Science of prosody.	عِلْمُ ٱلْعَرُوضِ
Broad.	عَرِيضٌ ج عِرَاضٌ
Opposition, objection.	إِعْتِرَاضٌ
Exposition.	مَعْرِضٌ
Opposition, contradiction.	مُعَارَضَةٌ
Offered, presented.	مَعْرُوضٌ
Transverse; obstructing.	مُعْتَرِضٌ
Parenthetic clause.	جُمْلَةٌ مُعْتَرِضَةٌ
Juniper-tree.	عَرْعَرٌ
To know.	عَرَفَ يَعْرِفُ

عَرَّفَ To make known. Define.
تَعَرَّفَ To be known.
إِعْتَرَفَ بِ To acknowledge.
عَرْفٌ Odour, (*sp.* fragrant).
عرفٌ Comb of a cock.
عرفُ ٱلدِّيكِ Cock's-comb, (plant).
عُرْفِيٌّ Common usage.
عَرَفَاتٌ Mount Arafât.
عَارِفٌ Knowing. Skilled.
عِرَافَةٌ The diviner's art.
عَرَّافٌ Diviner, astrologer.
عَرِيفٌ ج عُرَفَاءُ Overseer.
إِعْتِرَافٌ Confession.
تَعْرِيفٌ ج تَعْرِيفَاتٌ Tariff. Defining.
حرفُ ٱلتَّعْرِيفِ The definite article.
مَعْرِفَةٌ ج مَعَارِفُ Knowledge.
Determinate, noun.
مُعَرَّفٌ Determinate, definite.
مَعْرُوفٌ Known. Kindness.

عَرِقَ يَعْرَقُ عَرَقًا To sweat.
عَرَّقَ To cause to sweat.
أَعْرَقَ Extend its roots, (tree).
عَرَقٌ Sweat. Distilled spirits.
عِرْقٌ ج عُرُوقٌ Root. Vein.
عَرْقَانُ Sweating, perspiring.
بِلَادُ ٱلْعِرَاقِ Irak.
عَرِيقٌ Rooted. Noble.
مُعَرِّقٌ Diaphoretic.
عَرْقَبَ To hamstring (a beast).
عُرْقُوبٌ ج عَرَاقِيبُ Hamstring.
عَرْقَلَ To confuse, complicate.
تَعَرْقَلَ To be dangled, confused.
عَرَاقِيل Difficulties.
عَرَكَ يَعْرُكُ عَرْكًا To rub.
عَارَكَ مُعَارَكَةً وَعِرَاكًا To fight.
عَرِيكَةٌ ج عَرَائِكُ Nature.
لَيِّنُ ٱلْعَرِيكَةِ Gentle, tractable.
مَعْرَكَةٌ ج مَعَارِك Battle.

A heap.	عُرْمَةٌ ج عُرَمٌ
Numerous, (army).	عَرَمْرَمٌ
Covert, lair.	عَرِين وَعَرِينَةٌ
To be fall.	عَرَا ـ وَٱعْتَرَى
Loop, button-loop.	عُرْوَةٌ ج عُرًى
The firmest support.	ٱلْعُرْوَةُ ٱلْوُثْقَى
Overtaken (by).	مُعْتَرًى
To be naked ; free from.	عَرِيَ يَعْرَى
To strip, denude.	عَرَّى وَأَعْرَى
To be stripped.	تَعَرَّى
Nakedness.	عُرْيٌ وَعُرْيَةٌ
Naked ; free from.	عَارٍ ج عُرَاةٌ
Naked.	عُرْيَانٌ ج عُرْيَانُونَ
Naked, denuded.	مُعَرًّى
To be mighty, noble.	عَزَّ يَعِزُّ
To be distressing to.	عَزَّ عَلَيْهِ
God, exalted and magnified (be His name!).	ٱللّٰهُ عَزَّ وَجَلَّ
To render powerful.	عَزَزَ
To love.	اعَزَّ
To become powerful.	تَعَزَّزَ
To overcome.	إِعْتَزَّ وَٱسْتَعَزَّ عَلَى
Might. Honour.	عِزٌّ وَعِزَّةٌ
Self-respect.	عِزَّةُ ٱلنَّفْسِ
Mighty ; noble ; dear.	عَزِيزٌ ج أَعِزَّاءُ
The mighty God.	ٱلْعَزِيزُ
Governor of Egypt.	عَزِيزُ مِصْرَ
Dear, or dearer.	أَعَزُّ
Celibacy.	عُزْبَةٌ وَعُزُوبَةٌ
To be celibate.	عَزَبَ يَعْزُبُ
Unmarried.	أَعْزَبُ م عَزْبَاءُ ج عُزْبٌ
To punish ; reprove.	عَزَّرَ
Punishment.	تَعْزِيرٌ
The angel of death.	عِزْرَائِيل
To play upon a musical instrument.	عَزَفَ يَعْزِفُ
To furrow (the earth).	عَزَقَ يَعْزِقُ عَزْقًا
A hoe.	مِعْزَقٌ وَمِعْزَقَةٌ ج مَعَازِقُ
To set aside ; depose.	عَزَلَ يَعْزِلُ

عَزَّلَ To clean out.

إِعتَزَلَ To separate one's self.

عَزْلٌ Removal (of an officer).

عُزْلَةٌ Retirement. seclusion.

إِعتِزَالٌ وآنعِزَالٌ Retirement.

معزل Place of seclusion.

بِمَعْزِلٍ عَنْ Away, aloof from.

مُعتَزِلٌ Seceder.

مَعزُولٌ Removed, separated.

عَزَمَ يَعْزِمُ عَلَى To resolve to do.

عَزَّمَ To invite. Recite charms.

عَزْمٌ Resolution, firm purpose.

عَازِمٌ ج عَزَمَةٌ Firm, resolute.

عَزَّامٌ وَمُعَزِّمٌ Magician, charmer.

عَزُومٌ Determined, resolute.

عزّى تَعْزِيَةً To comfort.

تَعَزَّى To be comforted.

عَزَاءٌ Patience. Mourning.

مُعَزٍّ Comforter, consoler.

مُعَزًّى Consoled, comforted.

عَزَى يَعزُو To ascribe, attribute.

عَسَّ يَعُسُّ وَآعتَسَّ To patrol.

عَسٌّ وَعَسَسٌ Night-patrol.

يَعسُوبٌ Male-bee. Chief.

عوسَجٌ Bax-thorn.

عَسجَدٌ Gold. Gem.

عَسُرَ يَعسُرُ عُسْراً عَلَى To be difficult for.

عَسَّرَ To make difficult.

عَاسَرَ To treat harshly.

أَعسَرَ To become poor.

تَعَسَّرَ To become difficult.

إِستَعسَرَ To find difficult.

عُسرٌ وَعُسرَى وَمَعسَرَةٌ Difficulty.

عَسِرٌ وَعَسِيرٌ Difficult, hard.

أَعسَرُ م عَسرَاءُ Left-handed.

مُعسِرٌ Poor, indigent.

عَسَفَ يَعْسِفُ To treat unjustly.

عَسْفٌ Injustice, oppression.

To form a camp. عَسْكَرَ
Army, troops. عَسْكَرٌ ج عَسَاكِرُ
Soldier. عَسْكَرِيٌّ ج عَسَاكِرُ
Military service. عَسْكَرِيَّةٌ
Military camp. مُعَسْكَرٌ
Honey. عَسَلٌ
To make honey, (bees). عَسَّلَ
Tender shoot. عُسْلُجٌ ج عَسَالِجُ
Stiffness of the wrist. عَسَمٌ
Having stiff wrist or ankle. أَعْسَمُ
To become hard. عَسَا يَعْسُو
Thick, coarse, rough. عَاسٍ
It may be that, perhaps. عَسَى أَنْ
To make a nest. عَشَّشَ وَأَعْشَشَ
Bird's nest. عِشٌّ ج أَعْشَاشٌ
To produce herbage. أَعْشَبَ
Green herb. عُشْبٌ ج اعشَابٌ
To take tithes. عَشَرَ وَعَشَّرَ
To consort with. عَاشَرَ
To associate together. تَعَاشَرَ

Tithe ; a tenth. عُشْرٌ ج أَعْشَارٌ
Social intercourse. عِشْرَةٌ وَمُعَاشَرَةٌ
Ten. عَشَرَةٌ م عَشْرٌ ج عَشَرَاتٌ
Twenty. عِشْرُونَ
Tenth. عَاشِرٌ
Tithe-gatherer. عَشَّارٌ ج عَشَّارُونَ
Associate, friend. عَشِيرٌ ج عُشَرَاءُ
Kinsfolk. عَشِيرَةٌ ج عَشَائِرُ
Decimal. (*arith.*) أَعْشَارِيٌّ
Community. مَعْشَرٌ ج مَعَاشِرُ
Familiar friend. مُعَاشِرٌ
Companionship. مُعَاشَرَةٌ
To love passionately. عَشِقَ يَعْشَقُ
Passionate love. عِشْقٌ وَمَعْشَقٌ
Beloved one. عَشِيقٌ وَمَعْشُوقٌ
Passionate lover. عَاشِقٌ ج عُشَّاقٌ
To sup. عَشَا يَعْشُو وَتَعَشَّى
Weakness of sight. عَشاً وَعَشَاوَةٌ
Supper. عَشَاءٌ

The Eucharist. اَلْعَشَاءُ ٱلرَّبَّانِيُّ

Evening. عَشِيَّةٌ ج عَشَايَا

Yesterday evening. عَشِيَّةُ أَمْسِ

Darkness of night. عَشْوَةٌ وَعَشْوَاءُ

Cook. عَشِّيٌّ

To bind up. عَصَبَ وَعَصَّبَ

To defend a cause. تَعَصَّبَ فِي

To take the part of. تَعَصَّبَ لِ

To league against. تَعَصَّبَ عَلَى

To be leagued. إِعْتَصَبَ

Sinew. Nerve. عَصَبٌ ج أَعْصَابٌ

Male relations. عَصَبَةٌ ج عَصَبَاتٌ

Troop, band. عُصْبَةٌ ج عُصَبٌ

Nervous. عَصَبِيٌّ

Partisanship. Male relations. عَصَبِيَّةٌ

Bandage. Troop. عِصَابَةٌ ج عَصَائِبُ

Obstinacy, fanaticism. تَعَصُّبٌ

A zealous partisan. مُتَعَصِّبٌ

Bound, tied. مَعْصُوبٌ

To press, squeeze. عَصَرَ يَعْصِرُ

To be contemporary with. عَاصَرَ

To be pressed. تَعَصَّرَ وَٱنْعَصَرَ

A time, period. عَصْرٌ ج أَعْصُرٌ

Latter part of the day. عَصْرٌ

The afternoon prayer. صَلَاةُ ٱلْعَصْرِ

Juice, extract. عَصِيرٌ وَعُصَارَةٌ

A press. مِعْصَرَةٌ ج مَعَاصِرُ

Contemporary. مُعَاصِرٌ

Tail-bone. عُصْعُصٌ ج عَصَاعِصُ

To blow violently. عَصَفَ يَعْصِفُ

Hurricane. عَاصِفَةٌ ج عَوَاصِفُ

Chaff, straw. عُصَافَةٌ

Safflower. عُصْفُرٌ

Small bird. عُصْفُورٌ ج عَصَافِيرُ

To prevent ; defend. عَصَمَ يَعْصِمُ

To take refuge. اعْتَصَمَ وَٱسْتَعْصَمَ

Prevention, defence. عِصْمَةٌ

عَاصِمَةٌ	Capital of a country.
مَعْصَمٌ ج مَعَاصِم	Wrist.
مَعْصُومٌ	Preserved, protected.
عَصًا ج عِصِيٌّ	Staff, rod, cane.
عَصَا الرَّاعِي	Knot-grass.
عَصَى يَعْصِي	To disobey, rebel.
عَاصٍ ج عُصَاةٌ	Rebellious.
نَهْرُ العَاصِي	The river Orontes.
عِصْيَانٌ وَمَعْصِيَةٌ	Disobedience.
عَضَّ يَعَضُّ عَضًّا	To bite.
عَضَّ بِلِسَانِهِ	To defame.
عَضَدَ يَعْضُدُ وَعَاضَدَ	To aid, assist.
تَعَاضَدَ	To aid one another.
إِعْتَضَدَ بِ	To seek assistance of.
عَضْدٌ ج أَعْضَادٌ	Aid Assistance.
عِضْدٌ ج أَعْضَادٌ	The upper arm.
عِضَادَةٌ	Side, side-post.
عَضَلَ وَأَعْضَلَ	To be difficult.
عَضِلٌ	Muscular.
عَضَلَةٌ ج عَضَلٌ وَعَضَلَاتٌ	Muscle.
عُضَالٌ وَمُعْضِلٌ	Severe; difficult.
مُعْضِلَةٌ ج مُعْضِلَاتٌ	Difficult case.
عِضْوٌ ج أَعْضَاءٌ	Member, limb.
عَطِبَ يَعْطَبُ عَطَبًا	To perish.
اعْطَب	To destroy. Damage.
عَطَّرَ	To perfume.
تَعَطَّرَ	To perfume one's self.
عِطْرٌ ج أَعْطَارٌ	Perfume.
عِطْرُ الوَرْدِ	Ottar of roses.
عَطِرٌ م عَطِرَةٌ	Aromatic.
عَطَّارٌ ج عَطَّارُونَ	Grocer.
عِطَارَةٌ	Grocery.
عُطَارِدُ	The planet Mercury,
عَطَسَ يَعْطُسُ	To sneeze.
عَطَّسَ	To make one sneeze.
عَطْسَةٌ وَعُطَاسٌ	A sneezing.
عَطُوسٌ	Snaff.
عَطِشَ يَعْطَشُ عَطَشًا	To thirst.

To cause to thirst. عَطَّشَ وَأَعْطَشَ

Thirst. عَطَشٌ

Thirsty. عَطْشَانُ ج عَطَاشَى

To incline towards. عَطَفَ يَعْطِفُ إِلى

To be kind to. عَطَفَ وَتَعَطَّفَ عَلَى

To join one word to another by a conjunction. عَطَفَ كَلِمَةً

To turn away from. عَطَفَ عَنْ

To be bent, inclined. إِنْعَطَفَ

To seek favour. إِسْتَعْطَفَ

A conjunction. حَرْفُ عَطْفٍ

Side, flank. عِطْفٌ ج أَعْطَافٌ

Conjunctive particle. عَاطِفٌ

Kindness, pity. عَاطِفَة ج عَوَاطِفُ

Joined ; inclined. مَعْطُوفٌ

A word to which another is joined by a conjunction. مَعْطُوفٌ عَلَيْهِ

A bend. مُنْعَطَفٌ

To be without work. Be spoiled. عَطِلَ وَتَعَطَّلَ

To leave unemployed. Ruin. عَطَّلَ

Damage and loss. عُطْلٌ وَضَرَرٌ

Interest on money. عُطْلُ ٱلْمَالِ

Vacant time. عُطْلَةٌ وَعَطَالَةٌ

Spoiled, useless. عَاطِلٌ

Without work ; useless. مُعَطَّلٌ

Mouldiness. عَطَنٌ وَعَطْنَةٌ

Mouldy. عَطِنٌ وَمُعَطَّنٌ

To give present, offer. أَعْطَى

To beg. تَعَطَّى وَٱسْتَعْطَى

To engage in. تَعَاطَى

Gift. عَطًا وَعَطَاءٌ وَعَطِيَّةٌ

Giver. مُعْطٍ

To be great, large. عَظُمَ يَعْظُمُ

To be hard upon. عَظُمَ عَلَى

To make large ; magnify. عَظَّمَ

To be great ; proud. تَعَظَّمَ

To magnify one's self. تَعَاظَمَ

To regard as great. إِسْتَعْظَمَ

Bone. عَظْمٌ ج عِظَامٌ

عظمٌ وَعَظَمَةٌ	Pride ; majesty.
عَظِيمٌ ج عُظَمَاءُ وَعِظَامٌ	Great.
أَلْعَظِيمُ	The Great (God).
عَظِيمَةٌ ج عَظَائِمُ	A great thing.
أَعْظَمُ م عُظْمَى	Greater.
مُعْظَمٌ	Greater, or chief part.
مُعَظَّمٌ	Exalted, made great.
عَفَّ يَعِفُّ عَنْ	To abstain from wrong.
عَفِيفٌ ج أَعِفَّاءُ	Virtuous.
عِفَّةٌ	Continence, chastity.
عَفَرَ يَعْفِرُ	To cover with dust.
عَفْرٌ وَعَفَرٌ	Dust.
عِفْرِيتٌ ج عَفَارِيت	Demon.
عَفَشَ يَعْفِشُ	To heap up.
عَفْشٌ	Trash. Baggage.
عَفْصٌ	Galls.
عَفِنَ يَعْفَنُ وَعَفَّنَ وتَعَفَّنَ	To become decayed, rotten, mouldy.
وعُفُونَةٌ	Mildew.
عَفِنٌ وَمَعْفُونٌ ومُعَفَّنٌ	Decayed.
مُتَعَفِّنٌ	Putrid, mouldy.
عَفَا يَعْفُو عَنْ	To pardon, forgive.
عَافَى	To restore to health.
عَافَاكَ	Bravo ! Well done.
أَعْفَى مِن	To exempt, excuse.
تَعَافَى	To be restored to health.
إِسْتَعْفَى	To ask to be released.
عَفْوٌ	Pardon, amnesty. Young ass.
عَفْواً	Spontaneously ; easily.
عَافِيَةٌ ج عَوَافٍ وَعَافِيَاتٌ	Health.
إِسْتِعْفَاءٌ	Resignation.
مُعَافَاةٌ	Restoration to health.
مُتَعَافٍ	Convalescent.
عَقِيقٌ	Cornelian.
عَقَبَ ـُ عَقْباً	To succeed.
عَقَبَ وَأَعْقَبَ وَٱعْتَقَبَ	To follow.
عَاقَبَ	To punish.
تَعَقَّبَ	To follow out.

تَعَاقَبَ	To follow (one another).
عَقِبٌ ج أَعْقَابٌ	Heel of foot.
عَقَبَةٌ ج عِقَابٌ	Mountain road.
عُقْبَى	End, issue.
عَاقِبَةٌ ج عَوَاقِبُ	End, result.
عِقَابٌ وَمُعَاقَبَةٌ	Punishment.
عُقَابٌ ج أَعْقُبٌ وَعِقْبَانٌ	Eagle.
عَقِيبٌ	That which follows.
عَقَدَ يَعْقِدُ	To tie, knot. Conclude. Ratify.
عَقَدَ عَلَى	To determine upon.
عَاقَدَ	To make a contract with.
تَعَقَّدَ	To be complicated.
تَعَاقَدَ	To unite in a contract.
إِعْتَقَدَ	To believe firmly.
عَقْدٌ ج عُقُودٌ	Contract. Vault.
عِقْدٌ ج عُقُودٌ	Necklace.
عُقْدَةٌ ج عُقَدٌ	Knot. Joint.
عَقَّادٌ	Maker of silk-cord.
عَقِيدَةٌ	Ally, confederate.
عَقِيدَةٌ ج عَقَائِدُ	Article of faith.
إِعْتِقَادٌ	Belief, creed.
إِنْعِقَادٌ	Bond, contract, union.
تَعْقِيدٌ	Obscurity, complexity.
مُعَقَّدٌ	Very knotty ; tangled.
مُعْتَقَدٌ	Doctrine, belief.
عَقَرَ يَعْقِرُ عَقْرًا	To cut, wound.
عَاقَرَ	To persevere in.
إِنْعَقَرَ	To be wounded.
عَقْرٌ	Wounding, wound.
عُقْرٌ وَعُقْرَةٌ وَعَقَارَةٌ	Barrenness.
عَاقِرٌ ج عَوَاقِرُ	Barren.
عَقَارٌ ج عَقَارَاتٌ	Real estate.
عَقَّارٌ ج عَقَاقِيرُ	A drug.
عَقْرَبٌ ج عَقَارِبُ	Scorpion.
اَلْعَقْرَبُ	Scorpion (of the zodiac).
عَقَصَ يَعْقِصُ	To plait (the hair).
(عَقَصَ يَعْقُصُ وَعَقَّصَ)	To sting.
عَقِيصَةٌ ج عَقَائِصُ	Plait (of hair).

Hair-filet.	عِقَاصٌ
To crook, bend.	عَقَفَ يَعْقِفُ
To become bent.	تَعَقَّفَ وَٱنْعَقَفَ
Bent, hooked.	أَعْقَفُ وَمَعْقُوفٌ
To bind.	عَقَلَ يَعْقُلُ وَٱعْتَقَلَ
To understand.	عَقَلَ مَعْقُولاً
To conceive, know.	تَعَقَّلَ
To withhold, restrain.	إِعْتَقَلَ
Mind, intellect.	عَقْلٌ ج عُقُولٌ
Rational ; mental.	عَقْلِيٌّ
Intelligent.	عَاقِلٌ ج عُقَّالٌ وَعُقَلَاءُ
Rope cord.	عِقَالٌ ج عُقُلٌ
A noble woman.	عَقِيلَةٌ ج عَقَائِلُ
Fortress, refuge.	مَعْقِلٌ ج مَعَاقِلُ
Intelligible, reasonable.	مَعْقُولٌ
Mental science.	عِلْمُ ٱلْمَعْقُولَاتِ
To be barren.	عَقِمَ يَعْقَمُ
To render barren.	عَقَمَ وَأَعْقَمَ
Barrenness.	عُقْمٌ

Barren, sterile.	عَقِيمٌ ج عُقُمٌ
Acre, (town).	عَكَّةُ وَعَكَّاءُ
To become turbid.	عَكِرَ يَعْكَرُ وَتَعَكَّرَ
To render turbid.	عَكَّرَ وَأَعْكَرَ
Dregs, lees, sediment.	عَكَرٌ
Troubled, turbid.	عَكِرٌ وَمُعَكَّرٌ
To lean upon (a staff.)	عَكَزَ وَتَعَكَّزَ عَلَى
Staff ; crosier.	عُكَّازٌ ج عَكَاكِيزُ
To reverse, invert.	عَكَسَ يَعْكِسُ
To invert, oppose.	عَاكَسَ
To be inverted, reflected.	إِنْعَكَسَ
Inversion, reflection.	إِنْعِكَاسٌ
On the contrary.	بِٱلْعَكْسِ
Thick, dense.	عَكِشٌ
To detain.	عَكَفَ يَعْكُفُ عَكْفًا
To persevere in.	عَكَفَ عَلَى
To abide in.	عَكَفَ وَٱعْتَكَفَ فِي
Keeping to.	عَاكِفٌ
Religious seclusion.	إِعْتِكَافٌ

عكَمَ يَعْكِمُ To tie up. Muzzle.

عَلَّ علة To become ill.

علَّلَ بِ To Divert. Account for.

تَعَلَّلَ To offer excuses.

تعلل بِ To divert one's self.

إِعْتَلَّ To become diseased, sick.

علَّ وَلَعَلَّ May-be, perhaps.

علةٌ ج عِلَلٌ Cause. Malady.

حُرُوفُ ٱلعِلة The weak letters.

عِلِّيَّةٌ ج عَلَالِيٌّ Upper chamber.

عَلِيلٌ وَمَعْلُولٌ Sick, diseased.

تَعْلِيلٌ Assignment of a cause.

مُعْتَلٌّ Ill, diseased. Containing one of the weak letters.

عُلْبَةٌ ج عُلَبٌ Small box.

عَالَجَ To work at. Treat (a disease).

تَعَالَجَ To take medical treatment.

تعَالَجَ To strive with one another.

عِلَاجٌ وَمُعَالَجَةٌ Treatment of disease. Remedy, cure,

مُعَالَجَةٌ Dispute, contention.

عَلَفَ يَعْلِفُ To feed (a beast).

عَلَفٌ Fodder (for beasts).

عَلَّافٌ Seller of provender.

مَعْلَفٌ ج مَعَالِفُ Manger.

مُعَلَّفٌ Fattened (animal),

عَلِقَ يعلقُ وَٱعْتَلَقَ بِ To hang to.

عَلِقَ عُلُوقًا To conceive, (woman).

عُلِقَ عُلُوقًا بِهِ To love.

عَلِقَ يَعْلَقُ To begin to do.

عَلَّقَ To attach.

عَلَّقَ فِي To note down.

تَعَلَّقَ بِ To be attached to.

عَلَقَةٌ ج عَلَقَاتٌ وَعَلَقٌ Leech.

علاقةٌ ج عَلَائِقُ Connection.

عَلِيقٌ Forage, for animals.

عُلَّيْقٌ Climbing plant ; brier.

تَعَلُّقٌ Connection.

مُعَلَّقٌ Attached, suspended.

مُتَعَلِّقٌ بِ Attached to.

عَلْقَمٌ Very bitter plant.

عَلَكَ يَعْلُكُ عَلْكًا To chew.

عَلِمَ يَعْلَمُ To know, perceive.

عَلَّمَ To teach. To mark.

أَعْلَمَ To inform.

تَعَلَّمَ To learn.

إِسْتَعْلَمَ To desire to know ; ask.

عَلَمٌ ج أَعْلَامٌ Sign. Banner.

إِسْمُ عَلَمٍ Proper name.

عِلْمٌ ج عُلُومٌ Science, knowledge.

عِلْمِيٌّ Scientific.

عَالِمٌ ج عُلَمَاءُ Knowing ; learned.

عَالَمٌ ج عَوَالِمُ وعَالَمُونَ World.

عَالَمُ ٱلْحَيَوَانِ The animal kingdom.

عَالَمُ ٱلنَّبَاتِ The vegetable kingdom.

عَالَمُ ٱلْمَعَادِنِ The mineral kingdom.

عَلَّامٌ وَعَلَّامَةٌ Very learned.

عَلَامَةٌ Sign, mark.

عَلِيمٌ ج عُلَمَاءُ Learned, savant.

إِعْلَامٌ Announcement, notice.

تَعْلِيمٌ Instruction. Doctrine.

تَعْلِيمَاتٌ Instructions ; orders.

مُعَلَّمٌ Taught. Marked.

مُعَلِّمٌ Teacher, master.

مَعْلُومٌ Known. Active voice, (verb). Certainly, of course.

عَلَنَ يَعْلَنُ To be open, manifest.

أَعْلَنَ To publish, reveal.

إِعْتَلَنَ وَٱسْتَعْلَنَ To be manifest.

عَلِنٌ وَعَالِنٌ Manifest, open.

عَلَانِيَةً Openly, publicly.

إِعْلَانٌ Manifestation, announcement. Advertisement.

عَلَا يَعْلُو To be high ; ascend.

عَلَا عَلَى To overcome.

عَلَّى وَأَعْلَى To elevate.

تَعَلَّى وَتَعَالَى To be elevated.

أَللهُ تَعَالَى God, the exalted one.

تَعالَ	Come ! come here !
إِعتَلَى وَاستَعلَى	To rise high.
عَلاء وَعلى	Nobility ; eminence.
عُلُوّ	Height. Grandeur.
عِلاوَةٌ	In addition to.
عَلِيٌّ ج عَلِيُّونَ	High ; elevated ; noble.
أَلعَلِيُّ	God, the most High.
عِلِّيَّةٌ ج عَلالِيُّ	Upper chamber.
عالٍ	High, sublime.
أَلبَاب العَالِي	The Sublime Porte.
أَعلَى ج أَعالٍ	Higher, nobler.
أَلمُتَعَالِي	The exalted, (God).
عَلوَنَ	To address a letter.
عُلوَانٌ	Address ; title.
عَلَى يَعلِي عَلِيّاً وَعُلِيّاً	To ascend.
عَلَى	Upon, with, for, at.
عَلَيكَ أَن تَفعَلَ...	You ought to do ...
عَلَيهِ دَينٌ	He is in debt.
عَلَى عَهدِهِ	In his time.
عَلَى يَدِ فُلانٍ	By means of.
عَمَّ يَعُمُّ	To be general ; include.
عَمَّمَ	To generalize.
عَمٌّ ج أَعمامٌ	Paternal uncle.
عَمَّةٌ ج عَمَّاتٌ	Paternal aunt.
إِبنُ العَمِّ	Cousin on the father's side. Husband.
بِنتُ العَمِّ	Cousin on the father's side. Wife.
عَمَّ (عَن ما)	For what ?
عَمَّن (عَن مَن)	For whom ?
عَامٌّ	General, universal.
أَلعَامَّةُ	The common people.
جَاءَ القَومُ عَامَّةً	They all came.
أَلعَوَامُّ	To common people.
عَامِّيٌّ	Vulgar, common.
عِمَامَةٌ ج عَمَائِمُ	Turban.
عُمُومٌ	Universality, totality.
عُمُوماً	Ingeneral, universally.

عُمُومِيّ General, universal.

أَعَمّ More common or general.

مُعَمَّم ومُتَعَمِّم Turbaned.

عَمَدَ يَعْمِدُ To prop up, support.

عَمَدَ وتَعَمَّدَ To intend, purpose.

عَمَدَ إِلَى To aim at, seek, repair to.

عَمَدَ وعَمَّدَ To baptize.

تَعَمَّدَ واعْتَمَدَ To be baptized.

اعْتَمَدَ عَلَى To depend upon.

عَمْداً وتَعَمُّداً Intentionally.

عُمْدَة Prop. Committee.

عَمُود ج أَعْمِدَة Column, pillar.

خَطّ عَمُودِيّ Perpendicular line.

مُعْتَمَد Representative.

مَعْمُودِيَّة Baptism.

عَمَرَ يَعْمُرُ To live a long time.

عَمَرَ يَعْمُرُ To be inhabited.

عَمَرَ عِمَارَة To inhabit.

عَمَرَ عِمَارَة To build.

أَعْمَرَ To make inhabited.

عَمَرَ يَعْمُرُ To be flourishing.

عَمَّرَ To build, construct.

أَعْمَرَ واسْتَعْمَرَ To colonize.

عُمْر ج أَعْمَار Life-time ; age.

لَعَمْرِي By my life!

عُمْرَان Prosperity of a land. Civilization.

عِمَارَة ج عَمَائِر Edifice. Cultivation.

عَامِر وعَمِير ومَعْمُور Inhabited.

مِعْمَار ومِعْمَارِيّ ج مِعْمَارِيَّة Mason.

مُسْتَعْمَرَة Colony.

عَمَش Weakness of sight.

أَعْمَش Weak in sight.

عَمُقَ يَعْمُقُ To be deep.

عَمَّقَ وأَعْمَقَ To make deep.

تَعَمَّقَ فِي To go deeply into.

عَمْق وعُمْق ج أَعْمَاق Depth.

عَمِيق Deep, profound.

عَمِلَ يَعْمَلُ To work, do, make.

عَمِلَ فِي To act upon.

عَامَلَ To deal with. Treat.

اعْمَلَ To employ, use, exert.

تَعَامَلَ To deal with one another.

إِعْتَمَلَ To labour, work.

إِسْتَعْمَلَ To use ; employ.

عَمَلٌ ج اعْمَالٌ Work, service, deed, action ; occupation.

عَمْلَةٌ An evil deed.

عُمْلَة Money.

عَمَلِي Practical. Artificial.

عَمَلِيَّةٌ Operation.

عَامِلٌ ج عُمَّالٌ Workman, doer.

عَامِلٌ ج عَوَامِلُ A word that governs another (*in gram.*)

عَمِيلٌ Commercial agent.

إِسْتِعْمَالٌ Use, employment.

مَعْمَلٌ ج مَعَامِلُ Mill, factory.

مُعَامَلَةٌ ج مُعَامَلَاتٌ Transaction. Manner of treatment.

مَعْمُولٌ Made. Governed (word).

عَمِيَ يَعْمَى To become blind.

عَمِيَ عَنْ To be blind to.

عَمِيَ ٱلْأَمْرُ عَلَى To be obscure to.

اعْمَى To render blind.

تَعَامَى To feign blindness.

عَمًى Blindness.

أَعْمَى م عَمْيَاءُ ج عُمْيٌ Blind.

عَنْ For, from, at.

ذَهَبَ عَنَّا He left us.

عَنْ قَلِيلٍ After a little while.

عَنْ آخِرِهِمْ To the last man.

عَنْ يَمِينِهِ At his right hand.

نَفْسٌ عَنْ نَفْسٍ Life for life.

عَنْ وَعْدٍ Because of a promise.

عَنَّ يَعِنُّ عَنًّا To appear.

عَنَانٌ Clouds.

عِنَانٌ ج اعِنَّة Reins.

عِنَبٌ Grapes.

عُنَّابٌ Jujube tree and fruit.

عَنْبَرٌ Ambergris. Ship-hold. A kind of Mimosa.

عَنَّتَ To treat with rigour.

عِنْدَ At, near, with, on.

جِئْتُ مِنْ عِنْدِهِ I came from him.

عِنْدَ طُلُوعِ ٱلشَّمْسِ At sunrise.

جَلَسَ عِنْدَهُ He sat with him.

عِنْدِي مَالٌ I have property.

عِنْدِي كَذَا Such is my opinion.

عِنْدَ مَا صَارَ When it happened.

عِنْدَ ذٰلِكَ Then ; thereupon.

عَنَدَ يَعْنُدُ To be obstinate.

عَانَدَ عِنَاداً وَمُعَانَدَةً To resist.

تَعَانَدَ To oppose one another.

عَنِيدٌ ج عُنُدٌ وَمُعَانِدٌ Obstinate.

عَنْزٌ ج عُنُوزٌ وَعِنَازٌ She-goat.

عُنْصُرٌ ج عَنَاصِرُ Element. Origin.

أَلْعَنْصَرَةُ Feast of Pentecost.

عُنْصُرِيٌّ Simple, elemental.

عَنْصَلٌ Wild onion ; squill.

عَنُفَ يَعْنُفُ To be harsh ; rude.

عَنَّفَ وَأَعْنَفَ To upbraid.

عُنْفٌ Roughness, harshness.

عُنْفاً Violently.

عُنْفُوَانٌ The first of a thing.

عُنْفُوَانُ ٱلشَّبَابِ Prime of youth.

عَنِيفٌ Harsh, violent.

عَانَقَ وَٱعْتَنَقَ To embrace.

عُنُقٌ ج أَعْنَاقٌ Neck.

عِنَاقٌ وَمُعَانَقَةٌ Embrace.

أَلْعَنْقَاءُ Fabulous bird ; griffin.

عُنْقُودٌ ج عَنَاقِيدُ Bunch.

عَنْكَبُوتٌ ج عَنَاكِبُ Spider.

عَنَا يَعْنُو To trouble, distress.

عَنَا (لِ) To submit to.

عَنَّى وَأَعْنَى To subdue.

عَنْوَةٌ Force, violence.

عَانٍ ج عُنَاةٌ	Captive ; submissive.
عَنْوَنَ	To address a letter.
عُنْوَانٌ	Title ; address.
عَنَى يَعْنِي	To mean, intend.
عُنِيَ عِنَايَةً	To concern.
عَنَّى وَأَعْنَى	To distress, afflict.
عَانَى	To suffer, endure.
إِعْتَنَى بِ	To care for, manage.
عَنَاءٌ	Difficulty, trouble.
عِنَايَةٌ وَٱعْتِنَاءٌ	Care, solicitude.
أَلْعِنَايَةُ ٱلإِلَهِيَّةُ	Divine Providence.
مَعْنًى ج مَعَانٍ	Meaning, sense.
عِلْمُ ٱلْمَعَانِي	Rhetoric.
مَعْنَوِيٌّ	Ideal, mental.
عَهِدَ يَعْهَدُ عَهْدًا	To know.
عَهِدَ إِلَى	To enjoin, charge.
عَاهَدَ	To make an agreement.
عَاهَدَه	To swear to one.
تَعَهَّدَ وَتَعَاهَدَ	To be careful of.
تَعَاهَدَ	To make an engagement.
عَهْدٌ ج عُهُودٌ	Covenant, agreement. Time, epoch.
أَلْعَهْدُ ٱلْقَدِيمُ	The Old Testament.
أَلْعَهْدُ ٱلْجَدِيدُ	The New Testament.
وَلِيُّ ٱلْعَهْدِ	Presumptive heir.
عُهْدَةٌ	Compact. Responsibility.
مُعَاهَدَةٌ	Treaty, alliance.
مَعْهُودٌ	Stipulated. Known.
عَهْرٌ وَعَهَارَةٌ	Debauchery.
عَاجَ يَعُوجُ	To stop ; pass by.
عَوَّجَ	To crook, bend, contort.
تَعَوَّجَ وَٱعْوَجَّ	To become bent.
عَاجٌ	Ivory.
عِوَجٌ وَٱعْوِجَاجٌ	Crookedness.
أَعْوَجُ م عَوْجَاءُ ج عُوْجٌ	Crooked.
مُعَوَّجٌ	Crooked, tortuous.
عَادَ يَعُودُ إِلَى	To return to.
عَادَ وَأَعَادَ	To repeat.
عَادَ عِيَادَةً	To visit (the sick).

عوَّدَ	To accustom.
أعَادَ إلَى	To restore.
تَعَوَّدَ وَاْعتَادَ	To be accustomed.
عَادَةٌ ج عَادَاتٌ	Custom.
عَادِيٌّ	Old. Customary.
اْلعَادِيَّاتُ	Ancient monuments.
عَوْدٌ	Return ; repetition.
عُوْدٌ ج عِيدَانٌ	Stick. Lute.
اْلعُودُ	Aloes-wood.
عِيدٌ ج أعْيَادٌ	Festival, feast-day.
عَائِدٌ	A visitor, (*sp.* of the sick).
عَائِدَةٌ ج عَوَائِدُ	Benefit ; utility.
إعَادَةٌ	Repetition.
إعْتِيَادِيٌّ	Habitual, customary.
اْلمَعَادُ	The future life.
مُعَوَّدٌ وَمُعْتَادٌ	Habituated.
عَاذَ يَعُوذُ بِ	To seek protection.
عَوْذٌ وَعِيَاذٌ	Taking refuge.
مَعَاذٌ وَمَعَاذَةٌ	Refuge, asylum.
مَعَاذَ اْللهِ	God forbid !
عَوِرَ وَاْعوَرَّ	To lose one eye.
أعَارَ	To lend.
إسْتَعَارَ	To borrow.
عَوْرَةٌ ج عَوْرَاتٌ	Private parts.
إعَارَةٌ	Loan ; act of lending.
إسْتِعَارَةٌ	Borrowing. Metaphor.
إسْتِعَارِيٌّ	Metaphorical.
أعْوَرُ م عَوْرَاءُ ج عُورٌ	One-eyed.
مُسْتَعَارٌ	Borrowed. Metaphorical.
عَازَ يَعُوزُ وَأعْوَزَ	To want, lack.
أعْوَزَهُ اْلشَّيْءُ	He needed it.
أعْوَزَهُ اْلدَّهْرُ	Fortune has reduced him to poverty.
عَوَزٌ	Poverty, need.
عَوِزٌ وَعَائِزٌ وَأعْوَزُ وَمُعْوِزٌ	Needy.
مَعَاوِزُ	Wants.
عَوِصَ يَعْوَصُ	To be difficult.

Difficulty, obscurity. عَوَصٌ

Difficult. عَوِيصٌ م عَوْصَاءُ

To give something in exchange. عَاضَ يَعُوضُ وَعَوَّضَ

To receive in compensation for. تَعَوَّضَ وَٱعْتَاضَ عَنْ أَوْ مِنْ

Thing in exchange. عِوَضٌ

Compensation. عِوَضٌ وَتَعْوِيضٌ

Instead of. عِوَضًا عَنْ أَوْ مِنْ

To hinder. عَاقَ يَعُوقُ وَعَوَّقَ وَأَعَاقَ

To be hindered. تَعَوَّقَ

Delay. عَاقَةٌ

Obstacle. عَائِقٌ وَعَائِقَةٌ ج عَوَائِقُ

Capella (star). أَلْعَيُّوقُ

Act of retarding. إِعَاقَةٌ وَتَعْوِيقٌ

To support; nourish. عَالَ يَعُولُ

To be unfaithful in. عَالَ فِي

His patience was exhausted. عَالَ وَعِيلَ صَبْرُهُ

To wail. عَوَّلَ وَأَعْوَلَ وَٱعْتَوَلَ

To rely upon. عَوَّلَ عَلَى وَبِ

To sustain a family. أَعَالَ

Wailing. عَوْلٌ وَعَوْلَةٌ وَعَوِيلٌ

Family. عَائِلَةٌ ج عَائِلَاتٌ

A family, household. عِيَالٌ

Pickaxe. مِعْوَلٌ ج مَعَاوِلُ

To swim, float. عَامَ يَعُومُ عَوْمًا

A year. عَامٌ ج أَعْوَامٌ

Swimming. عَائِمٌ

To aid, assist. عَاوَنَ وَأَعَانَ عَلَى

To give mutual aid. تَعَاوَنَ

To seek the aid of. إِسْتَعَانَ بِ

Aid, assistance. عَوْنٌ وَمَعُونَةٌ

Aider, assistant. عَوْنٌ ج أَعْوَانٌ

Aid, assistance. إِعَانَةٌ وَمُعَاوَنَةٌ

Assistant, coadjutor. مُعَاوِنٌ

Bane, pest, blight. عَاهَةٌ

To howl, bark. عَوَى يَعْوِي عُوَاءً

عُوَاءٌ Howling, crying, barking.

عَابَ يَعِيبُ To be faulty.

عَابَ وَعَيَّبَ To find fault with.

عَيْبٌ ج عُيُوبٌ Blemish ; shame.

عَائِبٌ Defective, faulty.

مَعِيبٌ وَمَعْيُوبٌ Shameful.

عَاثَ يَعِيثُ To act corruptly.

عَيَّدَ To celebrate a feast.

عِيدٌ ج أَعْيَادٌ Feast, festival.

عِيدُ ٱلْمِيلَادِ Christmas.

عَارَ يَعِيرُ To go about ; journey.

عَيَّرَ To upbraid, reproach. To verify by weighing.

عَارٌ Disgrace, shame.

عِيَارٌ Standard of weight.

عِيسَى Jesus (Christ).

عِيسَوِيٌّ Christian.

عَاشَ يَعِيشُ عَيْشًا To live.

عَيَّشَ وَأَعَاشَ To nourish.

تَعَيَّشَ To seek means of living.

عَيْشٌ وَعِيشَةٌ Life.

عَيْشٌ Wheat, bread, food.

عَائِشٌ Living, living well.

مَعَاشٌ وَمَعِيشَةٌ Means of living.

عَيَّطَ To cry out, shout.

عِيَاطٌ Shouting.

عَافَ يَعَافُ وَيَعِيفُ To dislike.

عَالَ يَعِيلُ To become poor.

أَعْيَلَ To have a large family.

عَائِلَةٌ ج عِيَالٌ Family.

مُعْيِلٌ Having a large family.

عَيَّنَ To appoint ; specify.

عَايَنَ مُعَايَنَةً وعِيَانًا To see.

تَعَيَّنَ To be specified ; appointed.

عَيْنٌ ج أَعْيُنٌ وَعُيُونٌ Eye. Self.

اَلْأَعْيَانُ The chief men, notables.

عينٌ ج عيون Fountain.

هُوَ هُوَ عَيْنُهُ	It is he himself.
عَيْنُ ٱلْيَقِين	Certain knowledge.
عِيَانٌ ومُعَايَنَةٌ	Act of seeing.
عِيَانًا	Clearly, evidently.
عِيَانِيٌّ	Occular (witness).
عُوَيْنَاتٌ	Spectacles, eye-glasses.
تَعْيِينٌ	Specification, designation.
مُعَيَّنٌ	Designated, appointed.
مُعَيَّنٌ	A rhombus, (*geom.*).
الشَّبِيهُ بِالْمُعَيَّن	A rhomboid.
مُتَعَيِّن	Designated, appointed.
عَاهَةٌ	Bane, scourge, blight.
عَيِيَ يَعْيَى عَيًّا	To be unable.
أَعْيَا	To be disabled ; disable.
عَيَاءٌ	Weakness, disease.
عَيٌّ ج أَعْيَاءٌ	Weak.
عَيَّانٌ	Weak, incapable, sick.

غ

غ	As a numeral sign=1000.
غَبَّ ـُ	To visit at intervals.
غِبًّا	At intervals.
غِبَّ	After.
غَبَّرَ وَأَغْبَرَ	To raise the dust.
تَغَبَّرَ	To become dusty.
إِغْبَرَّ	To become dust-coloured.
غَبْرَةٌ و غَبَرَةٌ وَغُبَارٌ	Dust.
غَابِرٌ	Remaining. Passing away.
أَغْبَرُ م غَبْرَاءُ ج غُبْرٌ	Dust-coloured.
غَبَسٌ وغُبْسَةٌ	Duskiness.
اغْبَسُ م غَبْسَاءُ	Ash-coloured.

To be in a happy state.	إِغْتَبَطَ
Happy state.	غَبْطٌ وَغِبْطَةٌ
Channel of water.	غَبِيطٌ ج غُبُطٌ
Fortunate ; blessed.	مَغْبُوطٌ
To cheat.	غَبَنَ يَغْبِنُ غَبْنًا
To conceal.	غَبَنَ وَاغْتَبَنَ
To be deceived, or cheated.	إِنْغَبَنَ
Fraud, deceit.	غَبْنٌ وَغَبِينَةٌ
To be hidden from.	غَبِيَ عَلَى
Ignorance, heedlessness.	غَبَاوَة
Ignorant, stupid.	غَبِيٌّ ج أَغْبِيَاء
Lean, meagre.	غَثٌّ وَغَثِيثٌ
Ash-colour.	غُثْمَةٌ
To be nauseated.	غَثَا يَغْثِي غَثَيَانًا
Wen ; gland.	غُدَّةٌ ج غُدَدٌ
To deceive.	غَدَرَ يَغْدِرُ غَدْرًا بِ
To leave, abandon.	غَادَرَ
Perfidy, treachery.	غَدْرٌ
Treacherous.	غَادِرٌ وَغَدَّارٌ
Small pistol.	غَدَّارَةٌ ج غَدَّارَاتٌ
Pool of water.	غَدِيرٌ ج غُدْرَانٌ
To go forth early.	غَدَا يَغْدُو
To breakfast.	تَغَدَّى
To give breakfast.	غَدَّى
To-morrow.	غَدًا وَفِي ٱلْغَدِ
Day after to-morrow.	بَعْدَ ٱلْغَدِ
Morning meal ; lunch.	غَدَاءٌ
Early morning.	غُدُوٌّ وَغَدَاةٌ
To nourish (food).	غَذَا ـُ وَغَذَّى
To be fed.	تَغَذَّى وَٱغْتَذَى
Food nutriment.	غِذَاءٌ ج أَغْذِيَةٌ
Nourishing (food).	مُغَذٍّ
To beguile.	غَرَّ يَغُرُّ غُرُورًا
To be deceived.	إِغْتَرَّ
White mark on the forehead of a horse. The new moon. The best of anything.	غُرَّةٌ ج غُرَرٌ
Very deceitful.	غَرَّارٌ وَغَرُورٌ
Unexperienced, ignorant.	غِرٌّ ج أَغْرَارٌ

غُرُورٌ False things, vanities.

أَغَرُّ م غَرَّاءُ Beautiful. Noble.

مَغْرُورٌ Deceived, deluded.

غَرَبَ يَغْرُبُ To depart; set (sun).

غَرَّبَ وَأَغْرَبَ To go west.

تَغَرَّبَ To go to a strange land.

إِسْتَغْرَبَ To regard as strange.

غَرْبٌ The west.

غُرْبَةٌ وَتَغَرُّبٌ وَٱغْتِرَابٌ Travelling in a foreign land.

غُرَابٌ ج غِرْبَانٌ A crow.

غَرَابَةٌ Strangeness, obscurity.

غُرُوبٌ Setting, sun-set.

غَرِيبٌ ج غُرَبَاءُ A stranger.

غَرِيبَةٌ ج غَرَائِبُ Strange event.

مَغْرِبٌ ج مَغَارِبُ The west.

مَغْرِبُ ٱلشَّمْسِ Hour of sun-set.

مَغْرِبِيٌّ ج مَغَارِبَةٌ Moor, Arab of N. W. Africa.

غَرْبَلَ To sift; disperse.

غِرْبَالٌ ج غَرَابِيلُ Sieve.

غَرَدَ يَغْرُدُ وَغَرَّدَ To warble.

غَرَزَ يَغْرِزُ غَرْزًا ب To prick.

غَرَزَ وَغَرَّزَ وَأَغْرَزَ To insert.

غَرِيزَةٌ ج غَرَائِزُ Nature; natural, innate quality.

غَرِيزِيٌّ Natural, innate.

غَرَسَ يَغْرِسُ غَرْسًا To plant.

إِنْغَرَسَ To be planted.

غَرْسٌ ج أَغْرَاسٌ Planted tree.

مَغْرِسٌ ج مَغَارِسُ Plantation.

مَغْرُوسٌ Planted (tree).

غُرْشٌ ج غُرُوشٌ Piastre.

غَرَضٌ ج أَغْرَاضٌ Aim, object.

غَرْغَرَ To gargle.

غَرْغَرَةٌ A gargle.

غَرَفَ يَغْرُفُ وَٱغْتَرَفَ To dip out with a ladle.

غُرْفَةٌ ج غُرَفٌ Upper chamber.

غُرْفَةٌ ج غِرَافٌ Handful.

مِغْرَفَةٌ ج مَغَارِفُ — Ladle.

غَرِقَ يَغْرَقُ — To sink, be drowned.

غَرَّقَ وَأَغْرَقَ — To drown.

إِسْتَغْرَقَ — To take in, comprise.

غَرَقٌ — Drowning, sinking.

غَرِيقٌ ج غَرْقَى — Drowned.

غَرِمَ يَغْرَمُ — To pay a tax, fine.

غَرَّمَ وَأَغْرَمَ — To impose a fine.

اغْرِمَ ب — To be very fond of.

تَغَرَّمَ — To pay a tax ; fine.

غَرَامَةٌ — Fine, tax ; loss.

غَرَامٌ — Fond attachment.

غَرِيمٌ ج غُرَمَاءُ — Debtor ; litigant.

مُغْرَمٌ — Eagerly desirous.

غُرْنُوقٌ ج غَرَانِيقُ — Crane ; stork.

غَرَا يَغْرُو وَغَرَّى — To glue.

أَغْرَى — To incite, urge.

تَغَرَّى — To be glued.

غِرَاءٌ — Glue.

لَا غَرْوَ — No wonder !

إِغْرَاءٌ — Incitement, instigation.

مِغْرَاةٌ — Glue pot.

غَزَّ يَغُزُّ ب — To prick.

غَزَّةُ — Gaza, (town).

غَزُرَ يَغْزُرُ — To be copious.

غَزَارَةٌ — Abundance.

غَزِيرٌ ج غِزَارٌ — Abundant.

غَزَلَ يَغْزِلُ غَزْلاً — To spin.

تَغَزَّلَ — To say amatory words.

غَزْلٌ — Spun thread or yarn.

غَزَلٌ وَتَغَزُّلٌ — Amatory words.

غَزَالٌ ج غِزْلَانٌ — Gazelle.

غَزَالَةٌ — Female gazelle. The sun.

مِغْزَلٌ ج مَغَازِلُ — Spindle.

مَغْزُولٌ — Spun.

غَزَا يَغْزُو — To wage war, invade the enemy's country.

غَزْوٌ — Military expedition.

An incursion. غَزْوَةٌ ج غَزَوَاتٌ

Warrior ; invader. غَازٍ ج غُزَاةٌ

Sense, meaning. مَغْزَى ٱلْكَلَامِ

To become very dark. غَسَقَ يَغْسِقُ

Early darkness of night. غَسَقٌ

To wash. غَسَلَ يَغْسِلُ وَغَسَّلَ

To be washed. إِنْغَسَلَ

To wash one's self. إِغْتَسَلَ

Washing, ablution. غُسْلٌ

Washerwoman. غَسَّالَةٌ

Clothes that are washed. غَسِيلٌ

To deceive, falsify. غَشَّ يَغُشُّ

To be deceived. إِنْغَشَّ

Deceit, dishonesty, fraud. غِشٌّ

Deceitful. غَاشٌّ وَغَشَّاشٌ

Deceived ; falsified. مَغْشُوشٌ

Inexperience. غُشْمٌ

Inexperienced. غَشِيمٌ ج غُشَمَاءُ

Film (on the eyes) غَشَاوَةٌ

To cover, conceal. غَشِيَ يَغْشَى

To be dark, (night). غَشِيَ وَأَغْشَى

He swooned. غُشِيَ عَلَيْهِ غَشَيَانًا

To put a covering upon. غَشَّى

Cover ; membrane. غِشَاءٌ ج أَغْشِيَةٌ

Swoon. غَشْيَةٌ وَغَشَيَانٌ

Covered, enveloped. مُغْشًى وَمُغَشًّى

Swooning, senseless. مُغْشًى عَلَيْهِ

To be choked. غَصَّ يَغُصُّ

To choke. Grieve. أَغَصَّ

Choking. Grief. غُصَّةٌ ج غُصَصٌ

To force. غَصَبَ يَغْصِبُ غَصْبًا عَلَى
To take by violence.

To violate. غَصَبَ وَٱغْتَصَبَ مِنْ

Violence. غَصْبٌ

In spite of him. غَصْبًا عَنْهُ

Oppressor. غَاصِبٌ وَمُغْتَصِبٌ

Violence, tyranny. إِغْتِصَابٌ

Forced. مَغْصُوبٌ وَمُغْتَصَبٌ

Branch, twig. غُصْنٌ ج أَغْصَانٌ

To be fresh (plant). غَضَّ يَغِضُّ

To take no notice. غَضَّ ٱلطَّرْفَ

Fresh, juicy, luxuriant. غَضٌّ

To be angry. غَضِبَ يَغْضَبُ

To make angry. غَاضَبَ وَأَغْضَبَ

To be angry. تَغَضَّبَ

Anger, rage, passion. غَضَبٌ

Angry, enraged. غَضْبَانٌ ج غَضْبَى

Stern, austere, angry. غَضُوبٌ

Object of anger. مَغْضُوبٌ عَلَيْهِ

Ease of life, affluence. غَضَارَةٌ

Cartilage. غَضْرُوفٌ ج غَضَارِيفُ

Wrinkle, fold. غَضْنٌ

During. فِي غُضُونِ كَذَا

To become dark. غَضَا يَغْضُو

To close the eyes to. أَغْضَى عَنْهُ

To neglect, disregard. تَغَاضَى عَنْ

To immerse, dip. غَطَّ يَغِطُّ غَطًّا

To snore. غَطَّ يَغِطُّ غَطِيطًا

To be plunged, immersed. إِنْغَطَّ

To be proud. غَطْرَسَ غَطْرَسَةً

To immerse. To plunge. غَطَسَ يَغْطِسُ غَطْسًا فِي

To immerse. غَطَّسَ

Feast of Epiphany. عِيدُ ٱلْغِطَاسِ

Diver. غَطَّاسٌ

Bath-tub. مِغْطَسٌ ج مَغَاطِسُ

Magnet. مَغْنَطِيسٌ وَمَغْنَاطِيسٌ

To cover up, conceal. غَطَّى

To be covered, concealed. تَغَطَّى

Cover, covering. غِطَاءٌ ج أَغْطِيَةٌ

To cover, veil. غَفَرَ ـ وَغَفَّرَ

To forgive, pardon. غَفَرَ ـِ لِ

To ask for pardon. إِسْتَغْفَرَ

Guard, escort. غَفَرٌ

Pardon, forgiveness. غُفْرَانٌ

Forgiving, (God). غَفَّارٌ وَغَفُورٌ

Guard, sentinel.	غَفِيرٌ وَخَفِيرٌ
Pardon, forgiveness.	مَغْفِرَةٌ
To be heedless of.	غَفَلَ يَغْفُلُ عَنْ
To make one unmindful.	أَغْفَلَ
Forget, disregard.	أَغْفَلَ
To be unmindful of.	تَغَافَلَ عَنْ
To watch for one's unmindfulness.	إِسْتَغْفَلَ
Heedlessness.	غَفْلٌ وَغَفْلَةٌ وَغُفُولٌ
Unawares.	غَفْلَةً وَعَلَى غَفْلَةٍ
Unmindful, heedless.	غَافِلٌ
Simpleton.	مُغَفَّلٌ
To sleep.	غَفَا يَغْفُو وَغَفِيَ يَغْفَى
Sleepy ; sleeping.	غَافٍ
To fetter, shackle.	غَلَّ يَغُلُّ
To yield income.	أَغَلَّ وَغَلَّ
To take the proceeds.	إِسْتَغَلَّ
Rancour, malice.	غِلٌّ وَغَلِيلٌ
Manacle, shackle.	غُلٌّ ج أَغْلَالٌ
Burning of love &c.	غَلِيلٌ
Proceeds, revenue from land, crops.	غَلَّةٌ ج غَلَّاتٌ وَغِلَالٌ
Burning of love or grief.	غَلِيلٌ
Fruitful, productive.	مُغِلٌّ
Manacled, shackled.	مَغْلُولٌ
To conquer, subdue.	غَلَبَ يَغْلِبُ
To contend for victory.	غَالَبَ
To prevail, overcome.	تَغَلَّبَ عَلَى
To be overcome, defeated.	إِنْغَلَبَ
Victory, conquest.	غَلَبَةٌ
Victor, conqueror.	غَالِبٌ ج غَلَبَةٌ
Usually.	غَالِبًا وَفِي ٱلْغَالِبِ
Conquered, overcome.	مَغْلُوبٌ
The last darkness of night.	غَلَسٌ
At early dawn.	غَلَسًا
To make a mistake.	غَلِطَ يَغْلَطُ
To accuse one of mistake.	غَلَّطَ
Mistake, error.	غَلَطٌ ج أَغْلَاطٌ

غَلْطَةٌ	Single mistake, fault.
مغَلَّط وَمغلوطٌ	Erroneous.
مغالطَةٌ	Sophism.
غَلُظَ يَغلُظُ	To be thick, bulky.
غَلَّظَ على	To be hard, severe.
أَغْلَظَ لَهُ	To be rough, uncivil.
غلاظَةٌ	Thickness, incivility.
غَليظٌ ج غِلاظٌ	Thick; rough.
غَلَّفَ	To put into an envelope.
تَغَلَّفَ وَٱغْتَلَفَ	To have a cover.
غِلافٌ ج غُلفٌ	Covering, sheath.
(مُغلَّفٌ ج مُغلَّفَاتٌ)	Envelope.
أَغْلَفُ ج غُلفٌ	Uncircumcised.
أَغلَقَ	To close, shut.
إِنغلَقَ	To be closed, shut.
غَلَقٌ ج أَغْلاقٌ	Lock.
مُغْلَقٌ	Closed, locked.
غِلاقَة حِسَاب	Balance of account.
غُلامٌ ج غِلمَانٌ	Boy, youth.
غَيلَمٌ	Tortoise.
غَلَّنَ	To become calm, (sea).
(غَلّينَة)	Quiet, calmness of the sea.
غَلاَ يَغلُو غُلُوًّا	To be excessive.
غَلاَ غَلاءً	To be high in price.
غَلَّى	To make the price high.
غَالَى مُغَالاَةً في	To go too far.
إِستغلَى	To find it high-priced.
غَلاَءٌ	High price; dearness.
غُلُوٌّ	Excess, exaggeration.
غَلْوَةٌ ج غَلَوَاتٌ	Furlong.
غَالٍ	High-priced, dear.
أَغْلَى	Of higher price, dearer.
غَلَى يَغْلِي	To boil (pot).
غَلَّى وَأَغْلَى	To cause to boil.
غَليٌ وَغَلَيَانٌ	Boiling, ebullition.
غَلْيُونٌ ج غَلايِينُ	Tobacco-pipe.
غَلاَّيَةٌ	Vessel for heating water.

To cover, to grieve.	غَمَّ يَغُمُّ
To be grieved.	إِنغَمَّ وَاغتَمَّ
Grief, sorrow.	غَمٌّ ج غُمُومٌ
Clouds, (*coll*).	غَمَامٌ ج غَمَائِمُ
A cloud.	غَمَامَةٌ
Sorrowful, mournful.	مغمّ
Afflicted, grieved.	مَغمُومٌ
To sheathe; cover.	غَمَدَ يَغمُدُ وَأَغمَدَ
To cover, veil.	غَمَّدَ وَتَغَمَّدَ
Scabbard, sheath.	غِمْدٌ ج أَغْمَادٌ
To submerge (water).	غَمَرَ يَغمُرُ
To be abundant.	غَمُرَ يَغمُرُ
To be submerged.	إِنغَمَرَ وَاغتَمَرَ
Abundant (water).	غَمْرٌ
Deep water. Difficulty.	غَمْرَةٌ
Pangs of death.	غَمَرَاتُ ٱلْمَوْتِ
To wink. Press.	غَمَزَ يَغمُزُ غَمزًا
Sign made with the eye.	غَمْزٌ
To immerse, dip.	غَمَسَ يَغْمِسُ
To be plunged.	إِنغَمَسَ وَٱغْتَمَسَ
To be obscure.	غَمَضَ يَغمُضُ
To shut (the eyes).	غَمَّضَ وَاغمَضَ
To be closed, (eye).	إِنغَمَضَ
Obscure.	غَامِضٌ ج غَوَامِضُ
Closed (eye). Obscure.	مُغَمَّضٌ
Depth.	(غُمْقٌ)
Deep.	(غَمِيقٌ)
To swoon.	غُمِيَ عَلَيْهِ وَاغْمِيَ عَلَيْهِ
Swooning, swoon.	غَمْيٌ وَإِغْمَاءٌ
In a swoon.	مُغْمًى عَلَيْهِ
To be coquettish.	غَنِجَ
Coquetry.	غَنْجٌ وَغِنَاجٌ
Coquette.	غَنِجَةٌ وَغَنُوجَةٌ
To plunder ; obtain.	غَنِمَ يَغنَمُ
To give a free gift.	غَنَّمَ
To seize as spoil.	إِغْتَنَمَ

إِغْتَنَمَ وَٱسْتَغْنَمَ ٱلْفُرْصَةَ	To seize the opportunity.
غُنْمٌ وَغَنِيمَةٌ ج غَنَائِمُ	Booty.
غَنَمٌ ج أَغْنَامٌ	Sheep (*coll.*).
غَنَّامٌ	Shepherd.
غَانِمٌ	Spoiler ; successful.
غَنِيَ يَغْنَى	To be rich.
غَنِيَ بِ	To be content with.
غَنِيَ عَنْ	To be in no need of.
غَنَّى	To sing, chant.
أَغْنَى	To free from want.
إِغْتَنَى وَٱسْتَغْنَى	To become rich.
إِسْتَغْنَى عَنْ	To be in no need of.
غِنًى وَغَنَاءٌ	Wealth, opulence.
مَا لَهُ عَنْهُ غِنًى	He cannot do without it.
غِنَاءٌ وَأُغْنِيَّةٌ ج أَغَانٍ وَأَغَانِيُّ	Song.
غَنِيٌّ ج أَغْنِيَاءُ	Rich, opulent.
غَانِيَةٌ ج غَوَانٍ	Beautiful woman.
مُغَنٍّ ج مُغَنِّيَةٌ	Singer.
غَيْهَبٌ ج غَيَاهِبُ	Very dark, black.
غَاثَ يَغُوثُ وَأَغَاثَ	To aid, succour.
إِسْتَغَاثَ وَبِ	To seek aid.
غَوْثٌ وَإِغَاثَةٌ	Aid, succour.
إِسْتِغَاثَةٌ	Request of aid.
غَارَ يَغُورُ	To sink deep.
أَغَارَ عَلَى	To attack, invade.
غَارٌ	Laurel (plant).
غَارَةٌ ج غَارَاتٌ	Raid, incursion.
شَنَّ ٱلْغَارَةَ	He made a raid.
غَوْرٌ	Bottom, depth. Low land.
مَغَارَةٌ ج مَغَائِرُ	Cave, cavern.
غَاصَ يَغُوصُ فِي	To plunge into.
غَوَّصَ	To plunge dip (*v.t.*).
غَائِصٌ	One who plunges.
غَوَّاصٌ	Diver, (*sp.* pearl-fisher).
(غَوِيصٌ)	Deep.
غَاطَ يَغُوطُ	To dig, excavate. Sink.

تَغَوَّطَ To void excrement.
غَوْطٌ وَغَوْطَةٌ Low ground.
غائِطٌ Excrement, fæces.
غَالَ يَغُولُ وَٱغْتَالَ To destroy.
إِغْتَالَ To slay covertly.
غُولٌ ج غِيلَانٌ Goblin, demon.
غَائِلَةٌ ج غَوَائِلُ Evil, mischief.
غَوِيَ يَغْوَى غَوًى To err.
غَوَى وَأَغْوَى To seduce.
إِنْغَوَى To be led into error.
غَيٌّ وغَوَايَةٌ Error, leading astray.
غَيَّةٌ ج غَيَّاتٌ Error.
غَاوٍ ج غُوَاةٌ Erring ; deceiver.
غَابَ يَغِيبُ To be absent, distant.
غابَ غِيَابًا To set ; disappear.
غابَ عَنِ ٱلصَّوَابِ To lose one's reason.
غَابَ وَٱغْتَابَ To slander.
غَابَ وتَغَسَّ To go away, travel.

غَيَّبَ عَنْ To conceal from.
غَيْبٌ وَغَيْبَةٌ وَغِيَابٌ Absence.
غَيْبٌ ج غُيُوبٌ Hidden thing.
غَيْبًا وَعَلَى ٱلغَائِبِ From memory.
عَالَمُ ٱلغَيْبِ The unseen world.
غَابَةٌ ج غَابَاتٌ Forest.
غِيبَةٌ Calumny, backbiting.
غَائِبٌ Absent, hidden.
مَغِيبُ ٱلشَّمْسِ Time or place of the setting of the sun.
غَاثَ يَغِيثُ To water with rain.
غَيْثٌ ج غُيُوثٌ Rain.
غَادَةٌ Fresh, tender (woman)
أَغْيَدُ م غَيْدَاءُ ج غِيدٌ Tender.
غَارَ يَغَارُ To be jealous.
غَيَّرَ To alter, change.
أَغَارَ To make jealous.
تَغَيَّرَ To be changed.
غَايَرَ وَتَغَايَرَ To differ.

غَيْرُ Other ; another. Except.

وَغَيْرُ ذَلِكَ Et cætera.

غَيْرُ خَالِصٍ Not pure, impure.

مِنْ غَيْرِ ذَلِكَ Without that.

غَيْرَ أَنَّ Although.

لَا غَيْرُ Nothing else.

غَيْرَةٌ Jealously ; zeal.

غَيُورٌ Very jealous.

(مِغْيَارٌ) Unhealthy (climate).

غَيْضَةٌ ج غِيَاضٌ Thicket, wood.

غَاظَ يَغِيظُ وَأَغَاظَ To anger, enrage.

إِغْتَاظَ وَتَغَيَّظَ To become angry.

غَيْظٌ Anger, rage, wrath.

مُغْتَاظٌ Angry, enraged.

غَاقٌ Crow, raven.

(غَالٌ ج غَالَاتٌ) Lock.

غِيلٌ ج أَغْيَالٌ Thicket, jungle.

غِيلَةٌ Subterfuge, deception.

غَائِلَةٌ Rancour, malice ; evil.

غَامَ وَأَغْيَمَ وَتَغَيَّمَ To be cloudy.

غَيْمٌ ج غُيُومٌ Clouds (*coll.*)

غَايَةٌ ج غَايَاتٌ Extremity, term. Ultimate object.

إِلَى ٱلْغَايَةِ Extremely.

ف

ف And ; then. As a numeral sign=80.

فُؤَادٌ ج أَفْئِدَةٌ Heart ; soul ; mind.

فَارٌ ج فِئْرَانٌ Rat ; mouse.

فَأْرَةٌ ج فَارَاتٌ A mouse.

فَاسٌ ج فُؤُسٌ Axe ; hatchet.

تَفَأَّلَ وَتَفَاءَلَ بِ To draw a favourable augury.

فَأْلٌ وَتَفَاؤُلٌ Good or evil omen.

فِئَةٌ ج فِئَاتٌ Company, band.

فَتَّ يَفُتُّ To break in pieces.

تَفَتَّتَ وَانْفَتَّ To be crumbled.

فُتَاتٌ Small pieces ; crumbs.

فَتِيتٌ وَمَفْتُوتٌ Crumbled.

فَتِئَ يَفْتَأُ عَنْ To cease from.

مَا فَتِئَ يَفْعَلُ He continued to do.

فَتَحَ يَفْتَحُ To open. Conquer (a country).

فَتَحَ عَلَى To succour. Reveal.

فَاتَحَ To address one first.

تَفَتَّحَ وَانْفَتَحَ To be opened.

إِفْتَتَحَ To open, commence. Attack and conquer (a land).

إِسْتَفْتَحَ To begin. Seek succour.

فَتْحٌ ج فُتُوحٌ Victory, conquest.

فُتُوحَاتٌ Conquered countries.

فَتْحَةٌ The short vowel *fatha*.(َ)

فَتْحَةٌ An opening.

فَاتِحٌ Conqueror. Light-coloured.

فَاتِحَةٌ Introduction, preface.

اَلْفَاتِحَةُ First chapter of the Koran.

فَتَّاحٌ He who opens, conquers.

Introduction. Conquest.	افْتِتَاحٌ
Introductory.	افْتِتَاحِيٌّ
Key.	مِفْتَاحٌ ج مَفَاتِيحُ
Opened. Vocalized by the vowel *fatha*.	مَفْتُوحٌ
To subside ; be tepid.	فَتَرَ يَفْتُر
To desist ; abate.	فَتَرَ عَنْ
To allay. Make tepid.	فَتَّرَ
Measure between extended thumb and index finger.	فِتْرٌ
Intermission.	فَتْرَةٌ ج فَتَرَاتٌ
Languid ; lukewarm.	فَاتِرٌ
Lukewarmness, languor.	فُتُورٌ
To examine, investigate.	فَتَّشَ
Examination, inquest.	تَفْتِيشٌ
Examiner, inspector.	مُفَتِّشٌ
To crumble (*v.t.*).	(فَتَّتَ)
To cleave, slit, rip.	فَتَقَ يَفْتُق وفَتَّقَ
To be split ; ripped.	تَفَتَّقَ وَآنْفَتَقَ

Rupture, hernia. Rent.	فَتْقٌ وَفِتَاقٌ
Ruptured, ripped.	مَفْتُوقٌ
To assault ; kill.	فَتَكَ بِ
Bold, daring.	فَاتِكٌ ج فُتَّاكٌ
To twist.	فَتَلَ يَفْتِل فَتْلاً وَفَتَّلَ
To be twisted.	تَفَتَّلَ وَآنْفَتَلَ
Twister (of rope, &c.)	فَتَّالٌ
Twisted (rope, &c.)	فَتِيلٌ وَمَفْتُولٌ
Wick of a lamp.	فَتِيلَةٌ ج فَتَائِل
To please ; infatuate.	فَتَنَ يَفْتِن
To please ; seduce.	أَفْتَنَ
To lead, or to be led, into error.	اِفْتَتَنَ
Seduction. Trial, affliction. Sedition.	فِتْنَةٌ
Seducer ; charmer.	فَاتِنٌ ج فُتَّانٌ
Infatuated ; seduced.	مَفْتُونٌ
To be young.	فَتِيَ يَفْتَى فَتًى وَفَتَاءً
To answer a learned question.	أَفْتَى (الْعَالِمُ) فِي مَأْلَةٍ

تَفَتَّى To affect youth.

إِسْتَفْتَى To ask the solution of a learned question, *sp*. judicial.

فَتًى ج فِتْيَانٌ A young man.

فَتَاةٌ ج فَتَيَاتٌ A young woman.

فُتُوَّةٌ Manliness, generosity.

فَتْوَى ج فَتَاوِ Judicial sentence.

مُفْتٍ (اَلْمُفْتِي) A lawyer. Mufti.

فَجٌّ ج فِجَاجٌ Way, path.

فِجٌّ وَفَجٌّ Unripe (fruit).

فَجَأَ يَفْجَأُ وَفَاجَأَ To attack or befall suddenly.

فَجْأَةً Suddenly ; unawares.

فَجَرَ يَفْجُرُ To give exit to water.

فَجَرَ يَفْجُرُ To live in open sin.

تَفَجَّرَ وَٱنْفَجَرَ To flaw. Dawn.

فَجْرٌ Dawn, day-break.

فَاجِرٌ ج فُجَّارٌ Wicked (man).

فُجُورٌ Great wickedness.

فَجَعَ يَفْجَعُ فَجْعًا To give pain.

فَجِعَ To suffer pain from loss.

تَفَجَّعَ To grieve, complain.

فَاجِعٌ وَفَجُوعٌ Calamitous.

فَاجِعَةٌ ج فَوَاجِعُ Great calamity.

فُجْلٌ Radish (plant).

فَجَمَ يَفْجُمُ فَجْمًا To notch, blunt.

فَحُشَ يَفْحُشُ To be excessive ; foul.

فَحَشَ وَأَفْحَشَ To use foul words.

فُحْشٌ Shameless evil. Excess.

فَاحِشٌ Evil. Excessive.

فَاحِشَةٌ ج فَوَاحِشُ Atrocious sin.

فَحَصَ - وَتَفَحَّصَ To examine.

فَحْصٌ ج فُحُوصٌ Examination.

اِسْتَفْحَلَ To become formidable.

فَحْلٌ ج فُحُولٌ Male. Strong man.

فحول العُلَمَاءِ Elites in science.

فَحَمَ يَفْحَمُ To be silence.

فَحَّمَ To blacken.

أَفْحَمَ To silence by argument.
فَحْمٌ Charcoal.
فَحْمُ ٱلْحَجَرِ أَو فَحْمٌ حَجَرِيٌّ Coal.
فَحَّامٌ ج فَحَّامَة Seller of charcoal.
فُحْمَةٌ Blackness ; darkness.
مُفْحِمٌ (Answer) that silences.
فَحْوَى وَفَحْوَاءُ Meaning ; sense.
فَخٌّ ج فِخَاخٌ وفخوخ Trap, snare.
فَخَتَ يَفْخُتُ To break through.
إِنْفَخَتَ To be perforated.
فَخْت Hole, break, perforation.
فَخْذٌ ج أَفْخَاذ Thigh. Sub-tribe.
فَخَرَ يَفْخَرُ وَٱفْتَخَرَ To glory, boast.
فَخَرَ وَفَخَّرَ وَأَفْخَرَ عَلَى To prefer.
فَاخَرَ To compete or vie with.
فَخْرٌ Glory, excellence.
فَاخِرٌ Glorious ; excellent.
فَخَّارٌ Pottery ; earthen-ware.
فَخَّارِيٌّ وَفَاخُورِيٌّ Potter.

مَفْخَرَةٌ ج مَفَاخِر Glorious trait.
فَخُمَ يَفْخُم فَخَامَةً To be great.
فَخَّمَ To show great honour.
مُفَخَّمٌ Highly honoured.
أَفْدَعُ ج فُدْعٌ Club-footed.
فَدَغَ يَفْدَغُ To wound the head.
فَدَّان وَفَدَان ج فَدَادِين Yoke of oxen. Field-measure, acre.
فَادِنٌ ج فَوَادِن Plum-line.
فَدَى يَفْدِي To redeem, ransom.
إِفْتَدَى To ransom.
فِدَاءٌ Ransom. Redemption.
فِدَاكَ May it be a ransom to you !
الْفَادِي The Redeemer.
فَذَّ يَفُذُّ To become apart.
فَذٌّ One alone, single.
فَذَاذَى وَفُذَاذًا One by one.
فَذْلَكَةٌ Resumé, gist.
فَرَّ يَفِرُّ فَرًّا To flee ; escape.

فَارٌّ وفَرَّارٌ	Fleeing, fugitive.
فُرِّيٌّ	Snipe, quail.
فِرارٌ	Flight ; escape.
مَفَرٌّ	Escape. Place of escape.
فَرأٌ وفَراء	Wildass ; onager.
أَلْفُرَاتُ	The Euphrates (river).
(فُرْشِيكَة)	Fork.
(فُرْتُونَة)	Storm at sea.
فَرْثٌ	Excrement, fæces.
فَرَجَ يَفْرِجُ فَرْجاً	To relieve.
أَفْرَجَ بَين	To separate.
فَرَجَ لِ	To make place for.
فَرَّجَ	To open ; widen. Relieve.
فَرَّجَ عَلَى	To show,
تَفَرَّجَ	To see a new thing.
انفرج	To be opened, separate ; to diverge. Be relieved.
فَرَجٌ	Relief.
فُرْجَة ج فُرَجٌ	Opening Show.
فَرَجِيَّة	Over-garment.
فَرُّوجٌ ج فَرَارِيجُ	Chicken.
مَفْرُوجٌ	Open. Relieved.
مُنْفَرِجٌ	Diverging.
أَلزَّاوِيَةُ ٱلْمُنْفَرِجَة	Obtuse angle.
فَرِحَ يَفْرَحُ فَرَحاً بِ	To rejoice.
فَرَّحَ وأَفْرَحَ	To make glad.
فَرَحٌ	Joy, gladness, happiness.
فَرِحٌ ج فَرِحونَ	Happy, glad.
فَرْحَانٌ م فَرْحَانَةٌ	Glad, rejoicing.
فَرَّخَ وَأَفْرَخَ	To sprout ; hatch.
فَرْخ ج فُروخ	Sprout. Chick
فَرْخَةٌ	Chicken.
فَرِدَ عَنْ	To separate one's self.
افْرَدَ	To make single ; set apart.
تَفَرَّدَ وَٱنفَرَدَ	To be alone.
إِستَفْرَدَ	To seek privacy.
فَرْدٌ ج أَفْرَادٌ	One ; one of a pair. Individual.

Atom ; monad. اَلْجَوْهَرُ ٱلْفَرْدُ

Pistol. فَرْدٌ ج فُرُودَةٌ

Bale of goods. فَرْدَةٌ

One by one. فُرَادًا وَفُرَادَى

Unique, matchless. فَرِيدٌ

Precious gem. فَرِيدَةٌ ج فَرَائِدُ

Singular number (*gram.*). مُفْرَدٌ

Alone; insolated. مُنْفَرِدٌ

Paradise. فِرْدَوْسٌ ج فَرَادِيس

To set aside. فَرَزَ يَفْرِزُ وَأَفْرَزَ

To go aside, or away. إِنْفَرَزَ

Cornice, frieze. إِفْرِيزٌ ج أَفَارِيز

To perceive ; gaze ' تَفَرَّسَ

To capture (prey). اِفْتَرَسَ

Horse. فَرَسٌ ج أَفْرَاسٌ

Hippopotamus. فَرَسُ ٱلْبَحْرِ

Horseman. فَارِسٌ ج فُرْسَان

Persia. بِلَادُ فَارِسَ وَبِلَادُ ٱلْفُرْسِ

Persian. فَارِسِيٌّ وَفُرْسِيٌّ ج فُرْسٌ

The Persian language. اَلْفَارِسِيَّةُ

Horsemanship. فَرَاسَةٌ وَفُرُوسَةٌ

Skilful discernment. فِرَاسة

Physiognomy. عِلْم ٱلْفِرَاسَةِ

Prey (of a lion). فَرِيسَة

Pharisee. فَرِّيسِيٌّ ج فَرِّيسِيُّونَ

Parasang; league. فَرْسَخٌ ج فَرَاسِخ

To spread out. فَرَشَ يَفْرُشُ

To be spread out. إِفْتَرَشَ وَٱنْفَرَشَ

House-furniture. فَرْشٌ وَمَفْرُوشٌ

Brush. فُرْشَةٌ

Bed. فِرَاشٌ وَفَرْشَةٌ ج فُرُشٌ

Moth ; butterfly. فَرَاشَةٌ ج فَرَاشٌ

Furnished (house). مَفْرُوشٌ

To separate the feet. فَرْشَخَ

Occasion; chance. فُرْصَة ج فُرَصٌ

To avail one's self of an opportunity. إِنْتَهَزَ ٱلْفُرْصَةَ

To appoint ; ordain. فَرَضَ يَفْرِضُ
Estimate ; suppose. Allot.

فَرَضَ وفرَّضَ — To notch, cut.

فَرَضَ وآفتَرَضَ عَلَى — To impose.

إِفتَرَضَ — To enact (a law).

فَرْضٌ ج فُرُوضٌ — Decree. Supposition.

على فَرْضٍ — On the supposition.

فُرْضَةٌ ج فُرَضٌ — Harbour.

فَرِيضَةٌ ج فَرَائِضُ — Ordinance; duty. Alloted portion.

عِلْمُ الفَرَائِضِ — The science of the laws of inheritance.

إِفتِرَاضٌ — Enactment. Supposition.

مَفْرُوضٌ — Supposed. Enacted.

فَرَطَ يَفْرُطُ — To lose an opportunity.

فَرَطَ مِنْ — To do a thing hastily.

فَرَّطَ (في) — To miss ; neglect.

أَفْرَطَ افْرَاطًا — To go to excess.

فَرْطٌ ج أَفراط — Excess.

فرط — Cheap.

مُفْرَطٌ — Excessive, immoderate.

فَرْطَحَ — To flatten ; make broad.

مُفَرْطَحٌ — Broad ; flattened.

فَرَّعَ مِنْ — To derive, deduce.

تَفَرَّعَ — To ramify ; branch forth.

فَرْعٌ ج فروعٌ — Branch. Derivative.

فَرَّاعَةٌ — Hatchet.

تَفَرْعَنَ — To be very proud.

فِرْعَوْنٌ ج فَرَاعِنَةٌ — Pharaoh.

فَرَغَ يَفْرُغُ — To be empty, vacant.

فَرَغَ مِنْ — To finish a thing.

فَرَّغَ وأَفْرَغَ — To pour out. Empty.

تَفَرَّغَ مِنْ — To be free from, be at leisure.

تَفَرَّغَ لِ — To devote one's self to.

إِستَفْرَغَ — To exhaust ; vomit.

فَرِغٌ وفَارِغٌ — Empty, vacant.

فَرَاغٌ — Emptiness ; cessation.

فَرْفَرَ فَرْفَرَةً — To flap the wings.

فَرْفَارٌ — Light-headed, noisy.

فَرَقَ يَفْرُقُ بَيْنَ To divide. Distinguish.

فَرَّقَ To scatter ; disperse.

فَرَّقَ على To distribute among.

فَرَّقَ بَيْنَ To stir up dissention.

فَارَقَ To abandon. Die.

تَفَرَّقَ وآفْتَرَقَ To be separated.

تَفَارَقَ To leave one another.

إِنْفَرَقَ عَنْ To be separated from.

فَرْقٌ Difference, distinction.

الْفُرْقَانُ The Koran.

فِرْقَةٌ ج فِرَقٌ Party of men.

فُرْقَةٌ وآفْتِرَاقٌ Separation.

فِرَاقٌ Separation. Death.

فَرِيقٌ General of a division.

أَفْرِيقِيَةُ Africa.

تَفْرِيقٌ Separation, dispersion.

بِالتَّفْرِيقِ In parts, in detail.

مَفْرَقٌ ج مَفَارِقُ A point from which a road branches.

فَرَكَ يَفْرُكُ فَرْكاً To rub.

أَفْرَكَ To be mature, (grain).

إِنْفَرَكَ To be rubbed and pressed.

إِسْتَفْرَكَ To become full (grain).

فَرْكٌ Act of rubbing ; friction.

فَرِيكٌ Rubbed soft grain.

فَرَمَ يَفْرِم فَرْماً To mince.

فَرَّمَ To change the teeth, (child).

(فَرْمَةٌ) A small piece.

فَرَمَانٌ Firman.

فرنٌ ج أَفْرَانٌ Oven.

فَرَّانٌ Baker.

إِفْرَنْجٌ وفِرَنْجٌ Europeans. Franks.

فَرَنْسَا France.

فَرَنْسِيٌّ فَرَنْسَاوِيٌّ French.

فَرَّى تَفْرِيَةً To line with fur.

فَرْوٌ ج فِرَاءٌ Garment of fur.

فَرْوَةٌ Scalp. Fur-cloak.

فَرَّاءٌ Furrier.

إِفْتَرَى ٱلْكَذِب — To fabricate a lie.

فِرْيَةٌ ج فِرًى — Wilful lie.

فَرِيٌّ — Unusual thing.

فَزَّ ـِ — To be excited.

فَزَّ وَأَفَزَّ — To frighten, disturb.

إِسْتَفَزَّ — To excite, incite.

فَزَرَ يَفْزِرُ فَزْرًا — To cut ; break.

فَزِعَ يَفْزَعُ فَزَعًا — To be afraid.

فَزِعَ إِلَى — To flee for help to.

فَزَّعَ وَأَفْزَعَ — To frighten.

فَزَعٌ — Fear ; fright.

فَزِعٌ — Frightened, afraid.

مَفْزَعٌ — Refuge. Succour.

فُسْتُقٌ — Pistachio (tree and fruit).

فُسْتُقِيَّةٌ — Basin ; reservoir.

فُسْتَانٌ ج فَسَاتِينُ — Female gown.

فَسَحَ يَفْسَحُ وَأَفْسَحَ لَهُ فِي — To make place for ; permit.

فَسُحَ يَفْسُحُ — To be spacious, (place).

فَسَّحَ — To make roomy, wide.

إِنْفَسَحَ صَدْرُه — His bosom was dilated (with joy).

فُسْحَةٌ ج فُسَحٌ — Space ; court-yard.

فَسَاحَةٌ — Spaciousness, width.

فَسِيحٌ — Spacious, roomy, ample.

فَسَخَ يَفْسَخُ — To annul, abrogate.

فَسَّخَ — To split.

إِنْفَسَخَ — To be annulled, split.

فَسْخٌ — Abrogation. Separation.

فُسْخَةٌ — A part, a piece.

فَسِيخٌ — Salted fish.

فَسَدَ يَفْسُدُ — To become corrupt.

فَسَّدَ وَأَفْسَدَ — To corrupt.

أَفْسَدَ بَيْنَ — To stir up strife.

إِنْفَسَدَ — To be corrupted, bad.

فَسَادٌ — Corruption, mischief. Invalidity. Decomposition.

فَاسِدٌ — Bad. Invalid. Spoilt.

مُفْسِدٌ — Causing mischief or strife.

مَفْسَدَةٌ ج مَفَاسد Cause of evil.

فَسَّرَ To make plain ; explain.

إِسْتَفْسَرَ To seek an explanation.

تَفْسِيرٌ ج تَفَاسِير Explanation.

فُسْطَاطٌ Pavilion ; tent.

فُسْفُورٌ وَفُصْفُورٌ Phosphorus.

فَسَافِس Bugs ; bed-bugs.

فُسَيْفِسَاء Mosaic-pavement.

فَسَقَ يَفْسق To be impious.

فِسقٌ وَفُسُوقٌ Impiety.

فَاسِقٌ Impious, dissolute.

فَاسِقة Adulteress.

فَشَّ يَفُشُّ فَشًّا To pick a lock.

فشَّ خُلْقَهُ To vent one's anger.

فَشَخَ يَفْشَخُ Do take a wide step.

فَشْخَة A step.

فَشَرَ وَفَشَّر To talk incoherently.

فُشَّارٌ Incoherent talk ; babbling.

فَشَكَةٌ ج فَشَكٌ) Cartridge.

فَشِلَ يَفْشَلُ To be faint-hearted.

تَفَشَّلَ To fail, be disappointed.

فَشَلٌ Disappointment.

فَشَا يَفْشُو فَشْواً To be spread.

أَفْشَى To spread. Divulge.

تَفَشَّى To become wide ; extend.

فَصٌّ ج فُصُوصٌ Stone or gem of a signet-ring. Lobe.

فَصة A species of clover.

فَصَحَ يَفْصَح To break forth, (light).

افْصَح To appear clearly.

تَفَاصَح To affect eloquence.

فِصْحٌ Passover ; Easter.

فَصَاحَةٌ Lucidity ; eloquence.

فَصِيحٌ ج فُصَحَاء Elegant speaker.

فَصَدَ يَفْصِدُ فَصْداً To open a vein.

إِنْفَصَدَ To be bled.

فَصَّادٌ Bleeder, phlebotomist.

A person who is bled.	مَفْصُودٌ
Lancet.	مِفْصَدٌ
To cut off ; separate. Decide a disputed point.	فَصَلَ يَفْصِلُ
To divide into parts.	فَصَّلَ
To bargain for a price.	فَاصَلَ
To expire ; die.	أَفْصَلَ
To be separated ; detatched.	إِنْفَصَلَ
To go away from.	إِنْفَصَلَ عَنْ
Separation. Chapter. A season of the year.	فَصْلٌ ج فُصُولٌ
That which separates.	فَاصِلٌ
Decisive judgment.	حُكْمٌ فَاصِلٌ
Family ; species.	فَصِيلَةٌ ج فَصَائِل
Judge, arbiter.	فَيْصَلٌ ج فَيَاصِل
Detailed statement.	تَفْصِيلٌ ج تَفَاصِيلُ
In detail.	بِالتَّفْصِيلِ
Joint.	مَفْصِلٌ ج مَفَاصِل
Rheumatism.	دَاءُ الْمَفَاصِل
Cut out. Detailed.	مُفَصَّلٌ
In detail.	مُفَصَّلاً
Hinge.	مُفَصَّلَةٌ ج مُفَصَّلاتٌ
Detached.	مَفْصُولٌ ومُنْفَصِلُ
To break, crack.	فَصَمَ يَفْصِمُ
To be broken, cracked.	إِنْفَصَمَ
To break open.	فَضَّ يَفُضُّ فَضًّا
To cover with silver.	فَضَّضَ
To be dispersed.	إِنْفَضَّ
Silver. Para.	فِضَّةٌ
To divulge, disgrace.	فَضَحَ يَفْضَحُ
Disgrace.	فَضِيحَةٌ ج فَضَائِحُ
To remain over.	فَضَلَ يَفْضُلُ
To excel, surpass.	فَضَلَ وعَلَى
To prefer.	فَضَّلَ عَلَى
To show favour.	أَفْضَلَ وتَفَضَّلَ
Do me the favour.	تَفَضَّلْ
To leave a part.	إِسْتَفْضَلَ مِنْ

فَضْلٌ ج فُضُولٌ Excess Favour.
Superiority, excellence.

فَضْلاً عَن Besides.

فَضْلَةٌ Portion remaining.

فَاضِلٌ وَفَضِيلٌ Superior; excellent.

فُضُولٌ Officiousness.

فُضُولِيٌّ Meddlesome.

فَضِيلَةٌ ج فَضَائِل Virtue. Excellence.

أَفْضَل ج أَفَاضِل Better.

أَلأَفْضَلُ The best.

حِسَابُ ٱلتَّمَامِ وَٱلتَّفَاضُلِ Calculus
(integral and differential).

تَفْضِيلٌ Preference.

إِسْمُ ٱلتَّفْضِيلِ Adjective in the
comparative degree, *as* : أَكْبَرُ

مُفَضَّلٌ Preferable.

مِفْضَالٌ Distinguished for excellence.

فَضَا يَفْضُو فَضَاءً To be empty.

فَضَّى To empty, turn out.

أَفْضَى إِلَى To reach. Lead to.

تَفَضَّى لِ To have leisure for.

فَضَاءٌ Open space.

فَاضٍ Empty; unoccupied.

فَطْرًا To create, (God).

فَطَرَ وأَفْطَرَ To bre ak one's fast.

تَفَطَّرَ وَٱنْفَطَرَ To be broken.

فِطْرٌ Fungus.

عِيدُ ٱلْفِطْرِ Feast of Ramadan.

فِطْرَةٌ ج فِطَرٌ Innate quality.

فَاطِرٌ Creator.

فُطُورٌ Midday, meal.

فَطِيرٌ Unleavened.

عِيدُ ٱلْفِطْرِ Jewish feast of unleavened bread.

فَطِيرَةٌ ج فَطَائِرُ Pastry-cake.

فَطَسَ يَفْطِسُ فُطُوسًا To die.

فَطِسَ يَفْطَسُ To be suffocated.

فَطَّسَ To kill. Suffocate.

أَفْطَسُ م فَطْسَاءُ ج فُطْسٌ Flat-nosed.

فَطَمَ يَفْطِمُ	To wean (an infant).
إِنْفَطَمَ	To be weaned.
إِنْفَطَمَ عَنْ	To cease from.
فِطَامٌ	Weaning.
فَطِيمٌ ومَفْطُومٌ	Weaned (child).
فَطِنَ يَفْطِنُ بِ	To remember ; consider. Understand.
فَطَّنَ بِ	To remind.
تَفَطَّنَ ل	To understand. Remember.
فِطْنَةٌ	Understanding ; sagacity.
فَطِنٌ وفَطِينٌ	Intelligent.
فَظَّ يَفَظُّ فَظَاظَةً	To be rough, rude.
فَظٌّ ج فِظَاظٌ	Rough, rude.
فَظُعَ يَفْظُعُ فَظَاعَةً	To be horrid.
فَظِعٌ وفَظِيعٌ	Atrocious ; horrid.
فَعَلَ يَفْعَلُ	To do ; perform ; act.
إِنْفَعَلَ	To be affected. Be done.
افْتَعَلَ	To forge ; invent.
فِعْلٌ ج أَفْعَالٌ	Act, deed. Verb.
فَاعِلٌ ج فَعَلَةٌ	Doer. Agent or subject of the verb.
إِسْمُ ٱلْفَاعِلِ	Noun of agent.
نَائِبُ ٱلْفَاعِلِ	Agentor subject of the passive verb.
فَعَّالٌ	Effective, efficient.
إِنْفِعَالٌ ج إِنْفِعَالَاتٌ	Influence, impression.
إِنْفِعَالٌ نَفْسَانِيٌّ	Emotion.
تَفْعِيلٌ ج تَفَاعِيلُ	Foot (*in prosody*).
مَفْعُولٌ ج مَفَاعِيلُ	Something done. Impression ; influence.
مَفْعُولٌ بِهِ	Object of transitive verb.
إِسْمُ ٱلْمَفْعُولِ	Noun of patient.
مُفْتَعَلٌ	Invented. Done purposely.
فَعَمَ يَفْعَمُ	To fill (a vessel).
فَعِمَ يَفْعَمُ فُعُومَةً	To be full.
مُفْعَمٌ	Filled, full.
أَفْعَى وأُفْعُوانٌ ج أَفَاعٍ	Viper.
فَغَرَ يَفْغَرُ	To open (the mouth).
فَغَرَ وَٱنْفَغَرَ	To open.
فَقَأَ يَفْقَأُ	To open (an abscess). Put out an eye.

تَفَقَّأَ وَانْفَقَأَ To burst; break.

فَقَدَ يَفْقِدُ فَقْداً وَفُقْدَاناً To lose.

أَفْقَدَ To deprive of, cause to lose.

تَفَقَّدَ To seek a lost object.

إِفْتَقَدَ To miss, fail to find. Visit a sick person.

فَقِيدٌ وَمَفْقُودٌ Lost object. Dead.

فَقَرَ يَفْقُرُ To slit, perforate.

أَفْقَرَ To impoverish.

إِفْتَقَرَ To become poor.

إِفْتَقَرَ إِلَى To need.

فَقْرٌ Poverty; need.

فَقْرَةٌ ج فِقَرٌ Vertebra.

فَقِيرٌ ج فُقَرَاءُ Poor; needy.

فَقَسَ يَفْقِسُ فَقْساً To hatch eggs (bird).

تَفَقَّسَ وَانْفَقَسَ To be hatched.

فَقُّوسٌ Small melon.

فَقَشَ يَفْقُشُ فَقْشاً To break open.

فَقَطْ Only.

فَقَعَ To die from heat or grief.

إِنْفَقَعَ To be cleft or rent.

فَاقِعٌ Very bright-coloured.

فُقَّاعَةٌ ج فَقَاقِيعُ Bubble of air.

(فُقَّيْعٌ) Unripe figs.

فَقْرٌ مُفْقِعٌ Excessive poverty.

فَقِمَ يَفْقَمُ To be full, (vessel).

تَفَاقَمَ To become very serious.

فُقْمَةٌ وَفُقَّمَةٌ Seal. (sea-animal).

فَقِهَ يَفْقَهُ فِقْهاً To understand.

فَقُهَ يَفْقُهُ To be skilled in the Law.

فَقَّهَ وَأَفْقَهَ To teach.

تَفَقَّهَ To understand; learn.

فِقْهٌ Knowledge; intelligence.

عِلْمُ الْفِقْهِ Science of Law.

فَقَاهَةٌ Understanding; learning.

فَقِيهٌ ج فُقَهَاءُ Skilled in Law.

فَكَّ يَفُكُّ فَكًّا To separate; untie.
فَكَّكَ To separate ; disentangle.
إِنْفَكَّ To be separated ; untied.
مَا انْفَكَّ Not to cease.
إِسْتَفَكَّ To seek redemption.
فَكٌّ ج فُكُوكٌ Jaw-bone.
فَكَرَ يَفْكِرُ وَفَكَّرَ وتَفَكَّرَ وَافْتَكَرَ فِي To think of ; consider.
(فَكَّرَ) To remind.
فِكْرٌ ج أَفْكَارٌ Thought ; reflection.
فِكِّيرٌ Very thoughtful.
(فَاكُورَةٌ ج فَوَاكِيرُ) Latch.
فَكِهَ يَفْكَهُ فَكَاهَةً To be gay.
فَكَّهَ To cheer by wit.
تَفَكَّهَ بِ To enjoy.
تَفَاكَهَ To jest with another.
فَكِهٌ ج فَكِهُونَ Merry ; cheerful.
فَاكِهَةٌ ج فَوَاكِهُ Fruit.
فُكَاهَةٌ Jesting ; merriment.

فَلَّ يَفُلُّ فَلًّا To blunt or notch.
فُلٌّ Arabian Jasmine.
فَلَتَ يَفْلِتُ To free, liberate.
أَفْلَتَ وتَفَلَّتَ وانْفَلَتَ To escape
تَفَلَّتَ عَلَى To spring on.
فَلْتٌ Escape.
فَلْتَةٌ Sudden event.
فَلْتَةً Suddenly. Undesignedly.
(فَلَتِيٌّ) Vagabond.
فَالِتٌ Loose, free.
(كَلَامٌ فَالِتٌ) Improper language.
فُلِجَ وَانْفَلَجَ To be paralyzed.
انْفَلَجَ To shine, (day break).
فَالِجٌ Paralysis ; palsy.
مَفْلُوجٌ Paralysed ; paralytic.
فَلَحَ يَفْلَحُ To plough ; till.
أَفْلَحَ To prosper; be successful.
فَلْحٌ ج فُلُوحٌ Furrow.
فَلَاحٌ Prosperity ; success.

فَلاَحَةٌ	Agriculture.
فَلاَّحٌ ج فَلاَّحُونَ	Farmer, peasant.
فِلذة ج أَفْلاَذ	A piece.
فَالُوذ وَفَالُوذَجٌ	A sweet pastry.
فُولاَذٌ (بُولاَدٌ)	Steel.
فِلِزٌّ	Bronze. Metal.
فَلَّسَ	To proclaim bankrupt.
أَفْلَسَ	To become bankrupt.
فَلسٌ ج فُلُوسٌ	A small coin. *Pl.* scales of fish. Money.
إِفْلاَسٌ	Insolvency, bankruptcy.
مُفْلِسٌ	Bankrupt ; penniless.
فِلَسْطِينَ	Palestine.
تَفَلْسَفَ	To philosophize.
فَلْسَفَةٌ	Philosophy.
أَلْفَلْسَفَةُ ٱلطَّبِيعِيَّةُ	Physics.
أَلفَلْسَفَةُ ٱلعَقْلِيَّةُ	Psychology.
فَلْسَفِيٌّ	Philosophical.
فَيْلَسُوفٌ ج فَلاَسِفَة	Philosopher.
(فَلَشَ)	To spread out.
(إِنفَلَشَ)	To be spread out.
(فَلَصَ يَفْلُصُ مِنْ)	To escape from.
افْلَصَ وتَفَلَّصَ وَٱنْفَلَصَ	To escape.
فَلطَحَ	To flatten, make broad.
مُفَلطَحٌ	Flattened ; broad.
فَلْفَلَ	To pepper.
فُلْفُلٌ وَفِلْفِلٌ	Pepper (tree or fruit).
فُلَيْفِلَةٌ	Pepper plant.
مُفَلْفَلٌ	Peppered.
فَلَقَ يَفْلِقُ	To cleave ; split.
أَفْلَقَ وَٱفْتَلَقَ	To be skilled in.
تَفَلَّقَ وَٱنْفَلَقَ	To be split, cleft.
انْفَلَقَ ٱلصُّبْحُ	The dawn broke.
فَلَقٌ ج أَفْلاَق	Dawn. Stocks.
فِلْقَةٌ ج فِلَقٌ	Lobe. Cotyledon.
مُفْلِق	Distinguished (poet).
فَلَّكَ وَتَفَلَّكَ	To augur or predict.
فُلْكٌ	Ship. Noah's ark.

فَلَكٌ ج أَفْلَاكٌ — Celestial sphere.

عِلْمُ الْفَلَك — Astronomy.

فَلَكِيٌّ — Astronomer.

(فُلُوكَةٌ) — Small ship ; boat.

فُلَانٌ — A certain person.

فُلَانِيٌّ — Such and such.

(فَلَا) — Open space ; the open air.

فِلْوٌ ج فَلَاوَى وَأَفْلَاءٌ — Foal.

فَلَاةٌ ج فَلَوَاتٌ — Open country.

فَلَّى — To clean from lice.

فِلِّينٌ — Cork. Bottle-cork.

فَلْيُونٌ — God-son.

فَمٌ وَفَمٌّ — Mouth. (*see* فوه)

فَنٌّ ج فُنُونٌ — Form ; kind. Art.

تَفَنَّنَ — To be accomplished.

مُتَفَنِّنٌ — Accomplished ; skilful.

فِنْجَانٌ ج فَنَاجِينُ — Small cup.

فَنَّدَ — To state in detail. Accuse of untruth or error.

فِنْدٌ فُنُودٌ — Branch. Taper.

فُنْدُقٌ ج فَنَادِق — Inn ; hotel.

فَنَارٌ ج فَنَارَاتٌ — Lantern. Light-house.

فَانُوسٌ ج فَوَانِيسُ — Lantern. Lamp.

فَنِيَ يَفْنَى — To perish.

أَفْنَى — To annihilate ; destroy.

فَنَاءٌ — Destruction. Vanishing.

فَانٍ — Transient ; perishing.

فَهْدٌ ج فُهُود — Panther ; lynx.

فَهْرَسَ — To make index.

فِهْرِسٌ وَفِهْرِسْتٌ ج فَهَارِس — Catalogue. Index, table of contents.

فَهِمَ يَفْهَمُ — To understand.

فَهَّمَ وَأَفْهَمَ — To make understand.

إِنْفَهَمَ — To be understood.

إِسْتَفْهَمَ — To seek to know.

فَهْمٌ — Understanding.

فَهِيمٌ وَفَهَّامَة — Very intelligent.

إِسْتِفْهَامٌ — Interrogation.

إِسْمُ اسْتِفْهَامٍ — Interrogative pronoun.

مَفْهومٌ	Understood. Meaning.
فَاتَ يَفوتُ	To pass. Miss.
فَوَّتَ	To make pass ; omit.
تَفَاوتَ	To differ ; be dissimilar.
فَوتٌ وفواتٌ	Passing ; missing.
تَفاوتٌ	Dissimilarity ; difference.
فوجٌ ج أَفْواجٌ	Troop ; company.
افواجاً أفواجاً	In troops, crowds.
فاح يَفوح	To be diffused, (odour).
فار يَفور فَوراً وفوراَنَاً	To boil.
أَفَار وفَوَّر	To make boil.
فارٌ ج فيرانٌ	Mice.
فارةٌ	Mouse. Carpenter's plane.
علَى ٱلْفَور	Immediately ; at once.
فَوَّارةٌ	Jet d'eau ; fountain.
فازَ يَفوز	To win, succeed.
فاز بِ	To obtain ; attain.
فَوْزٌ	Success. Escape.
مفازَةٌ ج مفازاتٌ ومَفاوزُ	Desert.
(فاش يَفوش فَوْشاً)	To float.
فَوَّضَ إلى	To commit to.
فاوض	To converse with.
تَفاوض	To converse together.
فَوْضَى	Anarchy.
مُفاوضَةٌ	Conversation.
فُوطَةٌ ج فوطٌ	Napkin ; towel.
فاق يَفوق	To surpass; excel.
فَاقَ فَوَاقاً	To hiccough.
أَفاق واَستَفاق مِن	To awake.
فَوقُ	Above ; upon ; beyond.
إلى فوقُ	Upwards.
فَما فوقُ	And upwards.
فاقةٌ	Poverty ; want ; need.
فَوقانيٌّ	What is above.
فُواقٌ	Hiccough.
فائقٌ	Surpassing, excelling.
فائِقُ ٱلْوصف	Beyond description.
فولٌ (فولَةٌ *sing.*)	Horse-beans.

Cook or seller of beans.	فوّالٌ
Garlic.	فومٌ
To speak ; utter.	فَاهَ يفوهُ وتفوَّه
Mouth,	فوهٌ وفمٌ ج أفواهٌ وأفمَامٌ
Madder-root.	فوّةٌ وفوّةٌ
Opening.	فوّهةٌ ج فوّهاتٌ وأفواهٌ
In, among, with, at.	في
To shade.	فَاءَ وفَيأً
To shade one's self.	تفيّأ
Shadow.	فيءٌ ج أفياءٌ
Party ; company.	فئةٌ ج فئاتٌ
To flow.	فاحَ يفيح فيْحاً وفيحَانًا
To spill, shed.	أفَاح
Wide ; extensive.	أفيح م فيحاء
To benefit ; serve ; mean.	أفَاد
To be benefited ; acquire.	إستفاد
Benefit ; use ; profit. Interest (on money).	فَائدةٌ ج فوائد
Bestowal of benefit.	إفَادةٌ
Beneficial ; useful.	مفيدٌ
Turquoise (stone).	فيروزٌ
See under. فَصْلٌ	فيصلٌ
To abound ; overflow, (river.) Be full, (vessel).	فَاض يَفيض فيضَانًا
To pour (water) ; fill.	أفَاض
Abundance.	فَيْضٌ ج فيوضٌ
Periodic overflow or inundation of the Nile.	فيضَانُ النّيل
Waterless desert.	فيفَاءٌ ج فَيَافٍ
Elephant.	فيلٌ ج أفْيالٌ وفيلَة
An army-corps.	فَيْلَق ج فيالقُ
Why ? Wherefore ?	فيم (في ما)
To be niggardly.	فَان يَفين فينًا

ق

As a numeral sign=100. ق

To make convex. قَبَّبَ

Collar (to a shirt, &c.). (قَبَّةٌ)

Cupola, dome. قُبَّةٌ ج قُبَبٌ

Large steelyard. قَبَّانٌ ج قَبَابِين

Surmounted with a dome. مُقَبَّبٌ

To be ugly, vile. قَبُحَ يَقْبُحُ

To render, or deem ugly. قَبَّحَ

To revile, insult. قَابَحَ

To act meanly, shamefully. اقبح

To detest, abhor. إِسْتَقْبَحَ

Ugliness, foulness. قُبْحٌ وقَبَاحَةٌ

Fie on him! قُبْحًا لَهُ

Ugly, infamous. قَبِيحٌ ج قِبَاحٌ

Vile action. قَبِيحَةٌ ج قَبَائِح

To bury, inter. قَبَرَ يَقْبُرُ قَبْرًا

Grave, sepulchre. قَبْرٌ ج قُبُورٌ

Sky-lark, lark. قُنْبُرَةٌ ج قَنَابِر

Capers. قُبَّارٌ

Cemetery. مَقْبَرَةٌ ج مَقَابِر

Interred, buried. مَقْبُورٌ

Cyprus (island). قُبْرُس

Of Cyprus; Cypriote. قُبْرُسِيٌّ

To seek قَبَسَ يَقْبِسُ وَاقْتَبَسَ مِن
fire, or knowledge, from.

To quote an author. إِقْتَبَسَ مِن

A coal, a fire-brand. قَبْسَةٌ

To seize, grasp; قَبَضَ يَقْبِضُ
arrest. To contract.

To receive (money). قَبَضَ

God caused him to die. قَبَضَهُ

To die. قُبِض

To make a payment to. قَبَّض

To shrink. تَقَبَّض وٱنقَبَض

Grasping, taking possession. Constipation. قَبْضٌ

A grasp ; handful. قَبْضَةٌ

Handle, haft, hilt. قَبْضَةٌ

Astringent. قَابِضٌ

Contraction, constipation. إِنقِبَاضٌ

Handle, hilt. مَقْبَضٌ ج مَقَابِض

Seized ; received. Dead. مَقْبُوضٌ

Copts. قِبْطٌ وأَقْبَاط

A Copt ; Coptic. قِبْطِيٌّ

Hood, cowl. قُبْعٌ وقُبَّعَةٌ

Clogs. قَبْقَابٌ ج قَبَاقِيب

To receive, accept, admit ; consent, agree to. قَبِلَ يَقْبَل قَبُولاً

To take up. أَقْبَلَ عَلَى

To approach, be near. أَقْبَلَ

To kiss. قَبَّلَ

To correspond to ; meet. قَابَلَ

To compare, collate. قَابَلَ بِ

To receive, accept. تَقَبَّلَ

To meet ; be compared. تَقَابَلَ

To go to meet, receive. إِستَقبَل

Previously. قبلُ وَقَبْلاً ومِن قَبلُ

Side, direction. قِبلٌ

With respect to ; from. مِنْ قبله

Direction of Mecca. South. قبلةٌ

Kiss. قبلةٌ ج قبَلٌ . وتَقْبِيلٌ

Southern. قبليٌّ

Capable of, subject to. قَابِلٌ ل

Midwife. Receiver. قَابِلةٌ ج قوابلُ

Capacity ; appetite. قَابِليَّةٌ

Over against. قبالةٌ

Midwifery. قِبَالة

Consent ; reception. قبولٌ

As regards this. مِنْ هذَا القبيل

قبيلة ج قبائل	Tribe.
إقبال	Approach. Prosperity.
إستقبال	The future. Reception.
مقابلة	Meeting. Collation (of two texts). Antithesis.
مقبل	Coming, approaching.
مقابل	Opposite to, in front of.
مقبول	Accepted ; received.
مستقبل	The future ; Facing.
قبّن	To weigh with steelyard.
قبّان	Steelyard.
قبانة	Trade of a weigher.
قبّاني	One who weighs.
قبونة	Weighing.
قبا يقبو قبواً	To bend, curve.
قباء ج أقبية	Outer garment.
قبو ج أقبية	Vault.
قتب ج أقتاب	Small pack-saddle.
قتر وأقتر على	To be niggardly.
قتر وتقتير	Avarice, economy.
قاتر ومقتر	Parsimonious, economical.
قتل يقتل	To kill, murder.
قاتل مقاتلة	To fight against.
تقاتل واقتتل	To combat with one another, fight.
إستقتل	To seek death, stake one's life.
قتل	Murder ; execution.
قاتل ج قتلة	Murderer, assassin.
قتال ومقاتلة	Battle, combat.
قتّال	Deadly, causing death.
قتيل ج قتلى . ومقتول	Killed.
مقتل	Vital part (of the body).
مقاتل	Warrior, combatant.
قتام	Darkness.
قاتم وأقتم	Dark-coloured.
قثّاء	Cucumber.
قثّاء الحمار	*Elaterium.*
(قحّ يقحّ)	To cough.
قحّ ج اقحاح	Pure, unmixed.

A cough. (قَحَّة)

Cough. Prostitute. قَحْبَة ج قِحَابٌ

To be rainless. قَحِطَ يَقْحَطُ وأُقْحِطَ

Drought, famine. قَحْطٌ

Year of drought. عَامٌ مُقْحِطٌ

To sweep away. قَحَفَ يَقْحَفُ

Skull. قِحْفٌ ج أَقْحَافٌ

What is swept away. قُحَافَة

Winnowing-fan; dust-pan. مِقْحَفَة

To dry up, wither. قَحِلَ يَقْحَلُ قَحْلاً

To dry, cause to wither. أَقْحَلَ

Dryness, aridity. قُحُولَة

To rush. قَحَمَ يَقْحُمُ قُحُوماً في

To draw near to. قَحَمَ إلى

To rush upon. إِقْتَحَمَ

Anthemis, camomile. أُقْحُوان

Particle, e. g. Zeid has *just* risen. قد. قَدْ قَامَ زَيْدٌ

The liar *sometimes* speaks the truth. قَدْ يَصْدُقُ الكَذُوب

Verily he prospers. قَدْ أَفْلَحَ

To cut, cleave. قَدَّ يَقُدُّ قَدًّا

To cut and dry (meat). قَدَّدَ

To be cut and dried. تَقَدَّدَ

To be cut, slit, divided. إِنْقَدَّ

Stature, size. قَدٌّ ج قُدُودٌ

Equal to in measure. عَلَى قَدِّهِ

Goodly in form. حَسَنُ القَدِّ

Cured meat. قَدِيدٌ ومُقَدَّدٌ

To bore, pierce. قَدَحَ يَقْدَحُ

To strike fire. قَدَحَ واقْتَدَحَ

To revile, censure. قَدَحَ في

Drinking-cup. قَدَحٌ ج أَقْدَاحٌ

Slanderer, calumniator. قَادِحٌ

Gimlet. مِقْدَحٌ ومِقْدَاحٌ

To be able. قَدَرَ يَقْدِرُ عَلَى

To measure; compute. قَدَرَ وقَدَّرَ

To decree for. قَدَرَ وقَدَّرَ عَلَى

To prepare, assign. قدر لِ

To put a value upon. قدَّر
To enable. قَدر على
To be preordained. تقدَّر
To be powerful, or rich. اقْتَدر
Quantity, measure. قَدْرٌ
Fate ; divine decree. قَدْرٌ ج أَقْدارٌ
Powder, position.
Cooking-pot. قدْرٌ ج قُدورٌ
Might, power, authority. قدرةٌ
Powerful ; able. قَادرٌ وقديرٌ
The Omnipotent. ألقدير
Predestination. تقديرٌ ج تقادير
Suppositon. Implied meaning.
Evaluation.
Hypothetically. تقديراً
Quantity, fixed measure. مقدارٌ
As much as. بِمقْدارِ ما
Power, ability. مقْدرةٌ
Valuer, estimator. مقدِّرٌ
Predestinated. مقَدَّرٌ ومقدورٌ

To hallow ; sanctify. قدَّس
To be purified, sanctified. تَقدَّس
Holiness. قُدْسٌ وقداسةٌ
Jerusalem. القُدْس
The Holy Ghost. (ألروح ألقدس)
Mass, liturgy. قداسٌ ج قداديس
The All-Holy (God). القدوس
Saint. قدّيسٌ ج قدّيسونَ
Sanctification. تقْديسٌ
Jerusalem. بيت ألمَقدس
Sanctified. مقدسٌ ومُتقدّسٌ
The Holy Bible. ألكِتَاب ألمقدَّس
To arrive from. قدِم يقدُم من
To be old. قدم يقْدم . وتقادم
To prefer (a thing). قدَّمهُ علَى
To present, offer to. قَدم ل
To undertake boldly. اقْدم على
To advance, lead. تقدَّم
To advance towards. تقدَّم إِلى

تقدَّم على To surpass.

قِدْمٌ وقِدْمَةٌ Antiquity.

قِدَمٌ Precedence.

قدمٌ ج أَقْدَامٌ Foot.

قُدمَةٌ Priority, precedence.

قَادِمٌ Comer ; coming.

قُدَّام In front of, before.

قَدومٌ ج قُدُمٌ Courageous, bold.

قَدُومٌ وقدُّومٌ Hatchet, adze.

قَدِيمٌ ج قُدماءُ Ancient, old.

أَلْقَدِيم The Eternal (God).

قَدِيمًا وفي ٱلقديم Formerly.

من ٱلقديم In olden times.

اقدم ج أَقْدمون More ancient.

أَلأَقْدمون The ancients.

إِقْدَامٌ Boldness ; diligence.

تَقْدِمَةٌ ج تَقَادم Present ; offering.

تقديمٌ Presenting, offering.

تَقَدُّم Pre-eminence ; progress.

تَقَادُمٌ Antiquity, oldness, &c.

مُقَدَّمٌ Front part, fore part.

مُقَدَّمَةٌ Advance guard of (an army). Preface ; premise.

متقدّمٌ One who is in advance.

متقدّمٌ ذِكْره Afore-mentioned.

مِقْدامٌ Courageous, energetic.

اقتدَى ب To imitate, emulate.

قُدْوَةٌ Model for imitation.

قِدْيَةٌ Way, manner.

اقتِداءٌ Imitation.

قَذَرَ يَقْذُر وقذ ر يقذر To be unclean.

قَذَّرَ To foul, render unclean.

قذرٌ ج أَقْذارٌ وقاذورةٌ Filth.

قذرٌ Dirty, filthy ; unclean.

قذف يَقْذِف To throw. Row.

قذف بِ To accuse of.

قَذْف Throwing ; abusing.

قذَّافٌ Rower.

Oar. مقذافٌ ومقذفٌ ج مقاذيف

Mote, or small particle. قَذًى

To stay, dwell. قَرَّ يقِرُّ

To persist, persevere in. قَرَّ على

He was content. قَرَّ عيناً

To settle, fix, establish. قَرَّر

To cause one to stay. قَرَّر وأقرَّ

To cause one to confess. To settle, fix. قَرَّر

To decide upon. قَرَّر في نفسِه أن

To confess, avow. أقرَّ ب

To refresh, console. أقرَّ عينَه

To be stated, determined. تقرَّر

To dwell, inhabit. إستقرَّ في

Water-cress. Darling. قُرَّة العَين

Dwelling ; stability. قَرارٌ

Refrain, (music). قَرارٌ

Continent, firm-land. قارةٌ

Glass bottle. قارورةٌ ج قوارير

Consoled, content. قريرُ العَين

Affirmation ; confession. إقرارٌ

Report. تقريرٌ

Residence. مقرٌّ ومستقرٌّ

To read. قرأ يقرأُ قراءةً

To study with (a teacher). قرأ على

To send, or deliver, a greeting. أقرأه السلام

To investigate. إستقرأ

Act of reading. قراءةٌ ج قراءاتٌ

The Coran. القرآن

Reader, reciter. قارئٌ ج قرّاء

Read, recited. مقروءٌ ومقريٌّ ومقروٌّ

To approach. قَرِب يقرَب الى ومن

To bring near ; offer. قرَّب

To be near to. قارب

To be on the point of. قارب أن

To approach. تقرَّب تقرُّباً إلى

To be near one another. تقارب

To approach. إقترب

قُرْبٌ Nearness.
عن قُرب Near ; soon.
بِٱقْرب مِن In the vicinity of.
قُرْبَةٌ ج قِرَبَاتٌ وَقِرَبٌ Skin-bag.
قُرْبَانٌ ج قَرَابِين Offering to God.
قِرَابٌ ج اقربة Sheath, scabbard.
قرابةٌ وَقُربَى Kinship ; relations.
قَاربٌ ج قَوَارب Boat, skiff.
قَرِيبٌ ج أَقْرِبَاء Near ; related ; neighbour, followman ; relation.
عن قَرِيب Shortly, soon.
أَقْرَبُ Nearer ; more probable.
تَقْرِيبٌ Approximation.
تَقْرِيبًا و بِٱلتَّقْرِيب Approximately.
قَرْبُوسٌ ج قَرَابِيس Pommel.
قرح يَقْرِح قَرحًا To wound.
قرح يَقْرَح To finish teething (horse).
إِقْترح To invent ; improvise. Demand.
قَرحةٌ A wound ; an ulcer.

قَرَاحٌ Pure (water).
قَرِيحَة ج قرائح Talent, genius.
قِردٌ ج قُرودٌ Ape, monkey.
قُرادٌ ج أَقْرِدَةٌ Tick, (insect).
قردح To burn, blaze (coal).
قرداحيٌّ وَقَردَحْجِيٌّ Armourer.
قرس يَقْرِس قَرسًا To freeze.
قَارِسٌ وقَرِيسٌ Intense cold.
(قَرَاسِيَا) A kind of plum.
قرش ٱلْحَلِيب To curdle (milk).
قِرشٌ ج قُروشٌ Piastre.
قُرَيْشٌ Tribe of Koreish.
قُرَيشَةٌ Sweet curd.
(مُقَرِّشٌ) Rich.
قَرَص يَقْرُص قَرصًا To pinch.
قَرَّص To cut out (dough).
قُرصٌ ج أَقْرَاصٌ Disc ; cake.
قُرَّاصٌ وَ(قُرَّيْصٌ) Nettle (plant).
قُرصانٌ Corsairs, pirates.

قَرَضَ يَقْرِض — To cut ; nibble.

أَقْرَض — To lend one money.

إِنقَرَض — To die out, perish.

إِقتَرَض وآستَقرَض — To borrow.

قَرْضٌ ج قروضٌ — Loan, debt.

قُرَاضَةٌ — Cuttings, clippings.

قريضٌ — Poetry.

مِقْرَاضٌ ج مقَاريض — Scissors.

قَرَط يقرط — To cut.

قَرَّطَ عَلَى — To give little to.

قَرْطٌ ج أَقْراطٌ — Ear-ring. Cluster.

قيراطٌ ج قَراريط — Carat, inch.

قُرْطُبَة — Cordova (in Spain).

قُرْطَاسٌ ج قراطِيس — Paper.

قَرْطَلٌ ج قراطل — Reed-basket.

قَرَّظَ — To laud, eulogize.

تَقْرِيظٌ — Eulogy. Panegyric.

قَرَع يَقْرَع قَرعاً — To knock, rap.

قَرَّعَ — To scold, rebuke.

قَارَعَ مقارعةً وقِرَاعاً — To fight.

تَقَارَع — To cast lots, or play dice.

إِقترع فِي وعَلَى — To cast lots for.

قَرْعٌ — Knocking. Gourd.

قَرَعَةٌ — Baldness ; scald-head.

قَرْعَةٌ — A gourd, Chemical retort.

قُرْعَةٌ ج قُرَعٌ — Lot. Ballot.

أَلْقُرْعَةُ لَه — He wins.

اَلْقُرْعَةُ عَلَيْه — He loses.

قَارِعَةٌ — Middle part of the way.

اَلقَارِعَةُ — Day of judgement.

أَقْرَعُ — Bald, scald-headed. Bare.

مِقْرَعَةٌ ج مقَارِع — Whip, knocker.

قَرَف وقَرَّف ب — To suspect, blame.

قَرِف يَقْرَف قَرَفاً — To loathe.

أَقْرَف — To cause disgust.

إِقترف — To commit (a crime).

قَرَفٌ — Disgust, loathing.

قِرفةٌ — Suspicion. Cinnamon.

مُقرِفٌ	Disgusting.
قَرَقَ يقْرِق قَرَقاً	To cluck, (hen).
(قُرْقٌ)	Hernia in the scrotum.
(قُرْقَةٌ)	Sitting-hen.
(قرقَدَ)	To dry, become hard.
قَرقذانٌ وقَرْقَذَونٌ	Squirrel.
قَرْقَرَ	To rumble, (stomach).
قرقَرَةٌ ج قَرَاقِر	Rumbling.
(قَرقورٌ)	Lamb.
(قَرقَش)	To gnaw at.
(قَرْقَطَ)	To cut into small pieces.
(قَرقَع)	To rumble, clatter.
(قرقَعَةٌ)	A rattling, rumbling.
قَرَمَ يَقرُم قَرماً	To gnaw off.
أَلقَرَم	The Crimea.
قرمةٌ ج قرمٌ	Stump of a tree.
قِرميدٌ	Tile, brick.
قِرْمِزٌ	Cochineal ; crimson.
قرمزيٌّ	Of a crimson colour.
قرمطيٌّ	A Karmathian.
قَرَامِطَةٌ	Sect of Karmathians.
قرنَ يقرن قرناً بِ	To join.
أَقرنَ	To join together.
إِقترَنَ ب	To be joined ; married.
قَرْنٌ ج قرونٌ	Horn. Century, age.
ذو آلقَرْنَين	*Alexander the Great.*
وحيد القَرن	Rhinoceros.
قِرْنٌ ج أَقرانٌ	One's equal.
قَرنَةٌ	Projecting angle or corner.
قِرَانٌ وَمقارَنَةٌ	Close union.
قَرينٌ ج قُرَنَاءُ	Comrade ; husband.
قَرينَةٌ ج قَرَائِنُ	Wife. Context.
مُقَرَّنٌ	Horned ; angled.
مَقرونٌ ومقْترنٌ	Joined, yoked.
قَرْنَبيطٌ (قُنَّبيطٌ)	Cauliflower.
قَرَنفلٌ	Cloves. Carnation (plant).
كَبش آلقَرنفل	Cloves.

قَرَنفُلَة A pink, carnation.

قَرَا . واستَقرَى To follow out.

إستقراء (See إستقرأ) Analogy.

قَرَا يَقري To receive hospitably.

قِرى Entertainment ; feasting.

قَريَة ج قُرًى Village.

قَزَّ يَقِزُّ عَن To feel aversion to.

قَزّ Raw-silk, floss silk.

دود القَزّ Silk-worm.

قَزاز (زجاج) Glass, glass-ware.

قَزَّاز Silk, or glass merchant.

قُزَحيَّة Iris (of the eye).

قَزدير (عوض : قَصدير) Tin.

قَزَل يقزل قَزَلاً To limp.

قَزَل Limping.

أقزل قزلاء ج قزل Lame.

قَزم يَقزَم To be small, mean.

قَزَم وقِزم Mean, dwarfish.

قَسّ ج قسوس. وقِسّيس ج قِسّيسون Clergyman, minister.

مِقساس Sebesten plum. *Cordia Myxa L.*

قَسَر يقسر To force, compel.

قَسر Violence, compulsion.

قَسراً By force.

قسط يقسِط قَسطاً وقسوطاً To act unjustly, swerve from what is right, to separate, distribute.

قَسَط يقسط وأقسط To do justice.

قَسَّط To pay by instalments.

تقسَّط بَين To divide equally.

قِسط Justice ; just, equitable.

قِسط ج اقساط Part, portion.

قَسطَل ج قساطِل Pipe, conduit.

قَسَم يَقسِم قَسماً وقَسَّم To divide.

قاسَم To share mutually.

أقسم بِالله To swear by God.

تقَسَّم To be divided, separated.

تَقَاسَم وانقَسم To share.

تقاسم	To take mutual oaths.
إنقسم	To be divided.
قَسَمٌ ج أقْسَامٌ	Oath.
قِسْمٌ ج أقْسَامٌ	Part; share.
قِسْمَةٌ ج قِسَمٌ	Division, share, lot.
خارج القسمة	Quotient, (arith.).
قَسِيمٌ ج أقسِمَاءُ	Sharer ; lot.
مُقَسَّمٌ	Divided, distributed.
مقسومٌ	Dividend (arith.).
مقسومٌ عليه	Divisor, (arith.).
قسا يَقْسُو	To be hard, unyielding.
قَسَّى وأقسى	To harden.
قاسى	To endure, suffer.
قَسَاوة	Hard-heartedness.
قاس ج قُسَاة	Hard, severe.
قَشَّ يَقُشُّ	To gather, collect. Sweep. Skim.
قَشٌّ	Straw.
قشة	A single straw.
قَشَّاشٌ	Cleaner (sweeper).
مِقَشَّةٌ	Broom.
مِقَشَّةٌ	Demijohn.
قَشَبٌ	Chapped skin.
قِشْدَةٌ	Cream.
قَشَرَ يقشر قَشْراً	To peel, skin.
تَقَشَّرَ وانقشر	To be peeled.
قِشْرٌ ج قشورٌ	Rind, bark, shell.
قِشْرَةٌ وقشارةٌ	A rind, bark, shell.
مُقَشَّرٌ	Peeled.
قَشَطَ يقشط قَشْطاً عن	To strip off.
قَشَّطَ	To strip; rob.
تَقَشَّطَ وانقشط	To be stripped.
(قشطة)	Sugar-candy. Cream.
(قشاطٌ)	Leather strap.
(قَشَع يقشَعُ)	To see.
أقْشَعَ	To be dispersed, (clouds).
أقشَعَ عن	To be dispelled.

انقشع	To be seen. Dispelled.
إِقشعرَّ	To shudder, shiver.
قُشعريرةٌ	Shudder ; shivering.
قَشِفَ يَقشَفُ قَشَافة	To be wretched.
تقشَّف	To lead an ascetic life.
قشفٌ	Life in misery.
متقشِّفٌ	Ascetic.
(قُشلةٌ)	Barrack.
قَصَّ يَقُصُّ قَصًّا	To out off, clip.
قَصَّ يقصُّ على	To tell ; narrate.
قَاصَّ مُقَاصَّةً وقِصَاصاً	To punish.
انقصَّ	To be clipped, cut off.
اقتصَّ	To take vengeance. Tell.
قَصٌّ	Sternum.
قِصَّةٌ ج قِصَصٌ	Tale, story.
قِصَاصٌ	Punishment.
قُصَاصةٌ	Cuttings ; parings.
مِقَصٌّ ج مَقَاصُّ	Scissors.
قَصَبٌ	Reeds. Thread of gold.
قَصَبُ السُّكَّرِ	Sugar-cane.
قَصَبَةٌ ج قَصَبٌ	A reed or cane. City ; capital.
قَصَبَةُ المَرِيء	Œsophagus.
قصبةُ الرِّئَة	Windpipe.
قَصَبَةُ الأَنفِ	Bone of the nose.
قَصَابَةٌ	Butcher's trade.
قَصَّابٌ	Butcher.
مَقْصَبَةٌ	Slaughter-house.
قصد يَقصد	To purpose; repair to.
قصد واقتصد في	To economise.
قصدٌ	Intention, purpose, aim.
قاصدٌ ج قُصَّادٌ	Visitor. Legate.
مقصودٌ	Intended, desired.
قَصيدةٌ ج قَصَائد	A poem.
إِقتصَادٌ	Moderation ; economy.
مَقْصد ج مقاصد	Intention, aim.
قصديرٌ	Tin.
قصُر يقصر	To be short.
قَصَرَ أو قصر عن	To lack power.

قَصَّر وأقصر	To shorten.
قَصَر قَصْراً وقِصارة	To bleach.
قَصَرهُ في	To shut up, confine.
قَصَر على	To limit, restrict.
قَصَّر في	To lag, fall short of.
اقْصَر عن	To desist from.
تَقَصَّر	To shrink, contract.
إقتَصَر عَلَى	To limit one's self to.
قَصْرٌ وقِصَر	Shortness.
قصورٌ	Remissness.
قُصارى	End (of an affair).
قَصرٌ ج قصورٌ	Castle, palace.
قاصرٌ	Minor, under age.
قاصر اليد	Powerless.
قَصَّارٌ	Fuller, bleecher.
قِصارَة	Art of bleaching.
قَيْصَرٌ ج قَياصِرة	Cæsar, emperor.
قَصيرٌ ج قِصارٌ	Short; small.
أَقْصَرُ م قُصرى ج أَقَاصِرُ	Shorter.
تقصيرٌ	Abbreviation ; neglect.
مَقصورٌ	Limited. Bleached.
مقصورةٌ ج مقاصير	A large room.
قَصْعَةٌ ج قَصَعَاتٌ	Large dish.
قَصَف يقصِف قصفاً	To break.
قَصَف يقْصف	To roar, (thunder).
تَقَصَّف وانقصف	To be broken.
قَصِفٌ	Brittle, easily broken.
قَاصِفٌ	Breaking, roaring.
مَقصَفٌ	Pleasure-house.
قَصَل يقصِل قصْلا	To cut off, mow.
قَصَلٌ وقَصَالةٌ	Stubble, chaff.
قَصيل	Green food for animals.
قَصَم يقصِم قَصْماً	To break in pieces.
تقصَّم وانقصم	To be broken.
قَصِيمٌ	Brittle, fragile.
قصيمٌ ومقصومٌ	Broken shattered.
قَصَا يقصو	To be very distant.
تقصّى واستقصى في	To penetrate deeply ; follow out to the end.

Distance. قَصًا وَقَصَاءٌ

Very distant. قَاصٍ ج أَقْصَاءٌ

Investigation. إِسْتِقْصَاءٌ

More distant. أَقْصَى م قُصْوَى ج أَقَاصٍ

The extreme end ; highest purpose. الغَايَةُ ٱلقُصْوَى

The uttermost parts of the earth. أَقَاصِي ٱلأَرْضِ

To break, crush. قَضَّ يَقُضُّ قَضًّا

To swoop down (bird). To fall. إِنْقَضَّ

To cut off, prune. قَضَبَ وَٱقْتَضَبَ

To be pruned. تَقَضَّبَ وَٱنْقَضَبَ

Prunings. قُضَابَةٌ

Rod, stick. قَضِيبٌ ج قُضْبَانٌ

Improvised (speech). مُقْتَضَبٌ

To nibble at, gnaw. قَضِمَ يَقْضَمُ

Roasted peas. (قَضَامَةٌ أَوْ قَضَامِيٌّ)

To decide, fulfil (a duty) ; satisfy (a want) ; execute (an order). قَضَى يَقْضِي

To judge. قَضَى بَيْنَ يَقْضِي

To require. قَضَى عَلَى

To die. قَضَى أَوْ قَضَى أَجَلَهُ أَوْ نَحْبَهُ

To spend the time. قَضَى ٱلزَّمَانَ

To pay a debt. قَضَى ٱلدَّيْنَ

To judge in favour of. قَضَى لِ

To fulfil a purpose. قَضَى ٱلوَطَرَ

To execute, carry out. قَضَّى

To summon before a judge. قَاضَى

To be carried out ; cease. إِنْقَضَى

They had a law-suit. تَقَاضَيَا

To be required ; necessary. إِقْتَضَى

Judgment. قَضًى وَقَضَاءٌ ج أَقْضِيَةٌ

Event ; fact, matter ; question, proposition. قَضِيَّةٌ ج قَضَايَا

A judge. قَاضٍ ج قُضَاةٌ

Supreme Judge. قَاضِي ٱلقُضَاةِ

Death. أَلقَاضِيَة

End ; completion. إِنْقِضَاءٌ

Exigency ; requisite. إِقْتِضَاءٌ

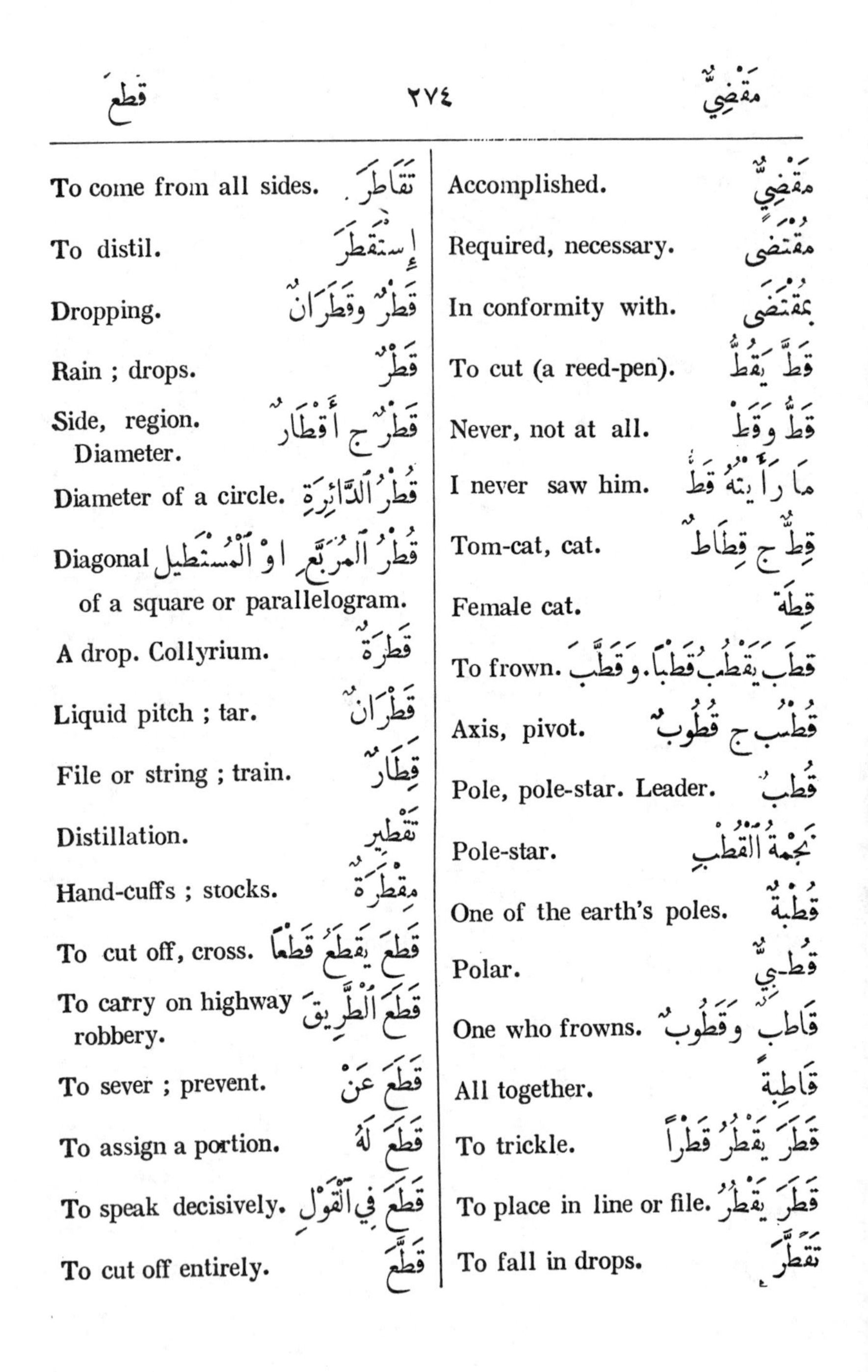

مَقْضِيٌّ Accomplished.

مُقْتَضًى Required, necessary.

بِمُقْتَضَى In conformity with.

قَطَّ يَقُطُّ To cut (a reed-pen).

قَطُّ وَقَطْ Never, not at all.

مَا رَأَيْتُهُ قَطُّ I never saw him.

قِطٌّ ج قِطَاطٌ Tom-cat, cat.

قِطَّةٌ Female cat.

قَطَبَ يَقْطِبُ قُطُوبًا . وَقَطَّبَ To frown.

قُطْبٌ ج قُطُوبٌ Axis, pivot.

قُطْبٌ Pole, pole-star. Leader.

نَجْمَةُ ٱلْقُطْبِ Pole-star.

قُطْبَةٌ One of the earth's poles.

قُطْبِيٌّ Polar.

قَاطِبٌ وَقَطُوبٌ One who frowns.

قَاطِبَةً All together.

قَطَرَ يَقْطُرُ قَطْرًا To trickle.

قَطَرَ يَقْطُرُ To place in line or file.

تَقَطَّرَ To fall in drops.

تَقَاطَرَ To come from all sides.

إِسْتَقْطَرَ To distil.

قَطْرٌ وَقَطَرَانٌ Dropping.

قَطْرٌ Rain ; drops.

قُطْرٌ ج أَقْطَارٌ Side, region. Diameter.

قُطْرُ ٱلدَّائِرَةِ Diameter of a circle.

قُطْرُ ٱلْمُرَبَّعِ أَوْ ٱلْمُسْتَطِيلِ Diagonal of a square or parallelogram.

قَطْرَةٌ A drop. Collyrium.

قَطْرَانٌ Liquid pitch ; tar.

قِطَارٌ File or string ; train.

تَقْطِيرٌ Distillation.

مِقْطَرَةٌ Hand-cuffs ; stocks.

قَطَعَ يَقْطَعُ قَطْعًا To cut off, cross.

قَطَعَ ٱلطَّرِيقَ To carry on highway robbery.

قَطَعَ عَنْ To sever ; prevent.

قَطَعَ لَهُ To assign a portion.

قَطَعَ فِي ٱلْقَوْلِ To speak decisively.

قَطَّعَ To cut off entirely.

To scan poetry. قَطَّعَ ٱلشِّعْرَ
To while away time. قَطَّعَ ٱلزَّمَانَ
To separate from. قَاطَعَ
To take across (a river). Give land as a fief. أَقْطَعَ
To be cut off. تَقَطَّعَ وَانْقَطَعَ
To be interrupted ; cease. إِنْقَطَعَ
To be devoted to. إِنْقَطَعَ إِلى
To cut off a part. إِقْتَطَعَ مِنْ
Amputation. Section. Size. قَطْعٌ
Hyperbola. قَطْعٌ زَائِدٌ
Ellipse. قَطْعٌ نَاقِصٌ
Parabola. قَطْعٌ مُكَافِئٌ
Conic section. قَطْعُ ٱلْمَخْرُوطِ
Certainly ; not at all. قَطْعًا
A part, piece. قِطْعَةٌ ج قِطَعٌ
Sharp ; decisive. قَاطِعٌ
Opposite side of a river. (قَاطِعُ ٱلنَّهْرِ)
Highway-man. قَاطِعُ ٱلطَّرِيقِ

Lent. قَطَاعَةٌ ج قَطَائِعُ
Herd, flock. قَطِيعٌ ج قُطْعَانٌ
Fief-land. Tax. قَطِيعَةٌ ج قَطَائِعُ
Separation ; interruption. إِنْقِطَاعٌ
Scanning. تَقْطِيعٌ تَقَاطِيعُ
Syllable. مَقْطَعٌ ج مَقَاطِعُ
Ford of a river. مَقْطَعُ ٱلنَّهْرِ
Province. مُقَاطَعَةٌ ج مُقَاطَعَاتٌ
Work by the job. (بِالْمُقَاطَعَةِ)
Cut into pieces. مُقَطَّعٌ
Separated, detached. مُنْقَطِعٌ
Cut off ; amputated. مَقْطُوعٌ
To cull, pluck, gather. قَطَفَ يَقْطِفُ وَاقْتَطَفَ
Act of gathering fruit. قَطْفٌ
Time of gathering. قِطَافٌ
A kind of sweet cake قَطَائِف
Basket, panier. مِقْطَفٌ
To cut off. قَطَمَ يَقْطِمُ قَطْمًا

Piece, fragment. قُطَيْمَةٌ

To inhabit (a place). قَطَنَ يَقْطُنُ فِي

Loins ; lumbar region. قَطْنٌ

Cotton. قُطْنٌ ج أَقْطَانٌ

Settled inhabitant. قَاطِنٌ ج قُطَّانٌ

Pumpkin, squash. يَقْطِينٌ

A kind of snipe. قَطَاةٌ ج قَطًا

To sit down ; dwell. قَعَدَ يَقْعُدُ

To lie in wait for. قَعَدَ لِ

To desist from. قَعَدَ عَنْ

To cause to sit, seat. اقْعَدَ

To be unable to walk. اقْعِدَ

To neglect. تَقَعَّدَ وَتَقَاعَدَ عَنْ

Eleventh month of the Arabian year. ذُو ٱلْقَعْدَةِ

Foundation, base; rule, canon ; model. قَاعِدَةٌ ج قَوَاعِدُ

Capital of a country. قَاعِدَةُ ٱلْبِلَادِ

Sitting ; inactivity. قُعُودٌ

A place of sitting. مَقْعَدٌ ج مَقَاعِدُ

Infirm ; cripple. مُقْعَدٌ

Pensioner. Neglectful. مُتَقَاعِدٌ

To be deep. قَعُرَ يَقْعُرُ قَعَارَةً

To make concave. قَعَّرَ

To dig deep. قَعَّرَ وَأَقْعَرَ

Bottom ; depth. قَعْرٌ ج قُعُورٌ

Dug ; hollow ; concave. مُقَعَّرٌ

To clatter, rattle. قَعْقَعَ ج قَعْقَعَةً

Magpie. قَعْقَعٌ وَقُعْقُعٌ ج قَعَاقِعُ

Large basket, panier. قُفَّةٌ ج قُفَفٌ

To track. قَفَرَ يَقْفُرُ قَفْرًا وَتَقَفَّرَ وَاقْتَفَرَ

To be waste, deserted. اقْفَرَ

Desert, waste (land). قَفْرٌ ج قِفَارٌ

Bee-hive ; basket. قَفِيرٌ ج قُفْرَانٌ

To jump, leap. قَفَزَ يَقْفِزُ قَفْزًا

Jump, leap. قَفْزَةٌ ج قَفَزَاتٌ

A certain measure. قَفِيزٌ ج أَقْفِزَةٌ

Bird-cage ; coop. قَفَصٌ ج أَقْفَاصٌ

To shiver from cold. قَفْقَفَ

To return. قَفَلَ يَقْفُلُ قُفُولاً

To guard, lock up. قَفَلَ يَقْفِلُ قَفْلاً

To lock, shut. قَفَّلَ وَأَقْفَلَ

To cause to return. أَقْفَلَ عَنْ

To be locked, bolted. إِنْقَفَلَ

Lock, bolt. Caravan. قُفْلٌ ج أَقْفَالٌ

Caravan. قَافِلَةٌ ج قَوَافِلُ

Vein in the arm. قِيفَالٌ

To walk behind, follow. قَفَا يَقْفُو

To send after. قَفَّى بِ

To follow, imitate. تَقَفَّى وَاقْتَفَى

To prefer, select, chose. اِقْتَفَى

Back side, reverse. قَفًا وَقَفَاءٌ

Rhyme, (final word). قَافِيَةٌ ج قَوَافٍ

Imitation ; preference. إِقْتِفَاءٌ

Rhymed prose. أَلْكَلَامُ ٱلْمُقَفَّى

Cardamon. قَاقُلَّة

To be little in quantity, be scarce, happen rarely. قَلَّ يَقِلُّ

Rarely, قَلَّمَا (قَلَّ مَا)

To bear, carry. قَلَّ قَلاًّ وَأَقَلَّ

To diminish, lessen. قَلَّلَ وَأَقَلَّ

To have little property. أَقَلَّ

To find small, paltry. إِسْتَقَلَّ

To be independent. إِسْتَقَلَّ بِ

Earthen water-jug. قُلَّةٌ ج قُلَلٌ

Littleness, small quantity. قِلَّةٌ

Plural which signifies from 3 to 10 objects. جَمْعُ ٱلْقِلَّةِ

A (monk's) cell. قِلِّيَّةٌ وَقِلَّايَةٌ

Few, little, scarce. قَلِيلٌ ج قَلِيلُونَ

Rarely, seldom, slightly. قَلِيلاً

Less, rarer. أَقَلّ

Least, rarest. أَلْأَقَلُّ

Poor, having but little. أَقَلّ وَمُقِلٌّ

Diminishing, lessening. تَقْلِيلٌ

Independence. إِسْتِقْلَالٌ

Independent. مُستَقِلّ

To change, alter. To overturn ; overthrow. قَلَبَ يَقلِبُ

To manipulate ; prove. قلَّب

To be turned ; be fickle. تَقَلَّبَ

To be turned upside down. انقَلَبَ

To return to. إِنقَلَبَ إِلَى

Change of letters (*in gram*). قَلْبٌ

Heart, mind, thought ; centre, core. قَلْبٌ ج قُلُوبٌ

Sincere, earnest, hearty. قَلْبِيٌّ

Mould, cast, last. قَالَبٌ ج قَوَالِب

Loaf of sugar. قَالِبُ سُكَّرٍ

Revolution ; overthrow. إِنقِلابٌ

Solstice. إِنْقِلَابُ ٱلشَّمْسِ

Change ; inconstancy. تَقَلُّبٌ

Vicissitudes. تَقَلُّبَاتٌ

Turned, turned over. مقلُوبٌ

Final resting place. مُنقَلَبٌ

To wind round ; adorn. Imitate. قَلَّدَ

To undertake an affair. تَقَلَّدَ الأَمْرَ

To put on the sword. تَقَلَّدَ ٱلسَّيفَ

Necklace ; collar. قِلَادَةٌ ج قَلَائِدُ

Imitation. Church tradition. تقليدٌ ج تَقَالِيدِ

Imitator, counterfeiter. مُقَلِّدٌ

Imitated, counterfeited. مُقَلَّدٌ

Management of affairs. مقَالِيدُ الامُورِ

Red Sea. بَحْرُ ٱلقُلْزُمِ

Hood, cap. قَلَنسُوَةٌ

Eel. أَنقَلِيسٌ وَإِنقِلِيس

To contract, shrink. قَلَصَ يَقْلِصُ

To be wrinkled, shrunk. تَقَلَّصَ

To tear from its place, pull out, uproot. قَلَعَ يَقلَعُ

To set sail. أَقلَعَ

To withdraw from. أَقْلَعَ عَنْ

To be taken away. إِنقَلَعَ

To pull out, uproot. إِقْتَلَعَ

قِلعٌ ج قُلُوعٌ	Sail.
قَلْعَةٌ ج قِلاعٌ	Castle, fortress.
قُلاعٌ	Sores in the mouth, (aphthæ).
مَقْلَعٌ ج مَقَالِعُ	Stone-quarry.
مِقْلاعٌ ج مَقَالِيعُ	Sling.
مَقْلُوعٌ	Uprooted, pulled out.
قَلَفَ يَقْلِفُ	To circumcise.
قَلَفَ وَقَلَّفَ	To calk a ship.
قَلَفَةٌ وَقُلْفَةٌ ج قُلَفٌ	Prepuce.
قِلافَةٌ	Trade of calking ships.
أَقْلَفُ	Uncircumcised.
قَلِقَ يَقْلَقُ قَلَقاً	To be agitated.
أَقْلَقَ	To agitate, disturb.
قَلَقٌ	Disquietude, trouble.
قَلِقٌ	Disturbed ; restless.
قُلْقَاسٌ	Colocassia (plant).
قَلْقَلَ قِلقَالاً	To move, shake.
تَقَلْقَلَ	To be moved, shaken.
قَلْقَلَةٌ	Agitation.
قَلَمَ ـ وَقَلَّمَ	To pare (the nails).
قَلَمٌ ج أَقْلامٌ	Pen ; handwriting. Style.
قَلَمُ رُصَاص	Pencil.
قَلَمُ حَجَرٍ	Slate-pencil.
قُلامَةٌ	Parings (of nails &c.).
إِقْلِيمٌ ج أَقَالِيمُ	Region, tract, province ; climate.
مُقَلَّمٌ	Cut, pared.
مَقْلَمَةٌ	Pen-case.
قَلَنْسُوَةٌ ج قَلانِسُ	Cowl, cap.
قَلا يَقْلُو قَلْواً وَقَلَى يَقْلِي قَلْياً	To fry.
قَلًى وَقِلْيٌ	Ash of alkaline plants.
قَلاَّيَةٌ	Cell of a monk.
قَلِيَّةٌ	Fried food.
مِقْلَى وَمِقْلاةٌ	A frying-pan.
مَقْلِيٌّ وَمُقْلَى	Fried, roasted.
قِمَّةٌ ج قِمَمٌ	Summit, top.
قَمْحٌ	Wheat.
قَمْحَةٌ	Grain of wheat; grain (weight).

قَمَرَ يَقْمِرُ To play a game of chance.

قَامَرَ مُقَامَرَةً وَقِمَاراً To gamble.

أَقْمَرَ To be moonlight.

تَقَامَرَ To play at dice.

قَمَرٌ ج أَقْمَارٌ Moon.

قَمِرَةٌ Moonlit (night).

قَمَرِيٌّ Lunar ; moonlike.

قَمَرِيَّةٌ Small window.

قِمَارٌ Gambling.

مُقْمِرَةٌ Moonlit (night).

مُقَامِرٌ Gambler.

قَمَزَ يَقْمِزُ قَمْزاً To jump.

قَمَسَ يَقْمُسُ قَمْساً To dive.

قَامُوسٌ ج قَوَامِيسُ Dictionary.

قَمْشَةٌ Whip.

قُمَاشٌ ج أَقْمِشَةٌ Woven stuff.

قُمَاشُ ٱلْبَيْتِ Household things.

قَمَصَ يَقْمِصُ To jump, leap.

تَقَمَّصَ To transmigrate (soul).

قَمِيصٌ ج أَقْمِصَةٌ وَقُمْصَانٌ Shirt.

تَقَمُّصٌ Transmigration (soul).

قَمَطَ وَقَمَّطَ To bind ; swaddle.

قِمَاطٌ ج قُمُطٌ Swaddling-cloth.

مُقَمَّطٌ Bound up, swaddled.

قَمَعَ يَقْمَعُ وَأَقْمَعَ To tame, subdue.

قَمَعَ وَأَقْمَعَ عَنْ To prevent.

إِنْقَمَعَ To be subdued, tamed.

قَمْعٌ وَإِقْمَاعٌ Subjugating.

قِمْعٌ ج أَقْمَاعٌ Funnel.

تَقَمْقَمَ To murmur, find fault.

قُمْقُمٌ ج قَمَاقِمُ Jar, cup; flask.

قَمْلٌ Lice, vermin.

قَمِلٌ وَمُقَمَّلٌ Infested with lice.

قَمْلَةٌ A louse.

قُمَّلٌ Very small insects.

قَمِينٌ Oven to heat baths.

قُنٌّ Poultry-house, hen-coop.

قُنَّةٌ ج قُنَنٌ	Small mountain. Peak.
قَانُونٌ ج قَوَانِينُ	Rule, canon, law. Kind of harp.
قَانُونِيٌّ	Canonical, legal.
قِنّينَةٌ ج قَنَانِيُّ	Glass bottle, phial.
قَنَأَ يَقْنَأُ قُنُوءً	To be very red.
أَحْمَرُ قَانِئٌ	Very dark red.
قُنَّبٌ	Hemp ; coarse rope.
قُنْبَرَاءُ وَقُنْبُرَةٌ ج قَنَابِرُ	Lark.
قُنْبُرَةٌ ج قَنَابِرُ	Crest of a cock.
قُنَّبِيطٌ وَقَرْنَبِيطٌ	Cauliflower.
قُنْبُلَةٌ ج قَنَابِلُ	Bomb-shell.
قَنَتَ يَقْنُتُ وَأَقْنَتَ	To obey God.
قَنُتَ يَقْنُتُ قَنَاتَةً	To eat sparingly.
قَانِتٌ م قَانِتَةٌ	Pious.
قُنُوتٌ	Piety, submission to God.
قِنْدِيلٌ ج قَنَادِيلُ	Lamp.
قَنَصَ يَقْنِصُ وَاقْتَنَصَ	To hunt.
قَنْصٌ وَاقْتِنَاصٌ	Hunting.
قَنَصٌ وَقَنِيصٌ	Prey ; game.
قَانِصٌ وَقَنَّاصٌ	Hunter.
قَانِصَةٌ ج قَوَانِصُ	Crop, gizzard.
قُنْصُلٌ ج قَنَاصِلُ	Consul.
قُنْصُلِيَّةٌ وَقُنْصُلَاتُو	Consulate.
قَنَطَ يَقْنِطُ وَقَنُطَ يَقْنُطُ	To despair.
قَنَّطَ	To throw into despair.
قَنَطٌ وَقُنُوطٌ	Despair.
قَنِطٌ	Discouraged ; despairing.
قَنْطَرَ وَتَقَنْطَرَ	To fall from a horse.
قَنْطَرَةٌ ج قَنَاطِرُ	Arch.
قِنْطَارٌ ج قَنَاطِيرُ	100 rottles.
قِنْطَارِيُونٌ	Centaury.
مُقَنْطَرٌ	Collected together.
قَنِعَ يَقْنَعُ	To be contented.
قَنَّعَ وَأَقْنَعَ	To convince, persuade.
تَقَنَّعَ	To veil one's self.
إِقْتَنَعَ بِ	To be content. To be persuaded, convinced.
قَنِعٌ وَقَنُوعٌ	Content, temperate.

قَانِعٌ	Contented.
قِنَاعٌ ج قُنُعٌ	Veil for the head.
قَنَاعَةٌ وَقُنُوعٌ	Contentedness.
مُقَنَّعٌ	Wearing an iron helmet.
قِنْفِذٌ ج قَنَافِذُ	Porcupine.
قَنَا يَقْنُو وَٱقْتَنَى	To acquire.
قَنَّى	To dig a canal.
أَقْنَى	To give one possession.
قُنْوَةٌ	Acquisition ; possession.
قَنَاةٌ ج قَنَوَاتٌ	Canal. Lance.
قِنْيَةٌ ج قِنًى	That which is acquired.
قَانٍ	Possessor, proprietor, owner.
أَقْنَى	Having an aquiline nose.
قَهَرَ يَقْهَرُ	To subdue, oppress.
قَاهَرَ	To treat with violence.
قَهْرٌ	Violence ; oppression.
قَهْرًا	By force, inspite of.
قَاهِرٌ	Victor, conqueror.
أَلْقَاهِرَةُ	Cairo, *i.e. Victirx.*
أَلْقَهَّارُ	God, the Almighty.
مَقْهُورٌ	Forced, conquered.
قَهْرَمَانٌ ج قَهَارِمَةٌ	Steward.
قَهْقَرَ وَتَقَهْقَرَ	To go backwards.
قَهْقَرَى	Retrograde movement.
قُهْقُورٌ (وَقَعْقُورٌ)	Pile of stones.
قَهْقَهَ	To laugh immoderately.
قَهْقَهَةٌ	Immoderate laughter.
قَهْوَةٌ	Coffee. Wine.
قَهْوَةٌ ج قَهَوَاتٌ	Coffee-house ; café.
(قَهْوَجِيٌّ)	Coffee-house keeper.
قَابُ قَوْسٍ	A bow's length.
قُوبَاءُ	Ring-worm, tetter.
قَاتَ يَقُوتُ	To nourish, feed.
تَقَوَّتَ وَٱقْتَاتَ	To be nourished.
قُوتٌ ج أَقْوَاتٌ	Food, victuals.
مُقِيتٌ	Sustainer, guardian.

قَادَ يَقُودُ وَٱقْتَادَ To lead, guide.

إِنْقَادَ وَٱقْتَادَ To be guided, led.

إِنقَادَ لِ To obey.

قَوْدٌ وَقِيَادَةٌ Leading, guiding.

قَائِدٌ ج قُوَّادٌ Guide ; leader.

مِقْوَدٌ ج مَقَاوِدُ Halter.

مَقُودٌ وَمَقْوُودٌ Led, guided.

قَارَةٌ ج قَارَاتٌ Small, isolated mountain.

مُقَوَّرٌ A thing with a hole in its middle.

قَاسَ يَقُوسُ وَٱقْتَاسَ To measure.

قَوِسَ يَقْوَسُ وَتَقَوَّسَ To be bent.

(قَوَّسَ) To shoot with a gun.

(تَقَوَّسَ) To be shot, fired.

قَوْسٌ ج قُسِيٌّ وَأَقْوَاسٌ Bow, arc.

قَوْسُ قُزَحَ Rainbow.

قَوَّاسٌ ج قَوَّاسَةٌ Cavass ; archer.

قُوَيْسَةٌ Sage (plant).

(قُوشٌ ج أَقْوَاشٌ) Crupper.

قَاضَ وَقَوَّضَ To demolish.

قَوْضٌ Exchange.

قَاعٌ ج قِيعٌ Plain ; bottom-land.

قَاعَةٌ ج قَاعَاتٌ Courtyard. Hall.

قَاقَ يَقُوقُ قَوْقًا To cackle (hen).

قَاوُوقٌ ج قَوَاوِيقُ Cylindrical hat.

قَالَ يَقُولُ To speak, say, propose.

قَالَ بِ To give as an opinion.

قَالَ عَلَى To speak against.

قِيلَ It is said, has been said.

قَاوَلَ To argue, bargain with.

تَقَوَّلَ To make a false report.

تَقَاوَلَ To converse together.

قَالٌ وَقِيلٌ Talk.

قَوْلٌ ج أَقْوَالٌ وَأَقَاوِيلُ Saying, word, speech ; promise.

قَائِلٌ Author of a saying.

مَقَالَةٌ Treatise ; chapter ; article.

مَقُولٌ Said ; word, sentence.

مُقاوَلَةٌ	Conference. Contract.
قُولَنْجٌ	Colic.
أَلقُولُونُ	Colon (intestine).
قَامَ يَقُومُ	To rise ; stand.
قَامَ عَلَى	To rise against, revolt.
قَامَ لِ	To rise to honour one.
قَامَ مَقَامهُ	To take one's place.
قَامَ بِ	To carry on (a matter).
قَامَ بِوَعْدِهِ	To keep a promise.
قَامَتْ تَنُوحُ	She began to cry.
قَوَّمَ	To erect ; straighten.
قَاوَمَ	To oppose, dispute with.
أَقَامَ	To set up ; establish.
أَقَامَ بِ	To stay (in a place).
اقَامَ عَلَى	To persevere in.
أَقَامَهُ على	To appoint to.
أَقَامَ عَلَيْهِ ٱلدَّعْوَى	He brought a charge against him.
تَقَوَّمَ	To be straightened.
إِسْتَقَامَ	To be upright, straight.
قَوْمٌ ج أَقْوَامٌ	People ; company.
أَلقَوْمُ	The enemy.
قَوَامٌ	Consistence.
قِوَامٌ	Support ; sustenance.
قَامَةٌ ج قَامَاتٌ	Stature ; fathom.
قِيمَةٌ ج قِيَمٌ	Price, value, worth.
قَائِمٌ	Upright, vertical ; firm.
قَائِمَقَام	Governor. Lt.-Colonel.
قَائِمُ ٱلزَّاوِيةِ	Right-angled.
زَاوِيَةٌ قَائِمَةٌ	Right angle.
قَائِمَةٌ ج قَوَائِمُ	Foot of a quadruped.
قَائِمَة ج قَوَائِمُ	List, catalogue.
قِيَامَةٌ	Resurrection.
قَيِّمٌ	Manager ; agent.
قَوِيمٌ ج قِيَامٌ	Straight ; true.
أَلقَيُّومُ	The Self-Existent (God)
إِقَامَةٌ	Abiding ; preforming.

إِسْتِقَامَةٌ Uprightness ; rectitude.

تَقْوِيمُ ٱلسَّنَةِ Calendar.

تَقْوِيمُ ٱلْبِلَادِ Valuation of a country for purposes of taxation.

مُقَامٌ Place, rank, office.

مُقَاوِمٌ Resisting ; adversary.

مُقَاوَمَةٌ Resistance, opposition.

مُسْتَقِيمٌ Straight. Upright.

قَوِيَ يَقْوَى To be, or grow, strong.

قَوِيَ عَلَى ٱلْأَمْرِ To be able to do it.

قَوَّى To strengthen.

تَقَوَّى وَٱسْتَقْوَى To grow strong.

قُوَّةٌ ج قُوَّات وَقُوًى Strength, faculty, ability ; potentiality.

أَلْقُوَى ٱلْعَقْلِيَّةُ The mental faculties.

أَلْقُوَّةُ ٱلنَّظَرِيَّةُ Perception.

أَلْقُوَّةُ ٱلْعَمَلِيَّةُ Reasoning.

أَلْقُوَّةُ ٱلْحَافِظَةُ Memory.

قَوِيٌّ ج أَقْوِيَاءُ Strong, powerful.

تَقْوِيَةٌ Act of strengthening.

مُقَوٍّ Strengthening, fortifying.

قَاءَ يَقِيءُ قَيْئًا To vomit.

قَيَّأَ تَقْيِئَةً وَأَقَاءَ To make vomit.

قَيْءٌ Act of vomiting.

مُقَيِّئٌ Emetic.

قِيثَارٌ ج قَيَاثِيرُ Guitar.

قَاحَ يَقِيحُ وَقَيَّحَ وَتَقَيَّحَ To suppurate.

قَيْحٌ Pus, suppuration.

قَيَّدَ To bind. Register. To restrict. (the sense of a word).

تَقَيَّدَ To be bound, registered.

تَقَيَّدَ بِ To be bound to.

قَيْدٌ ج قُيُودٌ Fetter, chain, limit.

تَقْيِيدٌ Limitation, restriction. Registration.

مُقَيَّدٌ Bound ; Registered.

قِيرٌ وَقَارٌ Pitch, tar.

أَلْقَيْرَوَانُ Cyrene.

قَاسَ يَقِيسُ To measure, compare.

قَايَسَ مُقَايَسَةً — To measure.

قَايَسَ بَيْنَ — To compare a thing with another.

إِنْقَاسَ — To be measured.

قِيَاسٌ ج أَقْيِسَة — Measure ; rule, analogy. Syllogism.

قِيَاسِيٌّ — According to rule.

مُقَايَسَة — Estimate by analogy.

مِقْيَاس ج مَقَايِيسُ — A measure.

مِقْيَاس النِّيلِ — Nilometer.

قَاضَ ـِ مِنْ — To exchange for.

قَايَضَ مُقَايَضَةً — To exchange with.

تَقَيَّضَ — To be broken down.

قِيَاضٌ وَمُقَايَضَة — Exchange.

(قَيطَانٌ) — Silk-cord.

قَاظَ يَقِيظ قَيْظًا — To be very hot.

قَيْظٌ — Heat of summer. Drought.

قَيْقَبٌ — Maple (tree).

قَالَ يَقِيلُ — To take a siesta.

أَقَالَ — To abrogate a sale.

إِسْتَقَالَ — To seek abrogation.

قِيلَة — Hydrocele.

قَيْلُولَة — Mid-day nap, siesta.

إِقَالَة — Annulment of a bargain.

مَقِيل — Place of a mid-day nap.

قَيْنَة — Maid-servant. Female singer.

ك

ك As a numeral sign=20.

كَ وكِ Pronominal suffix.

ضَرَبَكَ He struck thee.

كِتَابُكِ Thy book.

كَ As, like.

كَالاَسَدِ Like a lion.

كَئِبَ يَكْأَبُ وَٱكْتَأَبَ To be sad.

كَأْبٌ وَكَآبَةٌ Grief, sorrow.

كَئِبٌ وَكَئِيبٌ وَمُكْتَئِبٌ Grieved.

كَأْسٌ ج كَاسَاتٌ وَكُؤُوس Cup.

كَأْسُ ٱلْمَنِيَّةِ Death.

كَأَنَّ وَكَأَنْ As if, as though.

كَأَنَّ زَيْداً أَسَدٌ As if Zeid were a lion.

كَبَّ يَكُبُّ كَبًّا To invert; overthrow.

أَكَبَّ عَلَى To be intent upon.

إِنْكَبَّ To fall prostrate.

كُبَّةٌ ج كُبَبٌ Ball of thread.

كَبَابٌ Broiled bits of meat.

كَبَابَةٌ (نبات) Cubeb.

كَبَّابَةُ ٱلشَّوْكِ Hedge-hog.

مِكَبٌّ ج مِكَبَّاتٌ Thread-reel.

كَبُّوتٌ ج كَبَابِيتُ Over-coat.

كَبَحَ يَكْبَحُ To pull in a horse.

كَبَحَ عَنْ To restrain, prevent.

كَبَّدَ وَتَكَبَّدَ To be in the zenith.

كَابَدَ To suffer, endure.

كَبْدٌ	The middle of the sky.
كَبْدٌ وَكِبْدٌ ج أَكْبَادٌ وَكُبُودٌ	Liver.
كَبَدٌ	Interior ; middle.
كَبَّادٌ	Citron.
كَبِرَ يَكْبَرُ	To be advanced in age.
كَبُرَ يَكْبُرُ	To be large ; grow.
كَبُرَ عَلَيْهِ ٱلْأَمْرُ	It became formidable to him.
كَبَّرَ	To enlarge ; magnify.
تَكَبَّرَ وَٱسْتَكْبَرَ	To grow proud.
إِسْتَكْبَرَ	To deem great.
كُبْرٌ	Greatness, glory, pride.
كِبَرٌ	Greatness, advanced age.
كَبَرٌ وَ(كَبَّارٌ وَقَبَّارٌ)	Caper-bush.
كُبْرَى	Major proposition, (*logic*).
كِبْرِيَاءُ	Greatness ; pride.
كَبِيرٌ ج كِبَارٌ وَكُبَرَاءُ	Great, large.
كَبِيرَةٌ ج كَبَائِرُ	Great crime.
أَكْبَرُ	Greater ; older.
أَللّٰهُ أَكْبَرُ	God is great !
الْأَكَابِرُ	The grandees.
تَكَبُّرٌ	Pride, haughtiness.
تَكْبِيرٌ	Magnifying God.
مُتَكَبِّرٌ	Proud, haughty.
كِبْرِيت	Sulphur ; matches.
مُكَبْرَتٌ	Sulphuretted.
كَبَسَ يَكْبِسُ	To press. Surprise.
كَبَّسَ	To train an animal.
تَكَبَّسَ	To be pressed, squeezed.
كَبْسٌ	Assault. Pressure.
كَبْسَةٌ	A sudden attack.
كَابُوس ج كَوَابِيسُ	Nightmare.
كبيس	Pickles.
سَنَةٌ كَبِيسَةٌ	Leap year.
مِكْبَسٌ ج مَكَابِسُ	Hand-press.
مَكْبُوس	Assailed, pressed. Pickled.
كَبَشَ يَكْبُشُ كَبْشًا	To grasp.

كَبْشٌ ج كِبَاشٌ Ram, male sheep.

كَبْشُ ٱلتُّوتِ Mulberry-fruit.

كَبْشُ ٱلْقَرَنْفُلِ Cloves.

(كَبْشَةٌ) A handful.

كَبَلَ يَكْبِلُ وَكَبَّلَ To bind, fetter.

تَكَبَّلَ To be fettered.

كَبْلٌ ج كُبُولٌ Heavy fetter.

مُكَبَّلٌ وَمَكْبُولٌ Fettered.

(كُوبَانٌ) Horse-blanket.

كَبَا يَكْبُو كَبْوًا To fall, trip.

كَبْوَةٌ Trip, stumble.

كَتِيتٌ Charpie, lint.

كَتَبَ يَكْتُبُ كِتَابَةً To write.

كَتَبَ عَلَى To prescribe, appoint.

كَتَّبَ To arrange troops in order.

كَاتَبَ To correspond with.

تَكَتَّبَ To assemble in squadrons.

تَكَاتَبَ To write to one another.

اِكْتَتَبَ To enrol one's self.

إِسْتَكْتَبَ To ask to write.

كُتُبِيٌّ Book-seller.

كَاتِبٌ ج كُتَّابٌ Writer, clerk.

كِتَابٌ ج كُتُبٌ Writing, book.

أَهْلُ ٱلْكِتَابِ Christians. Jews.

كُتَّابٌ ج كَتَاتِيبُ School.

كِتَابَةٌ Writing ; calligraphy.

كَتِيبَةٌ ج كَتَائِبُ Squadron.

مَكْتَبٌ ج مَكَاتِبُ School. Office.

مَكْتَبَةٌ ج مَكَاتِبُ Library ; study.

مُكَاتِبٌ Correspondent.

مُكَاتَبَةٌ Correspondence by letter.

مُكْتَتِبٌ Inscribed, registered.

مَكْتُوبٌ ج مَكَاتِيبُ Written ; letter.

أَكْتَعُ م كَتْعَاءُ ج كُتْعٌ Crippled. Whole.

كَتَّفَ To tie the hands back.

تَكَنَّفَ To cross the arms.

Shoulder. كَتِفٌ ج أَكْتَافٌ

Heap, lump. كُتْلَةٌ ج كُتَلٌ

Catholic. كَاثُولِيكِيٌّ ج كَاثُولِيكٌ

To conceal, hide. كَتَمَ يَكْتُمُ

To be concealed, hidden. إِنْكَتَمَ

To confide a secret. إِسْتَكْتَمَ

Concealing. كَتْمٌ وَكِتْمَانٌ

Private secretary. كَاتِمُ ٱلْأَسْرَارِ

Constipation, costiveness. كُتَامٌ

Kept secret. مَكْتُومٌ وَمُكْتَتَمٌ

Flax, linen. كَتَّانٌ

Linseed. بِزْرُ كَتَّانٍ

Thick, dense. كَثٌّ وَكَثِيثٌ

To be much, many; increase, multiply. كَثُرَ يَكْثُرُ

To increase; do too much. كَثَّرَ

To be rich; increase, grow. أَكْثَرَ

To speak much. أَكْثَرَ فِي ٱلْكَلَامِ

To increase multiply. تَكَاثَرَ

To regard as much. إِسْتَكْثَرَ

To thank. إِسْتَكْثَرَ بِخَيْرِهِ

Great number, plenty, abundance كُثْرٌ وَكَثْرَةٌ

Much, many; abundant. كَثِيرٌ

Abundantly, often, very. كَثِيراً

Tragacanth, goat's thorn. كَثِيرَاءُ

More, more frequent. أَكْثَرُ

Most people. أَكْثَرُ ٱلنَّاسِ

Growth, increase. تَكَاثُرٌ

Rich. مُكْثِرٌ

To be thick, dense. كَثُفَ يَكْثُفُ

Thickness, denseness. كَثَافَةٌ

Thick, dense, compact. كَثِيفٌ

To apply collyrium, or paint, to one's eyes. تَكَحَّلَ وَٱكْتَحَلَ

An eye-salve or paint. كُحْلٌ

Black antimony-powder. كُحَالٌ

Horse of best breed. كَحِيلٌ ج كَحَائِلُ

أَكْحَلُ م كَحْلَاءُ ج كُحْل Having the eye-lashes black.

مِكْحَلٌ وَمِكْحَال Pencil with which the *kohl* is applied.

مُكْحُلَةٌ ج مَكَاحِلُ Vessel containing the *kohl*.

كَاخِيَةٌ ج كَوَاخٍ Secretary.

كَدَّ يَكُدُّ To toil hard. To weary.

كَدٌّ Toil ; effort, exertion.

كدودٌ Laborious.

كَدِرَ يَكْدَرُ To be muddy, turbid.

كَدَّرَ To trouble ; make turbid.

تَكَدَّرَ To be troubled ; muddy.

كَدَرٌ Turbidness ; vexation.

كَدِرٌ وَمُكَدَّرٌ Troubled ; turbid.

كَدَسَ يَكْدِسُ To heap reaped grain.

كُدْسٌ ج أَكْدَاسٌ Heap of grain.

كَدَشَ يَكْدِشُ To bite (horse).

كَدِيشٌ ج كُدْشٌ Pack-horse.

كَدَمَ يَكْدُمُ كَدْماً To bite.

كَدْمٌ ج كُدُومٌ Scar.

كَدَنَ يَكْدُنُ To yoke oxen.

كَذَا وَكَذَلِكَ Thus, like this.

كَذَا وَكَذَا So and so.

كَذَبَ يَكْذِبُ To lie, speak falsely.

كَذَّبَ To accuse of lying.

كَذَّبَ To discredit a thing.

كَذَّبَ وَأَكْذَبَ نَفْسَهُ To contradict one's self ; belie one's self.

كِذْبٌ وَأُكْذُوبَةٌ ج أَكَاذِيب Lie, fraud.

كَذُوبٌ وَكَاذِبٌ وَكَذَّابٌ Liar.

أَكْذَبُ More false.

مَكْذُوبٌ عَلَيْهِ Falsely accused.

مَكْذَبَةٌ ج مَكَاذِبُ Falsehood.

كَرَّ يَكُرُّ كُرُوراً To return.

كَرَّ كَرّاً To return against.

كَرَّرَ To repeat. Purify, refine.

تَكَرَّرَ To be repeated.

Return, return to attack.	كَرٌّ
Turn, time.	كَرَّةٌ ج كَرَّاتٌ
Globe, ball.	كُرَةٌ ج كُرَاتٌ
Succession of ages.	كُرُورُ ٱلدُّهُورِ
Repetition.	تِكْرَارٌ وَتَكْرِيرٌ
Repeatedly.	تَكْرَاراً
Repeated. Refined.	مُكَرَّر
To grieve.	كَرَبَ يَكْرُبُ كَرْباً
To offect with sorrow.	أَكْرَبَ
To be in distress, grief.	إِكْتَرَب
Grief, sorrow.	كَرْبُ ج كُرُوبٌ
Cherub.	كَرُوبٌ
Grieved.	كَرِيبٌ وَمَكْرُوبٌ
Horse-whip.	كُرْبَاجٌ ج كَرَابِيجُ
To impose a quarantine.	كَرْتَنَ
To be kept in quarantine.	تَكَرْتَنَ
Quarantine.	كَرَنْتِينَةٌ
Paste-board.	كَرْتُونٌ
To look after.	إِكْتَرَثَ لِ وَبِ
Leek.	كُرَّاثٌ
Georgia.	بِلَادُ ٱلْكُرْجِ
Georgian.	كُرْجِيٌّ
Kurd.	كُرْدٌ وَأَكْرَادٌ
A Kurd.	كُرْدِيٌّ
Neck chain.	(كُرْدَانٌ)
To divide into squadrons.	كَرْدَسَ
The Kurds country.	كُرْدِسْتَانُ
Squardon.	كُرْدُوسَةٌ ج كَرَادِيسُ
To preach.	كَرَزَ يَكْرِزُ كَرْزاً
Preaching.	كَرْزٌ وَكِرَازَةٌ
Cherry, cherry tree.	كَرَزٌ
The leading ram.	كَرَّازٌ
Earthen flask.	كَرَازٌ وَكَرَّارٌ
To consecrate.	(كَرَّسَ)
To be devoted to God.	تَكَرَّسَ
Pamphlet.	كُرَّاسَةٌ ج كَرَارِيس

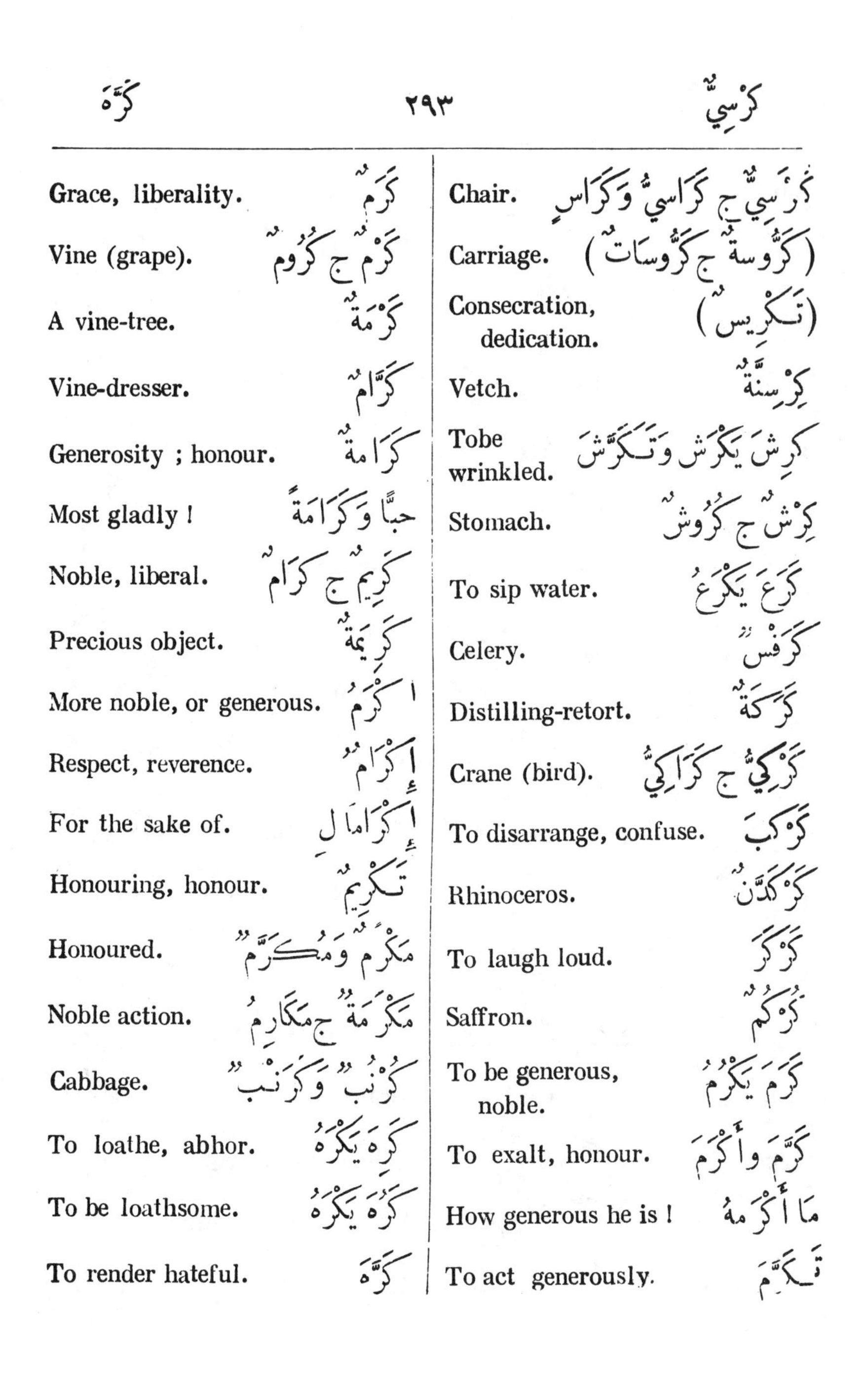

كُرْسِيٌّ ج كَرَاسِيُّ وَكَرَاسٍ	Chair.
(كَرُّوسَةٌ ج كَرُّوسَاتٌ)	Carriage.
(تَكْرِيسٌ)	Consecration, dedication.
كِرْسِنَّةٌ	Vetch.
كَرِشَ يَكْرَشُ وَتَكَرَّشَ	To be wrinkled.
كِرْشٌ ج كُرُوشٌ	Stomach.
كَرَعَ يَكْرَعُ	To sip water.
كَرَفْسٌ	Celery.
كَرَكَةٌ	Distilling-retort.
كَرْكِيٌّ ج كَرَاكِيُّ	Crane (bird).
كَرْكَبَ	To disarrange, confuse.
كَرْكَدَّنٌ	Rhinoceros.
كَرْكَرَ	To laugh loud.
كُرْكُمٌ	Saffron.
كَرُمَ يَكْرُمُ	To be generous, noble.
كَرَّمَ وَأَكْرَمَ	To exalt, honour.
مَا أَكْرَمَهُ	How generous he is !
تَكَرَّمَ	To act generously.
كَرَمٌ	Grace, liberality.
كَرْمٌ ج كُرُومٌ	Vine (grape).
كَرْمَةٌ	A vine-tree.
كَرَّامٌ	Vine-dresser.
كَرَامَةٌ	Generosity ; honour.
حُبًّا وَكَرَامَةً	Most gladly !
كَرِيمٌ ج كِرَامٌ	Noble, liberal.
كَرِيمَةٌ	Precious object.
أَكْرَمُ	More noble, or generous.
إِكْرَامٌ	Respect, reverence.
إِكْرَامًا لِ	For the sake of.
تَكْرِيمٌ	Honouring, honour.
مُكْرَمٌ وَمُكَرَّمٌ	Honoured.
مَكْرُمَةٌ ج مَكَارِمُ	Noble action.
كُرُنْبٌ وَكَرَنْبٌ	Cabbage.
كَرِهَ يَكْرَهُ	To loathe, abhor.
كَرُهَ يَكْرُهُ	To be loathsome.
كَرَّهَ	To render hateful.

أَكْرَهَ عَلَى	To force one to . .
تَكَرَّهَ وَتَكَارَهَ	To loathe.
إِسْتَكْرَهَ	To find loathsome.
كُرْهٌ وَكَرَاهَةٌ	Aversion, disgust.
كَرِهٌ وَكَرِيهٌ	Detestable.
كَرِيهَةٌ ج كَرَائِهُ	Adversity.
إِكْرَاهٌ	Compulsion.
مَكْرُوهٌ	Abhorred, detested.
كَرَوْيَا وَكَرَاوِيَا	Caraway.
كَرِيَ يَكْرَى كَرًى	To slumber.
كَارَى وَأَكْرَى	To let, rent.
إِكْتَرَى وَٱسْتَكْرَى	To hire, rent.
كِرَاءٌ وَكِرْوَةٌ	Hire, wages ; rent.
كُرَةٌ ج كُرَاتٌ وَكُرًى	Globe, ball.
كُرَةُ ٱلْأَرْضِ	Terrestrial globe.
كُرَوِيٌّ	Globular, spherical.
إِكْرَاءٌ	Act of renting, letting.
إِكْتِرَاءٌ	Act of hiring.
مُكَارٍ ج مُكَارُونَ	Muleteer.
مُكْرٍ	Hirer out, letter.
مُكْرًى	Hired, rented, let.
كَزَّ يَكُزُّ	To dry up; become rigid.
كُزَازٌ وَكُزَّازٌ	Tetanus.
كُزْبُرَةٌ وَكَزْبَرَةٌ	Coriander.
كَسَبَ يَكْسِبُ	To earn ; acquire.
كَسَّبَ وَأَكْسَبَ	To bestow; give.
إِكْتَسَبَ	To seek gain ; acquire.
كَسْبٌ	Earnings, gain.
إِكْتِسَابٌ	Acquiring, earning.
إِكْتِسَابِيٌّ	Acquired.
مَكْسَبٌ ج مَكَاسِبُ	Gain, profit.
مَكْسُوبٌ وَمُكْتَسَبٌ	Acquired.
(كَسْتَنَا)	Chestnut.
كَسَحَ يَكْسَحُ كَسْحًا	To cut off.
كَسِحَ يَكْسَحُ كَسَحًا	To be crippled.
كُسَاحَةٌ	Rickets. Sweepings.

كَسِيحٌ ج كُسْحَانٌ Lame, crippled.

أَكْسَحُ م كَسْحَاءُ ج كُسْحٌ A cripple.

كَسَدَ يَكْسُدُ To sell badly.

كَاسِدٌ Worthless ; selling badly.

كَسَرَ يَكْسِرُ To break ; rout, defeat.

كَسَّرَ To break into pieces.

كَاسَرَ To seek an abatement.

تَكَسَّرَ To be broken into pieces.

إِنْكَسَرَ To be broken ; routed ; become a bankrupt, fail.

كَسْرٌ Breach, fracture.

كَسْرٌ ج كُسُورٌ Fraction (*arith*).

كَسْرَةٌ ج كِسَرٌ Fragment.

كَسْرَةٌ ج كَسَرَاتٌ The vowel. (ِ) A fracture ; defeat.

كِسْرَى ج أَكَاسِرَةٌ Chosroes.

كَاسِرَةٌ ج كَوَاسِرُ Bird of prey.

كُسَارَةٌ A fragment.

إِكْسِيرٌ Elixir.

إِنْكِسَارٌ Defeat ; bankruptcy.

جَمْعُ ٱلتَّكْسِيرِ Broken plural.

مُكَسَّرٌ Broken into pieces.

مَكْسُورٌ Routed ; bankrupt.

كَسَفَ وَٱنْكَسَفَ To be eclipsed.

كُسُوفٌ وَٱنْكِسَافٌ Eclipse.

كَاسِفُ ٱلْبَالِ Heavy-hearted.

مَكْسُوفٌ وَمُنْكَسِفٌ Eclipsed.

كَسِلَ يَكْسَلُ وَتَكَاسَلَ To be lazy.

كَسَلٌ وَتَكَاسُلٌ Laziness, idleness.

كَسْلَانُ ج كَسَالَى Lazy, idle.

كَسْمٌ Mode, fashion.

كَسَا يَكْسُو وَأَكْسَى To clothe.

إِكْتَسَى To be dressed, clothed.

كِسَاءٌ ج أَكْسِيَةٌ Garment, dress.

كُسْوَةٌ ج كُسًى Clothing, dress.

(كَشَّ) To frown. Chase away.

كُشَّةٌ Lock of hair.

(كِشْتُبَانٌ) A thimble.

To disperse.	كَشَحَ ـُ
To retire from.	إِنْكَشَحَ عَنْ
Flank ; waist.	كَشْحٌ ج كُشُوحٌ
To snarl (beast).	كَشَرَ عَنْ نَابِهِ
To strip ; scrape.	كَشَطَ يَكْشِطُ
To be dispersed (clouds).	تَكَشَّطَ
To be taken off.	إِنْكَشَطَ
To uncover.	كَشَفَ يَكْشِفُ وَكَشَّفَ
To reveal, disclose.	كَاشَفَ بِ
To be uncovered.	إِنْكَشَفَ
To discover ; find out.	إِكْتَشَفَ
To try to discover.	إِسْتَكْشَفَ
Unveiling, revealing.	كَشْفٌ
Overseer. Test.	(كَاشِفٌ ج كَشَفَةٌ)
Uncovered, disclosed.	مَكْشُوفٌ
Discovery.	إِكْتِشَافٌ ج إِكْتِشَافَاتٌ
Discoverer.	مُكْتَشِفٌ
Ruffle of a garment.	كَشْكَشٌ
A beggar's bag.	كَشْكُولٌ
Currants.	كِشْمِشٌ
To surfeit (food).	كَظَّ يَكُظُّ
Indigestion ; surfeit.	كَظَّةٌ
To shut ; restrain.	كَظَمَ يَكْظِمُ
Silent, speechless.	كَاظِمٌ
Suppressing anger.	كَظِيمٌ
To cube (a number).	كَعَّبَ
Ankle. Cube, (*arith*).	كَعْبٌ
The kaba in Mecca.	أَلْكَعْبَةُ
Cubic ; cube.	مُكَعَّبٌ
The radius (bone).	كُعْبُرَةٌ
Biscuit, cake, bun.	كَعْكٌ
To muzzle.	كَعَمَ يَكْعَمُ
Muzzle of the camel.	كَعَامٌ
Muzzled.	كَعِيمٌ وَمَكْعُومٌ
To be timid.	كَعَا يَكْعُو
To defy.	(كَعَّى)

Paper. كَاغِدٌ

To hem, seam. كَفَّ يَكُفُّ كَفًّا

To prevent. To cease. كَفَّ عَنْ

To become blind. كُفَّ بَصَرُهُ

To abstain from. إِنْكَفَّ عَنْ

Palm of hand. كَفٌّ ج كُفُوفٌ

Scale (of a balance). كَفَّةٌ

Silk handkerchief. كَفِيَّةٌ

All. كَافَّةً

Equal ; daily bread. كَفَافٌ

Blind. كَفِيفٌ وَمَكْفُوفٌ ج مَكَافِيفُ

To reward. كَافَأَ مُكَافَأَةً وَكِفَاءً

To retreat ; turn back. إِنْكَفَأَ

Equality, likeness. كَفَأٌ وَكَفَاءَةٌ

Equal, like. كَفَاءٌ وَكُفْوءٌ

To face. كَفَحَ يَكْفَحُ وَكَافَحَ

To fight for, defend. كَافَحَ عَنْ

To drive back. أَكْفَحَ عَنْ

To encounter one another. تَكَافَحَ

Battle, combat. كِفَاحٌ وَمُكَافَحَةٌ

To cover. كَفَرَ يَكْفُرُ وَكَفَّرَ

To be an infidel. كَفَرَ يَكْفُرُ

To renounce, deny. كَفَرَ بِ

To expiate. كَفَّرَ

Village, hamlet. كَفْرٌ ج كُفُورٌ

Unbelief ; infidelity. كُفْرٌ

Infidel. كَافِرٌ ج كُفَّارٌ وَكَفَرَةٌ

Camphor. كَافُورٌ

Atonement ; expiation. كَفَّارَةٌ

Atonement ; expiation. تَكْفِيرٌ

To take charge of. كَفَلَ يَكْفُلُ

To stand security. كَفَلَ يَكْفِلُ

To make one give bail. كَفَّلَ

To guarantee. تَكَفَّلَ لَهُ بِ

Buttocks. كَفَلٌ ج أَكْفَالٌ

One who stands bail. كَافِلٌ

ألْكافِلُ	God.
كَفَالَةٌ	Bail, security, pledge.
كَفِيلٌ كُفَلاءُ	A surety.
مَكْفُولٌ	Guaranteed.
إِكْفَهَرَّ	To be very dark (night).
كَفَّنَ	To shroud the dead.
كَفَنٌ ج أَكْفَانٌ	Shroud.
كَفَى يَكْفِي	To suffice ; satisfy.
كَفَاهُ ٱلشَّرَّ	To prevent evil.
كَافَى بِـ	To recompense.
إِكْتَفَى	To be contented.
كَفِيٌّ وَكَافٍ	Sufficient.
كِفَايَةٌ	Sufficient quantity.
مُكَافَأَةٌ	Recompense, requital.
كَلَّ يَكِلُّ	To be tired, weary.
كَلَّ و كَلَّلَ	To be dim, dull.
كَلَّلَ	To crown. To join in wedlock, marry.
أَكَلَّ	To fatigue ; to dim.
تَكَلَّلَ	To be crowned.
كَلٌّ وَكَلَالٌ	Weariness ; dulness.
كَلٌّ وَكَلِيلٌ	Blunt ; dim.
كُلٌّ	All ; each, every.
كِلَا (كِلْتَا *dual fem*)	Both of.
كَلَّا	No ! by no means.
كُلَّةٌ ج كُلَلٌ	Cannon ball.
كُلَّمَا	As often as, whenever.
كُلِّيٌّ م كُلِّيَّةٌ	Universal, general.
أَلْكُلِّيَّةُ	General term, (*logic*).
بِالْكُلِّيَّةِ	Altogether, entirely.
كَالٌّ	Fatigued ; dim ; blunt.
إِكْلِيلٌ ج أَكَالِيلُ	Crown ; umbel.
مُكَلَّلٌ	Crowned.
كَلَأٌ	Forage ; herbage.
كَلِبَ	To have hydrophobia.
كَلْبٌ ج كِلَابٌ	Dog.
كَلْبُ ٱلْبَحْرِ	Shark.

Beaver. كَلْبُ ٱلْمَاءِ

Canis major. أَلْكَلْبُ ٱلْأَكْبَرُ

Canis minor. أَلْكَلْبُ ٱلْأَصْغَرُ

Hydrophobia. كَلَبٌ

Seized with hydrophobia. كَلِبٌ

Female dog, bitch. كَلْبَةٌ

Tongs, forceps. كَلْبتان

Hook ; grapnel. كُلَّابٌ ج كَلَالِيبُ

See : كِلَا Both, (*fem*). كِلْتَا

To frown. كَلَحَ يَكْلَحُ وأَكْلَحَ وتَكَلَّحَ

Austere, severe. كَالِحٌ

To plaster with lime. كَلَّسَ

Lime mortar. كِلْسٌ

Sock, stocking. (كَلْسَةٌ)

Lime-kiln. كَلَّاسَةٌ

Lime-burner; plasterer. مُكَلِّسٌ

Plastered with lime. مُكَلَّسٌ

Eel. أَنْكَلِيسٌ

To be freckled. كَلِفَ يَكْلَفُ كَلَفًا

To be devoted to. كَلِفَ بِ

To impose a difficult matter upon one. كَلَّفَ وَإِلى

To cost. كَلَّفَ

To take the trouble (to do anything). كَلَّفَ خَاطِرَهُ

Please do this ! كَلِّفْ خَاطِرَكَ

To take pains. تَكَلَّفَ

Ardent love. Freckles. كَلَفٌ

Trouble, labour, hardship. Cost, expense. كُلْفَةٌ ج كُلَفٌ

Freckled ; maculated. أَكْلَفُ

Trouble. تَكْلِيفٌ ج تَكَالِيفُ

Without ceremony. بِلَا تَكْلِيف

Expensive. مُكْلِفٌ وَمُكَلِّفٌ

Responsible agent. مُكَلَّفٌ

Intruder. مُتَكَلِّفٌ

Raft. كَلَكٌ

To wound. كَلَمَ يَكْلُمُ وَكَلَّمَ

كَلَّمَ	To speak ; speak to.
كَالَمَ	To converse with.
تَكَلَّمَ	To talk, converse.
كَلْمٌ ج كُلُومٌ وَكِلَامٌ	Wound.
كَلِمٌ	Incomplete sentence.
كَلِمَةٌ ج كَلِمَاتٌ	Word, sentence.
كَلَامٌ	Speech, saying.
تَكَلُّمٌ	Talking, speech.
مُتَكَلِّمٌ	Speaker, 1st person, (*gram*).
مَكْلُومٌ وَكَلِيمٌ	Wounded.
كِلَا م كِلْتَا	Both. (*dual*).
كُلْيَةٌ ج كُلًى	Kidney.
كَمْ	How much ? How many ?
كَمْ رَجُلاً	How many men ?
كُمْ	*Pronominal suffix.*
كِتَابُكُمْ	Your book (*pl. m.*).
كِتَابُكُمَا	Your book (*dual*).
كَمَا	As, even as, just as.
كَمَّ	To muzzle (an animal).
كَمٌّ وَكَمِّيَّةٌ ج كَمِّيَّاتٌ	Quantity.
كِمٌّ ج أَكْمَامٌ	Calyx, spathe.
كُمٌّ ج أَكْمَامٌ	Sleeve.
كِمَامَةٌ وَكِمَامٌ	Muzzle.
مَكْمُومٌ	Muzzled.
كَمْءٌ وَكَمْأَةٌ	Truffle.
كَمْبِيَالَةٌ	Bill ; cheque.
كَمْبِيُو	Rate, or bill of exchange.
كُمَيْتٌ	Dark brown, bay.
كُمِّثْرَى	Pear.
كُمِّثْرَاةٌ ج كُمِّثْرَيَاتٌ	A pear.
كَمْخَةٌ	Scum ; film.
كَمِدَ يَكْمَدُ كَمَداً	To be sad.
أَكْمَدَ	To make sad.
كَمَدٌ وَكُمْدَةٌ	Change of colour. Concealed grief.
كَمَرٌ ج أَكْمَارٌ	A kind of belt.
كُمْرُكٌ	Duty ; custom-house.

كُمْرُكْجِيٌّ Receiver of customs.

كَيْمُوسُ Chyme.

(كَمَشَ) To grasp.

إِنْكَمَشَ وَتَكَمَّشَ To be wrinkled.

(كَمْشَةٌ) A handful.

(كَمَّاشَةٌ) Carpenter's pincers.

كَمَلَ يَكْمُلُ وَتَكَمَّلَ وَتَكَامَلَ وَاكْتَمَلَ
To be complete, finished.

كَمَّلَ وَأَكْمَلَ To finish, complete.

كَامِلٌ Entire, complete.

كَمَالٌ Perfection.

تَكْمِيلُ Finishing; perfecting.

مُكَمَّلٌ Completed, finished.

كَمَنَ ـُ وَاكْتَمَنَ To hide; hide one's self.

كَمَنَ لِ To lie in ambush.

كَمْنَةٌ ج كِمَانٌ Ambush.

كُمُونٌ State of being hidden.

كَمُّونٌ Cumin.

كَمِينٌ ج كُمَنَاءُ Hidden; ambush.

مَكْمَنٌ ج مَكَامِنُ Place of ambush.

مُكْتَمِنٌ Hidden, concealed.

كَمَنْجَةٌ Violin.

كَمَهٌ Blindness.

أَكْمَهُ م كَمْهَاءُ ج كُمْهٌ Blind.

كُنَّ *Pronominal suffix.*

كِتَابُكُنَّ Your book, (*fem*).

كَنَّ يَكُنُّ To conceal, secrete.

إِكْتَنَّ To be concealed.

إِسْتَكَنَّ To retire; be quiet.

كِنٌّ ج أَكْنَانٌ Cover, shelter.

كَنَّةٌ ج كَنَائِنُ Son's wife.

كُنَّةٌ ج كِنَانٌ Roof for shelter.

كَانُونٌ ج كَوَانِينُ Hearth, stove.

كَانُونُ الأَوَّل December.

كَانُونُ الثَّانِي January.

كَنِينٌ وَمَكْنُونٌ Concealed.

كَنَبٌ Callousness (of hand).

Ingratitude. كُنُودٌ

Frankincense. كُنْدُرٌ

Shoe. (كُنْدُرَةٌ ج كَنَادِرُ)

Hem, border. كَنَارٌ

Canary bird. كَنَارِيٌّ

Lute, harp. كَنَّارَةٌ ج كَنَّارَاتٌ

To treasure, store. كَنَزَ يَكْنِزُ

To be firm, hard. إِكْتَنَزَ

Treasure. كَنْزٌ ج كُنُوزٌ

Firm and compact. مُكْتَنِزٌ

Hidden, buried (treasure). مَكْنُوزٌ

To sweep. كَنَسَ يَكْنِسُ كَنْسًا وكَنَّسَ

Sweeper. كَنَّاسٌ

Sweepings. كُنَاسَةٌ

Synagogue. كَنِيسٌ

Church. كَنِيسَةٌ ج كَنَائِسُ

Ecclesiastical. كَنَائِسِيٌّ وكَنَسِيٌّ

Broom. مِكْنَسَةٌ ج مَكَانِسُ

Canaan. كَنْعَانُ

The Canaanites. اَلْكَنْعَانِيُّونَ

To shelter. كَنَفَ يَكْنُفُ كَنْفًا

To surround. تَكَنَّفَ وَاكْتَنَفَ

Refuge. كَنَفٌ ج أَكْنَافٌ

A kind of sweet pastry. كُنَافَةٌ

Privy, sewer. كَنِيفٌ ج كُنُفٌ

Substance, essence. كُنْهٌ

To hint at. كَنَى يَكْنِي كِنَايَةً عَنْ

To give a surname. كَنَّى بِ

To take a surname. تَكَنَّى بِ

Surname. Epithet. كُنْيَةٌ

Metaphor, metonomy. كِنَايَةٌ

Instead or in place of. كِنَايَةً عَنْ

To electrify. كَهْرَبَ

Yellow amber. كَهْرَبَاءُ

Electric. كَهْرَبَائِيٌّ

Electricity. كَهْرَبَائِيَّةٌ

مُكَهْرَب	Electrified.
كَهْف ج كُهُوف	Cavern, cave.
كَهَلَ يَكْهَلُ	To be middle-aged.
كَهْل ج كُهُول	Middle-aged.
كُهُولَة وَكُهُولِيَّة	Mature age.
كَهَنَ يَكْهُنُ	To divine, foretell.
كَاهِن ج كَهَنَة	Soothsayer ; priest.
كِهَانَة	Soothsaying ; divination.
كَهْنُوت	Priesthood.
كُوب ج أَكْوَاب	A large cup.
(كُوبَان)	A horse cloth.
كَوْثَل	Stern of ship ; helm.
كُوخ ج أَكْوَاخ	Hut.
كَادَ يَكُودُ كَوْداً	To restrain, hinder.
كَاد يَفْعَلُ	He almost did.
مَا كَاد يَفْعَلُ	He hardly did.
كَار ج كَارَات	Art, profession.
كُور ج أَكْوَار	Furnace, forge.
كُورَة ج كُوَر	Small district.
كوارة نحل	Bee-hive
كُورَنْتِينا	Quarantine.
كَاز	Petroleum. Gas.
كُوز ج أَكْوَاز	Drinking-mug.
كَاس ج كُؤُوس	Drinking-cup.
كُوسا	Vegetable marrow.
كُوع ج أَكْوَاع	Elbow.
اَلْكُوفَة	Kufa (city).
كُوفِيّ	Kufic (writing) ; of Kufa.
كُوفِيَّة	Head-wrapper.
كَوْكَب ج كَوَاكِب	Planet, star.
كَوْكَبَة	A party ; assembly.
كوم	To make a heap.
كُومَة ج كُوَم وأَكْوَام	A heap.
كَان يَكُونُ	To be, exist.
كَان لَهُ مَال	He had wealth.
كَان قَائِمًا	He was standing.

He was doing.	كَانَ يَفْعَلُ
He had said.	كَانَ قَدْ قَالَ
To create, form.	كَوَّنَ
To be created, formed.	تَكَوَّنَ
Existence, nature.	كِيَانٌ
Nature ; universe.	كَوْنٌ ج أَكْوَان
Being ; creature.	كَائِنٌ
Incident, event.	كَائِنَةٌ ج كَائِنَاتٌ
All created things.	أَلْكَائِنَاتُ
Formation, creation.	تَكْوِينٌ
Book of Genesis.	سِفْرُ ٱلتَّكْوِينِ
Place.	مَكَانٌ ج أَمْكِنَةٌ وَأَمَاكِنُ
Adverb of place.	ظَرْفُ ٱلْمَكَانِ
Place ; rank.	مَكَانَةٌ ج مَكَانَاتٌ
Creator.	مُكَوِّنٌ
Window.	كُوَّةٌ ج كُوَّات وَكُوًى
To burn, cauterise.	كَوَى يَكْوِي
(To iron clothes).	كَوَى
To be cauterised.	إِكْتَوَى
Cauterisation, ironing.	كَيٌّ
Smoothing-iron.	مِكْوَاةٌ ج مَكَاوٍ
Cauterised ; ironed.	مَكْوِيٌّ
In order that.	كَيْ وَلِكَيْ
In order not...	كَيْ لَا وَلِكَيْ لَا
So and so.	كَيْتَ وَكَيْتَ
To deceive...	كَادَ يَكِيدُ كَيْداً وَكَايَدَ
Stratagem, guile.	كَيْدٌ
Same as. كَيْدٌ	مَكِيدَةٌ ج مَكَائِدُ.
To be shrewd.	كَاسَ يَكِيسُ
To put into a bag.	كَيَّسَ
Intelligence.	كَيْس وَكِيَاسَةٌ
Bag, purse.	كِيسٌ ج أَكْيَاسٌ
Clever ; handsome.	كَيِّس
Handsome, pretty.	(كُوَيِّسٌ)
More handsome.	أَكْوَسُ
To take a special form.	تَكَيَّفَ

كَيْفَ	How ; in what way ?
(كَيْف)	Enjoyment. Quality.
كَيفما كَانَ	Howsoever.
كَيفيَّةٌ ج كَيفيَّاتٌ	Quality ; form.
كَالَ يَكِيلُ وَكَيْلَ	To measure.
إِكْتَالَ	To measure out.
كَيْلٌ ج أَكْيَال	Measure of grains
(٦ أَمْدَادٍ)	= 6 *mudds*.
كَيْلَة ج كَيْلاَت	A small measure.
كِيَالة	Measuring, weighing.
كَيَّالٌ	One who measures.
مِكْيَلٌ	Measure of capacity.
مَكِيلٌ وَمَكْيُولٌ	Measured.
كَيْلُوسٌ	Chyle.
كَيْمَا (كَيْ مَا)	In order that.
كِيمِيَا وَكِيمِيَاء	Chemistry.
كِيمِيٌّ	Chemist ; chemical.
كِينَا	Quinine.
خَشَبُ ٱلْكِينَا	Cinchona bark.

ل

ل	As a numeral sign=30.
لِ	To, for.
لِيَكْتُبْ	Let him write.
لَعَمْرُكَ	By thy life !
لاَ	No ; not.
لاَ وَلاَ	Neither, nor.

لاَتَ No, there is not or no...

أَللاَّتُ An Arabian godess.

لاَزَوَرْدٌ Lapis lazuli.

لاَزَوَرْدِيٌّ Azure-blue.

مَلأَكٌ وَمَلَكٌ ج مَلاَئِكَةٌ Angel.

لأْلأَ وَتَلأْلأَ To shine, glitter.

لُؤْلُؤٌ Pearls.

لُؤْلُؤَةٌ ج لآَلِئُ A pearl.

لُؤْلُؤِيٌّ Pearl-coloured.

لأَمَ يَلأَمُ To bind up a wound.

لَؤُمَ To be of a low character.

لاَءَمَ To agree with.

لاَءَمَ بَيْنَ To reconcile.

إِلْتَأَمَ To assemble. Unite. *v. i.*

لُؤْمٌ Avarice, meanness.

لَئِيمٌ ج لِئَامٌ Base, sordid.

مُلاَئِمٌ Convenient ; suitable.

مُلاَءَمَةٌ Suitableness.

مُلْتَئِمٌ Assembled, gathered.

أَلَبَّ بِ To stay in.

لُبٌّ ج لُبُوبٌ Marrow, pith.

لُبٌّ ج أَلْبَابٌ Heart ; mind.

لَبِيبٌ ج أَلِبَّاءُ Intelligent.

لِبَأٌ First milk.

لَبُؤَةٌ ج لَبُؤَاتٌ Lioness.

لَبِثَ يَلْبَثُ ب To tarry, abide in.

مَالَبِثَ أَنْ فَعَلَ He did not delay to do.

لَبْثٌ وَلُبْثٌ وَلَبَاثٌ A tarrying.

لُبْثَةٌ A short stay, delay.

لَبَخَ يَلْبَخُ To beat. To abuse.

لَبَخٌ (وَلَبْخٌ) Persea (tree).

لَبْخَةٌ ج لَبَخَاتٌ Poultice, cataplasm.

لَبَدَ وَأَلْبَدَ بِ To abide, dwell in.

لَبَّدَ To cram, compress.

تَلَبَّدَ To be compact together.

تَلَبَّدَ ب To stick to, cleave to.

إِلْتَبَدَ To be pressed closely.

لَبَّادَةٌ Cap of cloth or felt.

لَبَسَ يَلْبِسُ عَلَى To make obscure.

لَبِسَ يَلْبَسُ To put on a dress.

لَبَّسَ To render obscure. To clothe.

أَلْبَسَ To cover, clothe.

إِلْتَبَسَ To be dark, obscure.

إِلْتَبَسَ بِ To be confused with.

لَبْسٌ وَٱلْتِبَاسٌ Ambiguity.

لُبْسٌ ج لُبُوسٌ Clothing, dress.

لِبَاسٌ ج أَلْبِسَةٌ Garment.

مَلْبَسٌ ج مَلَابِسُ Clothing.

مُلْتَبِسٌ Obscure; doubtful.

(مُلَبَّسٌ) Sugar-plums.

مَلْبُوسٌ ج مَلَابِيسُ Garment.

(لَبَّشَ) To collect pell-mell.

لَبَشٌ Baggage, chattels.

لَبَطَ يَلْبِطُ لَبْطًا To kick.

لَبْطَةٌ A kick.

لَبِقَ بِ To fit, become one.

لَبَقٌ وَلَبَاقَةٌ Wit and cleverness.

لَبِقٌ وَلَبِيقٌ Skilful, clever.

لَبَكَ يَلْبُكُ وَلَبَّكَ To mix; confuse.

تَلَبَّكَ وَٱلْتَبَكَ To be confused, embarrassed.

لَبْكٌ وَلَبْكَةٌ Confused affair.

مُلْتَبِكٌ وَمَلْبُوكٌ Embarrassed.

لَبْلَابٌ Egyptian bean.

لَبَنٌ ج أَلْبَانٌ Milk; sour milk. Sap.

لَبِنٌ وَلِبْنٌ Brick, tile.

لَبِنَةٌ A brick.

لُبْنَانُ Mount Lebanon.

لُبْنَانِيٌّ Of Mount Lebanon.

لُبَانٌ Frankincence. Pine.

لَبَّانٌ Brick-maker. Milk-man.

لَبْوَةٌ ج لَبَوَاتٌ Lioness.

لَبَّى To obey, respond.

Here I am! لَبَّيْكَ

To speak nonsense. لَتَّ يَلُتُّ لَتًّا

Two idols. أَللاَّت والعُزَّى

Who, which (*fem*). الَّتِي مث اللَّتَانِ

ج اللَّوَاتِي

To stammer, lisp. لَثِغَ يَلْثَغُ

Stammering, lisping. لَثَغٌ ولُثْغَةٌ

Lisper. أَلْثَغُ م لَثْغَاءُ ج لُثْغٌ

To kiss. لَثَمَ يَلْثُمُ وَلَثِمَ يَلْثَمُ لَثْمًا

To muffle the mouth. لَثَمَ ولَثَّمَ

A kiss. لَثْمَةٌ

Veil. لِثَامٌ

Gums (of the teeth). لِثَةٌ ج لِثَاتٌ

To persist, persevere. لَجَّ يَلِجُّ

To importune. لَجَّ عَلَى

To wrangle with. لاجَّ

High sea; the deep. لُجَّةٌ ج لُجَجٌ

Pertinacious. لاجٌّ وَلَجُوجٌ

Pertinacity. لَجَاجٌ وَلَجَاجَةٌ

To take refuge in, repair to. لَجَأَ يَلْجَأُ وَلَجِئَ يَلْجَأُ وَالْتَجَأَ إِلَى

To force, compel. لَجَّأَ وأَلْجَأَ إِلَى

To defend, protect. أَلْجَأَ

Refuge. لَجَأٌ ومَلْجَأٌ ج مَلاجِئُ

Seeking shelter. لاجِئٌ ومُلْتَجِئٌ

To stammer. لَجْلَجَ وَتَلَجْلَجَ

One who stutters. لَجْلاجٌ

To bridle (a horse). لَجَمَ وَأَلْجَمَ

To be bridled. إِلْتَجَمَ

Bridle, curb. لِجَامٌ ج أَلْجِمَةٌ وَلُجُمٌ

Bridled. مُلْجَمٌ

Committee. لَجْنَةٌ

To be close, near. لَحَّ يَلُحُّ لَحًّا

To persist in one's demands. أَلَحَّ فِي السُّؤَالِ

To importune, press. أَلَحَّ عَلَيْهِ

Importunity; persistence. إِلْحَاحٌ

One who insists. مُلِحٌّ وَمِلْحَاحٌ

لَحَدَ يَلْحَدُ لَحْداً وَأَلْحَدَ To bury.

أَلْحَدَ عن To swerve from.

أَلْحَدَ وَٱلْتَحَدَ To apostatize.

لَحْدٌ ج أَلْحَادٌ وَلُحُودٌ A grave.

إِلْحَادٌ Apostasy ; heresy.

مُلْحِدٌ ج مُلْحِدُون An apostate.

لَحَسَ ـَ لَحْساً To lick.

لَحَظَ يَلْحَظُ لَحْظاً To regard, observe.

لَاحَظَ To look at attentively.

لَحْظَةٌ Glance, moment.

مُلَاحَظَةٌ Observation.

مَلْحُوظٌ ج مَلْحُوظَاتٌ Regarded.

لَحَفَ يَلْحَفُ To wrap up

إِلْتَحَفَ To wrap one's self up.

لِحْفٌ Foot of a mountain.

لِحَافٌ ج لُحُفٌ Cover, blanket.

مِلْحَفَةٌ ج مَلَاحِفُ An outer dress.

لَحِقَ يَلْحَقُ To reach, overtake.

لَاحَقَ To pursue, follow.

أَلْحَقَ ب To annex, join to.

إِلْتَحَقَ ب To reach ; be annexed.

لَاحِقٌ Overtaking, reaching.

إِلْحَاقٌ Adding ; annexing.

مُلْحَقٌ Appendix ; supplement.

لَحِمَ يَلْحَمُ لَحْماً To be fleshy.

لُحِمَ لَحْماً To be killed, massacred.

لَحَمَ يَلْحُمُ لَحْماً To solder.

لَاحَمَ وَأَلْحَمَ ب To join, unite.

تَلَاحَمَ To kill one another.

إِلْتَحَمَ To be soldered, united.

اِلتحمَ To grow bloody, (combat).

لَحْمٌ ج لُحُومٌ Flesh, meat.

لُحْمَةٌ ج لُحَمٌ Woof (of a stuff).

لِحَامٌ Solder.

لَحَّامٌ Butcher ; flesh-monger.

إِلْتِحَامٌ Union ; alliance.

ملحمة ج ملاحم Combat, battle.

لحن يلحن To make grammatical mistakes in speaking.

لحن في القراءة To chant.

لحن ج ألحان Tone; chant, air.

Error of pronunciation.

صناعة الألحان Musical art.

تلحين Chanting.

إلتحى To let one's beard grow.

لحي مث لحيان ج لحي Jaw-bone.

لحاء Bark, (*sp*. inner bark).

لحية ج لحى Beard.

لحية التيس Wild salsify.

لخة Obscurity in speech.

لخص To extract; sum up.

تلخيص Abstract. Explanation.

ملخص Summary, abstract

لد يلد لدا To quarrel; oppose.

ألد Violent in opposition.

لدغ يلدغ لدغا To sting, bite.

لدغة Sting, poisonous bite.

لدن يلدن To be pliable, flexible.

لدن ج لدن Soft; supple.

لدن At, by, to, with, near to.

لدانة ولدونة Softness, flexibility.

لدى At, by, to, with.

لديك Near or by thee; to thee.

لذ يلذ To be sweet, agreeable.

لذ والتذ واستلذ ب To enjoy.

تلذذ To delight.

لذة ج لذات Pleasure, delight.

لذيذ Sweet, pleasant.

ملذة ج ملاذ Delight, pleasure.

لذع يلذع لذعا To burn, brand.

إلتذع To feel a burning pain.

لذعة A burn.

لذاع Stinging pungent.

لوذع ولوذعي Ingenious; witty.

أَللاَّذِقِيـَّةُ Latakia (*city*).

أَلَّذِي مث أَللَّذانِ ج أَلَّذِينَ Who, which.

لَزَّ يَلُزُّ لَزًّا To press.

أَلْتَزَّ بِهِ To adhere to it.

لَازِبٌ Necessary; constant.

لَزِجَ يَلْزَجُ To stick, adhere.

لَزِجٌ Viscid, sticky, cohesive.

لُزُوجَةٌ Viscidity, stickiness.

لَزِقَ يَلْزَقُ وَأَلْتَزَقَ بِ To stick to.

لَازَقَ To adhere to another.

أَلْزَقَ وَلَزَّقَ To glue together.

لِزْقٌ That which adjoins.

لَزْقَةٌ وَلَزُوقٌ Poultice, plaster.

لَزِمَ يَلْزَمُ To adhere to; persist in; be necessary, follow of necessity.

لَازَمَ To cling to, persevere in.

أَلْزَمَ إِلْزَامًا To impose as a duty, compel.

إِلْتَزَمَ To be responsible; be forced. To farm taxes.

اِسْتَلْزَمَ To find necessary.

لَازِمٌ Necessary, unavoidable. Intransitive verb (*Gram.*).

لُزُومٌ Necessity.

اِلْزَامٌ Compulsion.

إِلْتِزَامٌ ج إِلْتِزَامَاتٌ Necessity; obligation. Renting; farming

(مِلْزَمَةٌ ج. مَلاَزِمُ) Hand-vice; press.

مُلاَزِمٌ Lieutenant (*mil.*).

مُلاَزَمَةٌ Assiduity, application.

مَلْزُومٌ Obliged, compelled.

مُلْتَزِمٌ Farmer of revenues.

لَسَعَ يَلْسَعُ لَسْعًا To sting.

لَسِنَ يَلْسَنُ لَسَنًا To be eloquent.

لَسِنٌ ج لُسْنٌ Eloquent.

لِسَانٌ ج أَلْسُنٌ Tongue; language. Cape of land.

لِسَانُ ٱلْمِزْمَارِ Epiglottis.

لِسَانُ ٱلْحَالِ Speaking for itself.

لِسَانًا By word of mouth.

ذُو لِسَانَيْنِ Double dealer, false.

لِسَانِيٌّ Lingual.

To destroy, annihilate.	لاشَى
To vanish, perish.	تَلاشَى
Annihilation.	مُلاشَاةٌ وَتَلاشٍ
Thief, robber.	لِصٌّ ج لُصُوصٌ
Robbery, thieving.	لُصُوصِيَّةٌ
To stick to.	لَصِقَ يَلْصَقُ وَٱلْتَصَقَ بِ
To cling to, be devoted to	لاصَقَ
To fasten, join.	أَلْصَقَ بِ
A dressing (for wounds).	لَصُوقٌ
Contiguous.	مُلاصِقٌ
Contiguity, adherence.	مُلاصَقَةٌ
To soil with.	لَطَخَ يَلْطَخُ وَلَطَّخَ بِ
To be soiled with.	تَلَطَّخَ بِ
A soil, stain.	لُطْخَةٌ
To be kind.	لَطَفَ يَلْطُفُ بِ
To soften, mitigate.	أَطَفَ
To treat with kindness.	لاطَفَ
To be polite, courteous to.	تَلَطَّفَ لِ

To find pretty or nice.	إِسْتَلْطَفَ
Friendliness. Favour.	لُطْفٌ
Light illness.	حَرَكَةٌ لُطْفٍ
Delicacy. Tenuity.	لَطَافَةٌ
Graceful ; kind. Rare (not dense).	لَطِيفٌ ج لُطَفَاءُ
God.	ٱللَّطِيفُ
Witty saying.	لَطِيفَةٌ ج لَطَائِفُ
Friendliness ; courtesy.	تَلَطُّفٌ
Friendly treatment.	مُلاطَفَةٌ
To slap.	لَطَمَ يَلْطِمُ لَطْمًا
To clash, collide.	تَلاطَمَ وَٱلْتَطَمَ
Slap on the face.	لَطْمَةٌ ج لَطَمَاتٌ
To take shelter.	لَطَا يَلْطُو
To cleave to.	لَظَّ يَلُظُّ
To blaze (fire).	لَظِيَ يَلْظَى لَظًى
To be enflamed.	تَلَظَّى وَٱلْتَظَى
Fire ; flame	لَظًى
To play, sport, jest.	لَعِبَ ـ لَعِبًا

To play, sport with. لَاعَبَ

Play, sport. لَعْبٌ وَلَعِبٌ

Gambling. لَعْبُ ٱلْقِمَارِ

A game, sport. لُعْبَةٌ ج لُعَبٌ

Saliva, spittle. Mucilage. لُعَابٌ

Mucilaginous, slimy. لُعَابِيٌّ

Professional player. لَعَّابٌ وَلِعِّيبٌ

Play, pleasantry. أُلْعُوبَةٌ

Sporting, jesting. تَلَاعُبٌ

Place to play in. مَلْعَبٌ ج مَلَاعِبُ

Toy, plaything. مَلْعَبَةٌ

A trick in play. (مَلْعُوبٌ ج مَلَاعِيبُ)

To pain, burn. لَعَجَ يَلْعَجُ لَعْجًا

Burning pain. لَاعِجٌ ج لَوَاعِجُ

To lick. لَعِقَ يَلْعَقُ لَعْقًا

Electuary. لَعُوقٌ

Spoon. مِلْعَقَةٌ ج مَلَاعِقُ

Perhaps, may be. لَعَلَّ وَعَلَّ

It may be that Zeid is standing. لَعَلَّ زَيْدًا قَائِمٌ

To shine, gleam. لَعْلَعَ وَتَلَعْلَعَ

To curse. لَعَنَ يَلْعَنُ لَعْنًا

To curse one another. تَلَاعَنَ

Imprecation. لَعْنٌ وَلَعْنَةٌ ج لَعَنَاتٌ

Satan. أَللَّعِينُ

Cursed. مَلْعُونٌ ج مَلَاعِينُ

To be very tired. لَغَبَ ـُ

To chase long. تَلَغَّبَ

Riddle ; enigma. لُغْزٌ ج أَلْغَازٌ

Enigmatic, ambiguous. مُلْغَزٌ

To speak indistinctly. لَغَطَ يَلْغَطُ

Noise ; sound. لَغْطٌ ج أَلْغَاطٌ

Mine, blast. لُغْمٌ ج لُغُومٌ

Miner ; blaster. لُغْمَجِيٌّ

To speak. لَغَا يَلْغُو

To exclude, abolish. أَلْغَى

Language, dialect ; idiom, expression. لُغَةٌ ج لُغَاتٌ

عِلْمُ اللُّغَةِ Lexicography.

أَهْلُ اللُّغَةِ Lexicographers.

لَغْوٌ Faulty language, nonsense.

لُغَوِيّ Etymological ; linguistic.

إِلْغَاءٌ Abolishing, annulling.

مُلْغًى Suppressed, abolished.

لَفَّ يَلُفُّ لَفًّا To wrap up, roll.

اِلْتَفَّ To wrap one's self up.

إِلْتَفَّ To be entwined.

(لَفَّةٌ ج لَفَّاتٌ) A turban.

لِفَافَةٌ ج لَفَائِف Bandage.

لَفِيفٌ Mixed crowd.

مَلْفُوفٌ Wrapped up. Cabbage.

لَفَتَ يَلْفِتُ لَفْتاً To twist, turn.

إِلْتَفَتَ إِلَى To consider, regard.

لِفْتٌ Turnip, rape.

لَفْتَةٌ ج لَفَتَات Side-glance.

إِلْتِفَاتٌ Attention ; favour.

لَفَحَ يَلْفَحُ لَفْحاً To burn, scorch.

لَفُوحٌ وَلَافِحٌ ج لَوَافِحُ Scorching.

لُفَّاحٌ Mandrake (plant).

لَفَظَ يَلْفُظُ To pronounce. Dei.

لَفَظَ وَتَلَفَّظَ بِ To utter.

لَفْظٌ ج أَلْفَاظٌ Utterance ; word.

لَفْظاً وَمَعْنًى As regards the wording and the meaning.

لَفْظَةٌ ج لَفَظَاتٌ A word ; an utterance.

لَفْظِيٌّ Verbal.

لَفَقَ يَلْفُقُ لَفْقاً To seam.

لَفَّقَ To interpolate, falsify, lie.

مُلَفَّقٌ Embellished by falsehood.

لَفْلَفَ To wrap up, envelop.

تَلَافِيفُ الدِّمَاغِ Convolutions of the brain.

أَلْفَى إِلْفَاءً To find.

تَلَافَى To mend ; take up.

لَقَّبَ بِ To give a title

لَقَبٌ ج أَلْقَابٌ Surname ; title.

مُلَقَّبٌ Surnamed; having a title.

لَقَحَ يَلْقَحُ لَقْحاً To fecundate.

لَقِحَ يَلْقَحُ لَقَحاً To be fecundated.

لَقَّحَ وأَلْقَحَ To fecundate.

لَقْحٌ Fecundation.

لِقَاحٌ Pollen.

(تَلَقَّسَ) To delay, be late.

لَقَطَ يَلْقُطُ To pick up; glean.

تَلَقَّطَ وَٱلْتَقَطَ To glean. Catch.

لَاقِطٌ م لَاقِطَةٌ Freed slave.

لِقَاطٌ Picking up; gleaning.

لُقَاطَةٌ What is picked up.

لَقِيطٌ ج لُقَطَاءُ Foundling.

مِلْقَطٌ ج مَلَاقِطُ Pincers; tongs.

لَقِفَ وَٱلْتَقَفَ To snatch away.

لَقْلَقٌ وَلَقْلَاقٌ ج لَقَالِقُ Stork.

لَقِمَ يَلْقَمُ لَقْماً To swallow.

لَقَّمَ وأَلْقَمَ To feed.

تَلَقَّمَ وَٱلْتَقَمَ To swallow.

لُقْمَةٌ ج لُقَمٌ Morsel, mouthful.

لَقِنَ يَلْقَنُ To understand readily.

لَقَّنَ To instruct, teach.

تَلَقَّنَ To learn.

لَقِنٌ Of quick understanding.

لَقْوَةٌ Facial paralysis.

لَقِيَ يَلْقَى To meet; see, find.

لَاقَى لِقَاءً To go to meet, meet.

أَلْقَى بِ To throw away, fling.

أَلْقَى عَنْ To cast away from.

أَلْقَى على To propound, propose.

تَلَقَّى To receive. To encounter.

تَلَاقَى وَٱلْتَقَى To meet one another.

إِسْتَلْقَى عَلَى To lie on one's back.

تِلْقَاءَ Towards.

مِنْ تِلْقَاءِ نَفْسِهِ Spontaneously.

تَلَاقٍ Mutual encounter.

يوْمُ ٱلتَّلاقِي The day of resurrection.
ملْتقًى عَلَى Leaning or resting upon.
مُلْتقًى ومُلْتقًى Meeting-place.
ملاقاةٌ Meeting.
لَكٌّ Lac (resin); sealing wax.
لكٌّ ج ألْكاكٌ Ten millions. Lac.
لكز يلكُزُ لكزاً To push, thrust.
لكِعَ يلكَعُ لكَعاً ولكاعة To be vile.
لكَعٌ م لكاعِ Dirty, vile, abject.
لكمَ يلكُمُ لكْماً To strike with the fist.
مُلاكمةٌ Boxing, fighting.
لكِنْ ولكِنَّ But, yet, however.
(لَكنٌ ج ألْكانٌ) Large copper basin.
ألْكَنُ م لكناءُ ج لُكْنٌ Stammerer.
لكَيْ ولِكَيْما In order that.
لمْ Not, not yet.
لمْ يأْكل He has not eaten.
لِمْ Why? (*for* لِمَا)

ألَمْ وأَفَلَمْ وأَوَلَمْ Was it not?
لَمَّ يلُمُّ لمَّاً To gather, amass.
ألَمَّ ب To come upon, befall.
لمَّا When. Not yet.
لمَّا كانَ Inasmuch as...
لِمَاذَا (لِمَا ـ ذَا) Why?
لمَّةٌ Calamity; misfortune.
لِمَّةٌ ج لِمَمٌ ولِمَامٌ Lock of hair.
لَمَمٌ Slight madness.
إلْمَام Knowledge, experience.
مُلِمَّةٌ ج مُلِمَّاتٌ Calamity; chance.
ملْمُومٌ Collected. Slightly mad.
لُمْجَةٌ Light meal before lunch.
لمَحَ يلْمَحُ إلى To glance at.
لمح بالْبَصَر To direct the sight.
لَمَحَ يلْمَحُ To shine, gleam.
لَمَّحَ إلَى To hint at, suggest.
لَمْحَةٌ A glance resemblance.

لاَمِحٌ ولُمُوحٌ Gleaming, shining.

تَلْمِيحٌ Allusion, hint.

مَلاَمِحُ Points of resemblance.

لَمَسَ يَلْمِسُ لَمْساً ولاَمَسَ To touch.

تَلَمَّسَ To seek for repeatedly.

إِلْتَمَسَ مِنْ To entreat, ask for.

لَمْسٌ ومَلْمَسٌ Touch, feeling.

إِلْتِمَاسٌ Entreaty supplication.

مَلْمُوسٌ Touched.

لَمَعَ يَلْمَعُ وَالْتَمَعَ To shine, flash.

أَلْمَعَ بِ To beckon with.

لَمْعٌ ولَمَعَان Flash, brightness.

لَمْعَةٌ ج لُمَعٌ A small quantity.

لاَمِعٌ ج لُمَّعٌ That which shines.

أَلْمَعِيٌّ Having a sharp genius.

أَلْمَعِيَّةُ Genius, wit.

مُلَمَّعٌ Mottled, spotted.

لَمْلَمَ To gather, get together.

تَلَمْلَمَ To be gathered.

لَمْلَمٌ A numerous army.

لَنْ Not. By no means.

لَهِبَ يَلْهَبُ To flame, blaze(fire).

لَهَّبَ وأَلْهَبَ To make to blaze.

تَلَهَّبَ وَالْتَهَبَ To flame, blaze.

لَهَبٌ ولَهِيبٌ Flame.

إِلْتِهَابٌ ج إِلْتِهَابَاتٌ Inflammation.

أَللاَّهُوتُ The divine nature.

عِلْمُ اللاَّهُوت Theology.

لاَهُوتِيٌّ Theologian.

لَهَثَ يَلْهَثُ To pant. Thirst.

لَهْثَانُ Thirsty ; out of breath.

لَهِجَ يَلْهَجُ بِ To be addicted to.

أُلْهِجَ بِ To be taken up with.

لَهْجَةٌ Voice, tone.

لَهِفَ يَلْهَفُ وتَلَهَّفَ على To regret.

لَهْفٌ Regret, grief, sadness.

يا لَهفاهُ وَيالهفي على Oh ! Alas !

لَهفانُ م لهفى Grieved.

لهم يَلْهَمُ والْتَهم To swallow at one gulp.

الْهَمَ To inspire.

لَهِمٌ Greedy, voracious.

إِلْهامٌ ج إِلْهَاماتٌ Divine guidance.

لَها يَلْهُو لَهْواً To play.

لَهَا بِ To be infatuated with.

(لها عنْ) To forget ; neglect.

لَهَّى وأَلْهى (عنْ) To preoccupy.

تلاهَى وَالْتهَى To be diverted.

لَهْوٌ Amusement ; diversion.

لُهَاةٌ ج لَهَواتٌ Soft palate.

لَهَوِيٌّ Palatial.

لاَهٍ Diverted, thoughtless.

مَلْهًى ج مَلاهٍ Amusement.

لَوْ If. O that.

وَلَوْ Although, though.

لَوْ لَمْ Unless ; if not.

لَوْلاَ وَلَوْ ما Were it not for...

لاَبَ يَلُوبُ To thirst. Be restless.

لُوباءُ ولُوبِيَا Beans.

أَللوَاتي Pl. of. أَلَّتِي

لَوَّثَ To stain ; soil. Mix.

تَلَوَّثَ تَلَوُّثاً To be soiled.

لاَحَ يَلُوحُ To glimmer ; appear.

لَوْحٌ ج أَلْوَاحٌ Plate ; tablet. Shoulder-blade.

لاَئِحَةٌ ج لَوَائِح Schedule.

لَوائحُ Appearances.

لاَذَ يَلُوذُ (ب) To take refuge in

مَلاَذٌ Refuge ; fortress.

لَوْزٌ Almond (tree and fruit).

(أَللَّوزَتَان) The tonsils.

لاَسَ يَلُوسُ لَوْساً To taste.

لاَعَ يَلُوعُ To be impatient.

لَوَّعَ تَلْوِيعاً To torture.

لَوْعَةٌ — Pain ; anguish ; torture.

لُوفٌ — A plant, the Arum.

لَاكَ يَلُوكُ لَوْكًا — To masticate.

(لُوكَنْدَةٌ) — Hotel (*Ital*).

لَوْلَا — Were it not for....

لَوْلَبٌ ج لَوَالِبُ — Screw.

لَوْلَبِيٌّ — Spiral.

لَامَ يَلُومُ لَوْمًا — To blame censure.

تَلَاوَمَ — To blame ; one another.

لَوْمٌ — Blame ; censure.

لَائِمٌ — Blamer ; censurer.

مَلَامٌ وَمَلَامَةٌ — Blame ; censure.

مَلُومٌ — Blamable ; reprehensible.

أَلْعَظْمُ ٱللَّامِيُّ — Hyoid bone.

(لُومَانٌ) — State-prison.

لَوَّنَ تَلْوِينًا — To colour.

تَلَوَّنَ — To be coloured.

لَوْنٌ ج أَلْوَانٌ — Colour. Kind.

مُتَلَوِّنٌ — Changeful.

(لَوَنْدَا) — Lavander.

لَوَى يَلْوِي لَيًّا — To twist.

لَوَّى وَأَلْوَى — To bend.

إِلْتَوَى — To be bent, deflected.

لِوَاءٌ ج أَلْوِيَةٌ — Flag, standard. District.

أَمِيرُ ٱللِّوَاءِ — A general of the army.

إِلْتِوَاءٌ — Curvature.

لَيْتَ — O that ! Would that !

لَيْتَ زَيْدٌ ذَاهِبٌ — Would that Zeid were going !

لَيْتَنِي فَعَلْتُهُ — Would that I had done it !

لَيْثٌ ج لُيُوثٌ — Lion.

لَيْسَ — Not.

لَيْسَ ٱللّٰهُ بِظَالِمٍ — God is not unjust.

لِيفٌ — Fiber of palm, &c.

لَاقَ يَلِيقُ — To be fit, suitable.

لَائِقٌ — Suitable, proper.

لَيْلٌ ج لَيَالٍ . وَلَيْلَةٌ ج لَيْلَاتٌ — Night.

لِئَلَّا (From لِأَنْ لَا) Lest.

لِئَلَّا يَقُولَ Lest he should say.

لِيمُونٌ Lemon.

لَانَ يَلِينُ To be soft, tender.

لَيَّنَ تَلْيِيناً وأَلَانَ إِلَانَةً To soften.

لَايَنَ مُلَايَنَةً To conciliate.

تَلَيَّنَ To become soft, tender.

تَلَيَّنَ لَهُ To coax, conciliate.

لَيِّنٌ ج لَيِّنُونَ Tender, flexible.

لِينٌ Softness. Diarrhœa.

لُيُونَةٌ Softness, pliability.

مُلَيِّنٌ Laxative, aperient.

(لِيوَانٌ) إِيوَانٌ Portico.

م

م As a numeral sign=40.

مَا What?

مَا فَعَلَ What has he done?

مَا صَنَعَ What he has done.

أَمْرٌ مَا A certain affair.

مَا دُمْتُ حَيًّا As long as I live.

مَا أَجْمَلَهُ How beautiful!

مَا أَدْرِي I do not know.

مَاذَا What?

مَاذَا تَفْعَلُ What art thou doing?

لِمَاذَا جِئْتَ Why hast thou come?

مَاهِيَّةٌ Nature, essence.

Wages, pay. ماهِيَّة ج مَاهِيات

Water (*see* موه) مَاء ج مِياه

Inner angle of the eye. مُوق

To provide. مأن يَمأن مَأنًا

Provisions. مؤُونة ومؤُنة ج مُؤَن

One hundred. مِئَة ومائة ج مِئات

Centenary. مِئَويّ

Metre (measure). مِتر ج امتار

To grant. مَتَّع وأمتع ب

To enjoy. تمتّع بِ ومن

Enjoyment, privilege. متعة ج مُتَع

Furniture, effects. متاع ج امتِعَة

Enjoyment, privilege. تمتّع واستمتاع

To be firm. مَتن يمتُن مَتانة

Text of a book. مَتْن

Solidity, firmness. مَتانة

Strong, solid, robust. مَتين

When? When. مَتى

When, at the time when. مَتى مَا

To resemble. مثل يَمثُل وَمَاثَل

To compare to. مَثَّل وَمَاثَل بِ

To stand before someone. مَثُل يَمثُل بَيْن يديه

He imagined (a thing). تَمثَّل لَهُ

To imitate. تَمثَّل بِ

To resemble each other. تَماثَل

To be nearly convalescent. تَماثَل مِن علّته

To obey order. إمتَثَل الأمر

Similar, like. مِثْل ج أمثال

As well as. مِثلما

Proverb; a saying. مَثَل ج أمثال

To give an example. ضَرب مَثَلاً

Model. Example. مِثال ج امثِلة

Lesson. (مَثالة ج مثالات وَمثائل)

Resembling. مثيل ج مُثُل

The best. أمثل م مثلى ج اماثِل

Example. Lesson. أُمثُولَة

تِمْثَالٌ ج تَمَاثِيلُ	Image, figure.
تَمْثِيلُ	Assimilation. Analogy.
مَثَانَةٌ ج مَثَانَاتٌ	Bladder.
مَجَّ يَمُجُّ مَجًّا	To spit; reject.
مَجُدَ يَمْجُدُ	To be great, glorious.
مَجَّدَ	To glorify; exalt, honour.
تَمَجَّدَ	To be glorified, praised.
مَجْدٌ ج أَمْجَادٌ	Glory, praise.
تَمْجِيدٌ	Glorification, praising.
مَجِيدٌ وماجِدٌ	Noble, glorious.
أَلْمَجِيدُ	The Glorious (God).
أَمْجَدُ ج أَمَاجِدُ	More glorious.
مَجَرٌ	Hungarian.
بِلَادُ ٱلْمَجَرِ	Hungary.
مَجُوسٌ	Magians.
أَلْمَجُوسِيَّةُ	Creed of the Magians.
مَجَلَّةٌ	Code, book, (*see* جلل)
مَجَنَ يَمْجُنُ مُجُونًا	To jest.
مَجَّانٌ	Buffoon, jester.
مَجَّانًا	Gratuitously; freely.
مُحٌّ	Yolk of an egg.
مَحَّارَةٌ	Litter, panier.
مَحَصَ يَمْحَصُ مَحْصًا بِ	To purify.
مَحَّصَ	To purify. To try, prove.
مَحُضَ يَمْحُضُ مَحْضًا لَهُ	To be sincere.
مَحْضٌ	Pure, unmixed.
مَحَقَ يَمْحَقُ مَحْقًا	To blot out, efface.
إِمْتَحَقَ وٱمَّحَقَ	To be effaced.
مَحْقٌ	Perdition, annihilation.
مُحَاقٌ	Waning of the moon.
مَحَكَ يَمْحَكُ مَحْكًا	To brawl, dispute.
مَاحَكَهُ	To quarrel with one.
مُمَاحَكَةٌ	A quarrel, brawl.
مَحِكٌ ومَاحِكٌ	Quarrelsome.
مَحَلَ يَمْحَلُ وَأَمْحَلَ	To be sterile.
مَحْلٌ	Sterility, barrenness.

Cunning, deceitful.	مَحَّالٌ
Barren, unfruitful.	ماحِلٌ وَمُمْحِلٌ
To try, test.	مَحَنَ يَمْحَنُ محنًا
To try, examine.	إِمتَحن
Trial, affliction.	محنَةٌ ج مِحَنٌ
Experience; examination.	إِمتِحانٌ
To efface, blot out.	مَحا يَمْحُو مَحْوًا
To be blotted out.	امَّحى (إِنمحى)
Effected; blotted out.	ممحوٌّ
A wiper.	مِمحاةٌ
Marrow; brain.	مُخٌّ ج مِخاخٌ
To plough the water.	مَخَرَ يَمْخَرُ
A ship.	ماخِرةٌ ج مَواخِرُ
Wine shop. House of ill-fame.	ماخُورٌ
To churn.	مَخَضَ يَمخَضُ مَخْضًا
To suffer the pains of childbirth.	مَخَضَتْ تَمْخَضُ وَتَمخَّضتْ
To be churned.	تَمخَّضَ وَامتخض
Labour of childbirth.	مَخاضٌ
Butter-milk.	مخيضٌ
A churning-vessel.	مِمخضٌ
To blow the nose.	مَخَطَ يَمْخُطُ
Mucus.	مُخَاطٌ
Gossamar.	مُخاطُ الشَّيطانِ أَو الشَّمْسِ
Mucous.	مُخاطيٌّ
Lever.	مُخْلٌ ج أَمخالٌ ومُخُولٌ
To rinse the mouth.	(مَخمَضَ فاهُ وتَمَخمَضَ)
To spread, extend.	مدَّ يمدُّ مدًّا
To dip the pen in ink.	مدَّ القَلَمَ
To help, aid, assist.	مَدَّ وأَمَدَّ
To reach; extend to.	إِمتدَّ إِلى
To be extended, lie down.	تمدَّدَ
To seek help.	إِستمدَّ
Tide; flux.	مَدٌّ ج مُدُودٌ
The sign. (آ)	مَدٌّ ومدَّةٌ
A dry measure.	مُدٌّ ج أَمدادٌ
Period; while.	مدَّةٌ ج مُدَدٌ

Assistance.	مددٌ وَإمدادٌ
Ink. Oil (f a lamp).	مدادٌ
Matter.	مَادَّةٌ ج مَوادُّ
Material.	مادِّيٌّ
Long.	مديدٌ
Extensin ; dilatati n.	تمدُّدٌ
Prolonged ; extended.	مُمْتَدٌّ
A letter with. (ٓ) مَدة	ممدودٌ
To braise, extol.	مَدَحَ يمدحُ
To praise, Be extended.	إمتَدَحَ
Eulogy.	مَدحٌ .ومَديحٌ ج مَدَائحُ
Panegyrist.	مادِحٌ ومَدَّاحٌ
Village, town, city.	مدَرٌ
Inhabitants of towns.	أهلُ آلْمدَرِ
To build cities ; civilize.	مَدَّنَ
To become civilized.	تَمدَّنَ
Refinement, civilizatin.	تمدُّنٌ
City, town.	مَدِينَةٌ ج مُدنٌ ومَدائِنُ
Medina (in Arabia).	أَلْمدِينَةُ
Bagdad.	مَدينَةُ آلسَّلام
Citizen, townsman.	مَدَنِيٌّ
To grant one a delay.	مادَى
To take a long time.	تمادَى
Distance, extent ; end.	مدًى
Large knife.	مُدْيَةٌ ج مدًى
Since.	مُذْ
To become rotten.	مَذِرَ يمذَرُ
To disperse, scatter.	مَذَّرَ
Hither and thither.	شَذَرَ مَذَرَ
Spoilt, rotten (egg) ; foul.	مذِرٌ
Insincere, dissembler.	مُماذِق
To pass, pass by.	مَرَّ يمُرُّ
To embitter, make bitter.	مَرَّرَ
He caused him to pass.	أمرَّهُ
To continue ; last.	إستَمرَّ
Course, succession.	مَرٌّ ومُرُورٌ

Bitter. Myrrh (plant).	مُرٌّ
Once.	مَرَّةٌ ج مِرارٌ وَمرَّاتٌ
Several times, often.	مِرارًا
Gall ; bile.	امرّةٌ ج مررٌ
Aforesaid.	أَلْمارُّ ذِكْرُه
Bitterness. Gall-bladder.	مَرارةٌ
More bitter.	أمرُّ
Passage ; pathway.	مَمَرٌّ
Continued, continual.	مُستمِرٌّ
To be healthy (food).	مَرئَ يَمْرأ
Man.	مَرْءٌ وامْرُؤٌ
Woman.	مرْأةٌ وامْرأةٌ
Courage, bravery.	مروءةٌ ومُرُوَّةٌ
Gullet, œsophagus.	مَرِيٌّ
To moisten, soak.	مرث يمرُث
Meadow, pasture.	مَرْجٌ ج مُرُوجٌ
Confusion, disorder.	هرجٌ وَمرْجٌ
Coral.	مرْجانٌ
To be very gay.	مَرِحَ يَمْرَحُ
Very gay.	مرحٌ ج مرْحى وَمَرَاحى
(*See* رحب)	مَرْحَباً
To anoint.	مرخ يَمْرَخُ مَرْخًا
Liniment.	مَرُوخٌ
Mars (planet).	أَلْمِرِّيخُ
To rebel, revolt.	مرد يَمْرُدُ وَتَمرَّدَ
To be proud, insolent.	تمرَّدَ على
Rebellious.	مارِدٌ ج مَرَدَة
Beardless (youth).	أَمْرَدُ ج مُرْدٌ
Marjoram.	مرْدَقُوشٌ وَمَرْزَنْجُوشٌ
To steep, soak.	مَرَسَ يَمْرُسُ
To exercise, practice.	مارَسَ
Rope, cord.	مَرَسةٌ ج مَرَسٌ وأمْراس
Exercise, practice.	مُمارَسةٌ
Myrtle-tree.	مرْسِين
Hospital.	مارِسْتانٌ
To fall ill, be sick.	مَرِضَ يَمْرَضُ

مَرَّضَ To nurse the sick.

أَمْرَضَ To make ill, or sick.

تَمَارَضَ To feign illness.

مَرَضٌ ج امْرَاضٌ Disease, illness.

مَرِيضٌ ج مَرْضَى Sick, ill.

مَرَطَ يَمْرُطُ مَرْطًا To pull out (hair).

أَمْرَطُ م مَرْطَاء Scanty-haired.

مَرَغَ يَمْرَغُ مَرْغًا To graze (cattle).

مَرَّغَ To roll one in the dust.

تَمَرَّغَ To roll in the dust.

مَرَقَ يَمْرُقُ مِنْ To penetrate, pass.

مَرَقٌ وَمَرَقَةٌ Broth ; gravy, sauce.

مَارِقٌ A heretic.

مَرْمَرٌ Marble.

مَرُنَ يَمْرُنُ To become elastic.

مَرَنَ عَلَى To be accustomed to.

مَرَّنَ عَلَى To train, habituate.

تَمَرَّنَ عَلَى To be habituated to.

مَرِنٌ Elastic, flexible.

مُرُونَةٌ Elasticity, flexibility.

مَارُونِيٌّ ج مَوَارِنَةٌ Maronite.

تَمْرِينٌ وَتَمَرُّنٌ Practice; exercise.

مُمَرَّنٌ Trained ; inured.

مَرْهَمٌ ج مَرَاهِمُ Ointment.

مَارِ وَمَارِي Saint *(Syriac)*.

مِرْيَةٌ Dispute, quarrel.

مَزَّ يَمُزُّ مَزًّا To suck.

مُزٌّ وَمَزَّةٌ Sourish. Insipid.

مَزَجَ يَمْزُجُ مَزْجًا To mix.

مَازَجَ To associate with.

إِمْتَزَجَ ب To get mixed with...

إِمْتِزَاجٌ Mixture, amalgamation.

مَزِيجٌ Mixture, alloy.

مِزَاجٌ ج امْزِجَةٌ Temperament.

مَزَحَ يَمْزَحُ مَزْحًا To joke, jest.

تَمَازَحَ To jest together.

Jesting, bantering. مُزاحٌ

A kind of beer. مِزْرٌ

To tear to pieces. مَزَق يَمْزِق وَمَزَّق

To disperse (a crowd). مَزَّق

To be torn into pieces. تَمَزَّق

Merit; trait. مَزِيَّةٌ ج مزايا

To touch. مَسّ يَمَسّ مَسًّا

To touch one another. تَمَاسَّ

Touch; contact. Insanity. مَسٌّ

Urgent business. حاجةٌ مَاسةٌ

Tangent *(geom.)*. مُمَاسٌّ

Touched. Insane. مَمْسُوسٌ

A kind of shoe. مِسْتٌ ج مُسُوتٌ

To wipe; anoint. مَسح يَمْسَح مَسْحًا

To measure land. مَسح الارْض

Wiping. Anointing. مَسْحٌ

Sack-cloth. مِسْحٌ ج مُسُوحٌ

Land-survey. مِسَاحَةٌ

Mensuration. عِلْمُ ٱلْمِسَاحَةِ

Anointed. مسيحٌ ج مُسَحاء وَمَسْحَى

Christ, the Messiah. أَلْمسيحُ

Antichrist. أَلْمسيحُ ٱلدَّجَّالُ

Christian. مَسِيحِيٌّ ج مَسِيحِيُّون

Christianity. أَلْمَسِيحِيَّةُ

Land-surveyor. مسَّاحٌ ج مَسَّاحون

Flat barren land. مسحاء

Crocodile. تِمْساحٌ ج تماسيحُ

To change ; distort. مَسَخ يَمْسَخ مَسْخًا

Distorted, corrupted. مِسْخ

To plait or twist. مَسَد يَمْسُدُ

To rub with the hand. (مَسَّدَ)

Cord of fibres. مَسدٌ ج مِسَادٌ

Massage. (تَمْسِيدٌ)

To hold, seize. مَسَكَ يَمْسُكُ وَأَمْسَك

To retain, hold back. أَمْسَكَ

To refrain from. أَمْسَكَ عن

مِسْكٌ	Musk.
إِمْسَاكٌ	Avarice. Abstinence.
مُمَسَّكٌ	Scented with musk.
مَسَّى	To wish one good evening.
أَمْسَى	To enter into the evening.
مَسَاءٌ	Eve, evening.
مَسَاءَ ٱلْخَيْر	Good evening.
مَشَطَ يَمْشُطُ وَمَشَّطَ	To comb (the hair).
مِشْطٌ ج أَمْشَاطٌ	Comb; rake.
مُشْطُ ٱلرِّجْلِ	Instep of the foot.
مَاشِطٌ م مَاشِطَةٌ	Hair-dresser.
مَشْقٌ	Slenderness.
مُشَاقَةٌ	The refuse of silk.
مَمْشُوقٌ	Slim, Slender.
مِشْمِشٌ	Apricots.
مِشْمِشَةٌ	An apricot.
مَشَى يَمْشِي وَتَمَشَّى	To walk; go.
مَشَّى وَأَمْشَى	To cause to walk.
مَاشَى	To walk with one.
مَشْيٌ	Walking, marching.
مَاشٍ ج مُشَاةٌ	Walker on foot; foot-soldier.
مَاشِيَةٌ ج مَوَاشٍ	Flocks, cattle.
مَمْشًى ج مَمَاشٍ	Corridor.
مَصَّ يَمُصُّ وَٱمْتَصَّ	To suck; sip.
إِمْتَصَّ	To absorb.
مُصَّةٌ ومُصَاصٌ	What is sucked.
(قَصَبُ ٱلْمَصِّ)	Sugar-cane.
خَيْطٌ مَصِيصٌ	Twine, pack-thread.
مَمَصٌّ	Siphon; sucking tube.
إِمْتِصَاصٌ	Absorption.
مَصَّرَ	To build cities.
مِصْرُ	Egypt. Cairo.
مِصْرٌ ج أَمْصَارٌ	Great city. Limits.
مِصْرِيٌّ ج مِصْرِيُّونَ	Egyptian.
مُصْرَانٌ ج مَصَارِينُ	Intestines.
مُصْطَكَى	Mastic (kind of gum).

مَصَلَ يَمْصُلُ	To drop, trickle.
مَصْلٌ	Whey. Serum.
مَضَّ يَمُضُّ وَأَمَضَّ	To cause pain.
مُضٌّ وَمَضَّةٌ وَمَضَضٌ	Pain, grief.
مضغ يَمْضغ	To masticate, chew.
مضغٌ	Mastication, chewing.
مُضْغَةٌ ج مُضَغٌ	Morsel.
مَضْمَضَ	To rinse, wash.
مضى يَمْضِي	To pass; go, depart.
مضى على	To sign (a letter).
مضى بِ	To take, carry off.
أَمْضَى	To execute, accomplish.
تَمَضَّى	To pass off, carried out.
إِمْضَاء	Execution, Signature.
الْمَاضِي	The past; past tense.
مُمْضٍ	Signer; subscriber.
مطَّ يَمُطُّ	To draw; stretch.
مَطَر يَمْطُرُ وَامطر	To rain.
إِسْتَمْطَرَ	To pray for rain.
مَطَرٌ ج امْطَارٌ	Rain; heavy rain.
مَاطِرٌ وَمُمْطِرٌ	Rainy (weather).
مطرةٌ	A water-skin.
مُطْرَانٌ ج مطارِنَةٌ	Bishop.
مَطَلَ وَمَاطَلَ	To defer, put off.
مَطْلٌ وَمُمَاطَلَةٌ	Delay, putting off.
مُمَاطِلٌ	One who puts off.
مَمْطُولٌ	Deferred.
أَمْطَى وَامْتَطَى	To mount, ride.
مَطِيَّةٌ ج مَطَايَا	Beast of burden.
مع وَمَعَ	With, together with.
مع ذَلِك	Nevertheless, yet.
مع أَنْ	Although.
معاً	Together, simultaneously.
معيةٌ	Company, attendance.
معدةٌ ومِعدةٌ ج مِعدٌ	Stomach.
معزٌ ومعزى	Goats *(coll noun)*.

A goat.	ماعِزٌ ج مَواعِزُ
Goat-herd.	معّازٌ
To crush.	(مَعَسَ يَمْعَسُ مَعْساً)
To pull out (hair).	مَعَطَ يَمْعَطُ
Hairless.	أَمْعَطُ م معْطاءُ ج مُعْطٌ
To rub.	معَكَ يَمْعَكُ مَعْكاً
To delay paying.	ماعَك بدَيْنِهِ
Tumult of battle.	مَعْمَعَةٌ ج مَعامِعُ
To consider.	أَمْعَنَ ٱلنَّظَرَ. وَتَمَعَّنَ
Consideration.	إِمْعانٌ وَتَمَعُّنٌ
Utensil ; boat.	ماعُونٌ ج مَواعِينُ
Running water.	مَعِينٌ ج مُعُنٌ
Intestine.	معيٌ ومِعًى ج أَمْعاءٌ
Red earth for dyeing.	مَغْرَةٌ
To suffer from colic.	مُغِصَ
Colic gripes.	مَغْصٌ
To stretch.	مَغَطَ يَمْغَطُ. وَمَغَّطَ
To be stretched.	تَمَغَّطَ وَٱمْتَغَطَ
To draw (a sword).	إِمْتَغَطَ
To speak indistinctly.	مَغْمَغَ ٱلْكلام
To magnetize.	(مَغْطَسَ)
The magnet.	مَغْنَطِيسٌ
To hate, detest.	مَقَتَ يَمْقُتُ مَقْتاً
Hatred ; aversion.	مَقْتٌ
Hated, detested.	مقيتٌ وَمَمْقوتٌ
Sebesten (*Cordia myxa*).	مقْساسٌ
To look at.	مَقَلَ يَمْقُلُ مَقْلاً
The eye ; eye-ball.	مُقْلَةٌ ج مُقَلٌ
Mecca (city in Arabia).	مَكَّةُ
Meccan.	مكِّيٌّ وَمَكّاوِيٌّ
Weaving-shuttle.	مَكُّوكٌ
To abide,dwell.	مَكَثَ يَمْكُثُ
Sojourn, stay.	مَكْثٌ
To deceive.	مكَرَ يَمْكُرُ وَمَاكَرَ
Trick, deceit, fraud.	مكْرٌ
Cunning, deceitful.	ماكِرٌ ج مَكَرَةٌ

مكَّارٌ	Deceiver ; trickster.
مَكَسَ وَمَكَّسَ	To collect taxes.
مَكْسٌ ج مُكوسٌ	Custom duties.
ماكِسٌ وَمَكَّاسٌ	Tax-gatherer.
مَكُنَ يَمْكُنُ	To be strong.
مَكَّنَ	To strengthen.
مَكَّنَ وَأَمْكَنَ مِنْ	To enable.
أَمْكَنَهُ	To be possible for (him).
يُمْكِنُ أَنْ	It is possible that...
تَمَكَّنَ	To be stable, firm, solid.
تَمَكَّنَ مِنْ	To be able, overcome.
مَكِنَةٌ	Possibility. Power.
مَكانٌ ج أَماكِنُ	Place ; station.
مَكانَةٌ	Influence ; power.
إِمْكانٌ	Possibility ; power.
مُمْكِنٌ	Possible.
مُتَمَكِّنٌ	Declinable noun.
مَلَّ يَمُلُّ مَلًّا	To tack, baste.
مَلَّ يَمَلُّ مِنْ	To tire of.
أَمَلَّ	To cause weariness.
تَمَلَّلَ	To be restless, tired.
مِلَّةٌ ج مِلَلٌ	A religion, creed.
مَلَلٌ ومَلالٌ ومَلالَةٌ	Weariness.
مُلاَّ	Mollah, a Turkish judge.
مَلُّولٌ	Acorn-tree ; kind of oak.
مَلأَ يَمْلأُ مَلأً	To fill up.
مَلِئَ يَمْلأُ وَامْتَلأَ مِنْ	To be filled.
مَلَّأَ تَمْلِئَةً	To fill, fill up.
مِلْءٌ	Quantity which fills up.
مَلأٌ ج أَمْلاءٌ	An assembly.
مُلاءَةٌ ومُلايَةٌ	A kind of garment.
مَلآنٌ م مَلأَى وَمَلآنَةٌ	Full.
إِمْتِلاءٌ	Fullness Plethora.
مَمْلُوءٌ وَمَمْلُوٌّ وَمُمْتَلِئٌ	Full.
مَلَحَ يَمْلَحُ وَمَلَّحَ	To salt (food.)
مَلُحَ يَمْلُحُ مُلُوحَةً	To be salty. Be beautiful.

How handsome he is! ما أمْلحهُ

Salt. مِلْحٌ ج أمْلاحٌ

Pleasant anecdote. مُلْحةٌ ج مُلَحٌ

Beauty, goodliness. مَلاحةٌ

The art of navigation. مِلاحةٌ

Sailor. Salt merchant. مَلّاحٌ

Salt-works, salt mine. مَلّاحةٌ

Saltness. ملوحةٌ

Goodly, pretty. مَليحٌ ج مِلاحٌ

Salted. مُملَّحٌ

Salt-cellar. مملْحةٌ ج ممالحُ

Jew's mallow. ملوخيةٌ وملُوخيا

To be smooth. مَلُسَ يملُسُ

To make smooth. ملَّس

Twilight, dawn. مَلَسُ الظَّلام

Smoothness. مَلاسةٌ

Smooth. أمْلسُ م ملْساء ج ملْسُ

To escape. ملصَ وَتملَّصَ مِنْ

To plaster. مَلَطَ يملط وَملَّطَ

Plaster. مِلاطٌ

Malta (Island). مالِطةٌ

Maltese. مالطيٌّ

Scanty-haired. أمْلطُ م ملْطاء

To flatter. مَلِقَ يملَقُ . وَماالَقَ

To flatter, cajole. تَمَلَّقَ تملّقاً

Flattery. مَلَقٌ وَتَمليقٌ وَتملقٌ

Adulator, flatterer. مَلِقٌ وملّاقٌ

To possess. مَلَكَ يملِكُ وتملَّكَ

To reign or rule over. مَلَكَ على

To give in possession. ملَّك

To rule, possess. تملَّك

To abstain from. تمالَكَ عَنْ

Property; goods. مِلْكٌ ج امْلاكٌ

Power, authority, reign. مُلْكٌ

Angle. مَلَكٌ وَمَلاكٌ ج مَلائكةٌ

King. مَلِكٌ ج مُلُوكٌ

Queen. مَلَكَةٌ

Custom, habit. مَلَكَةٌ ج مَلَكات

Royalty. Kingdom. مَلَكُوتٌ

Royal, Kingly. مَلَكِيٌّ وَمُلُوكِيٌّ

Possessor, proprietor. مالِكٌ

Heron (bird). مالِكُ الْحَزين

Possessor. King. مَلِيكٌ ج مُلَكاء

Kingdom. مَمْلَكَةٌ ج مَمالِكُ

Mamluk. مَمْلُوكٌ ج مَمالِيكُ

To be restless. تَمَلْمَلَ

Melancholy; black bile. مَلَنْخوليا

To dictate a writing. أَمْلَى عَلَى

A long time. مَلِيًّا مِنَ الدهر

Dictation. إِمْلاءٌ ج أَمالٍ

Million. مِلْيُونٌ ج مَلايِين

For what? From what? مِمَّا (مِنْ ما)

Who? Whoever. مَنْ

From; of; for; than. مِنْ

Some *of* them say. مِنْهُمْ مَنْ يَقُولُ

He drew nigh *to* him. قَرُبَ مِنْهُ

Better *than*. أَفْضَلُ مِنْ

He came at once. جاءَ مِنْ ساعَتِهِ

To be gracious. مَنَّ يَمُنُّ وَامْتَنَّ

To reproach for benefits. مَنَّ وَمَنَّنَ

Gift, benefit. Manna. مَنٌّ

By the grace of God. بِمَنِّهِ تَعالى

Grace, bounty. مِنَّةٌ ج مِنَنٌ

Generous. مَنَّانٌ

God, the Giver of good. أَلْمَنَّانُ

Death. Ill-fortune. أَلْمَنُونُ

Reproach for benefit. إِمْتِنانٌ

Under obligation. (مَمْنُونٌ)

Obligation. (مَمْنُونِيَّةٌ)

Battering-ram. مَنْجَنِيقٌ وَمَنْجَلِيقٌ

To give, grant. مَنَحَ يَمْنَحُ مَنْحًا

Gift, favour. مِنْحَةٌ ج مِنَحٌ

مُنْذُ وَمُذْ — Since.

مَنَعَ يَمْنَعُ عَنْ وَمِنْ — To refuse; prohibit.

مَنُعَ يَمْنُعُ — To be inaccessible.

مانَعَ — To refuse; oppose.

تَمَنَّعَ عَنْ — To abstain from.

تَمَنَّعَ بِ — To intrench one's self.

إِمْتَنَعَ — To be impossible.

إِمْتَنَعَ وتَمَنَّعَ — To refrain from.

مَنْعٌ — Prevention.

مَنِيعٌ — Impregnable, inaccessible.

مانِعٌ — Something which prevents.

مُمْتَنِعٌ — Impossible.

مَمْنُوعٌ — Interdicted, prohibited.

مَنَّى تَمْنِيَة — To grant one's desire.

تَمَنَّى — To wish, desire.

مَنا ج أَمْناء — A measure.

مَنِيَّةٌ ج مَنايا — Death. Destiny.

مُنْيَة ج مُنًى — Wish, desire.

أُمْنِيَّةٌ ج أَمانِيّ — Wish, vain wish.

مُهْجَةٌ ج مُهَج — Soul, life.

مَهَدَ يَمْهَدُ ومَهَّد — To level; prepare.

تَمَهَّد — To be made easy.

مَهْدٌ ج مُهُودٌ — Bed; child's cradle.

مَهَرَ يَمْهَرُ — To be skilful.

تَمَهَّرَ — To become skilful.

مَهْرٌ ج مُهُورٌ — Dowry.

مُهْرٌ ج مِهارٌ — Foal. Signet.

مُهُرْدارٌ — Seal-bearer, secretary.

مُهْرَةٌ ج مُهُرات — Filly.

مَهارَةٌ — Skilfulness, dexterity.

ماهِرٌ ج مَهَرَة — Skilful.

مَهَلَ يَمْهَلُ . وتَمَهَّلَ — To act slowly.

مَهَّلَ وَأَمْهَلَ — To grant a delay.

إِسْتَمْهَلَ — To ask for a delay.

مَهْلٌ — Deliberate action.

مَهْلاً — Go slowly; softly!

إِمْهَالٌ	Concession of a delay.
تَمَهُّلٌ	Slowness, delay.
مَهْمَا	Whatever.
مَهَنَ يَمْهَنُ	To serve. Overwork.
إِمْتَهَنَ	To employ. Despise.
مِهْنَةٌ ج مِهَنٌ	Art, trade.
مَهَاةٌ ج مَهًا	Antelope.
مَاتَ يَمُوتُ مَوْتًا	To die, expire.
مَوَّتَ وَأَمَاتَ	To kill.
تَمَاوَتَ	To feign death.
اِسْتَمَاتَ	To act desperately.
مَوْتٌ وَمَوْتَة	Death, decease.
مَوْتَانٌ ومُوتَانٌ	Cattle-plague.
مَائِتٌ ج مَائِتُونَ	Dying.
مَيْتٌ وَمَيِّتٌ ج أَمْوَاتٌ	Dead.
مِيتَة	Kind of death.
مَمَاتٌ	Death, decease.
مُمِيتٌ	Deadly, mortal, fatal.
مُسْتَمِيتٌ	Bold, desperate.
مَاجَ يَمُوجُ وَتَمَوَّجَ	To be agitated.
مَوْجٌ ج أَمْوَاجٌ	Wave, billow.
تَمَوُّجٌ	Commotion ; fluctuation.
مَارِسْتَانٌ	A hospital; asylum.
مَوْزٌ	Banana (tree or fruit).
مَاسٌ	Diamond.
مُوسَى أَوْ مُوسًى و (مُوسٌ) ج مَوَاسٍ	A razor.
مُوسَى	Moses.
مُوسِيقَى	Music.
مُوسِيقِيّ	Musician. Musical.
مَاشٌ	Indian peas.
مُوقٌ	Inner angle of the eye.
مَالَ يَمُولُ	To be wealthy, rich.
تَمَوَّلَ	To become rich.
مَالٌ ج أَمْوَالٌ	Goods, riches.
بَيْتُ ٱلْمَالِ	Public Treasury.

Financial ; pecuniary.	ماليّ
Finance; ministry of...	ألْمالِيةُ
Minister of Finance.	وزيرُ ٱلْمالية
A wealthy man.	مُتموّلٌ
A kind of bitumen.	مومياً
Mummy.	مومْيةٌ ج مُوميات
To furnish.	مَان يمُونُ . ومَوّن
To lay in a store.	تموَّن
Provisions.	مُونةٌ (مؤُنةٌ)
Store-room.	بيْتُ ٱلْمُونةِ
To gild, or silver.	موّه
To falsify (news).	موَّه
Water.	ماء ج امْواهٌ ومياهٌ
Watery; fluid. Aquatic.	مائيّ
Nature, essence. Salary.	ماهيةٌ
Falsified (narrative).	مُموَّه
Equivocation.	تمْويهٌ
To give a gift.	مَاحَ يَميحُ
To seek a gift.	إستماح
A table.	مَائِدةٌ ج مَائدَاتٌ وموائدُ
Race-field; arena.	ميدانٌ ج مَيادِين
Taxes.	مِيريٌّ أوْ مِيرةٌ (أميريٌّ)
To detect, distinguish.	مَيَّز
To be distinguished.	تميّز وآمتاز
Separation ; distinction.	تَمييزٌ
The age of reason.	سِنُّ ٱلتَّمييز
Distinction; privilege ; preference.	إمْتيازٌ
Distinguishing.	مُتميّزٌ
Distinguished.	مُتميّزٌ ومُمْتازٌ
Hackberry tree.	مَيْسٌ
To flow (liquid).	ماعَ يميعُ
Incense, perfume. Balm.	مَيْعةٌ
Fluid, liquid.	مَائعٌ
To be inclined to.	مال يميلُ إلى
To deviate from.	مال عَنْ
To be adverse to...	مال على

مالَ يميلُ To decline, (sun).

تمايَلَ To reel in walking.

إستمالَ To conciliate.

ميَّلَ وأمالَ To incline, bend.

مَيْلٌ ج مُيُولٌ Inclination.

مِيلٌ ج أميالٌ A probe. A mile.

مائِلٌ Bent, inclined.

ميَّالٌ Very much inclined.

مانَ يمينُ To lie, tell a falsehood.

مَيْنٌ ج مُيُونٌ A lie, falsehood.

مينا A harbour, port. Enamel.

ن

ن As a numeral sign=50.

نارَجيلٌ ونارجيلٌ Cocoa-nut.

نأى ينأى عن To be far from.

انتأى عن To go far from.

ناءٍ One who is far away, remote.

أنبوبٌ ج أنابيب A tube, pipe.

نبا على To assault.

نبأ ب To lead to.

نبّأ وأنبأ To announce, inform.

تنبّأ To prophesy; foretell.

إستنبأ To seek information.

نبأ ج أنباء News; information.

نبوءة ونبوّة A prophecy.

نبويّ Prophetic.

A prophet.	نبيٌّ ج أَنْبياء وَنبيُّون
To sprout (plant).	نَبَتَ يَنْبتُ
To cause to sprout.	أَنْبَتَ
A plant; herb; sprout.	نَبْتٌ
Plant, vegetation.	نَباتٌ ج نباتات
Botany.	عِلْم النبات
The vegetable world.	عَالَم النّبات
Botanist. Vegetable.	نَباتيٌّ
Sprouting, germinating.	نابتٌ
A club.	نبُّوتٌ ج نَبابيتُ
Herbarium. Origin.	مَنْبَتٌ ج منابتُ
To bark (dog).	نَبَحَ يَنبحُ نَبحاً
Barking.	نُباحٌ
To throw; give up.	نبذَ يَنبذُ
The rabble, mob.	أَنباذُ النَّاس
Section, article.	نُبذةٌ ج نُبَذٌ
Wine.	نَبيذٌ ج أَنبذةٌ
To speak loud.	نَبرَ يَنبِرُ نَبْراً
A store; granary.	نِبْرٌ ج أَنابِر
Emphasis (in speaking).	نَبْرَةٌ
Stage, pulpit.	مِنبَرٌ ج مَنابِرُ
A lamp.	نِبْراسٌ ج نَبارِيس
To unearth, dig up.	نَبَشَ يَنْبُشُ
Earth or pit dug out.	نَبيشةٌ
A digger.	نَبَّاشٌ
To pulsate, throb.	نَبَضَ يَنبِضُ
Pulsation; pulse.	نَبْضٌ
A throb, pulsation.	نَبْضَةٌ
To invent (something).	إِسْتَنْبَطَ
The Nabathæns.	نَبَطٌ ج أَنْباطٌ
A vulgar word.	كَلِمَةٌ نَبَطيّةٌ
Discovery, invention.	إِسْتِنْباطٌ
To spring, gush (water).	نَبَعَ يَنبعُ
Spring of water.	نَبْعٌ
Source, origin.	مَنبَعٌ ج مَنابِعُ
A fountain.	يَنبُوعٌ ج يَنابيع

نَبَغَ يَنبُغُ To arise ; appear.

نَابِغَةٌ ج نَوَابِغُ Distinguished.

انْبِيقٌ ج أَنَابِيقُ Chemical retrot.

نَبَلَ يَنبُلُ نَبْلاً To shoot arrows.

نَبُلَ يَنبُلُ To have genius, skill.

تَنَبَّلَ To become skilful.

نَبْلٌ ج نِبَالٌ Arrows, darts.

نَبِيلٌ ج نِبَالٌ Highly intelligent.

نَبلةٌ An arrow, dart.

نَبَالَةٌ Ability; ; superiority.

نَبِهَ يَنبَهُ نَبْهًا لِ To perceive.

نَبِهَ نَبْهًا مِنَ ٱلنَّوْمِ To awake.

نَبَّهَهُ مِنَ النَّوْمِ To wake ; one up.

نَبَّهَ عَلَى أَوْ إِلَى To warn inform.

تَنَبَّهَ وَٱنْتَبَهَ To awake.

تَنَبَّهَ لِ To be awake to.

إِنْتَبَهَ لِ To perceive.

نَبَاهَةٌ Celebrity. Intelligence.

إِنْتِبَاهٌ Attention; wakefulness.

تَنبِيهٌ Warning. Notice.

مُتَنَبِّهٌ وَمُنْتَبِهٌ Awake, Attentive.

نَتَأَ يَنْتَأُ نُتُوءًا To project.

نَاتِىءٌ Projecting; jutting out.

نَتَجَ يَنْتِجُ To bring forth.

نَتَجَ عَنْ To arise, result from...

إِسْتَنْتَجَ To deduce, infer.

نَتِيجَةٌ ج نَتَائِجُ Conclusion. Result; consequence.

نَتَرَ يَنتُرُ To pull, snatch.

نَتَشَ يَنْتِشُ نَتْشًا To snatch, pluck.

نَتَفَ يَنْتِفُ To pluck, pull out.

تَنَتَّفَ To be plucked off.

نُتْفَةٌ ج نُتَفٌ A small quantity.

نَتُنَ يَنْتُنُ نَتْنًا وَأَنْتَنَ To stink.

نَتْنٌ وَنَتَانَةٌ Stench.

نَتِنٌ وَمُنْتِنٌ Stinking, putrid.

نتوءٌ ج نتوّاتٌ Tuberosity.

ناتِ	Swollen. Projecting.
نَثَرَ يَنْثُرُ	To disperse, scatter.
تَنَاثَرَ وَانْتَثَرَ	To be scattered.
نَثْرٌ . (نَظْم	Prose, (*opp. to* نَظْم).
مَنْثُورٌ	Gilly-flower.
نَجُبَ يَنْجُبُ	To be noble.
إِنْتَجَبَ	To choose, select.
نَجَابَة	Nobility.
نَجِيبٌ ج نُجَبَاء	Noble.
نَجَائِب	The choicest parts.
نَجَحَ يَنْجَحُ	To succeed, prosper.
نَجَّحَ وَأَنْجَحَ	To give success.
نُجْحٌ وَنَجَاحٌ	Success, prosperity.
نَاجِحٌ	Succĕssful, thriving.
نَجَدَ يَنْجُدُ . وَأَنْجَدَ	To help, aid.
نَجَّدَ	To upholster.
نَاجَدَ مُنَاجَدَةً	To bring help to.
إِسْتَنْجَدَ	To invoke assistance.
نَجْدٌ ج أَنْجُدٌ	High land.
نَجْدَةٌ ج نَجَدَاتٌ	Help, succour.
نَجَّادٌ وَمُنَجِّدٌ	An upholsterer.
نَجَرَ يَنْجُرُ	To plane (wood).
نِجَارَةٌ	Carpentry.
نُجَارَة	Shavings chips of wood.
نَجَّارٌ ج نَجَّارُونَ	Carpenter.
نَجَزَ يَنْجُزُ وَنَجَّزَ	To finish a thing.
نَجِزَ يَنْجَزُ	To come to an end.
أَنْجَزَ	To achieve; accomplish.
نَجْز وَنَجَاز	Achievement.
نَاجِزٌ وَنَجِيزٌ	Ready, present.
نَجِسَ يَنْجَسُ نَجْساً	To be impure.
نَجَّسَ وَأَنْجَسَ	To defile, pollute.
تَنَجَّسَ	To become polluted.
نَجَاسَةٌ	Filth. Legal impurity.
نَجْسٌ ج أَنْجَاسٌ	Impure, filthy.
النَّجَاشِيُّ	Title of the Abyssinian kings.

To benefit, profit. نَجَعَ يَنْجَعُ

Profitable, useful. Dark red blood. نَجِيعٌ

Child, son. نَجْلٌ ج أَنْجَالٌ

Gospel. إِنْجِيلٌ ج أَنَاجِيلُ

Evangelical ; evangelist. إِنْجِيلِيٌّ

A sickle. مِنْجَلٌ ج مَنَاجِلُ

To appear. نَجَمَ يَنْجُمُ وَأَنْجَمَ

To arise, or result from. نَجَمَ عَنْ

A star. Shrub. نَجْمٌ ج أَنْجُمٌ وَنُجُومٌ

Astronomy. عِلْمُ ٱلنُّجُومِ

Astrology. عِلْمُ ٱلتَّنْجِيمِ

Astronomer. Astrologer. مُنَجِّمٌ

Mine. Source. مَنْجَمٌ ج مَنَاجِمُ

To escape. نَجَا يَنْجُو نَجَاةً

To confide a secret to. نَاجَى

To save deliver. نَجَّى وَأَنْجَى مِنْ

To commune secretly. تَنَاجَى

Deliverance. نَجَاةٌ وَنَجَاءٌ

An asylum. مَنْجًى ج مَنَاجٍ

Secret communication. مُنَاجَاةٌ

To weep, cry, wail. نَحَبَ يَنْحَبُ

Bitter weeping. Death. نَحْبٌ

To die. قَضَى نَحْبَهُ

Wailing. Lamenation. نَحِيبٌ

To cut, hew, carve. نَحَتَ يَنْحُتُ

Fragments, chips. نُحَاتَةٌ

Stone-cutter. Sculptor. نَحَّاتٌ

Cut, hewed. نَحِيتٌ وَمَنْحُوتٌ

Sculptor's chisel. مِنْحَتٌ ج مَنَاحِتُ

To kill (an animal). نَحَرَ يَنْحَرُ

To contend together. تَنَاحَرَ

To commit suicide. إِنْتَحَرَ

Skilled. نِحْرِيرٌ ج نَحَارِيرُ

Lower part of neck. نَحْرٌ ج نُحُورٌ

Throat. مَنْحَرٌ

To cover with copper. نَحَّسَ

نحس ج نحوس Ill-luck.

نحس ومنحوس Unlucky.

نحاس Brass.

نحاس أحمر Copper.

نحاسة A piece of copper.

نحّاس A copper merchant.

نحف ينحف نحافة To be slim.

أنحف To make thin.

نحافة Leanness ; slenderness.

نحيف ج نحاف Thin, meagre.

نحل ينحل To become thin.

أنحل To make thin.

تنحل وانتحل To plagiarize.

انتحل To embrace a religion.

نحل Bees.

نحلة A bee.

نحلة ج نحل A religious sect.

نحول Thinness, leanness.

نحيل Thin, emaciated.

نحن We.

نحا ينحو To move towards.

نحى عن To send away.

تنحى عن To go aside.

نحو Towards. Nearly, about. For example.

نحو ج أنحاء Region. Method.

علم النّحو Grammar, *sp.* syntax.

ناحٍ ج نحاة Grammarian.

نحويّ Grammatical.

ناحية ج نواحٍ Side, direction.

نخب ينخب وانتخب To select.

نخب وانتخاب Choice, election.

نخبة ج نخب Chosen. Choice.

منتخِب Elector.

منتخَب Chosen ; elected.

نخر ينخر To snore ; snort.

نخر ينخر نخرا To be rotten.

نَخِرٌ وَنَاخِرٌ Rotten, decayed.

مِنْخَرٌ ج مَنَاخِيرُ Nostril ; nose.

نَخَرَ يَنْخُرُ بِ To prick with.

نَخَسَ يَنْخَسُ نَخْساً To prick.

نِخَاسَةٌ Cattle-trade ; slave-trade.

نَخَّاسٌ Cattle, or slave trader.

مَنْخَسٌ ج مَنَاخِسُ A goad, spur.

تَنَخَّعَ To hawk, clear the throat.

نُخَاعٌ ج نُخُعٌ Marrow. Brain.

نُخَاعَةٌ Phlegm, mucus.

نَخَلَ يَنْخُلُ To sift, bolt flour.

نَخْلٌ وَنَخِيلٌ The palm-tree.

نَخْلَةٌ A palm-tree.

نُخَالَةٌ Bran.

مُنْخُلٌ ج مَنَاخِلُ A sieve.

تَنَخَّمَ To blow the nose.

نُخَامَةٌ Mucus ; phlegm.

نخى وأنخى To incite, instigate.

نَخْوَةٌ Pride. Sense of honour.

نَدَّدَ بِ To expose one's faults.

نَدٌّ A kind of perfume.

نِدٌّ ج أَندادٌ Similar to, an equal.

نَدَبَ يَنْدُبُ To weep, lament.

نَدَبَ وَٱنْتَدَبَ To call, appoint.

نَدِبَ يَنْدَبُ To be cicatrized.

إِنْتَدَبَ لِ To respond to a call.

نَدْبَةٌ ج نُدُوبٌ وَأَنْدَابٌ Scar.

نَدَبَةٌ An elegy, a lamentation.

نَادِبٌ A weeper, lamenter.

مَنْدُوبٌ Mourned. Commissioner.

مَنْدُوحَةٌ Liberty of action.

نَدَرَ يَنْدُرُ To be rare.

نَدْرَةٌ Rarity ; infrequency.

نَادِرٌ ج نَوَادِرُ A rare thing.

نَادِراً ؛ وَفِي ٱلنَّادِرِ Rarely, seldom.

نَدَفَ يَنْدِفُ To card (cotton).

نِداَفةٌ	Trade of carding.
نَدَّافٌ	Wool or cotton carder.
مَندوفٌ	Carded.
مَنديلٌ ج مَناديلُ	A towel. Veil.
ألأندلُسُ	Andalusia. Spain.
اندلُسِيٌّ	Andalusian.
نَدِمَ يندَمُ . وتَنَدَّمَ على	To regret.
نادَمَ مُنادَمَة	To associate with.
نَدَمٌ ونَداَمةٌ	Regret, repentance.
نَادِمٌ	Repentant contrite.
نَديمٌ ج نُدَماء	Associate, friend.
نَدِيَ يندَى	To be wet.
ندَّى تندِيَةً	To dampen, wet.
نادَى مُناداَةً ونداءً	To call.
نادَى ب	To proclaim ; publish.
أندَى إِنداءً	To be liberal.
تَندَّى	Ta become wet.
انتَدَى	To assemble *v.i*
نَدىً ج أنداء	Moisture. Dew.
نداء	Call. Proclamation.
حرفُ النِّداء	Vocative particle.
نَدوَةٌ	An assembly, a meeting.
نَادٍ ج أندِيَةٌ	Place of assembly.
مُنادٍ	A public crier.
منتدًى	Assembly-hall.
نَذَرَ ـُ	To make a vow; dedicate
أنذرَ إِنذاراً ب	To warn.
نَذْرٌ ج نُذورٌ	A vow.
إِنذارُ	A warning. Prognosis.
نَذيرٌ ج نُذُرٌ	Vowed. Preacher.
مَنذُورُ	Vowed, consecrated.
نَذُلَ يَنذُلُ نَذالَةً	To be abject.
نذْلٌ ج أنذالٌ	Vile, mean.
نرْجِسٌ	Narcissus (plant).
نارِجيلٌ وَنارَجيلٌ	Cocoa-nut.
نارَجيلةُ	Nargileh.

Backgammon.	نَرْدٌ
Spikenard.	نَارَدِينٌ وَنَرْدِينٌ
Orange.	نَارَنْجٌ
Thrashing-harrow.	نَوْرَجٌ
To exude.	نَزَّ يَنِزُّ نَزًّا
Leakage.	نَزٌّ ج نُزُوزٌ
To exhaust a well.	نَزَحَ يَنْزَحُ
To emigrate.	نَزِحَ بِهِ وَانْتَزَحَ
Distant, Emigrant.	نَازِحٌ وَنَزِيحٌ
Little ; mean.	نَزْرٌ
To remove.	نَزَعَ يَنْزَعُ وَٱنْتَزَعَ
To fight, dispute with.	نَازَعَ
To contend among themselves.	تَنَازَعَ
To be taken away.	إِنْتَزَعَ
Agony of death.	نَزْعٌ وَنِزَاعٌ
Contention.	نِزَاعٌ وَمُنَازَعَةٌ
Taken away, removed.	مَنْزُوعٌ
To be exhausted (well).	نُزِفَ
To have a flow of blood.	نَزَفَ
Hemorrhage	نَزْفُ ٱلدَّمِ
Quick, hot-tempered.	نَزِقٌ
A falling star.	نَيْزَكٌ ج نَيَازِكُ
To descend.	نَزَلَ يَنْزِلُ نُزُولاً
To stop at a place.	نَزَلَ فِي وَعَلَى
To bring down.	نَزَّلَ وَأَنْزَلَ
To reveal.	نَزَّلَ وَأَنْزَلَ عَلَى
To fight with.	نَازَلَ
To renounce.	تَنَزَّلَ عَنْ
To condescend.	تَنَازَلَ
To seek or offer hospitaliy.	اِسْتَنْزَلَ
Place where men gather.	نَزْلٌ
Guests.	نُزُولٌ ج أَنْزَالٌ
A cold in the head.	نَزْلَةٌ
Calamity.	نَازِلَةٌ ج نَوَازِلُ
A guest.	نَزِيلٌ ج نُزَلَاءُ
A revelation.	إِنْزَالٌ وَتَنْزِيلٌ

Condescension, affability. تَنَازُلٌ

Hostlery ; house. مَنْزِلٌ ج مَنَازِلُ

Domestic economy. تَدْبِيرُ ٱلْمَنْزِلِ

Degree, rank. مَنْزِلَةٌ

To abstain from evil. نَزِهَ يَنْزَهُ

To walk, divert one's self. تَنَزَّهَ

To be free from. تَنَزَّهَ عَنْ

Purity of the soul. نُزْهٌ وَنَزَاهَةٌ

Pure, upright. نَزِيهٌ ج نُزَهَاءُ

Amusement. نُزْهَةٌ ج نُزَهٌ

Place of recreation. مُنْتَزَهٌ

To attribute, ascribe. نَسَبَ إِلَى

To resemble. Be suitable. نَاسَبَ

To correspond with. تَنَاسَبَ

To trace one's genealogy. إِنْتَسَبَ

To approve. إِسْتَنْسَبَ

Lineage. نَسَبٌ ج أَنْسَابٌ

Arithmetical proportion. نِسْبَةٌ

Relation, affinity. نِسْبَةٌ ج نِسَبٌ

Kinsman. نَسِيبٌ ج أَنْسِبَاءُ

Proportion. مُنَاسَبَةٌ وَتَنَاسُبٌ

Suited to, convenient. مُنَاسِبٌ

Proportioned. مُتَنَاسِبٌ

Ascribed, imputed. مَنْسُوبٌ إِلَى

Human nature. نَاسُوتٌ

To weave. نَسَجَ يَنْسُجُ نَسْجاً

To be woven. إِنْتَسَجَ

The art of weaving. نِسَاجَةٌ

Weaver. نَسَّاجٌ

Woven tissue. نَسِيجٌ ج نُسُجٌ

Loom. مِنْسَجٌ

Woven ; tissue. مَنْسُوجٌ

To abrogate. نَسَخَ يَنْسَخُ نَسْخاً

abolish To copy, transcribe.

To follow successively. تَنَاسَخَ

To copy a (book). إِنْتَسَخَ وَٱسْتَنْسَخَ

To annul, abrogate. إِنْتَسَخَ

نَسْخٌ Abrogation. Transcribing.

نُسْخَةٌ ج نُسَخٌ Copy ; manuscript.

تَناسُخٌ Transmigration of souls.

مَنْسُوخٌ Abolished. Copied.

نَسْرٌ ج نُسُورٌ An eagle ; vulture.

نَاسُورٌ ج نَوَاسِيرُ A fistula, sinus.

مِنْسَرٌ ج مَنَاسِيرُ Beak of a bird.

نِسْرِينٌ A scented white rose.

نُسْطُورِيٌّ ج نَسَاطِرَةٌ Nestorian.

نَسَفَ يَنْسِفُ To demolish winnow.

نُسَافَةٌ Chaff. Froth.

مِنْسَفٌ ج مَنَاسِفُ Winnowing-fan.

مِنْسَفَةٌ A razing machine.

نَسَقَ يَنْسُقُ نَسْقًا To compose.

نَسَّقَ To place in order; arrange.

تَنَسَّقَ وتَنَاسَقَ To be arranged.

نَسَقٌ Order ; system, method.

نَسَكَ وتَنَسَّكَ To lead an ascetic's life.

نَسْكٌ وَنُسُكٌ A hermit's life.

نَاسِكٌ ج نُسَّاكٌ A hermit.

نَسَلَ يَنْسُلُ نَسْلًا To beget.

تَنَاسَلَ To multiply (men).

نَسْلٌ Posterity, progeny.

تَنَاسُلٌ Descent by generation.

نَسَمَ يَنْسِمُ To blow gently.

تَنَسَّمَ To breathe.

نَسَمَةٌ ج نَسَمَاتٌ Breath of life. Man.

نَسِيمٌ A soft breeze.

نِسْنَاسٌ An ape.

نُسْوَةٌ وَنِسَاءٌ وَنِسْوَانٌ Women.

عِرْقُ ٱلنَّسَا Sciatica.

نَسِيَ يَنْسَى نَسْيًا وَنِسْيَانًا To forget.

نَسَّى وَأَنْسَى To cause to forget.

تَنَاسَى To feign forgetfulness.

نَسْوَةٌ وَنِسْيَانٌ Forgetfulness.

مَنْسِيٌّ Forgotten.

نَشَّ يَنِشُّ	To dry up ; ooze.
وَرَقٌ نَشَّاشٌ	Blotting-paper.
نَشَأَ يَنْشَأُ وَنَشُوَ يَنْشُو	To grow up (child). To live, orginate. Rise.
نَشَأَ مِن	To follow, proceed from.
أَنْشَأَ	To create ; originate. Train up.
أَنْشَأَ يَقُولُ	He began to say.
نُشُوءٌ	Growing, developing.
نَاشِئٌ	Growing. Resulting.
إِنْشَاءٌ	Composition ; style. Origination.
مَنْشَأٌ	Native country. Source.
مُنْشِئٌ	A creator. Author.
نَشِبَ ـ بَيْنَ	To break out (war).
نُشَّابٌ	An arrow (of wood).
نَشَّابٌ	An archer.
نَشَدَ يَنْشُدُ	To seek a lost object.
نَشَدَهُ اللهَ	To abjure by God.
نَاشَدَ	To cause to swear.
أَنْشَدَ	To recite (verses).
نَشِيدٌ	Chanting. Song.
نَشِيدُ آلأَنْشَادِ	The Song of Songs.
نَشِيدَةٌ ج نَشَائِدُ	A poem. Song.
نِشَادِرٌ وَنُوشَادِرٌ	Ammonia.
نَشَرَ يَنْشُرُ	To spread out. To saw.
نَشَرَ يَنْشُرُ	To publish.
نَشَرَ يَنْشَرُ	To resuscitate, raise to life.
تَنَشَّرَ وَآنْتَشَرَ	To be extended.
إِنْتَشَرَ	To be published.
نَشْرٌ	Resurrection. Publication.
يَوْمُ آلنُّشُورِ	Day of Resurrection.
نَشْرَةٌ	A written open paper.
نُشَارَةٌ	Shavings, saw-dust.
نِشَارَةٌ	Art of sawing.
إِنْتِشَارٌ	Dissemination.
مَنْشُورٌ وَمُنْتَشِرٌ	Dispersed.
مِنْشَارٌ ج مَنَاشِيرُ	A saw.
مَنْشُورٌ	Prism. Circular.

مَنْشُورِيٌّ Prismatic form.

نَشِطَ يَنْشَطُ. وَتَنشط To be active.

نشطَ يَنشطُ To knot (a cord).

نَشَّطَ إِلَى وَفِي To encourage in.

نَشَاطٌ Ardour, energy.

نَشِيطٌ ج نشاط Active, energetic.

أُنشُوطَةٌ ج أَنَاشِيط A knot, noose.

نَشَفَ يَنشف To become dry.

تَنَشَّفَ To dry, wipe (the body).

نَاشِفٌ Dry.

تَنْشِيفٌ Wiping, drying up.

مِنشَفَةٌ ج مَنَاشِفُ A towel.

نَشِقَ يَنشَقُ. وَٱستَنشق To inhale.

أَنشَقَ To cause one to inhale.

نَشُوقٌ Snuff.

نَشَلَ يَنشلُ وَٱنتَشَلَ To snatch ; steal.

نَشَّالٌ A pickpocket.

مِنْشَلٌ وَمِنْشَالٌ ج مَنَاشِلُ A ladle.

نَشِيَ ـ نَشْوًا وَنَشْوَةً To be drunk.

نَشِيَ وَاسْتَنْشَى To smell. Be drunk.

نَشَّى To starch (linen).

نَشًا وَنَشَاءٌ Starch.

نَشْوَةٌ Odour. Exhiliration of wine..

نَشْوَانُ م نَشْوَى ج نَشَاوَى Drunk.

نَصَّ ـُ ل To dictate a writing.

نَصٌّ ج نُصُوصٌ Text (of a book).

مَنْصُوصٌ عَلَيْهِ Clearly stated.

نَصَبَ يَنْصُبُ To fix, plant ; raise.

نَصِبَ ـَ نَصَبًا To strive, toil.

نَصَّبَ To appoint to an office.

نَاصَبَ To resist, oppose.

إِنْصَبَ To rise ; stand erect.

نُصْبٌ ج أَنْصَابٌ Idol, statue.

نُصْبَ عَيْنِي Before my eye.

نِصَابٌ ج نُصُبٌ Origin Handle.

نَصَّابٌ Swindler.

Portion ; lot. نَصِيبٌ ج أَنْصِبَةٌ

Fatiguing, toilsome. نَاصِبٌ

Rank ; place. مَنْصَبٌ ج مَنَاصِبُ

Elevated, erected. مَنْصُوبٌ

To listen to نَصَتَ يَنْصِتُ وَأَنْصَتَ ل

To silence. أَنْصَتَ

To listen. تَنَصَّتَ

To advise, counsel. نَصَحَ يَنْصَحُ

To act sincerely. نَصَحَ نَصْحاً

To receive advice. إِنْتَصَحَ

A sincere adviser. نَاصِحٌ

Sincere. نَصُوحٌ وَنَصِيحٌ

Advice, counsel. نَصِيحَةٌ ج نَصَائِحُ

To assist aid. نَصَرَ يَنْصُرُ

To become a Christian. تَنَصَّرَ

To strive to assist. تَنَصَّرَ ل

To help one another. تَنَاصَرَ

To conquer, vanquish. اِنْتَصَرَ عَلَى

To seek aid from. إِسْتَنْصَرَ ب

Help. Victory. نَصْرٌ وَنُصْرَةٌ

A Christian. نَصْرَانِيٌّ ج نَصَارَى

Christianity. أَلنَّصْرَانِيَّةُ

Victory, triumph. إِنْتِصَارٌ

Helper. نَاصِرٌ ج نُصَّارٌ وَأَنْصَارٌ

Helper. نَصِيرٌ ج نُصَرَاءُ

Victorious, conquering. مُنْتَصِرٌ

Aided Conqueror. مَنْصُورٌ

To be pure, unmixed. نَصَعَ يَنْصَعُ

Pure, unmixed (color) نَاصِعٌ

To divide into two halves. نَصَّفَ

To be just, equitable. أَنْصَفَ

To get one's due. إِنْتَصَفَ

To be mid-day. إِنْتَصَفَ ٱلنَّهَارُ

Half. Middle. نِصْفٌ ج أَنْصَافٌ

Justice, equity. إِنْصَافٌ

Middle (of anything). مُنْتَصَفٌ

To come out. (نَصَلَ يَنْصُلُ نَصْلاً)
Blade ; arrow-head. نَصْلٌ ج نِصَالٌ
Forelock. نَاصِيَةٌ ج نَوَاصٍ
To ooze, flow out. نَضَّ يَنِضُّ نَضًّا
Remainder, rest. نُضَاضَةٌ
To be well cooked ; ripe. نَضِجَ يَنْضَجُ
Cooked well, ripe. نَاضِجٌ
Of mature judgment. نَضِيجُ الرَّأْيِ
To ooze ; exude. نَضَحَ يَنْضَحُ نَضْحًا
To sprinkle with. نَضَحَ بِ
To pile up. نَضَدَ يَنْضُدُ . وَنَضَّدَ
Laid in layers. نَضِيدٌ وَمَنْضُودٌ
To be soft. Blooming. نَضَرَ يَنْضُرُ
Bloom, freshness. نَضْرَةٌ وَنَضَارَةٌ
Blooming, verdant. نَضِرٌ وَنَضِيرٌ
To defend. نَاضَلَ عَنْ
Combat. نِضَالٌ وَمُنَاضَلَةٌ
A horse-shoe. نَضْرَةٌ

To jump, skip. (نَطَّ يَنِطُّ نَطًّا)
To butt. نَطَحَ يَنْطَحُ نَطْحًا
To butt one another. تَنَاطَحَ
Butted ; gored. نَطِيحٌ وَمَنْطُوحٌ
To guard. To wait. نَطَرَ يَنْطُرُ
Keeper (of gardens). نَاطُورٌ ج نَوَاطِيرُ
A watch-tower. مَنْطَرَةٌ ج مَنَاطِرُ
Very learned. نَطِسٌ وَنِطَاسِيٌّ
To speak utter. نَطَقَ يَنْطِقُ
To gird. نَطَّقَ
To gird one's self. تَنَطَّقَ وَانْتَطَقَ
To question, examine. إِسْتَنْطَقَ
Speech ; articulation. نُطْقٌ
Belt, girdle. نِطَاقٌ ج نُطُقٌ
Endowed with speech. نَاطِقٌ
The human soul. أَلنَّفْسُ النَّاطِقَةُ
Speech, language. Logic. مَنْطِقٌ
Logical. Logician. مَنْطِقِيٌّ

مِنْطَقَةٌ ج مَنَاطِقُ	A girdle, belt.
مِنْطَقَةُ ٱلْبُرُوجِ	The Zodiac.
مَنْطُوقٌ	Proper signification.
مُسْتَنْطِقٌ	Examiner *(law)*.
نَطَلَ يَنْطُلُ . وَنَطَّلَ	To foment.
نَطُولٌ ج نُطُولَاتٌ	A fomentation.
نَظَرَ يَنْظُرُ وَإِلَى	To see, look at.
نَظَرَ يَنْظُرُ فِي	To consider.
نَاظَرَ	To resemble ; rival. Debate. Superintend, inspect.
تَنَاظَرَ	To debate with one another.
إِنْتَظَرَ وَٱسْتَنْظَرَ	To expect.
نَظَرٌ ج أَنْظَارٌ	Vision. Favour.
نَظَرًا وَبِالنَّظَرِ إِلَى	As regards.
نَظْرَةٌ	A look, a glance.
نَظَرِيٌّ	Theoretical. Subjective.
نَظَرِيَّةٌ ج نَظَرِيَّاتٌ	A problem.
نَاظِرٌ ج نُظَّارٌ	Inspector. Director.
نَاظِرُ ٱلنُّظَّارِ	Prime Minister.
نَاظِرُ الأَشْغَالِ	Minister of Works.
نَاظِرُ ٱلْمَعَارِفِ العُمُومِيَّةِ	Minister of Public Instruction.
نَاظِرُ ٱلمَالِيَّةِ	Minister of Finance.
نَاظِرُ ٱلخَارِجِيَّةِ	Minister of Foreign Affairs.
نَاظِرُ الدَّاخِلِيَّةِ	Minister of the Interior.
نَاظِرُ ٱلحَرْبِيَّةِ	Minister of War.
نَاظِرُ ٱلحَقَّانِيَّةِ	Minister of Justice.
نِظَارَةٌ	Administration. Ministry.
نَظَّارَةٌ وَنَاظُورٌ	A telescope.
نَظَّارَاتٌ	Spectacles.
نَظِيرٌ ج نُظَرَاءُ	Similar, equal to.
إِنْتِظَارٌ وَٱسْتِنْظَارٌ	Expectation.
مَنْظَرٌ ج مَنَاظِرُ	View. Aspect.
مِنْظَارٌ	Speculum.
مُنَاظِرٌ	Similar to. Inspector.
مُنَاظَرَةٌ	Rivalry. Inspection.
نَظُفَ يَنْظُفُ	To be clean ; comely.
نَظَّفَ	To cleanse, purify.

تَنَظَّفَ To become clean.

نَظَافَةٌ Cleanliness. Beauty.

نَظِيفٌ ج نظفاء Clean; comely.

نَظَمَ ـِ To arrange ; compose (verses).

تَنَظَّمَ وَٱنْتَظَمَ To be arranged.

نَظْمٌ Arrangement. Poetry.

نِظَامٌ ج أَنْظِمَةٌ System , method.

مُنَظَّمٌ Well-arranged.

مَنْظُومٌ Arranged, composed.

نَعَتَ يَنْعَتُ نَعْتًا To describe.

نَعْتٌ Qualification; attribute.

نَعْتٌ ج نعوت Adjective.

منعوت A qualified noun.

نَعْجَةٌ ج نعاج A sheep, an ewe.

نعّارٌ A kind of finch (bird).

(نَعارَةٌ ج نَعائِرُ) Earthen cooler.

ناعُورَةٌ ج نَوَاعِير Irrigating wheel.

نَعَسَ يَنْعَسُ To grow sleepy.

أَنْعَسَ To make sleepy.

تَناعَسَ To feign sleep.

نعاسٌ Sleepiness; drowsiness

ناعِسٌ وَنَعْسانٌ ج نعَّسٌ Sleepy.

نَعَشَ يَنْعَشُ . وَأَنْعَشَ To cheer, refresh.

إِنْتَعَشَ To be revived, animated.

نَعْشٌ Bier.

بنات نَعْشٍ الكبرى Ursa Major.

نَعَقَ يَنْعَق To croak, (crow).

نَعَلَ يَنْعَلُ نَعْلًا To shoe (an animal).

نَعْلٌ ج نِعالٌ Shoe. Horse-shoe.

نَعِمَ يَنْعَمُ To live in ease.

نَعُمَ يَنْعُمُ To be soft to the touch.

نِعْمَ الرَّجلُ Excellent man !

نِعِمَّا Excellent! Good !

نَعَّمَ To make one easy in life.

أَنْعَمَ عَلَيْهِ To bestow, confer on.

تَنَعَّمَ To enjoy life ; enjoy.

Yes, certainly, assuredly. نَعَمْ

Cattle, camles. نَعَمٌ ج أَنْعَامٌ

Blessing, favour. نِعْمَـةٌ ج نِعَمٌ

Opulent, rich. وَاسِعُ ٱلنِّعْمَـةِ

An ostrich. نَعَامَةٌ ج نَعَائِمُ وَنَعَامَاتٌ

Softness, smoothness. نُعُومَةٌ

Anemone. شَقَائِقُ ٱلنُّعْمَانِ

Soft, tender. نَاعِمٌ م نَاعِمَـةٌ

Contented, tranquil. نَعِيمُ ٱلْبَالِ

Goodness, favour. إِنْعَامٌ ج إِنْعَامَاتٌ

Luxury; enjoyment. تَنَعُّمٌ

Benefactor ; beneficent. مُنْعِمٌ

Mint (plant). نَعْنَعٌ وَنَعْنَاعٌ

To announce death. نعى يَنْعَى

News of death. نَعِيَّـةٌ

Announcer of death. نَاعٍ ج نُعَاةٌ

To be troubled. نغص يَنْغَصُ نَغْصاً

To trouble, vex. نَغَّصَ وَأَنْغَصَ عَلَى

To be annoyed (in life). تَنَغَّصَ

To be inflamed, (wound). نَغَلَ يَنْغَلُ

Bastard. Hinny. نَغْلٌ

To sing softly. نَغَمَ يَنْغُمُ . وَنَغَّمَ

Melody, tune. نَغْمَـةٌ ج نَغَمَاتٌ

To spit out. نَفَثَ يَنْفُثُ

Expectoration. Puff. نَفْثٌ

To blow (wind). نَفَحَ يَنْفَحُ نَفْحاً

A breath. A gift. نَفْحَةٌ ج نَفَحَاتٌ

To blow with the mouth. نَفَخَ يَنْفُخُ

To be puffed up proud. إِنْتَفَخَ

Breath, puff; blowing. نَفْخٌ

A water-bubble. Vesicle. نُفَّاخَةٌ

Bellows. مِنْفَاخٌ وَمِنْفَخٌ ج مَنَافِخُ

Inflated, swollen, مَنْفُوخٌ

To be spent, consumed. نَفِدَ يَنْفَدُ

To consume. أَنْفَـدَ وَٱسْتَنْفَدَ

To pierce through. نَفَذَ يَنْفُذُ مِنْ

نَفَذَ To be executed (an order).
نَفَذَ إِلى To reach, arrive at.
نَفَّذَ وأَنفذ To send, execute.
نفاذٌ ونفوذٌ Execution; efficiency.
نافذٌ Efficacious, effective.
نَافِذَةٌ ج نَوَافِذُ Window.
مَنفَذٌ ج منافذُ Outlet, passage.
نفرَ يَنفرُ مِنْ To turn away from.
نَفَّرَ To cause aversion.
تَنافرَ To have mutual aversion.
نَفَرٌ ج أَنْفار A number of men.
تَنَافُرٌ Contest, repulsion.
نفيرٌ A trumpet, bugle.
نَفُسَ يَنفسُ To be precious.
نَفِسَتْ تَنْفَسُ To give birth.
تَنَفَّسَ To breathe.
تَنَفَّسَ الصُّعداء To sigh deeply.
تَنافَسَ To contend together.
نفسٌ ج نفوسٌ وأَنفُسٌ Soul, self.
جاءَ نفسُهُ He himself came.
نُفَساء A woman at child-birth.
نَفْسُ الشَّيء The thing itself.
نَفَسٌ ج أَنفاسٌ Breath. Style.
نفاسٌ Confinement, child-birth.
تَنَفُّس Respiration, breathing.
نَفيسٌ ج نَفائِسُ A valuable thing.
أَنفَسُ More precious.
نَفَشَ ـ وَنَفَّشَ To teaze (cotton).
تَنَفَّشَ To bristle (hair), ruffle (feathers).
نَفَضَ ـُ ونَفَّضَ To shake, shake off.
مِنفضةٌ ج مَنافِض A plate for ashes.
نَفطٌ Matches.
نِفطٌ Naptha, bitumen.
نَفطةٌ Pustule, vesicle.
مُنفِطٌ A vesicating medicine.
نَفَعَ يَنفعُ نَفعاً To be useful.

To profit by.	إنتفعَ بِ ومِنْ
To seek benefit.	إستنفعَ
Advantage, benefit.	نَفعٌ ومنفعة
Useful, profitable.	نافِعٌ
To have a brisk sale. To be exhausted.	نفقَ ينفُقُ نفاقاً
To sell well.	نفّقَ وأنفقَ
To be hypocritical.	نافقَ
To exhaust one's means.	انفقَ
Cost, expenses.	نفقةٌ ج نفقاتٌ
Selling briskly.	نافِقٌ
Hypocrisy.	نفاقٌ ومنافقة
A hypocrite ; deceiver.	منافِقٌ
A supererogatory deed.	نفْلٌ
Booty. Present.	نفلٌ ج أنفالٌ
Clover.	نفلةٌ
To expel ; deny, exclude.	نفى ينفِي
To banish, exile.	نفى مِنْ
To oppose, be incompatible.	نافى
To be excluded, rejected.	إنتفى
Banishment. Negation.	نفْيٌ
Particle of negation.	حرْفُ ٱلنَّفْيِ
Rejected as useless.	نفاوةٌ ونُفاية
Excluded. Exiled.	منفِيٌّ
Incompatibility.	تنافٍ ومنافاةٌ
Exile.	منفًى ج منافٍ
To dig through.	نقبَ ينقُبُ نقباً
To travel over.	نقّبَ في
To examine.	نقّبَ عنْ
To put on a veil.	تنقّبَ وانتقبَ
A hole in a wall.	نقبٌ ج انقابٌ
Veil of a woman.	نِقاب ج نقبٌ
Chief. Magistrate.	نقيبٌ ج نقباء
Worthy deed.	منقبةٌ ج مناقبُ
To revise, correct.	نقّحَ وأنقحَ
Revision, correction.	تنقيحٌ
To peck (bird).	نقدَ ينقُدُ نقداً

نَقَد لِ To pay in cash.

نَقَدَ وَتَنَقَّدَ To sort, pick out.

نَقدٌ Ready money, cash.

نُقُودٌ وَنَقدِيَّةٌ Money, cash.

إِنْتِقَادٌ Testing ; criticism.

مِنقَادٌ ج مَنَاقِيدُ Beak (of a bird).

نَقَذَ يَنقُذُ وأَنقَذَ To deliver, save.

نَقْذٌ Rescue, deliverance.

مُنقِذٌ Deliverer.

نَقَرَ يَنقُرُ To cut into (stone, wood) ; peck (bird).

نَقَرَ وَنَقَّرَ عَنْ To examine.

نَاقَرَ مُنَاقَرَةً To dispute with.

نَقرٌ Cavity. Carving.

نُقرَةٌ ج نُقَرٌ Hollow, cavity.

نَقَّارٌ Sculptor, carver.

(نَقَّارَةٌ وَنُقَيرَةٌ) A small tambourine.

نَاقُورٌ ج نَوَاقِيرُ Hunting-horn.

مِنقَارٌ ج مَنَاقِيرُ Beak of a bird.

نِقرِسٌ Gout.

نَقَزَ يَنقِزُ To skip.

نَاقُوسٌ ج نَوَاقِيسُ A church-bell.

نَقَشَ يَنقُشُ To paint; sculpture.

نَاقَشَ مُنَاقَشَةً To reckon with.

نَقْشٌ ج نُقُوشٌ Painting. Tracing.

نِقَاشَةٌ Painting. Sculpture.

نَقَّاشٌ Painter. Engraver.

مِنقَشٌ وَمِنقَاشٌ Brush. Chisel.

نَقَصَ يَنقُصُ To reduce, decrease.

تَنَاقَصَ To decrease gradually.

إِنْتَقَصَ To defame.

نَقصٌ وَنُقصَانٌ Diminution ; loss.

نَاقِصٌ Diminished, defective.

نَقِيصَةٌ ج نَقَائِصُ Fault ; vice.

نَقَضَ يَنقُضُ To demolish; annul.

نَاقَضَ To contradict.

إِنْتَقَضَ To be annulled.

نَقْضٌ Destruction, dissolution.

نَقْضَةٌ Beam, joist.

نقيضٌ The contrary, opposite.

تَناقضٌ ومناقَضة Contrariety.

نَقَطَ يَنقُطُ ونقَّطَ To mark with dots.

نقطةٌ ج نقطٌ Dot of a letter. Geometrical point. A drop.

نقطةُ الدَّائرة Centre of a circle.

داء النقطة Epilepsy.

نقع ينقع To soak, macerate.

إستنقع To become stagnant.

ناقعٌ Penetrating, pervading.

نقيعٌ ومنقوعٌ Infusion.

(نقوعٌ) Dried apricots.

مستنقعٌ ونقعٌ A marsh, swamp.

إنتقف To take out.

نقل ينقل To remove, transport.

نقل عنْ To copy from ; quote.

انتقل منْ إلى To emigrate.

إنتقل إلى رحمة الله To die.

نقلٌ Transpsrt. Quotation.

ناقلٌ Narrator. Bearer. Copyist.

منتقلٌ Movable (estate).

منقولٌ Transferred ; quoted.

إنتقم منْ To punish, chastise.

نقمةٌ وانتقامٌ Vengeance.

ناقمٌ ومنتقمٌ An avenger.

نقه ينقه نقهاً To recover (from illness).

ناقهٌ ونقهٌ ج نقّه Convalescent.

نقي ينقى To be pure.

نقّى وأنقى To clean, purify.

تنقّى وانتقى To choose, select.

إستنقى To cleanse one's body.

نقاء ونقاوة Purity. Innocence.

نقيّ Pure. clean. Innocent.

أنقى Purer, cleaner.

نكب ينكب نكباً To afflict.

To swerve from. نَكَبَ عَنْ

Adversity. نَكْبَةٌ ج نَكَبَات

Shoulder; side. مَنْكِبٌ ج مَنَاكِب

Afflicted, smitten. مَنْكُوبٌ

To find fault with. نَكَّتَ عَلَى

Speck. Witty saying. نُكْتَةٌ ج نُكَتٌ

Criticism. تَنْكِيتٌ

To break a compact. نَكَثَ يَنْكِثُ

To be broken (promise). إِنْتَكَثَ

Broken, violated. مَنْكُوثٌ

To marry. نَكَحَ يَنْكِحُ نِكَاحاً

To give in marriage. أَنْكَحَ

Marriage contract. نِكَاحٌ

To be hard. نَكِدَ ـ نَكَداً

To molest, annoy. نَكَّدَ وَنَاكَدَ

To molest each other. تَنَاكَدَ

Irritable, peevish. نَكِدٌ م نَكْدَاء

Annoyance, molestation. تَنْكِيدٌ

Unfortunate. مَنْكُودُ ٱلْحَظّ

To be ignorant of. نَكِرَ يَنْكَرُ

To deny. أَنْكَرَ

To disapprove of. أَنْكَرَ عَلَى

To be disguised. تَنَكَّرَ

To deny. To censure. إِسْتَنْكَرَ

Cunning. نُكْرٌ وَنَكَارَةٌ

Indefinite noun. نَكِرَةٌ ج نَكِرَات

Denial. Repudiation. إِنْكَارٌ

Disguise. تَنَكُّرٌ

Illicit deed. مُنْكَرٌ ج مُنْكَرَات

Indeterminate noun. مُنَكَّرٌ

To push; prick. نَكَزَ يَنْكُزُ نَكْزاً

To upset. نَكَسَ يَنْكُسُ وَنَكَّسَ

To be upset, inverted. تَنَكَّسَ

To have a relapse. نُكِسَ وَٱنْتَكَسَ

A relapse. نُكْسٌ وَٱنْتِكَاسٌ

Reversed. مَنْكُوسٌ وَمُنْتَكِسٌ

نَكَشَ يَنْكُشُ — To exhaust. To dig.

مِنْكَاشٌ ج مَنَاكِيشُ — Pickaxe.

نَكَصَ يَنْكُصُ عَنْ — To withdraw from.

نَكَصَ عَلَى عَقِبَيْهِ — To turn back.

نَكَفَ يَنْكُفُ عَنْ — To abstain from, reject.

تَنَاكَفَ — To discuss, contend.

إِسْتَنْكَفَ — To disdain, scorn.

نَكَلَ وَنَكَّلَ بِ — To punish severely.

نِكْلٌ ج أَنْكَالٌ — A strong fetter.

نَكَالٌ — Chastisement; warning.

نَكْهَةٌ — Smell of breath.

نَكَى يَنْكِي نِكَايَةً — To overcome; vex.

نَمَّ ـ بَيْنَ — To make mischief.

نَمَّامٌ وَنَمُومٌ — A calumniator.

نَمِيمَةٌ ج نَمَائِمُ — Calumny, slander.

(نَمَّرَ) — To mark with numbers.

نِمْرٌ ج نُمُورَةٌ — Leopard; panther. Tiger.

(نمرة ج نُمَرٌ) — Number *(For)*.

نِمْسٌ ج نُمُوسٌ — Ichneumon; weasel.

نَامُوسٌ ج نَوَامِيسُ — Law. Mosquito.

نَامُوسِيَّةٌ — Mosquito-net.

نَمَشٌ — Freckles.

انمشةٌ — A straight sword.

نَمِشٌ م نَمْشَاءُ ج نُمْشٌ — Freckled.

نَمِيصٌ — Cropped grass.

نَمَطٌ ج نِمَاطٌ — Manner; fashion.

نَمَّقَ — To write well, embellish.

نَمِلَ ـ نَمَلاً — To be numb.

نَمْلَةٌ ج نَمْلٌ — An ant. A pustule.

أَنْمُلَةٌ ج أَنَامِلُ — Tip of the finger.

نَمْنَمَ — To embellish, adorn.

نَمَا يَنْمُو — To grow, develop.

نَمَا إِلَى — To attribute, ascribe, to.

نُمُوٌّ — Growth, increase.

نَمُوذَجٌ ج نَمُوذَجَاتٌ — Example.

نَمَى يَنْمِي — To grow, increase.

نمى إلى — To ascribe to one.

أنمى — To cause to grow.

إنتمى إلى — To trace one's origin to.

نامٍ — Growing, increasing.

نَهَبَ يَنْهَبُ وَآنْتَهَبَ — To plunder.

نَهْبٌ — Pillage, rapine.

نُهْبَةٌ — Booty, plunder, spoil.

نَهَّابٌ — Pillager, depredator,

مَنْهُوبٌ — Pillaged, plundered.

نَهَجَ يَنْهَجُ — To follow (the way).

نَهَجَ يَنْهَجُ — To be out of breath:

نَهَجٌ — Rapid breathing, panting.

مَنْهَجٌ ومِنْهاجٌ ج مَناهج — A plain road. Way.

ناهَدَ — To contend with in battle.

تَنَهَّدَ — To sigh, groan.

نَهَرَ يَنْهَرُ نَهْراً — To flow.

نَهَرَ وآنْتَهَرَ — To chide, check.

نَهْرٌ ج أَنْهُرٌ وأَنْهارٌ — River.

نَهارٌ ج نُهُرٌ — Day.

نَهَزَ يَنْهَزُ نَهْزاً — To be near.

ناهَزَ — To approach, be close to.

إنْتَهَزَ — To seize an opportunity.

نُهْزَةٌ ج نُهَزٌ — Opportunity.

نَهَشَ يَنْهَشُ نَهْشاً — To bite.

نَهَضَ يَنْهَضُ عَنْ — To rise, get up.

نَهَضَ عَلى — To revolt, rise against.

نَهَضَ إِلى — To rush towards.

أَنْهَضَ — To urge ; cause to rise,

إنْتَهَضَ — To rise up.

إسْتَنْهَضَ لِ — To urge, incite.

نُهُوضٌ — Lifting ; rising.

نَهَقَ يَنْهَقُ نُهاقاً وَنَهِيقاً — To bray.

نَهَكَ يَنْهَكُ — To overcome, wear out.

نَهَكَ عِرْضَهُ وآنْتَهَكَ — To defame.

نَهَكَ وآنْتَهَكَ — To weaken.

مَنْهُوكٌ — Enfeebled, weakened.

نَهِلَ يَنْهَلُ نَهلاً To drink.

مَنْهَلٌ ج مَناهِلُ A watering place.

نَهِمَ يَنْهَمُ To be ravenous.

نَهْمٌ An insatiable avidity.

نَهِمٌ وَنَهِيمٌ Greedy ; glutton.

نَهَى يَنْهَى عَنْ To prohibit.

أَنْهى To accomplish, achieve.

أَنْهى إِلى To inform.

إِنتَهى إِلى To lead to.

تَناهَى وَٱنْتَهَى To be completed.

تَناهَى وٱنْتَهَى عَنْ To abstain from.

نَهْيٌ Prohibition, interdiction.

نُهى Intelligence.

نِهايَةٌ ج نِهايَاتٌ End, utmost.

نَاهٍ One who forbids.

نَاهِيكَ مِنْ رَجُلٍ What a man !

إِنْتِهاءٌ End, termination ; limit.

مَنْهِيٌّ عَنْهُ Prohibited.

أَلْمَناهِي Prohibited things.

غَيْرُ مُتَناهٍ Infinite ; endless.

مُنْتَهى End, extremity ; limit.

مُنْتَهَى ٱلجُمُوعِ The final plural.

نَوْءٌ ج أَنْوَاءٌ Storm ; tempest.

نَابَ يَنُوبُ عَنْ To take one's place.

نابَ وَأَنَابَ إِلَى اللهِ To repent.

نَابَ وَٱنْتَابَ To overtake, befall.

أَنَابَ To appoint a substitute.

تَناوَبَ عَلَى To do a thing in turn.

نُوبٌ وَنُوبَةٌ The Nubians.

نُوبِيٌّ A Nubian.

نَوْبَةٌ ج نُوَبٌ A turn ; time.

نَوْبَةٌ ج نَوْبَاتٌ Musical concert.

نِيابَةٌ Lieutenancy, vicarship.

نِيابَةً عَنْ In place of, instead of.

نَائِبٌ ج نُوَّابٌ Substitute, deputy.

نَائِبُ ٱلفَاعِلِ The subject of a passive verb.

مَجْلِسُ آلنوّابِ Parliament.

نائِبةٌ ج نَوائِبُ Misfortune.

نُوتِيٌّ ج نوتيّةٌ Mariner, sailor.

ناحَ يَنوحُ To wail ; coo (pigeon).

ناحَ على To bewail the dead.

نَوْحٌ وَنُواحٌ وَنِياحٌ Lamentation.

نائِحٌ A mourner, weeper.

نائِحةٌ ج نَوائِحُ وَنائِحاتٌ Wailing women.

أناخَ To cause a camel to kneel.

أناخ بِالْمكانِ To abide in a place.

مُناخٌ ج مُناخاتٌ Climate.

نارَ يَنورُ وَأنارَ To shine, sparkle.

نَوَّرَ وَأنارَ To flower, blossom (plant).

نَوَّرَ وَأنارَ To light up.

إستنارَ بِ To be enlightened by.

نارٌ ج نيرانٌ Fire.

جَبلُ ٱلنّارِ A volcano.

مَرْكبُ ٱلنّارِ A steam-ship.

نورٌ ج أنْوارٌ Light.

نُوريٌّ ج نَوَرٌ Gipsy.

إنارةٌ وتَنْويرٌ Illumination.

نَيِّرٌ م نَيِّرةٌ Shining, bright.

مُنيرٌ Giving light ; shining.

مَنارةٌ A light-house. Minaret.

نَوْرَجٌ A threshing-harrow.

ناسٌ Men; people. (*for* أناسٌ)

ناوُوسٌ ج نَواوِيسُ Sarcophagus.

ناوَشَ To engage in a combat.

تَناوَشَ To attack one another.

إنتاشَ To take out.

ناصَ يَنوصُ عَنْ To flee away.

مَناصٌ A refuge, an asylum.

ناطَ يَنوطُ وَأناطَ بِ To suspend to.

مَنوطٌ بِ Dependent on.

نَوَّعَ To divide, classify, specify.

تنوَّعَ To be of different kinds.

Kind, sort species. نَوْعٌ ج أنْواعٌ

Diversified ; diverse, مُتَنَوِّعٌ

To overlook, surmount. نَافَ ـ عَلَى

More, upwards of. نَيِّفٌ وَنَيْفٌ

Upwards of ten. عَشَرَةٌ وَنَيِّفٌ

Water-lily. نَوْفَرٌ

Jet d'eau. نَوْفَرَةٌ

She-camel. نَاقَةٌ ج نُوقٌ وَنِياقٌ

Dainty, fastidious. نَيِّقٌ

To give to, hand over. نَاوَلَ

To procure for one. أَنَالَ

To obtain, receive. تَنَاوَلَ

A loom. نَوْلٌ ج أنْوالٌ

Freight money. نَاوُلُونٌ

Mode, manner, fashion. مِنْوالٌ

To sleep. نَامَ يَنامُ نَوْماً وَنِياماً

To put to sleep. نَوَّمَ وَأنَامَ

To feign sleep تَنَاوَمَ

Sleep, slumber. نَوْمٌ

Sleeping ; sleeper. نَائِمٌ ج نِيامٌ

Sleep. A dream. مَنامٌ

A dormitory. مَنامٌ وَمَنامَةٌ

Hypnotic, soporific. مُنَوِّمٌ

To mark with the double vowels (ٌ) (ٍ) و (ً) . نَوَّنَ تَنْوِيناً

A dimple on chin. نُونَةٌ

To purpose, resolve. نَوَى يَنْوِي

Distance, absence. نَوًى

A fruit stone. Nucleus. نَوَاةٌ ج نَوًى

Intention. نِيَّةٌ ج نِيَّاتٌ

Intended, purposed. مَنْوِيٌّ

Raw, underdone. نِيءٌ وَنِيٌّ

Canine tooth ; tusk. نَابٌ ج أنْيابٌ

To give rest. (نَيَّحَ)

To die. تَنَيَّحَ

Yoke. نِيرٌ ج أنْيارٌ وَنِيرانٌ

نِيرٌ ج أنيارٌ Woof.

نِيرَةٌ Tooth-gum.

نيسانُ April.

نيشانٌ ج نَياشين A decoralion.

ناف يَنيفُ على To surpass, exceed.

نيافة Eminence, (*title of honour*).

نيِّفٌ و نيْفٌ . نوف *See under*

نالَ يَنالُ To obtain, acquire.

نالَ وأنالَ To cause to obtain.

نِيلٌ Indigo-plant ; indigo.

ألنِّيلُ The Nile.

نيلوفَرٌ ونِينوفَرٌ Nenuphar, lotus.

نينَوَى Nineveh.

نايٌ ج نايات A kind of flute.

ه

ه As a numeral sign = 5.

ه His, him, it.

هَا Her, it.

هَا Lo ! Behold !

هاكَ Take thou ! Here you are !

هَبْ Grant ! (*Imp, of* وَهَبْ

هَبْني قلت Suppose I said.

هَبَّ يَهُبُّ To blow (wind).

هَبَّ وأهَبَّ To shake (a sword).

هَبَّ يَفْعَلُ To begin to do.

هَبَّ مِنَ ٱلنَّوْمِ To awake from sleep.

هَبابٌ Fine dust in the air.

Blowing (of wind).	هُبوب
Place of blowing of wind.	مَهَبّ
Flesh, a piece of meat.	هَبْر
A wind raising dust.	رِيح هباريّة
Flakes. Scurf.	هِبْرِيَّة
To descend ; fall.	هَبطَ يَهْبُط
To cause to come down.	أَهبطَ
Fall ; abatement.	هَبْط وهُبوط
A fall; a descent.	هَبْطة
To take a vapour bath.	(تهبَّلَ)
Vapour; steam.	(هَبْلة)
Fumigation.	(تَهبيل)
Dust flying in the a ir.	هباء
To defame.	هَتَرَ يَهتِر هَتراً
To be reckless; neglect.	إِستَهتَرَ
To call, shout.	هَتَفَ يَهتِف هُتافاً
Call, cry, shauting.	هُتاف
To tear off ; divulge.	هتك يَهتِك
To defame, disgrace.	هَتَكَ سِتره
To be disclosed, divulged.	تَهتَّكَ
Solution of continuity.	هَتْك
Disgrace, dishonour.	(هَتيكة)
Rapid, quick (march).	هَجاج
To subside.	هَجأَ يَهجأ هَجأً
To spell (a ward).	تَهجَّأَ
To forsake, renounce.	هَجَرَ يَهجُر
To emigrate.	هاجَرَ مِنْ
Forsaking.	هَجْر وهِجران
Separation; flight.	هِجرة
The Hegira, Moslem Era.	أَلهِجرة
Hot mid-day.	هاجِرة وهَجيرة
Emigrant.	مُهاجِر
Emigration.	مُهاجَرة
Deserted, forsaken.	مَهجور
To occur to the mind.	هَجَسَ يَهجِس
A troubled thought.	هاجِس

To sleep; subside. هجع يهجع هجوعاً

Part of the night. هجيع من الليل

To assail, surprise. هجم يهجم على

To attack suddenly. هاجم

A surprise, sudden attack. هجمة

Sudden attack or surprise. هجوم

To be low, vile. هجن يهجن هجنة

To consider mean. إستهجن

Fault, meanness. هجنة

Fast dromedary. هجين

To mock, ridicule. هجا يهجو هجواً

To spell. هجا وهجى وتهجى

A satire, lampoon. هجاء

Spelling. هجاء وتهجية وتهجٍّ

The alphabet. حروف الهجاء

Satire. هجوة واهجية ج أهاجي

To pull down, demolish. هدّ يهدّ

To threaten, menace. هدّد وتهدّد

To be pulled down. إنهدّ

Destruction, demolition. هدّ

Threatening. تهديد وتهدّد

Sledge-hammer. مهدّة

To subside, calm down. هدأ يهدأ

To calm, appease. هدّأ تهدئة

Rest, tranquillity, quiet. هدوء

Eye-lashes; fringe. هدب ج أهداب

To be spent uselessly. Squander. هدر يهدر

Roaring (of waves, &c.) هدير

To approach. هدف يهدف إلى

Target, aim. هدف ج أهداف

To let down. هدل ـ هدلاً

To hang down. هدل وتهدّل

A bovine epidemic. Rinderpest. أبو هدلان

To pull down. هدم يهدم هدماً

To be destroyed. تهدّم وانهدم

Destruction, demolition. هدم

Clothes, garments.	(هدوم)
Death.	هادِمُ اللَّذاتِ
Destroyed, demolished.	مهدوم
To come to an agreement.	هادَنَ
To make a truce.	تهادن
Armistice, truce.	هدنة ومهادنة
Hoopoo (bird).	هدهد ج هداهد
To lead aright, guide.	هدى يهدي
To give a present.	أهدى
To make mutual presents.	تهادى
To be rightly guided.	اهتدى
To ask for guidance.	إستهدى
The right path.	هداية وهدى
A present, gift.	هَدِيَّة ج هدايا
Guide, leader,	هادٍ ج هداة
Rightly guided, offered.	مهديّ
To ponder over.	هذّ ـ هذيذا في
This.	هَذا م هَذهِ وَهَذي

Dual of هَذا	هذان
To trim; improve.	هذّب
To be educated; improved.	تهذّب
Education. Correction.	تهذيب
Refined. polished.	مهذّب ومتهذب
To babble,	هَذر يهذر هَذْرا
Fem of. هذا	هَذه
To talk irrationally.	هَذى يهذي
Delirium.	هذاء وَهَذيان
A cat.	هرّ ج هررة
A she-cat.	هرّة ج هرر
Whining, yelping.	هَرير
To become tattered,	هرئ يهرأ
To run away, flee.	هَرب يهرب
To put to flight; smuggle.	هرّب
Escape, flight.	هَرب
A fugitive.	هَارب
Place of refuge.	مَهرب ج مهارب

To joke, jest. هَرَّجَ

Agitation, tumult. هَرْجٌ

Jester ; buffoon. هارِجٌ وَمُهَرِّجٌ

To pound, crush. هَرَسَ يَهْرُسُ

To excite discord. هَرَّشَ بَيْنَ

To sport. تَهارَشَ وَاهْتَرَشَ

Tumult, row. هَرَاشٌ

Heretic. هَرْطُوقِيٌّ ج هَرَاطِقَةٌ

To walk fast. هَرَعَ يَهْرَعُ هَرَعًا

To pour out. هَرَقَ يَهْرِقُ. وهَرَّقَ

Effusion, shedding. إِهْرَاقٌ

Heraclius *(Emperor)*. هِرَقْلُ

To be decrepit. هَرِمَ يَهْرَمُ

To cut, hash. هَرَمَ يَهْرِمُ. وَهَرَّمَ

To render one old. هَرَّمَ وَأَهْرَمَ

Decrepitude. هَرَمٌ

A pyramid. هَرَمٌ ج أَهْرَامٌ

Very old. هَرِمٌ ج هَرِمُونَ

To walk fast. هَرْوَلَ

A cudgel. هِرَاوَةٌ ج هَرَاوَى

To wear out. (هَرَى يَهْرِي هَرْيًا)

To get worn out. (إِهْتَرَى)

Granary. هُرْيٌ ج أَهْرَاءٌ

To shake, brandish. هَزَّ يَهُزُّ هَزًّا

Ta be shaken. إِهْتَزَّ وَانْهَزَّ

Earthquake. هَزَّةٌ

Sound. Rustling. هَزِيزٌ

To mock at. هَزَأَ وَهَزِئَ يَهْزَأُ بِ

To ridicule. تَهَزَّأَ وَاسْتَهْزَأَ بِ

Mockery. هُزْءٌ وَهُزُوءٌ وَاسْتِهْزَاءٌ

Part of the night. هَزِيجٌ مِنَ اللَّيْلِ

A song. أُهْزُوجَةٌ ج أَهَازِيجُ

Part of the night. هَزِيعٌ مِنَ اللَّيْلِ

Fear. Tumult. هَيْزَعَةٌ

To joke, jest. هَزَلَ يَهْزِلُ هَزْلًا

To emaciate. هَزَلَ هُزْلًا. وَهَزَّلَ

To be emaciated. هَزَلَ يَهْزُلُ

Sport, jest, joke. هَزْلٌ وهَزَالةٌ

Thinness, emaciation. هزالٌ

Thin, meagre. هزيل ومَهْزول

To put to flight. هَزَم يهزِم

To be put to flight. إنهزام

Rout, defeat. هَزْم وهَزيمة

Thunder. Rain. هزيم

To shake, agitate. هزْهَزَ

To be cheerful. هشَّ يهِشُّ

Joyous cheerful. هشٌّ

Tender, soft. هَشٌّ وهَشاشٌ

To roam about. (هشَلَ يهشِل هَشْلاً)

To drive away, expel. (هَشَلَ)

To crush, break. هشَم يهْشِم وهَشَّم

To be crushed. تهشَّم وانهشَم

A hill. هَضْبَةٌ ج هِضابٌ

To break. To digest. هضَم يَهْضِم

To oppress. هَضَمَ وتهضَّم واهْتَضَم

To wrong. هَضَم حقّه

To be digested (food). إنهضَم

Digestion. هَضْم وانهضام

Indigestion. سوء الهَضْم

Injury, wrong. هَضيمة ج هَضائِم

To rain. هَطَل يَهْطِل هَطلاً

Fine but continuous rain. هَطلٌ

To rustle; walk quickly. هَفَّ يهِفُّ

To long for. هَفَّ إلى

To fly up and down. هَفَت يَهفِت

To rush to, or into. تهافَت على

A slip, fault. هفوة ج هَفوات

Famished. هاف

Thus, so. هكذا

To mock at, deride. تهكَّم على

Mockery. Irony. Sarcasm. تهكُّمٌ

Particle of Interrogation. هَلْ

Did you write ?	هَلْ كَتَبْتَ
Is not ? Why not ?	هَلَّا
Come! Hasten!	حَيَّ هَلْ
To appear, (new moon).	هَلَّ يَهِلُّ
To praise God.	هَلَّلَ
To exult, be joyous.	تَهَلَّلَ
To pour down (rain).	إِنْهَلَّ
The new moon.	هِلٌّ وَهَلَّةٌ
New moon. Crescent.	هِلَالٌ
Semi-lunar, crescentic.	هِلَالِيٌّ
Act of parising God.	تَهْلِيلٌ
Elliptical. Oval.	أَهْلِيلَجِيٌّ
To perish, die.	هَلَكَ يَهْلِكُ
To ruin. destroy.	هلك وأَهْلَكَ
To squander, exhaust.	إِسْتَهْلَكَ
Ruin, loss. Death.	هَلَاكٌ
Perishing, lost, dead.	هَالِكٌ
Perdition, ruin.	تَهْلُكَةٌ
Dangerous place.	مَهْلَكَةٌ
Here ! Come here !	هَلُمَّ
And so on, *et cœtera.*	هَلُمَّ جَرًّا
Jelly.	هُلَامٌ
Jelly-like, gelatinous.	هُلَامِيٌّ
They ; their ; them.	هُمْ
Their book.	كِتَابُهُمْ
He struck them.	ضَرَبَهُمْ
To cause anxiety.	هَمَّ يَهُمُّ . وَأَهَمَّ
To desire, seek.	هَمَّ يَهُمُّ هَمًّا بِ
To be grieved.	إِهْتَمَّ
To take pains in...	إِهْتَمَّ بِ
To be solicitous about	إِهْتَمَّ لِ
Care, anxiety.	هَمٌّ ج هُمُومٌ
Concern ; energy.	هِمَّةٌ ج هِمَمٌ
Reptile, insect.	هَامَّةٌ ج هَوَامُّ
Energetic.	هُمَامٌ
More important.	أَهَمُّ

إِهْتِمَامٌ Care, effort.

مُهِمٌّ ج مَهَامٌّ Important matter.

مُهِمَّاتٌ Provisions, necessaries.

مَهْمُومٌ Preoccupied, anxious.

هَمَجٌ Stupid, savage people.

هَمَدَ يَهْمُدُ هُمُودًا To subside.

هَمَّدَ وأَهْمَدَ To extinguish ; clam.

هَمَرَ يَهْمُرُ To pour out.

إِنْهَمَرَ To be poured out, flow.

هَمَزَ يَهْمِزُ هَمْزًا To beat ; push.

هَمْزَةٌ ج هَمَزَاتٌ A hemza = (ء)

مِهْمَازٌ ج مَهَامِيزُ A spur, goad.

مَهْمُوزٌ Marked with a hemza.

هَمَسَ يَهْمِسُ هَمْسًا To mumble.

هَامِشٌ Margin of a book.

هَمَعَ يَهْمَعُ To shed tears.

هَمَكَ يَهْمُكُ To press, urge.

إِنْهَمَكَ في To be engrossed in.

هَمَلَ يَهْمُلُ To rain quietly.

أَهْمَلَ To neglect, forget.

(تَهَامَلَ في) To be negligent.

(تَهَامُلٌ) Negligence, carelessness.

مُهْمَلٌ Unused, obsolete (word).

مُهْمَلٌ Neglected.

هَمْهَمَ To mumble, mutter.

هَمَا يَهْمُو To fall, flow, run.

هِمْيَانٌ ج هَمَايِينُ Belt.

هَمَايُونٌ وَهَمَايُونِيٌّ Royal.

هُنَّ They ; their · them, *fem.*

هَنَّأَ ب To congratulate.

هَنِئَ يَهْنَأُ ب To enjoy, relish.

تَهَنَّأَ تَهَنُّؤًا ب To enjoy, relish.

هَنِيءٌ Wholesome. Pleasant.

تَهْنِئَةٌ Congratulation.

أَلْهِنْدُ India, the Indies.

جَوْزُ الهِنْدِ Cocoa-nut.

هنديّ ج هنود	An Indian.
هندباء	Endive, wild chicory.
هندس	To make a plan.
هندسة	Engineering. Architecture.
علم الهندسة	Geometry.
هندسيّ	Geometrical.
مهندس	Geometrician. Architect. Engineer.
هندم	To arrange, adorn.
هنا وهَهنا	Here (*adv*).
هنا وهنالك	There, yonder.
هنية وهنيهة	A little while, trifle.
هو	He, it.
هوّة ج هوت	An abyss.
هاد وتهوّد	To become a Jew.
هاود	To abate price.
يهود	Jews.
يهوديّ	Jew.
يهودية	Jewess. Judea.
هودج ج هوادج	Camel-litter.
هوذا	Lo ! Behold !
تهوّر	To roll down, fall down.
تهوّر	To rush imprudently.
تهوّر	Rashness. Collapse.
هوس	Folly. Passionate desire.
(هويس)	Scorched green wheat.
هاش يهوش	To be agitated ; (bark).
هوشة ج هوشات	Tumult.
هاع يهاع و يهوع هوعاً	To vomit.
هال يهول	To frighten.
هوّل عليه بـ	To threaten with.
إهتال	To be terrified.
هول ج أهوال	Terror, fright.
أبو الهول	The sphinx.
هائل ومهول	Frightful, terrible.
هالة ج هالات	Halo (of moon).
هامة ج هامات	Head. Chief.

To be easy. هانَ يَهُونُ هَوْنًا عَلى

To be despised. هَان يَهُونُ هُونًا

To facilitate. هَوَّنَ على

To despise. أهانَ

To neglect. تهاوَنَ ب

Contemptibleness. هَوانٌ

Disdain ; insult. إهانَةٌ ج إِهانات

Negligence ; idleness. تهاوُن

Mortar (for pounding). هَاوُنٌ

Light, easy to do. هيّنٌ وَهيْنٌ

Lighter, easier. أهْوَن

Disdained ; injured. مُهانٌ

Contempt, shame. مَهانَةٌ

To fall. هوى يهوي هَوِيًّا

To love ; desire. هوي يَهْوَى

To ventilate. هَوَّى تهْوِيَة

To fall down ; descend. أهْوى

Passionate desire. هوى ج أهْواء

Ringing in the ears. هَوِيٌّ

Air, atmosphere. هَواء ج أهْوِيَةٌ

Atmospherical. هَوائِيٌّ

The lower world ; hades. اَلْهاوِيَةُ

She, it ; they. هِيَ ج هُنَّ

To prepare. هَيَّأَ تَهيِئَة

To be prepared for. تَهَيَّأَ لِ

Form, aspect. هَيئَةٌ ج هَيئات

Astronomy. عِلْمُ ٱلْهيئة

To fear ; revere. هابَ يَهابُ وٱهْتابَ

Imp. of هَاب and وَهَب هَبْ

Respect, awe, veneration. هَيبَةٌ

More respected. أهيب

Venerable ; respected. مَهيبٌ

Fear ; veneration, respect. مَهابَة

Give ! هاتِ ج هاتُوا

To be agitated, excited. هاجَ يَهيج

To excite, agitate. هَاجَ وَهَيَّجَ

To be agitated. تهيّج و اهتاج

Agitation, excitement. هيجانٌ

Battle, combat ; strife. هيجاء

Agitated, excited. هائجٌ

Diarrhœa. هيضةٌ

Slim. أهيفُ م هيفاء ج هيفٌ

Temple ; alter, هيكلٌ ج هياكل

The skeleton. الهيكلُ العظميّ

Matter. هيولى

Material (*adj*). هيوليّ و هيولانيّ

To love passionately. هام يهيم

Passionate love. هيامٌ

Love stricken. هائمٌ ج هيّمٌ و هيّامٌ

Starless night. ليلٌ أهيمُ

Heart lost in love. قلبٌ مستهامٌ

God (the Protector). المهيمن

Easy. هيْنٌ و هيّنٌ

Far ! Far away ! هيهات

Come ! Quick ! هيّا و هيّ

و

As a numeral sign=6. و

And. و

By God ! والله

Oh ! Ah ! Alas ! وا

Shame. Dishonour. إبةٌ

Pestilence. وباء و وباء ج أوبئةٌ و أوباء

Epidemic ; pestilential. وبائيّ

Pestilential. وبيء و موبوء

وبّخ To rebuke, reprimand.

تَوْبِيخٌ Scolding, rebuking.

وَبْرٌ ج وُبُورٌ وَوِبَارٌ Cony.

وَبْرٌ Soft hair (of animals).

أَهْلُ ٱلْوَبَرِ Nomad people.

وَبَشٌ ج أَوْبَاشٌ Low people.

وَبَلَ يَبِلُ وَبْلاً To rain.

وَبُلَ يَوْبُلُ To be unhealthy, (land).

وَبْلٌ وَوَابِلٌ A heavy shower.

وَبَالٌ Unhealthiness. Hardship.

وَبِيلٌ Unhealthy. Hard.

وَتَدَ يَتِدُ وَوَتَّدَ To make firm.

وَتِدٌ ج أَوْتَادٌ Wooden peg. A kind of foot *(Prosody)*.

أَوْتَادُ ٱلْأَرْضِ Mountains.

وَتَرَ وَوَتَّرَ وَأَوْتَرَ To string a bow.

توتّر To be strained hard.

تواتَر To follow one another.

وِتْرٌ Single ; odd number.

وَتَرٌ وَوِتْرٌ Cord of a circle.

وَتَرٌ ج أَوْتَارٌ String of a bow, or musical instrument. Tendon

تَوَاتُرٌ Succession.

مُتَوَاتِرٌ Repeated at intervals.

مُتَوَاتِراً Often, repeatedly.

وَثْءٌ وَوَثَاءَةٌ A bruise or wound.

وَثَبَ يَثِبُ وَثْباً وَوُثُوباً To leap.

وَثْبَةٌ A leap, jump. An assault.

وَثِقَ يَثِقُ بِ To rely upon.

وَثُقَ يَوْثُقُ وَثَاقَةً To be firm.

وَثَّقَ To make firm.

وَاثَقَ To make a covenant with.

أَوْثَقَ بِٱلْوِثَاقِ To fetter, tie fast.

إِسْتَوْثَقَ مِنْ To trust, rely upon.

ثِقَةٌ Confidence.

وِثَاقٌ A tie, fetter, rope, strap.

وَثِيقٌ Firm or solid. Reliable.

وَثِيقَةٌ ج وَثَائِقُ Compact, alliance.

Firmer, firmest.	أوثق م وُثْقَى
The strongest hold.	ألعُرْوَةُ ٱلوُثْقَى
Covenant.	مِيثَاقٌ ج مَوَاثِيقُ
An idol.	وَثَنٌ ج أوْثَانٌ
Idolater ; heathen.	وَثَنِيٌّ ج وَثَنِيُّونَ
A sprain.	وَثْيٌ
To be necessary, due.	وَجَبَ يَجِبُ
To make binding.	أوْجَبَ
To be worthy of.	إسْتَوْجَبَ
A set of the same kind.	وَجْبَةٌ
Necessity, duty.	وُجُوبٌ
Affirmation.	ايجَابٌ
Affirmative, positive.	إيجَابِيٌّ
Necessary, obligatory.	وَاجِبٌ
Duty.	وَاجِبٌ ج وَاجِبَاتٌ
Cause, motive, reason.	مُوْجِبٌ
According to.	بِمُوجِبِ
To find.	وَجَدَ يَجِدُ
To be ; to exist.	وُجِدَ
To create, produce.	أوْجَدَ إيجَاداً
To be grieved for.	تَوَجَّدَ لِ
Wealth, competence.	جِدَةٌ
Love ; joy ; grief.	وَجْدٌ
Inner consciousness.	وُجْدَانٌ
Existence.	وُجُودٌ
Found ; existing.	مَوْجُودٌ
Existing things.	ألمَوْجُودَاتُ
Grotto, cave.	وَجْرٌ ج أوْجَارٌ
Den, lair.	وِجَارٌ ج أوْجِرَةٌ
To be brief in speech.	وَجَزَ يَجِزُ
To abbreviate, abridge.	أوْجَزَ
Abridged, concise.	وَجِيزٌ ومُوجَزٌ
Conciseness, brevity.	إيجَازٌ
To feel pain.	وَجِعَ يَوْجَعُ وَيَيْجَعُ
To cause or inflicl pain.	أوْجَعَ

To feel pain.	تَوَجَّعَ
To feel pain for.	توجع لَ
Beer, ale.	جِعَةٌ
Pain. Disease.	وَجَعٌ ج أَوْجَاعٌ
Painful ; sore.	وجيعٌ ومُوْجِعٌ
Fire-place, hearth.	وُجَاقٌ وأُوْجَاقٌ
To fear.	وَجِلَ يَوْجَلُ
Fear, terror.	وَجَلٌ ج أَوْجَالٌ
Timorous.	وجلٌ ج وَجِلُون
Cheek (face).	وجنةٌ ج وَجَنَاتٌ
Mallet.	ميجنةٌ ج مَوَاجِنُ
To be respected.	وجُهَ يَوْجُهُ
To turn a thing towards.	وَجَّهَ
To send.	وَجَّهَ
To meet one.	واجَهَ مُواجهةً
To repair to.	توَجَّهَ نحْوَ وإلى
To have an interview.	(تَوَاجَهَ)
To turn towards.	
Face. Chief. Manner. Aim. Surface.	وَجْهٌ ج أَوْجُهٌ وَوُجُوهٌ
To do for God.	عملهُ لِوجهِ اللهِ
In some manner.	بوجهٍ
Side. Dimension. *(Geom).*	جِهَةٌ ج جِهَاتٌ
Concerning.	مِنْ جِهَتِهِ
Consideration, position.	وَجَاهَةٌ
Opposite to, in front of.	تُجَاهَ
Chief, prince.	وَجِيهٌ ج وَجَهَاءُ
Going, turning to.	مُتَوَجِّهٌ
To be alone.	وَحَدَ يَحِدُ
To reduce to one ; unify.	وَحَّدَ
To be one, single, alone.	تَوَحَّدَ
To be united.	إتَّحَدَ
Separately.	عَلَى حِدَةٍ
Alone.	وَحْدَهُ
Unity, being unique.	وَحْدَانيَّةٌ
Solitude, isolation.	وَحْدَةٌ

وَاحِـدٌ	One; single; unique.
الوَاحِـد	The only one.
اَحدٌ م إِحْـدى ج آحادٌ	One.
الأَحدُ	Sunday.
وحيدٌ م وحيدَةٌ	Unique.
إِتّحادٌ	Union ; harmony ; accord.
تَوْحيدُ	Unification. Belief in the unity of God.
تَوحّد	Isolation, solitude.
تَوحّـدٌ	A unitarian.
مُتَوحّـدٌ	Isolated, alone. One.
وَحَشَ وَتَوَحّشَ	To be unpeopled.
تَوَحّشَ	To grow savage.
إِسْتَوْحَشَ	To feel lonely.
وَحْشٌ ج وحُوشٌ	Wild beast.
حِمارُ وَحْشٍ	Onager, wild ass.
وَحْشَةٌ	Grief ; solitude.
وحْشيٌّ	Wild, ferocious cruel.
تَوَحُّشٌ	Savage state. Barbarity.
مُتَوحّشٌ	Savage, brute-like.
وحْلٌ ج وُحُولٌ	Thin mud, mire.
وحِلٌ	Muddy, miry.
وَحنَ يحِنُ	To be spiteful.
أَوْحى إِلى	To inspire. Send.
وَحيٌ	Divine inspiration.
وَحًى	Haste, hurry.
وَاخَذ مواخَذةً	To find fault with.
(لا تُواخِذْني)	Excuse me.
وَخزَ يخِزُ وخْزاً	To prick.
وَخطهُ الشَّيْب	To be grizzled.
وَخُمَ يَوْخُمُ	To be unhealthy.
أَتخَمَ	To surfeit (food).
إِتّخم	To be ill (from food).
وَخِمٌ وَوَخيمٌ	Dirty unclean.
تخمَةٌ	Indigestion.
وخّى وَتوخّى	To seek diligently.
(وَاخَى مُواخَاة)	To fraternize with.

To love; wish for.	وَدَّ يَوَدّ
To show love to.	تَوَدَّدَ إلى
To have mutual love.	توادَّ توادًّا
Love ; friendship.	وُدٌّ وَوِدادٌ
It is my wish.	بودّي (بدّي)
Lover, affectionate.	وُدٌّ وَوَدُود
Affection, friendship.	مَوَدَّة
Mutual, love.	موادَّة وَتوَادٌّ
Jugular vein.	وَداج مث وَدَاجان
To forsake, leave.	وَدَعَ يَدَعُ
Let me, allow me !	دَعْني
To take leave of.	وَدَّعَ يُوَدِّع
To conciliate.	ودع وداعًا
To deposit with.	أَوْدَعَ عِنْد
To bid farewell. Deposit.	إِستَوْدَعَ
White shell.	وَدْعَةٌ ج وَدَعاتٌ
Bidding adieu, farewell.	وَداعٌ

Mildness, gentleness.	وَداعَة
Rest, quiet ; gentleness.	دَعَة
Quiet, gentle.	وديع ج ودَعاء
Deposit ; trust, charge.	وَديعَةٌ
Depositor.	مستَوْدِعٌ
Depository.	مستَوْدَعٌ
Race-field.	ميدان ج مَيادين
To send.	وَدَّى
To perish.	أَوْدى إِيداء
Blood-money.	دِيَة ج دِيَاتٌ
Valley.	وَادٍ ج أَوْدِيَة
Let him alone.	وذَرَ ـَ — ذَرْهُ
Behind. Beyond.	وَرَاء
To equivocate.	وَارَب مُوارَبَة
Obliquity. Diagonal.	(وَرْبٌ)
To inherit.	وَرِثَ يرِثُ إِرْثًا وَوِرَاثَة
To bequeath.	وَرَّثَ وَاوْرَثَ
To bring on (an evil).	أَوْرَث

To inherit.	تَوارَثَ
Inheritance.	إرْثٌ وَوِراثة
Heir.	وارثٌ ج وَرَثةٌ وَوُرّاثٌ
Inherited ; hereditary.	مَوْرُوثٌ
Inheritance.	مِيراثٌ ج مَواريثُ
To come, arrive.	وَرَدَ يَرِدُ وُرُوداً
Flower. Rose.	وَرْدٌ ج وُرُودٌ
A rose.	وَرْدَةٌ
Cockroach.	بِنْتُ وَرْدانَ
Red, rose-coloured.	وَرْدِيٌّ
Coming, arriving.	واردٌ
Revenue.	إيرادات
Vein.	وريدٌ ج اوْرِدَةٌ
Jugular vein.	حبْلُ الوَرِيدِ
Access, entrance.	مَوْرِدٌ ج مَوَارِد
Of a rose colour, rosy.	مورَّدٌ
Brick, restless.	ورِشٌ
Work-shop.	(ورْشةٌ)

To throw into difficulty.	وَرَّطَ
To fall into difficulty.	تَوَرَّطَ
Difficulty.	وَرْطَةٌ ج وَرَطاتٌ
To be pious.	وَرِعَ يَرِعُ
Fear of God. Piety.	وَرَعُ
A pious man.	وَرِعٌ ج أوْراعٌ
Foliage, paper.	وَرَقٌ ج أوْراقٌ
To put forth leaves.	أوْرَقَ
A leaf (of a tree) ; a piece of paper ; ticket.	وَرَقةٌ
Stationer. Plasterer.	مُوَرِّقٌ
Hip bone ; hip.	وَرِكٌ وَوِرْكٌ
A large lizard.	وَرَلٌ ج وِرْلانٌ
To swell.	وَرِمَ يَرِمُ وَرَماً . وَتَوَرَّمَ
To cause to swell.	وَرَّمَ
Swelling. Tumour.	وَرَمٌ ج أوْرَام
Bee-eater (bird).	وَرْوَارٌ ج وَرَاوِير
To conceal.	وَرَّى وَوَارَى
To hide one's self.	تَوَارَى عَن

وَرَى	Creatures ; mankind.
وَرَاءَ	Behind.
تَوْرَاةٌ	The Pentateuch. Bible.
تَوْرِيَةٌ	Using a word in a double sense.
وَزّ (اوز)	Geese.
وَزَّةٌ	A goose.
وَزَبَ يزب وُزُوبا	To flow.
ميزاب ج مَيَازِيبُ	Water-drain.
وَزَرَ يَزِرُ	To commit a sin.
وَازَرَ عَلَى	To aid, help.
تَوَزَّرَ	To become a vizier.
إِتَّزَرَ	To put on a وَزْرَة .
وِزْرٌ ج أَوزَارٌ	Burden. Crime.
وِزْرَةٌ ج وِزْرَاتٌ	Loin-cloth.
وِزَارَةٌ	Office of a vizier.
وَزِيرٌ ج وُزَرَاءُ	Vizier.
مُوَازِرٌ	Assistant.
وَزَّعَ وَأَوْزَعَ بَيْنَ	To distribute.
تَوَزَّعَ	To be divided, distributed.
(وَزَّالٌ)	Scotch broom.
وَزَنَ يَزِنُ وَزناً وَزِنَةً	To weigh.
وَزَنَ ٱلشِّعرَ	To compose (a verse) according to measure scan.
وَزُنَ يَوْزُنُ وَزَانَةً	To be heavy.
وَازَنَ	To be equal in weight.
وَازَنَ بَيْنَ	To compare.
تَوَازَنَ	To be equal in weight.
وَزْنٌ وَزِنَةٌ	Weighing ; weigh.
وَزْنٌ ج أَوْزَانٌ	Weight; measure; metre of a verse.
وَزْنَةٌ ج وَزَنَاتٌ	A weight. Talent.
وَازِنٌ	A weigher. Of full weight.
وَزِينُ ٱلرَّأْيِ	Prudent, reflecting.
مُوازِنٌ	Equal, equivalent to.
مُوازَنَةٌ	Equilibrium.
مَوْزُونٌ	Weighed ; measured.
مِيزَانٌ ج مَوَازِينُ	Scales, balance. Standard. Measure.
أَلمِيزَانُ	Libra (zodiac).

To correspond to, be parallel with. وازَى

To correspond to. توَازى

Correspondence. مُوازاةٌ

Parallel (line). مُتَوَازٍ

To be foul, soiled. وسِخَ يوْسَخ

To soil. وسَّخَ وَأوْسخ

Dirt, uncleanness. وَسَخ ج أوْساخٌ

Dirty, unclean, soiled. وسِخٌ

To prop with a pillow. وسد

A pillow, cushion. وسادٌ ج وُسُد

A pillow. وَسادَة ج وَسادات

To put in the middle. وسَّطَ

To take a middle position. توَسَّطَ

To mediate between. توَسَّطَ بَيْن

Middle, centre. وَسَطٌ وَوَسْط

Means. واسِطَةٌ ج وَسائِط

By means of, through. بوَاسِطةِ

Intermediation. وَساطَة وَتوسُّط

Mediator. وَسيط ج وُسَطاء

The middle finger. الوُسْطَى

Intermediate. Mediator. مُتَوَسِّط

Mediterranean. ألبَحْرُ المُتَوَسِّطُ

To be spacious, wide. وَسُعَ يوْسُع

To contain, hold. وَسِع يَسَع سَعَةً

Thou canst not. لا يَسَعُكَ انْ

To widen, enlarge. وَسَّعَ وَأوْسَعَ

To enrich (God). وسَّعَ وَأوْسَعَ على

To be at ease. توَسَّعَ في

To be enlarged. إتَّسع وَاسْتوْسَعَ

Power, ability. وسْعٌ وَسِعةٌ

Width; capacity. سعَة واتّساع

Extent, dilatation. إتّساعُ

Spacious. واسع وَوَسيع وَمُتَّسع

Wider, more vast. اوْسَع

Rich, wealthy, opulent. مُوسِعٌ

To load; to freight. وَسِقَ يَسِقُ وسقًا

وَسْقٌ ج أَوْسَاقٌ A load; cargo.

مُوْسُوقٌ Freighted, loaded.

تَوَسَّلَ إِلى To implore, seek.

وسيلةٌ ج وَسَائِل Means.

تَوَسّل Supplication.

وَسَمَ يَسِمُ وَسْماً وَسِمَةً To brand.

وَسْمٌ ج وُسُوم. سِمَةٌ ج سِمات Sign, mark.

وِسَامٌ Badge of honour.

مُوْسِمٌ ج مَوَاسِم Season.

مَوْسُوم Marked. Branded.

وَسِنَ يَوْسَن To slumber.

سِنَةٌ Slumber; unconsciousness.

وَسْوَسَ لِ To suggest wicked things.

وَسْوَاسٌ ج وَسَاوِس Hallucination.

إلوَسْوَاس Satan.

مُوسَى وَ (موس) A razor.

مُوسَى Moses.

مُوسَوِيٌّ Mosaic; a Jew.

وَشَّح To adorn.

تَوَشَّحَ وَٱتَّشَحَ To put on.

وُشَاح A sash set with jewels.

مُوَشَّحَةٌ Double-rhymed poetry.

وَشَرَ يَشِر To saw (wood).

مَوْشُورج مَوَاشِير A prism.

مِيشَار A saw.

وَشُكَ يَوْشُك وَشْكاً To be quick.

أَوْشَكَ أَنْ To be on the point of.

وَشَك Celerity; haste, hurry.

وَشِيك Swift; on the point of.

وَشَمَ يَشِمُ وَشْماً وَوَشَّم To tattoo.

وَشْوَشَ وَتَوَشْوَشَ To whisper.

وَشَى يَشِي. وَوَشَّى To embellish.

وَشَى بِفُلانٍ إِلى To slander.

وَاشٍ ج وُشَاةٌ وَوَاشُونَ Slanderer.

مُوَشَّى Coloured; embroiderd.

وَصَبٌ ج أَوْصَابٌ Illnes, pain.

أوْصَدَ To shut, close (a door).

مُوصَدٌ Shut, closed.

وصَفَ يَصِفُ To describe, qualify.

وَصَفَ لِ To prescribe medicine to a sick person, (physician).

إتَّصَفَ To be qualified.

وَصْفٌ ج أوْصَافٌ Description.

وَصفةٌ Prescription of physician.

وَصفيٌّ Descriptive.

صِفةٌ ج صِفاتٌ Quality ; adjective.

وصيف ج وصَفاء Young servant.

مَوْصُوف Qualified noun.

وَصَلَ يَصِلُ ب To unite, join.

وَصَلَ إلى To reach, arrive at.

وَصَلَ To give, bestow.

وَصَّلَ وَأوْصَلَ إلى To bring to.

واصَلَ To persevere in.

توَصّلَ إلى To arrive at.

تواصَلَ To be joined.

إتَّصَلَ To be continuous.

إتَّصَلَ إلى To arrive at, reach.

إتَّصَلَ بِ To be united to.

وصلٌ Connection. Receipt.

وُصْلةٌ وَاتّصالٌ Junction, union.

وَصالٌ Union of the friends.

صِلةٌ ج صِلاتٌ Union. Gift.

وُصول ج وُصُولاتٌ Arrival. Receipt.

إتّصالٌ Continuity ; connexion.

مُواصَلةٌ Continuity. Union.

مُوصِلٌ Connective.

مُتّصِلٌ Joined. Continual.

الضَّمِيرُ المُتَّصِلُ Suffixed pronoun.

مَوْصُولٌ United, joined.

ألاسْمُ المَوْصُول Relative Pronoun.

وَصْمٌ وَوَصْمَةٌ Fault; shame.

وَصْوَصَ To peep through a hole.

وَصّى وأوْصى To bequeath.

To recommend.	وَصَّى إِلَى بِ
To charge, commend.	وصَّى وَأَوْصى
A testator, Executor of a will. Guardian.	وصِيٌّ ج أَوْصياء
An order, charge. Will, testament.	وَصِيةٌ ج وَصَايَا
Testator.	مُوصٍ
What is bequeathed.	مُوصًى بِهِ
A legatee, legatory.	مُوصًى له
To be clean.	وَضُوءَ يَوْضُوء وضُوءًا
To perform ablutions.	تَوَضَّأَ
Water for ablutions.	وَضُوء
Cleanliness ; beauty.	وَضاءَة
Ablutions before prayers.	تَوَضُّوء
To be clear, evident.	وَضَحَ يَضِحُ
To explain clearly.	وضَّحَ وَأَوضَحَ
To become clear.	تَوَضَّحَ وَآتَّضَحَ
To ask for explanation.	إِسْتَوْضَحَ
Distinctness.	وُضوحٌ وَآتِّضاح
Clear, manifest, evident.	واضِحٌ
Clear exposition.	إِيضاحٌ وَتَوْضيح
Evident, manifest, clear.	مُتَّضِحٌ
To lay put down.	وَضَعَ يَضَعُ
To give birth.	وَضَعَتْ تَضَعُ
To humiliate, abase.	وَضَعَ فُلانًا
To be humble.	تَوَاضَعَ وَآتَّضَعَ
To be humbled.	إِتَّضَعَ
Position, site.	وَضْعٌ ج أَوْضاع
Humiliation.	ضِعَةٌ
Laying down. Founder.	وَاضِعٌ
Humble, low.	وَضِيعٌ ج وُضَعَاء
Humility.	تَوَاضُعٌ وَآتِّضاعٌ
Place, site, spot.	مَوْضِعٌ ج مَوَاضِع
Humble, meek.	مُتَّضِعٌ وَمُتَوَاضِع
Object; subject.	مَوْضُوعٌ ج مَوَاضيع
To tread upon.	وَطِئَ يَطأُ
To mount.	وَطِئَ (آلفَرَسَ)
To prepare, render easy.	وَطَّأَ

To agree upon. واطأ وتواطأ على

Low ground. وطاء ووطء

Pressure, violence. وطأة

Low. واطئ

Foot-stool. موطئ ج مواطئ

To fix, make firm. وطد يطد ووطّد

To be made firm, fixed. توطّد

Mountains. أوطاد

Firm, solid, immovable. وطيد

Object purpose. وطر ج أوطار

To reside in. وطن يطن. وأوطن ب

To inhabit. وطّن واستوطن

To resolve. وطّن نفسه

Native place. وطن ج أوطان

Abode, home. موطن ج مواطن

A bat. وطواط ج وطاويط

To lower, let down. وطّى

وظب يظب وظوباً وواظب على
To persevere in.

Perseverance, assiduity. مواظبة

To give an office to one. وظّف

To be employed. توظّف

Pay, Office, function, employment. وظيفة ج وظائف

Physiology. علم وظائف الأعضاء

Functionary; official. متوظّف

To take up wholly. وعب يعب

To fill up; complete. أوعب إيعاباً

To contain, hold. إستوعب

To promise. وعد يعد

To make an appointment. واعد

To threaten. توعّد

To promise one another. تواعد

A promise. عدة ووعد ج وعود

Menaces, threats. وعيد

Appointed time موعد ج مواعد

Appointed time or place. ميعاد

Rugged place. وعر ج وعور

وعِر Rugged, difficult.

وَعزَ وَأَوْعَزَ إِليهِ فِي To intimate.

وَعَظ يَعِظ To exhort, warn.

إتعظَ To listen to warning.

وعظٌ وَعظةٌ وَمَوعِظةٌ Sermon ; exhortation.

واعِظُ ج وعّاظُ A preacher.

توَعَّكَ To be ill, indisposed.

وَعْكةٌ An illness.

وَعلٌ ج أوْعَالُ Antelope.

وَعِمَ — عِمْ صَباحاً Good morning.

وَعَى يَعي To gather ; contain.

أوْعَى إيعاء To put into a vessel.

توَعَّى وَآستوْعَى To be careful.

وَعيٌ Attention, care.

وِعاء ج أوْعِيةٌ Vessel, receptacle.

وَاعٍ Remembering. Cautious.

وغر يَغِر وَغراً To be very hot.

وغرٌ Intense heat. Anger.

وَغى وَوَغيٌ Tumult ; battle.

وَفد يَفِدُ على To come, arrive.

وَفد وأوْفد To send (an envoy).

وفدٌ ج وفودٌ A deputation.

وَافدٌ ج وفودٌ Epidemic.

وَفرَ يَفِرُ To increase, multiply.

وَفَّرَ To economise ; save.

وَفرٌ ج وفورٌ Wealth, affluence.

وَفرٌ وَتوْفِيرٌ Economy ; saving.

وَافرٌ Abundant, plentiful.

أوْفرُ More abundant.

وَفَّقَ To make fit. To assist.

وَفَّقَ وَوَافقَ بَيْنَ To reconcile.

وَافَقَ To agree or accord with.

توَفَّقَ To succeed.

توَافَقَ في To agree together.

إتَّفَقَ عَلى أوْ في To agree upon.

إتفَقَ لِ To happen, occur.

Accord, agreement. وِفْقٌ وَوِفَاقٌ

In accordance with. وِفْقًا لِ

Agreement, fitness. مُوَافَقَةٌ

Coincidence. Accord. إِتِّفَاقٌ

Accidental, by chance. اِتِّفَاقِيّ

Success. Prosperity. تَوْفِيقٌ

Convenient, suitable. مُوَافِقٌ

Prosperous, successful. مُتَوَفِّقٌ

To keep one's promise. To pay a debt. وفى يَفِي وَأَوْفَى

To be perfect, complete. وفى وَفِيًّا

To come to, meet. وَافَى

To pay the whole. وَفَّى حَقَّهُ

To die. تُوُفِّيَ وَتَوَفَّاهُ اللّٰه

Payment of a dept. وَفَاءٌ وإِيفَاءٌ

Death, decease. وَفَاةٌ ج وَفَيَاتٌ

Complete. وَافٍ

Cavity, hole. وَقْبٌ ج أَوْقَابٌ

To appoint a time. وقت وَوَقَّتَ

Time, season. وَقْتٌ ج أَوْقَاتٌ

Then, at that time. وَقْتَئِذٍ

Immediately. لِلْوَقْتِ وَلِوَقْتِهِ

Temporal, provisional. وَقْتِيٌّ

To be impudent. وَقَحَ يَقِحُ وَتَوَقَّحَ

Impudent, brazen-faced. وَقِحٌ

Impudence. وَقَاحَةٌ وَقِحَةٌ

To burn, blaze (a fire). وَقَدَ يَقِدُ . وَتَوَقَّدَ وَٱتَّقَدَ

To kindle (a fire); light. أَوْقَدَ

Fuel. وَقُودٌ وَوَقِيدٌ

Fire-grate. مَوْقِدٌ وَمَوْقِدَةٌ

Lit, kindled. مَوْقُودٌ وَمُتَّقِدٌ

To honour, respect. وَقَّرَ

To load (an animal). أَوْقَرَ إِيقَارًا

Load, burden. وِقْرٌ ج أَوْقَارٌ

Dignified bearing. وَقَارٌ

Venerable. وَقُورٌ

To fall, fall down. وَقَعَ يَقَعُ

To happen, occur to one. وقَعَ لِ

To slander, insult one. وقَعَ في

To attack, assail. وقَعَ وَأَوْقَعَ ب

To let fall. Seal, sign. وقَّعَ

To charge, rush upon. واقَعَ

To tune, put in tune. أوقَعَ

To expect. توقَّعَ وَآستوْقَعَ

To fight together. تواقَعَ

To beseech humbly. توَاقَعَ عَلى

Event. Battle. وَقعة ج وَقَماتٌ

Imploring help. وقيعٌ

Actually, in fact. في الوَاقع

Event, catastrophe. وَاقعةٌ

Harmony of sounds. إيقاع

Expectation ; hope. توقع

Signature. توقيع ج توَاقيع

Place. موقع ج مواقع

To stop ; stand. وقفَ يَقِفُ

To endow. وَقفَ ل وَعلى

To inform. Know. وَقفَ وُقُوفًا على

To seize. To arrest. وَقَّفَ وَأَوْقفَ

To contend with. وَاقفَ في

To hesitate. توَقَّفَ في

To abstain from. توَقَّفَ عَنْ

To depend on. توَقَّفَ عَلى

Endowment. وَقفٌ ج أوْقافٌ

Standing. Pause. وَاقِفٌ ج وُقوفٌ

Standing ; stopping. وقُوفٌ

Hesitation ; arrest. توَقُّف

Suspension ; arrest. توْقيف

A stand, station. موْقِفٌ ج مَوَاقِفُ

Dependent on, stopped. Endowed. موْقُوف

To guard, protect. وقى يَقي

To be on one's guard. توَقى وَآتقى

To fear God. إتقى يَتقي

Protection. وِقايَةٌ وَوِقاء

تقًى و تقْوى Fear of God, piety.

تقيٌّ ج أتقياء Pious, God-fearing.

اوْقيةٌ ج أواقٍ Sixty drams. A pharmaceutical ounce.

متّقٍ A man who fears God.

تَوكّأ وَاتّكأ على To lean upon.

اِتّكأ To sit leaning on the side.

متّكأٌ ج متّكآت A staff ; a couch.

وكب يكب To advance slowly.

موْكبٌ ج مَواكب A procession.

وكّد وأكّد To affirm, confirm.

توكّد وتأكّد To be confirmed.

أكيدٌ ومؤكّدٌ Certain, affirmed.

توْكيدٌ وتأكيدٌ Affirmation, confirmation. Emphasis.

بالتّأكيدِ Certatinly.

وكْرٌ ج أوْكار Nest of a bird.

وَكز ـــ To push, thrust.

وُكس ـــ To be defective.

وكسٌ Diminution of value ; loss.

بَاعَ بالوَكس To sell at a loss.

وكفَ يكِف To drop, trickle.

وَكفٌ Trickling, leaking.

وكلَ يكلُ إلى To confide to.

وَكّل To appoint as an agent.

تَوكّل وَاتّكل على To trust in.

وَكالةٌ ج وكالات Agency.

وَكيلٌ ج وُكلاء Substitute, agent.

إتّكالٌ Trust, confidence.

موْكُول إلى Committed to.

وِلَج يَلِجُ وُلُوجاً وَفي To enter.

ولّج وَإلى To commit to.

ولد يَلِد To beget bring, forth.

ولّد To act as a midwife.

تولّد منْ To originate from.

وَلدٌ ج أوْلادٌ Child, son.

ولادةٌ Birth, parturition.

عِلمُ الولادَةِ Midwifery.

Father; sire. والد ج والدون

Mother; dam. والدة ج والدات

Father and mother. الوالدان

Generation. مولد ج موالد

Birthday. ميلاد ج مواليد

Christmas. عيد الميلاد

Unclassical (word) مولدة

Midwife. مولدة

Born. Child. مولود ج مواليد

To be attached to. ولع يولع ب

To light or kindle. ولع

Material for lighting with. (ولعة)

Violent love, passion. ولع

Passionately addicted. مولع ب

To associate with. والف موالفة

To entertain. اولم

Entertainment. وليمة ج ولائم

To grieve much. وله يله

Grief, passion, love. وله

Overcome with grief. ولهان م ولهى

To wail, lament. ولول ولولة

To follow. ولى وولي يلي

To rule. ولي ولاية وعلى

To make one a ruler. ولى

To turn away from. ولى عن

He turned and fled. ولى هاربا

He turned his face. ولى وجهه

To help, protect. والى موالاة

To do a good deed. أولى معروفا

To take charge of. تولى

To follow one another. توالى

To take possession. إستولى

Master, lord. ولي ج أولياء

Friend of God. ولي الله

Province. Rule. ولاية ج ولايات

Heir apparent. ولي العهد

Benefactor. وليُّ آلنعَمِ

Ruler, governor. وَال ج وُلاةٌ

More deserving, fit. أوْلى بِ

Master, lord. موْلى ج مَوَال

Invested with power. متَوَلٍّ

Successive. متوال

A Sheïte. متوَال ج متاولةٌ

To beckon to. وَمَأَ يَمَأُ . وَأوْمَأَ إلى

Indication by sign. وَمْأ وَإِيماء

Indicated. ألمومَا إليْهِ

A prostitute. مومِسةٌ ومومِس

To flash. وَمَض يَمِض . وَأوْمَض

Lightning; flash; gleam. وَمِيضٌ

To reprove, reprimand. وَنبَ

To be faint, weak. وَنى يَني. وَوَني

To relax one's efforts. توَانى في

Fatigue, faintness. وَنًى وَوَناء

Slowness, slackness. تَوَانٍ

Lazy, languid; slow. متوَان

Enamel. مينا

Port, harbour. مينا وَميناء ج مَوَان

To grant, give. وَهب يَهَب

Grant! (*Imp. of* وَهَبْ) هبْ

To ask for a present. إستوْهَب

Gift, present. هبةٌ ج هِبات

Donation, gift. موْهبةٌ ج مواهب

Mohammedan Wahhabite. وهَّابيٌّ

To blaze, burn. وَهج يَهج

To kindle (a fire). أوْهج إيهاجاً

To glow burn. توهَّج

Glow, heat (of fire, sun). وَهَج

Intensely glowing. وهَّاجٌ

Deep pit; abyss. وهدة ج وَهَدٌ

To lead into evil. وهَّط وأوْهَط

To rush rashly into. توهَّط في

Precipice, abyss. وهْطةٌ ج وهْط

وَهَلٌ وَوَهلة Terror, fear, fright.

أوّل وهلةٍ At first sight.

أوهم يهم To imagine, fancy.

وهّم وأوهم To lead into error.

إتّهم ب To suspect, accuse.

توهّم To suppose, imagine.

أتهم ب To be suspected.

وَهْمٌ ج أوهام Opinion, idea.

القوّة الوهمية The imagination.

وهميٌّ Imaginary, hypothetical.

إيهامٌ Ambiguity. Misleading.

تهمةٌ ج تُهَم Suspicion, charge.

متّهمٌ Suspected person.

توهّمٌ Fanciful imagination.

وَهن يهن . وَوهنـ To be weak.

وهّن وأوهن To weaken.

واهنٌ ج وهُن Weak, frail.

وَهى وَوهي يهي To be weak.

أوهى . To weaken, break.

واهٍ م واهية ج واهون Feeble, frail.

واهاً ل Wonderful! Alas!

ويك Woe to you!

واحةٌ ج واحات Oasis.

ويحٌ ويلٌ Woe to!

وَيلٌ Disaster, calamity.

وَيلي Woe to me!

ويلةٌ ج ويلات Disgrace.

ي

ي As a numeral sign=10.

ي My, me, e. g.

كِتَابي My book.

معي With me.

ضَرَبَني He struck me.

يّ *A particle of relation, e.g.*

مِصْريٌّ Egyptian.

يا *Interjection,* O *e.g.*

يا زَيدُ O Zeid!

يَئِسَ يَيْأَسُ وَيَيْئِسُ مِنْ To despair of,

يَأْسٌ Despair, loss of hope.

يَؤُسٌ وَيَؤُوسٌ Despairing.

يَبِسَ يَيْبَسُ To dry up, wither.

يَبَّسَ وأَيْبَسَ To cause to dry.

أليَبْس والْيابسة To dry land.

يابِسُ Dry.

يُبوسة Dryness.

يَتَّمَ To make one an orphan.

تَيَتَّم To become an orphan.

يُتْم State of orphanage.

يتيمٌ ج يتامى وأيْتامُ Orphan.

درة يتيمة A rare pearl.

(يَخنَةٌ) A kind of stew.

يَد ج ايدٍ وأيادٍ Hand; arm. Power. Handle.

عنْ يَد By force.

بَيْنَ يَديهِ In his presence.

لهُ يد بيضاء He is well versed.

أليد الطولى Power, influence.

يَدِيٌّ ويَدَوِيٌّ	Manual.
ايدِي سَبا	Scattered.
يَرْبُوعٌ	Jerboa (animal).
يَرَاعٌ	Glow-worm. Reed-pen.
يَرَقانٌ	Jaundice. Blight.
يسر ييسر يُسْراً	To be easy.
يَسَّرَ	To facilitate, make easy.
تَيَسَّرَ واستيسرَ	To become easy.
تَيَسَّرَ لَهُ	To be feasible to one.
يُسْرٌ	Facility, ease; affluence.
يَسارٌ ج يُسْرٌ	Left side. Ease.
يَسِيرٌ	Easy. Small quantity.
أَيْسَرُ	More easy.
الأَيْسَرُ واليُسْرَى	The left side.
مُوسِرٌ ج مَياسِيرُ	Rich, affluent.
مَيْسِرٌ	Gambling.
مَيْسُرَةٌ	Ease, affluence, wealth.
مَيْسَرَةٌ ج مَياسِرُ	Left side.
مَيْسُورٌ ج مَياسِيرُ	Feasible, easy
(يَسَقْ)	Arrest, interdicted.
(يسقجيٌّ)	A cavass (*Turk*).
ياسَمِينٌ	Jasmine (jessamine).
يَعْسُوبٌ	Male bee. Chief.
يَافُوخٌ	Fontanelle.
يافِعٌ ج يَفَعَةٌ	A young man. Lad.
ياقُوتٌ	Ruby.
يَقِظَ يَيْقَظُ	To be awake.
يَقَّظَ وأَيقَظَ	To awaken.
تَيَقَّظَ واستيقظ	To wake up.
يَقَظَةٌ	Wakefulness. Attention.
يَقِظٌ ويَقْظانُ	Awake, watchful.
يَقِنَ ييقَنُ	To be certain, sure.
أَيقنَ واستيقنَ	To believe firmly.
تَيَقَّنَ	To know, be sure of.
يَقِينٌ	Certain belief, conviction.
هُوَ على يقينٍ منهُ	He is sure of it.
يَقِيناً	Certainly, undoubtedly.
عِلمُ اليقينِ	Certain knowledge.

حقُّ اليقين	Indubitable truth.
يقينيَّات	Certain truths; axioms.
موقنٌ	Confident, sure.
يمٌّ ج يموم	Sea, ocean.
يمام ويمامة	Wood-pigeon.
يمَّن ويامن	To go to the right.
تيمَّن ب	To seek a blessing.
إستيمن	To exact an oath.
يمنٌ	Blessing, success, luck.
يمنة	Right side or hand.
اليمنُ	Yemen (Arabia Felix).
يُمنى ج يمنيات	Right hand.
يَمينٌ	Right side, right hand.
يمينٌ ج أيمنٌ وأيمانٌ	Oath.
أيمُ وآيمُ الله	By God.
التيمن	The South.
ميمنةٌ ج ميامنُ	Right Side. Right wing of an army.
ميمونٌ ج ميامين	Fortunate.
ميمونُ الطَّائر	Auspicious.
ينبوعٌ	Fountain.
يانسونٌ (أنيسونٌ)	Anise.
ينعَ يينعُ . وأينع	To ripen (fruit).
يانعٌ ويَنيعٌ ج ينعٌ	Ripe (fruit).
يهوديٌّ ج يهود . (See هود)	Jew (See هود)
يومٌ ج أيَّام	Day. Time; season
يوماً فيوماً	Day by day.
من يومهِ	The same day.
يوماً ما	Once, some day.
ذات يوم	On a certain day, once.
أليومُ	To-day.
يوميٌّ	Daily.
يومياً	Day by day, daily.
يومئذ	On that day.
يُونس (يونانٌ)	Jonah.
أليُونانُ	The Greek nation.
بلادُ أليونان	Greece.
يونانيٌّ ج يُونانيُّون	Greek. Grecian.
أليُونانيَّة	The Greek language.

SUPPLEMENT

ARABIC-ENGLISH

It was impossible, for technical reasons, to follow the conventional arrangement according to roots in this Arabic-English supplement. The words are, therefore, arranged strictly alphabetically.

metabolism *n.* إِبْدَالُ ٱلْمَوَادِّ فِى ٱلْجِسْمِ

Soviet Union *n.* إِتِّحَادُ ٱلسُّوفْيَت

authorize *v.* أَجَازَ

authorization *n.* إِجَازَةٌ

patent *n.* إِجَازَةُ ٱلْحَصْرِ

living wage *n.* أَجْرٌ كَافٍ

minimum wage *n.* ٱلْأَجْرُ ٱلْأَصْغَرُ

red tape *n.* إِجْرَاءَاتٌ عَقِيمَةٌ

enemy alien *n.* أَجْنَبِىٌّ عَدَائِىٌّ

inferiority complex *n.* إِحْسَاسُ ٱلْإِنحِطَاطِ

statistician *n.* إِحْصَائِىٌّ

statistics *n.* إِحْصَائِيَّةٌ

jurisdiction *n.* إِخْتِصَاصٌ

specialist *n.* إِخْتِصَاصِىٌّ

nutritionist *n.* إِخْتِصَاصِىٌّ بِٱلْغِذَاءِ

chiropodist *n.* إِخْتِصَاصِىٌّ لِمُعَالَجَةِ ٱلْأَقْدَامِ

fingerprint *v.* أَخَذَ طَابِعَ ٱلْأَصَابِعِ

camouflage *v.* أَخْفَى

defrost *v.* أَذَابَ ٱلْجَلِيدَ فِى خِزَانَةِ ٱلثَّلْجِ

broadcast *v.* أَذَاعَ

telecast *v.* أَذَاعَ بِٱلتِّلْفَزَةِ

broadcast *n.* إِذَاعَةٌ

newscast *n.* إِذَاعَةُ ٱلْأَخْبَارِ

telecast *n.* إِذَاعَةٌ تِلْفِزِيَّةٌ

radio broadcast *n.* إِذَاعَةٌ لَاسِلْكِيَّةٌ

mixup *n.* إِرْتِبَاكٌ

traffic jam *n.* إِرْتِبَاكُ ٱلْحَرَكَةِ

terrorism *n.* إِرْهَابٌ

terrorist *n.* إِرْهَابِىٌّ

أَرْهَبَ	terrorize *v.*
أَسْبِيرِينٌ	aspirin *n.*
إِسْتِبْدَادٌ	dictatorship *n.*
إِسْتَرَقَ إِلَى	infiltrate *v.*
إِسْتِعْرَاضٌ	revue *n.*
إِسْتِفْتَاءُ الشَّعْبِ	plebiscite *n.*
إِسْتِقْلَالٌ	autonomy *n.*
إِسْتِكْشَافٌ	reconnaissance *n.* (mil.)
إِسْتِهْلَاكٌ	amortization *n.*
إِسْتَهْلَكَ	amortize *v.*
أُسْطُوَانَةٌ	record *n.* (phonograph)
إِسْعَافٌ	first aid *n.*
إِسْمٌ مُسْتَعَارٌ	pseudonym *n.*
أَسِيرٌ	internee *n.*
إِشَارَةٌ	tip-off *n.*
إِشَارَةُ الْخَطَرِ	alert *n.*
إِشْتِرَاكِيٌّ	socialist *n,* socialist(ic) *a.*
إِشْتِرَاكِيَّةٌ	socialism *n.*
أَشِعَّةُ رِنْتْجِن أَوْ إِكْس	x-ray *n.*
أَصْلَحَ	ameliorate *v.*
إِضْرَابٌ	walkout *n.*
إِطْفَائِيَّةٌ	fire department *n.*
إِعَادَةُ إِذَاعَةٍ	rebroadcast *n.*
إِعَادَةُ التَّنْظِيمِ	reorganization *n.*
إِعَانَةٌ	subsidy *n.*
إِعْتِدَاءٌ	aggression *n.*
إِعْلَانٌ	advertisement *n.*
إِعْلَانُ الطَّلَبِ	want ad *n.*
إِعْلَانٌ مُبَوَّبٌ	classified ad *n.*
إِفْتِتَاحِيَّةٌ	editorial *n.*

إِقْتِدَارٌ	efficiency *n.*
إِقْطاعِيَّةٌ	feudalism *n.*
إِكْثَارٌ	boost *n.*
إِلْتِهَابُ ٱلْمَفَاصِلِ	arthritis *n.*
أَلِالْتِهَابُ ٱلسَّحَائِيُّ	meningitis *n.*
إِلْحَاقٌ	annexation *n.*
أَلْحَقَ	annex *v.*
أَلْفُ مِلْيُونٍ	billion *n.*
آلَةٌ اسْتِكْتَابِيَّةٌ	dictaphone *n.*
آلَةُ ٱلْبَيْعِ	vending machine *n.*
آلَةُ ٱلتَّسْخِينِ	heater *n.*
آلَةُ ٱلتَّصْفِيحِ	rolling mill *n.*
آلَةُ ٱلتَّصْوِيرِ	camera *n.*
آلَةُ ٱلتَّفْرِيخِ	incubator *n.*
آلَةٌ حَاسِبَةٌ	calculating machine *n.*
آلَةٌ لِحَرْقِ ٱلْفَضَلَاتِ	incinerator *n.*
آلَةُ ٱلْخِيَاطَةِ	sewing machine *n.*
آلَةُ ٱلْغَسْلِ	washing machine *n.*
آلَةُ ٱلْكِتَابَةِ	typewriter *n.*
آلَةُ لَعْبِ ٱلْقِمَارِ	slot machine *n.*
آلَةٌ مُسَخِّنَةٌ	radiator *n.*
إِلْهَابٌ	ignition *n.*
إِمْكَانِيَّةٌ	potential *n.*
الأَمْنُ ٱلْمُشْتَرَكُ	collective security *n.*
أَمِينٌ	trustee *n.*
إِنْتِظَارُ ٱلْحَيَاةِ	life expectancy *n.*
إِنْتِقَادٌ	book review *n.*
إِنْهِيَالُ ٱلْأَرْضِ	landslide *n.*
أُورْيُومِيسِين	aureomycin *n.*
إِبْنْسُولِين	insulin *n.*

بَابٌ دَوَّارٌ	turnstile *n.*
أَلْبَحْرِيَّةُ ٱلتِّجَارِيَّةُ	merchant marine *n.*
بَدَلَ	pinch-hit *n.*
بِدُونَ ٱسْمٍ	anonymous *a.*
بِدُونَ تَطَوُّرٍ كَافٍ	underdeveloped *a.*
بَرَّادَةٌ	air conditioner *n.*
بَرْقِيَّةٌ	cablegram *n.*
أَلْبَرِيدُ ٱلْجَوِّيُّ	air mail *n.*
بُرُوتِئِينٌ	protein *n.*
بَسْتِيلِيَّةٌ لِلسُّعْلَةِ	coughdrop *n.*
بَطِّيخٌ أَصْفَرُ	honeydew melon *n.*
بَقَايَا	leftover *n.*
بَقَايَا عَمَلٍ	backlog *n.*
بِلَادٌ مُتَوَقِّفَةٌ	satellite country *n.*
بْلُوتُونِيُومٌ	plutonium *n.*
بَنْزِينٌ	gasoline *n.*
بِنِيسِلِّينٌ	penicillin *n.*
بِيجَامَا	pajamas *n. pl.*
تَاجِرُ ٱلْجُمْلَةِ	wholesaler *n.*
تَأْلِيفٌ فَحَّاشٌ	pornography *n.*
تَأْمِينٌ ٱجْتِمَاعِيٌّ	social security *n.*
تَأْمِينٌ ضِدَّ ٱلأَمْرَاضِ	health insurance *n.*
تَأْمِينٌ عَلَى ٱلْحَيَاةِ	life insurance *n.*
تَأْمِينٌ عَلَى ٱلْمَسْؤُولِيَّةِ	liability insurence *n.*
تَبَادُلُ ٱلْخَوَاطِرِ	telepathy *n.*
تَجْرِيبٌ	trial balloon *n.*
تَحَالُفٌ	coalition *n.*
تَحْتَ ٱلْمِقْيَاسِ	substandard *a.*

تَحْكِيمٌ arbitration *n.*

تَحْلِيلٌ analysis *n.*

تَحْلِيلٌ نَفْسِيٌّ psychoanalysis *n.*

تَخْدِيرٌ anesthesia *n.*

تَخْزِينٌ storage *n.*

تَدْبِيرٌ نَجْمِيٌّ installment plan *n.*

تَدَرُّنٌ tuberculosis *n.*

تَدْمِيجٌ shorthand *n.*

تَذْكِرَةُ ٱلْأَصْلِ certificate of origin *n.*

تَذْكِرَةُ إِثْبَاتِ ٱلشَّخْصِيَّةِ identification *n.*

تَرَامٌ trolley car *n.*

تَرْتِيبٌ layout *n.*

تَرْوِيسَةٌ headline *n.*

تَسْجِيلٌ registration *n.*

تَسْخِينٌ heating *n.*

أَلتَّسْيِيرُ ٱلنَّفَّاثِيُّ jet propulsion *n.*

تَسْوِيَةٌ بِمِقْيَاسٍ أَحَدٍ standardization *n.*

تَشْخِيصُ مَرَضٍ diagnosis *n.*

تَشْرِيحٌ autopsy *n.*

تَشَنُّجِيٌّ spastic *a.*

تَصَوَّرَ visualize *v.*

تَصْوِيرٌ وَقْتِيٌّ time exposure *n.*

تَضَخُّمٌ نَقْدِيٌّ inflation *n.*

تَطَوَّرَ develop *v.*

تَعَطُّلٌ unemployment *n.*

تَعْقِيمٌ sterilization *n.*

تَفَرُّجٌ sightseeing *n.*

تَكْيِيفُ ٱلْهَوَاءِ air-conditioning *n.*

تَلْخِيصٌ synopsis *n.*

تَلْفَزَ televise *v.*

تَلْفَزَةٌ television *n.*

تَلْقِيحٌ vaccination *n.*

تِلْمِيذَةٌ coed *n.*

تَلِيفُونٌ phone *n.*

تَمْوِيجٌ permanent wave *n.*

تَنْزِيلُ ٱلْأَثْمَانِ بِٱلتَّزَاحُمِ price-cutting *n.*

تَنْزِيلُ ٱلثَّمَنِ markdown *n.*

تَنْزِيلٌ نَقْدِيٌّ devaluation *n.*

تَنْظِيفُ ٱلْأَظْفَارِ manicure *n.*

تَنْظِيفُ أَظْفَارِ ٱلْأَرْجُلِ pedicure *n.*

تَنْوِيمٌ hypnosis *n.*

تَنْوِيمٌ narcosis *n.*

تَوَاتُرٌ عَالٍ high frequency *n.*

تَوَاتُرٌ لَاسِلْكِيٌّ radio frequency *n.*

تَوْزِيعٌ مُسْتَعْجَلٌ special delivery *n.*

تَوْصِيلٌ مُتَكَاثِرٌ hookup *n.*

تَيَّارٌ current *n.*

تَيَّارٌ مُتَبَادَلٌ alternate current *n.*

ثَمَنُ ٱلتَّذْكِرَةِ carfare *n.*

ثَوْرَوِيٌّ subversive *a.*

ثِيَابٌ لِطِفْلٍ وَلِيدٍ layette *n.*

جَانِبِيٌّ collateral *n.*

جَذْبٌ جِنْسِيٌّ sex appeal *n.*

جَذْمُ ٱلزَّائِدَةِ ٱلدُّودِيَّةِ appendectomy *n.*

جَذْمُ ٱللَّوْزَتَيْنِ tonsilectomy *n.*

جُرْثُومَةٌ bacillus *n.*

جَرِيدَةٌ نَاطِقَةٌ	newsreel *n.*
جِسْرٌ مُعَلَّقٌ	suspension bridge *n.*
جَمْعِيَّةٌ تَعَاوُنِيَّةٌ	co-operative *n.*
جُنْدِيُّ ٱلْمِظَلَّة	parachutist *n.*
جَهَّزَ بِصَنَائِعَ	industrialize *v.*
جَوْلَةٌ	hike *n.*
جَوْلَةٌ وَعَوْدَةٌ	roundtrip *n.*
جَوِّيٌّ	atmospheric *a.*
حَاجِبُ ٱلْهَوَاءِ	airtight *a.*
حَارِسُ ٱلْمُقَاوَمَةِ ٱلْجَوِّيَّة	air warden *n.*
حَاطِمَةُ ٱلْجَلِيدِ	ice breaker *n.*
حَافِزٌ	initiative *n.*
حَافِلَةٌ	bus *n.*
حَاكٍ	phonograph *n.*
حَاكٍ	loudspeaker *n.*

حَامِضٌ بُورِقِيٌّ	boric acid *n.*
حَامِلَةُ ٱلطَّائِرَاتِ	aircraft carrier *n.*
حِجَابٌ حَرِيرِيٌّ	silkscreen *n.*
حُجْرَةٌ مُظْلِمَةٌ لِتَوْصِيحِ تَصَاوِيرَ	darkroom *n.*
حَرَارِيَّةٌ	calorie *n.*
حَرَّاقَةٌ	torpedo *n.*
أَلْحَرْبُ ٱلْبَرِيدَةُ	cold war *n.*
حَرْبُ ٱلطَّبَقَاتِ	class struggle *n.*
حَرَكَةٌ سِيَاسِيَّةٌ سِرِّيَّةٌ .	underground *n.* (polit.)
أَلْحُرُوفُ ٱلْمَجْمُوعَةُ	typesetting *n.*
حِزَامُ ٱلْأَمْنِ	safety belt *n.*
حِسَابٌ	bank account *n.*
حِسَابُ ٱلتَّفَاضُل	differential calculus *n.*

حِسِّيَاتٌ — emotions *n.*

حَصْرُ التَّمْوِينِ — rationing *n.*

حِصَّةٌ فِي الرِّبْحِ — dividend *n.* (profit share)

حِفْظٌ — upkeep *n.*

حُقْنَةٌ — injection *n.*

حَقِيبَةٌ — suitcase *n.*

أَلْحُكْمُ الْمُطْلَقُ — totalitarianism *n.*

حَلُّ الْجَيْشِ — demobilization *n.*

حَلَّ الْجَيْشَ — demobilize *v.*

أَلْحَمَوَانِ — in-laws *n.*

حَوَالَةٌ سَفَرِيَّةٌ — travelers' check *n.*

خَالِصٌ مِنَ الْكُمْرُوكِ — duty-free *a.*

خَانَ — doublecross *v.*

خَدَّرَ — anesthesize *v.*

خِدْمَةٌ اجْتِمَاعِيَّةٌ — social service *n.*, social work *n.*

أَلْخِدْمَةُ السِّرِّيَّةُ — secret service *n.*

خِزَانَةُ الثَّلْجِ — icebox *n.*

خِزَانَةُ الثَّلْجِ — refrigerator *n.*

خِزَانَةُ الْمِلَفَّاتِ — filing cabinet *n.*

خَصَّصَ — earmark *v.*

خَطِرٌ — touch-and-go *a.* [risky]

خَيَالِيٌّ — utopian *a.*

دَافِعُ الضَّرَائِبِ — taxpayer *n.*

دَائِرَةٌ قَصِيرَةٌ — short circuit *n.*

دَائِرَةُ الْمَعَارِفِ — encyclopedia *n.*

دَبَّابَةٌ — tank *n.* (mil.)

دَبُّوسٌ إِنْكِلِيزِيٌّ — safety pin *n.*

دَرَّاجَةٌ — bicycle *n.*

أَلدَّرَجَةُ الثَّالِثَةُ فِي سَفِينَةٍ — tourist class *n.*

دَرَجَةُ الْعَقْلِ — I.Q. *n.*

دَعَاوَةٌ	propaganda *n.*
دُكَّانُ جَرَائِدَ	newsstand *n.*
دُكَّانُ ٱلعِطَارَةِ	drugstore *n.*
دَلِيلٌ	directory *n.*
دَوْرَةُ ٱلبَرْدِ	cold wave *n.*
دَوْرَةُ ٱلحَرَارَةِ	heatwave *n.*
أَلدُّوَلُ ٱلمُوَقِّعَةُ	signatory powers *n. pl.*
دَوْلَةٌ مُتَوَسِّطَةٌ وَمُتَحَايِدَةٌ	buffer state *n.*
دُونَ ٱلأَحْمَرِ	infrared *a.*
ذَرِّيٌّ	atomic *a.*
ذَرِيرَةٌ طَلْقِيَّةٌ	talcum powder *n.*
ذُو رَادِيُوم فَاعِلٍ	radioactive *a.*
ذُو ٱللاسَامِيَّةِ	antisemite *n.*, anti-semitic *a.*
رَابِحٌ	profiteer *n.*
رَأْسُ ٱلجِسْرِ	bridgehead *n.*
رَأْسْمَالِيٌّ	capitalist *n.*
رَأْسْمَالِيَّةٌ	capitalism *n.*
رَامِي ٱللَّهِيبِ	flame thrower *n.*
رَئِيسٌ بِٱلإِسْمِ	figurehead *n.*
رَبْطَةُ ٱلسَّاقِ	suspender *n.*
رَثٌّ	hack *a.*
رَثْيَةٌ	rheumatism *n.*
رَدَّ	refund *v.*
رَدُّ ٱلفِعْلِ ٱلمُسَلْسَلِ	chain reaction *n.*
رَدُّ ٱلنُّقُودِ	refund *n.*
رِسَالَةٌ لاسِلْكِيَّةٌ	radiogram *n.*
رَسْمٌ قَلْبِيٌّ	cardiogram *n.*

رَسْمٌ هَنْدَسِيٌّ — blueprint *n.*

رِشْوَةٌ — hush money *n.*

رَقَّاسٌ — tugboat *n.*

رَفْتٌ — lay-off *n.*

رِوَايَةٌ بُولِيسِيَّةٌ — detective story *n.*

رَوْضَةُ ٱلْأَطْفَالِ — kindergarten *n.*

رَوْضَةُ ٱلْأَطْفَالِ — nursery school *n.*

رِيَاضَةٌ — sport *n.*

رِيحٌ وَرَائِيَّةٌ — tail wind *n.*

زَائِدَةٌ دُودِيَّةٌ — appendix *n.*

زَعِيمٌ — ringleader *n.*

زِيَادَةٌ مُفْرِطَةٌ — hypertrophy *n.*

زَيْتُ تَشْحِيمٍ — lubricating oil *n.*

زِينَةُ ٱلْوَجْهِ — make-up *n.*

سَاعَةُ يَدٍ — wristwatch *n.*

سَائِقٌ — chauffeur *n.*

سَائِقُ سَيَّارَةٍ — motorist *n.*

سِبَاقٌ — track meet *n.*

سَبُّورَةٌ — blackboard *n.*

أَلسِّتَارُ ٱلْحَدِيدِيُّ — iron curtain *n.*

سُتْرَةٌ صُوفِيَّةٌ — pullover *n.*

سَحْنَةٌ — physiognomy *n.*

سِرَاجُ ٱلْحَرَكَةِ — traffic light *n.*

سِرِّيٌّ جِدًّا — top-secret *a.*

سِعْرُ ٱلصَّرْفِ — rate of exchange *n.*

سِعْرُ ٱلْفَائِدَةِ — bank rate *n.*

سَفَّاحٌ — cutthroat *n.*

سَفَرٌ فِي ٱلْفَضَاءِ — space travel *n.*

سَفِينَةٌ فَضَائِيَّةٌ — space ship *n.*

سَكَارِينٌ — saccharine *n.*

subway *n.* سِكَّةُ تَحْتَ ٱلأَرْضِ

elevated railway *n.* سِكَّةُ ٱلْحَدِيدِ ٱلْمُرْتَفِعَةُ

barbed wire *n.* سِلْكٌ شَائِكٌ

escalator *n.* سُلَّمٌ مُتَحَرِّكٌ

fire escape *n.* سُلَّمُ ٱلنَّجَاةِ

fertilizer *n.* سَمَادٌ

audition *n.* سَمَاعٌ

telephone receiver *n.* سَمَّاعَةٌ

poison ivy *n.* أَلسُّمَّاقُ ٱلسَّامُّ

broker *n.* سِمْسَارٌ

stockbroker *n.* سِمْسَارُ ٱلأَسْهُمِ

brokerage *n.* سَمْسَرَةٌ

IOU *n.* سَنَدٌ

stock market *n.* سُوقُ ٱلأَسْهُمِ

labor market *n.* سُوقُ ٱلْعَمَلِ

standardize *v.* سَوَّى بِمِقْيَاسٍ أَحَدٍ

automobile *n.* سَيَّارَةٌ

taxicab *n.* سَيَّارَةُ ٱلأُجْرَةِ

armored car *n.* سَيَّارَةٌ مُصَفَّحَةٌ

motor truck *n.* سَيَّارَةُ ٱلنَّقْلِ

network *n.* شَبَكَةٌ

radio network *n.* شَبَكَةٌ لاسِلْكِيَّةٌ

diagnose *v.* شَخَّصَ مَرَضًا

military police *n.* أَلشُّرْطَةُ ٱلْعَسْكَرِيَّةُ

patrolman *n.* شُرْطِيٌّ

insurance company *n.* شِرْكَةُ ٱلتَّأْمِينِ

holding company *n.* شِرْكَةُ ٱلشَّرِكَاتِ

subsidiary *n.* (fin.) شِرْكَةٌ مُسَاعِدَةٌ

Inc. *a.* شِرْكَةٌ مُسَجَّلَةٌ

شَرِيطٌ غِرَائِي	Scotch tape *n.*
شَرِيطٌ ناطِقٌ	soundtrack *n.*
شَرِيكُ ٱلدِينِ	correligionist *n.*
شَرِيكُ ٱلمُدَّعَى عَلَيْهِ	codefendant *n.*
شُغْلٌ جانِبِي	side line *n.*
شَقّ	fission *n.*
شَقُّ ٱلذَرَّةِ	atomic fission *n.*
شُقَّةٌ	compartment *n.*
شَقْلَبَةُ طائِرَةٍ	tail spin *n.*
أَلشَّلَلُ ٱلطِّفْلِيُّ	polio(myelitis) *n.* infantile paralysis *n.*
شَمْعَةُ ٱلشَّرَارَةِ	spark plug *n.*
شَهِدَ قَانُونِيًّا	notarize *v.*
شُيُوعِي	communist *n.*
شُيُوعِيَّةٌ	communism *n.*
صَاحِبُ دَارِ ٱلزِينَةِ	beautician *n.*
صَارُوخٌ	rocket *n.*
صِبَاغٌ	pigment *n.*
صِبْيَانِي	juvenile *a.*
صَعَدَ	take off *v.* (av.)
صُعود	take-off *n.* (av.)
صَفُّ ٱلدَمِ	blood group *n.*
صِنَاعِي	industrial *a.*
صُنْدُوقُ سِينَمَاءَ أَوْ مَرْسَحٍ	box office *n.*
صُنْدُوقُ ٱلقُمَامَةِ	garbage can *n.*
صُنْدُوقُ مُسَجِّلٍ	cash register *n.*
صُنْدُوقٌ لِلمَكَاتِيبِ	mailbox *n.*
صُورَةٌ حَالِيَّةٌ	snapshot *n.*
صُورَةٌ مُتَحَرِّكَةٌ	motion picture *n.*
صُورَةٌ هَزْلِيَّةٌ	cartoon *n.*
ضَابِطُ ٱلصَفِّ	petty officer *n.*
ضَرَبَ طِفْلًا	spank *v.*
ضَغْطٌ عَالٍ	high pressure *n.* high tension *n.*

ضَنَى ٱلْحَرْبِ battle fatigue *n.*

ضَوْءٌ خَلْفِي rear light *n.*

ضَوْءٌ نِيونِي neon light *n.*

طَابِعُ ٱلْأَصَابِعِ fingerprint *n.*

طَالِبُ السَّنَةِ ٱلأُولَى freshman *n.*

طَالِعٌ فِي ٱلتَّنْجِيمِ horoscope *n.*

طَائِرَةٌ airplane *n.* aircraft *n.*

طَائِرَةُ ٱلاِنْقِضَاضِ dive bomber *n.*

طَائِرَةٌ بَحْرِيَّةٌ hydroplane *n.*

طَائِرَةٌ شِرَاعِيَّةٌ glider *n.*

طَائِرَةٌ عَمُودِيَّةٌ helicopter *n.*

طَائِرَةُ ٱلْقِتَالِ ٱلْقَذَّافَةُ fighter bomber *n.*

طَائِرَةُ ٱلْمُطَارَدَةِ pursuit plane *n.*

طَائِرَةٌ نَفَّاثَةٌ jet plane *n.*

أَلطِّبُّ ٱلطِّفْلِيُّ pediatrics *n.*

أَلطِّبُّ ٱلْمُشْتَرَكُ socialized medicine *n.*

أَلطِّبُّ ٱلنَّفْسَانِيُّ psychiatry *n.*

طَبَقَةُ ٱلتُّرْبَةِ ٱلْفَوْقَانِيَّةُ topsoil *n.*

الطَّبَقَةُ السُّفْلَى ground floor *n.*

طَبِيبُ أَمْرَاضِ ٱلْأَطْفَالِ pediatrician *n.*

طَبِيبٌ تَشْخِيصِي diagnostician *n.*

طَبِيبٌ مُوَلِّدٌ obstetrician *n.*

طَرِيقٌ عَامٌ highway *n.*

طَرِيقَةُ ٱلشِّفَاءِ therapy *n.*

طَعَامٌ جَانِبِي side dish *n.*

طِفْلٌ sibling *n.*

طَيَّارٌ aviator *n.*

طَيَرَانٌ aeronautics *n.*

عَازِلٌ insulator *n.*

عاهِرَةٌ	streetwalker *n.*
عَجَلَةٌ نارِيَّةٌ	motorbike *n.*
عَدَسَةٌ	lens *n.*
عَرَبَةُ ٱلأَكْلِ	dining car *n.*
عُرْيانِيَّةٌ	nudism *n.*
عُزْلَةٌ سِياسِيَّةٌ	isolationism *n.*
عَساكِرُ ٱلهُجُومِ	shock troops *n. pl.*
عُصْبَةُ ٱلأُمَمِ	League of Nations *n.*
عَطّارٌ	druggist *n.*
عَفّارَةٌ	atomizer *n.*
عَقْدٌ فَرْعِيٌّ	subcontract *n.*
أَلْعَقْلُ ٱلباطِنُ	subconscions *n.*
عِلاجٌ كَهْرَبائِيٌّ	diathermy *n.*
عَلّاقٌ	hanger *n.*
عَلامَةٌ تِجارِيَّةٌ	trade mark *n.*
عِلْمُ ٱلإِجْتِماعِ	sociology *n.*
عِلْمُ ٱلأَحْياءِ	biology *n.*
عِلْمُ ٱلجَراثِيمِ	bacteriology *n.*
عِلْمُ ٱلذَّرّاتِ	nuclear physics *n.*
عِلْمُ ٱلصِّحَّةِ	hygiene *n.*
عِلْمُ ٱلطَّبِيعَةِ	physics *n.*
عِلْمُ ٱلكَهارِبِ	electronics *n.*
عِلْمُ وَظائِفِ ٱلأَعْضاءِ	physiology *n.*
أَلعَمَلُ بِالقِطْعِ	piecework *n.*
عَمَلِيَّةٌ قَيْصَرِيَّةٌ	caesarian section *n.*
عَمُودٌ كَهْرَبائِيٌّ	electrode *n.*
عِنْتَرِي	bra(ssiere) *n.*
غارَةٌ جَوِّيَّةٌ	air raid *n.*
غازَلَ	flirt *v.*
غُدَّةٌ دَرَقِيَّةٌ	thyroid gland *n.*
غُدَّةٌ صَمّاءُ	endocrine gland *n.*
غُرْفَةُ ٱلإِنْتِظارِ	waiting room *n.*

غُرْفَةُ ٱلشَّحْن	shipping room *n.*
غُرْفَةٌ لِحفْظِ ٱلثِّيَاب	checkroom *n.*
غَشَيَانٌ بَعْدَ ٱلشُّرْب	hangover *n.*
غِلْطَةٌ كَبِيرَةٌ	boner *n.*
غَوَّاصَةٌ	submarine *n.*
فَاشِيّ	fascist *n.*
فَاشِيَّةٌ	fascism *n.*
فَاعِلٌ إِلَى ٱلْمَاضِي	retroactive *a.*
فَالِجٌ	paralysis *n.*
فَائِقٌ	topnotch *a.*
فَتَّاحَةٌ.	can opener *n.*
فَتَحَ	turn on the radio
فَحْصٌ	checkup *n.* (med.)
فَحْصُ ٱلدَّم	blood test *n.*
فُرَاطَةٌ	small change *n.*
فِرْقَةُ ٱلإِعْدَام	firing squad *n.*
فُسْحَةُ ٱلْوَاقِفِين	standing room *n.*
فَشَلٌ	washout *n.* (sl.) [failure]
فُلُورِيٌّ	fluorescent *a.*
أَلْفَوْزُ ٱلأَكْبَرُ فِي ٱلْمُقَامَرَة	jackpot *n.*
قَابِلٌ	receiver *n.*
قَارِبٌ نَارِيٌّ	motorboat *n.*
قَاطَعَ	boycott *v.*
أَلْقَائِدُ ٱلْعَامّ	supreme commander *n.*
قَاعِدَةٌ جَوِّيَّةٌ	airbase *n.*
قَائِمَةٌ	catalogue *n.*
قَائِمَةٌ سَوْدَاء	black list *n.*
قَائِمَةُ ٱلطَّعَام	menu *n.*
قَتَلَ بِالْكَهْرَبَاء	electrocute *v.*
قَتْلٌ بِالْكَهْرَبَاء	electrocution *n.*

قَدَّاحٌ	lighter *n.*
قَدَّمَ إِعَانَةً	subsidize *v.*
قَرَأَ مَكْتُوبًا شِفْرِيًّا	decode *v.*
قَطَعَ	turn off the radio
قَلَّبَ	revolutionize *v.*
قَلْبِيٌّ	cardiac *a.*
قَلَمُ ٱلْحِبْرِ	fountain pen *n.*
قَلَمُ ٱلْحِبْرِ ٱلْجَافِّ	ball point pen *n.*
قَمَرَةُ ٱلدَّرَجَةِ ٱلْأُولَى	stateroom *n.*
قُنْبُلَةٌ دَمْعِيَّةٌ	tear bomb *n.*
قُنْبُلَةٌ ذَرِّيَّةٌ	atom bomb *n.*
قُنْبُلَةٌ مُضَادَّةٌ لِلْغَوَّاصَاتِ	depth charge *n.*
قُوَّةُ حِصَانٍ	horsepower *n.*
قُوَّةُ عِرَاكٍ	task force *n.*
قُوَّةُ ٱلنَّارِ	fire power *n.*
كَاذِبٌ	phony *a.*, *n.*
كَاسِبٌ	wage earner *n.*
كَاسِرُ ٱلْإِضْرَابِ	strikebreaker *n.*
كَافِرٌ	atheist *n.*
كِتَابُ ٱلْمَرْجِعِ	reference book *n.*
كِتَابَةٌ بِٱلْآلَةِ	typewriting *n.*
كِتَابَةٌ عَلَى ٱلسَّمَاءِ	skywriting *n.*
كَرَاهَةُ ٱلْأَجَانِبِ	xenophobia *n.*
كُرْسِيٌّ دَائِرٌ	swivel chair *n.*
كَشْفِيٌّ	boyscout *n.*
كَشْكُولٌ	scrapbook *n.*
كَعْكَةُ طَاجِنٍ	pancake *n.*
كُفْرَانٌ	atheism *n.*
كَفَلَ	sponsor *v.*
كَفِيلٌ	sponsor *n.*

كَلامُ ذِي لِسانَيْنِ	double talk *n.*
كَهْرَبٌ	electron *n.*
كَهْرَبائِيٌّ	electrician *n.*
كَهْرَبَةٌ	electrification *n.*
كَهارِبِيٌّ	electronic *a.*
كُوخٌ	shack *n.*
كِيمِياءُ أَحْيائِيَّةٌ	biochemistry *n.*
كِينا	quinine *n.*
لاسامِيَّةٌ	antisemitism *n.*
لاسِلْكِيٌّ	radio *n.*, wireless *a.*
لاقِطَةُ الأَلْغامِ	mine sweeper *n.*
لَجْنَةٌ تَحْكِيمِيَّةٌ	arbitration board *n.*
لُصُوصِيَّةٌ	stickup *n.*
لَعْبُ كُرَةِ الْقَدَمِ	soccer *n.*
لِفافَةُ الْكِتابِ	book jacket *n.*
لُغْزُ قِطَعٍ كَثِيرَةٍ	jig saw puzzle *n.*
لَقَّحَ	vaccinate *v.*
لُقْمَةٌ ذاتَ كُرًى	ball bearing *n.*
لَوْلَبٌ	spring *n.* (techn.)
مائِيٌّ	hydraulic *a.*
مُبارَاةُ نُصْفِ نِهائِيٍّ	semifinal *n.*
مُبَدِّلُ الأُسْطُوانات	record changer *n.*
مَتْحَفٌ	museum *n.*
مُتَحَرِّكٌ بِذاتِهِ	automatic *a.*
مُتَطَرِّفٌ	extremist *n.*
مُتَفَرِّقٌ	sporadic *a.*
مَثَّلَ	assimilate *v.*
مِجْرافٌ بُخارِيٌّ	steam shovel *n.*
مُجَرَّدٌ عَنِ الْماءِ	dehydrated *a.*
مَجَلَّةٌ نُصْفُ شَهْرِيَّةٍ	semimonthly *n.*
مِجْهَرٌ	microscope *n.*
مُحارَبَةٌ ذَرِّيَّةٌ	atomic warfare *n.*

مُحَاصَرَةٌ blockade *n.*

مُحْتَرِفٌ professional *a.*

مُحْتَرَفٌ studio *n.*

مِحْرَاثٌ آلِيٌّ motor plough *n.*

مُحَرِّرٌ editor *n.*

مُحَرِّضٌ لِلْحَرْبِ warmonger *n.*

مُحَرَّمٌ عَلَى ٱلْعَسَاكِرِ off limits *n.*

مَحَطَّةٌ لاسِلْكِيَّةٌ radio station *n.*

مِحَفَّةٌ stretcher *n.*

مُحَكِّمٌ arbitrator *n.*

مَحَلُّ إِحْرَاقِ ٱلْجُثَثِ crematory *n.*

مَحَلُّ ٱلْبَنْزِينِ gas station *n.*

مُحَلَّفٌ juror *n.*

مُخْبِرُ جَرِيدَةٍ reporter *n.*

مُخْبِرٌ شُرْطِيٌّ plainclothes man *n.*

مُخَدِّرٌ anesthetic *n.*

مَخْرَجٌ عِنْدَ ٱلضَّرُورَةِ emergency exit *n.*

مَخْزَنُ ٱلدَّمِ blood bank *n.*

مَدْخَلٌ intake *n.*

مَدْخَلٌ لِلسَّيَّارَاتِ driveway *n.*

مُدَرَّبٌ trainee *n.*

مَدْرَسَةٌ أَوَّلِيَّةٌ elementary school *n.*

مَدْرَسَةٌ تِجَارِيَّةٌ commercial college *n.*

مَدْرَسَةُ ٱلصَّنَائِعِ vocational school *n.*

مُدْرِكٌ طَبَقَتَهُ class-conscious *a.*

مِدْفَعٌ مُضَادٌّ لِلدَّبَّابَاتِ tank destroyer *n.*

مُدَمِّجٌ stenographer *n.*

مُدِيرُ ٱلْجَوْقِ band leader *n.*

مُرَاقِبٌ	spotter *n.*
مُرَتِّبٌ	moderator *n.*
مِرْحَاضٌ	water closet *n.*
مُرْسِلَةٌ	radio transmitter *n.*
مَرَضُ ٱلبَوْلِ ٱلسُّكَّرِيِّ	diabetes *n.*
مَرَضٌ سِرِّيٌّ	venereal disease *n.*
مِرْفَعَةٌ	derrick *n.*
مَرْكَزُ ٱلتِّلِيفُونِ	switchboard *n.*
مِرْوَحَةٌ	propeller *n.*
مِرْوَدٌ	lipstick *n.*
مَرِيضٌ نَفْسِيٌّ	psychopath *n.*
مُزَخْرِفٌ	interior decorator *n.*
مِزْلَقَانِ ذَوَا عَجَلَاتٍ	roller skate *n.*
مُسْتَخْدَمَةُ ٱلإِسْتِقْبَالِ	receptionist *n.*
مُسْتَرَاحٌ	rest room *n.*
مُسْتَقْبِلٌ	receiver *n.* (radio)
مُسْتَقْبِلُ أَمْوَالِ ٱلإِفْلَاسِ؛	(in bankruptcy)
مُسْتَقِلٌّ	autonomous *a.*
مُسْتَوَى ٱلحَيَاةِ	standard of living *n.*
مُسَدَّسٌ	revolver *n.*
مُشَهٍّ	appetizer *n.*
مَشَى عَلَى غَفْلَةٍ	jaywalk *v.*
مِصْبَاحُ ضَوْءٍ فَوْقَ ٱلبَنَفْسَجِيِّ	sunlamp *n.*
مَصَحٌّ	sanitarium *n.*
مِصْعَدَةٌ	elevator *n.*
مِصْفَاةُ ٱلقَهْوَةِ	percolator *n.*
مَصْلَحَةُ ٱلتَّرْبِيَةِ	board of education *n.*

board of health *n.* مَصْلَحَةُ ٱلصِّحَّةِ

microphone *n.* مِصْوَاتٌ

contraceptive *n.* مُضَادَّاتٌ لِلْحَبَلِ

insecticide *n.* مُضَادَّاتٌ حَشَرِيَّةٌ

airfield *n.* مَطَارٌ

fire extinguisher *n.* مِطْفَأَةٌ

detergent *n.* مُطَهِّرٌ

spectroscope *n.* مِطْيَافٌ

parachute *n.* مِظَلَّةٌ وَاقِيَةٌ

tax-exempt *a.* مُعَافىً مِنَ ٱلْمُكُوسِ

collective agreement *n.* مُعَاهَدَةٌ جَمَاعِيَّةٌ

nonaggression pact *n.* مُعَاهَدَةُ عَدَمِ ٱلإِعْتِدَاءِ

overpass *n.* مَعْبَرٌ

aggressor *n.* مُعْتَدٍ

commissar *n.* مُعْتَمَدٌ شُيُوعِيٌّ

toothpaste *n.* مَعْجُونُ ٱلأَسْنَانِ

coefficient *n.* مُعَدَّلٌ

concentration camp *n.* مُعَسْكَرُ ٱلاعْتِقَالِ

ceiling price *n.* مُعْظَمُ ٱلثَّمَنِ

disinfectant *n.* مُعَقِّمٌ

aseptic *a.* مُعَقَّمٌ

visual aid *n.* مِعْوَانٌ نَظَرِيٌّ

flirt *n.* مُغَازَلَةٌ

electromagnet *n.* مِغْنَطِيسٌ كَهْرَبَائِيٌّ

vacationist *n.* مُفَرِّصٌ

commentator *n.* مُفَسِّرُ ٱلأَخْبَارِ

heckler *n.* مُقَاطِعُ ٱلكَلَامِ

subcontractor *n.* مُقَاوِلٌ فَرْعِيٌّ

antagonism *n.*	مُقاوَمَة
budget *n.* (pol.)	مُقَرَّر ٱلميزانيّة
toaster *n.*	مُقَمِّر كَهْرَبائي
bomber *n.*	مُقَنْبِلَة
spool *n.*	مَكَبّ
amplifier *n.*	مُكَبِّر
employment agency *n.*	مَكْتَب ٱلتَّخْديم
lending library *n.* rental library *n.*	مَكْتَبة إعارِيّة
subtenant *n.*	مُكْتَرٍ ثانٍ
typescript *n.*	مَكْتوب بِآلَة ٱلكِتابَة
refugee *n.*	مُلْتَجِئ
bunker *n.*	مَلْجَأ عَسْكَرِيّ
analogy *n.*	مُماثَلَة
screen actor *n.*	مُمَثِّل سينَمائي
eraser *n.*	مِمْحاة
potential *a.*	مُمْكِن
maneuver *n.*	مُناوَرَة
scholarship *n.* (grant)	مِنَح نَفَقَة لِتِلْميذ
apartment house *n.* tenement house *n.*	مَنْزِل
shower bath *n.*	مَنْضَح
balloon *n.*	مُنْطاد
dialectic *a.*	مَنْطِقِيّ
periscope *n.*	مَنْظَر ٱلغَوّاصَة
executive *n.*	مُنَفِّذ
vacuum cleaner *n.*	مِنْفَضَة
ventilator *n.*	مِهْواة
time table *n.*	مَواقيت
short wave *n.*	مَوْج قَصير
parking lot *n.*	مَوْقِف
motorcade *n.*	مَوْكِب سَيّارات

مُوَلِّدٌ generator *n.*

مُؤَلِّفٌ author *n.*

مِيعادٌ آخِرٌ deadline *n.*

مِيكانِيٌّ mechanized *a.*

مِينا جَوِّيَّةٌ airport *n.*

ناطِحَةُ ٱلسَّحابِ skyscraper *n.*

نائِبٌ عامٌ public prosecutor *n.*

نَباتِيٌّ vegetarian *n.*

نَزْعُ ٱلسِّلاحِ disarmament *n.*

نَزْلَةٌ صَدْرِيَّةٌ bronchitis *n.*

نَزْلَةٌ وَافِدَةٌ grippe *n.*

نُزُولٌ مَجْبُورٌ forced landing *n.*

نُزُولِيٌّ bearish *a.*

نَزِيفٌ hemorrhage *n.*

نَسّافَةٌ torpedoboat *n.*

نِسْبَةُ ٱلْمَوْتِ death rate *n.*

نِسْبِيَّةٌ relativity *n.*

نُسْخَةٌ فُوتُوغْرافِيَّةٌ photostat *n.*

نَسَقُ ٱلْأَفْكارِ ideology *n.*

نَسَقٌ مُوَظَّفِيٌّ bureaucracy *n.*

نَشْرٌ بِتَسَلْسُلٍ serialization *n.*

نَشَرَ بِتَسَلْسُلٍ serialize *v.*

نُصْبَةٌ signpost *n.*

نِصْفُ شَهْرِيٍّ semimonthly *a.*

نَظَرِيَّةُ ٱلْكَمِّ quantum theory *n.*

نِفْطٌ kerosene *n.*

نَقابَةٌ syndicate *n.*

نَقابَةٌ union *n.* (labor)

نَقابَةُ ٱلْعُمّالِ trade union *n.*

نَقّادٌ reviewer *n.*

نَقْلُ ٱلدَّمِ blood transfusion *n.*

نَكَّتَ	wisecrack *v.*
نُكْتَةٌ	wisecrack *n.*
نَهْبٌ	holdup *n.*
نُورٌ كَاشِفٌ	searchlight *n.*
نُورٌ كَشَّافٌ	floodlight *n.*
هُجُومٌ بِالْغَازِ	gas attack *n.*
هَنْدَسَةٌ	technology *n.*
هَوَائِي	pneumatic *a.*
هَوَائِيٌّ	aerial *n.*
هُورْمُونٌ	hormone *n.*
هِيدْرُوجِينٌ	hydrogen *n.*
هَيْئَةُ أَرْكَانِ الْحَرْبِ	general staff *n.*
وَرَقَةُ سُؤَالَاتٍ	questionnaire *n.*
وَزْنٌ ثَقِيلٌ	heavyweight *n.*
وَغْدٌ	hoodlum *n.*
وَكْرٌ	hangar *n.*
وَكَالَةُ الْإِشْهَارِ	advertising agency *n.*
يُودٌ	iodine *n.*